Distant Corner

Seattle Architects and the

Legacy of H. H. Richardson

Distant Corner

Seattle Architects and the
Legacy of H. H. Richardson

JEFFREY KARL OCHSNER

and DENNIS ALAN ANDERSEN

University of Washington Press Seattle and London

Publication of *Distant Corner* is supported by a grant from the Graham Foundation for Advanced Studies in the Fine Arts.

The authors and publisher gratefully acknowledge additional support for publication from three individuals—Priscilla Bullitt Collins, Victoria Reed, and John Nesholm—and the Johnston-Hastings Endowment of the College of Architecture and Urban Planning at the University of Washington.

Library of Congress Cataloging-in-Publication Data
Ochsner, Jeffrey Karl.
    Distant corner : Seattle architects and the legacy of H. H. Richardson / Jeffrey Karl Ochsner and Dennis Alan Andersen.
        p. cm.
    Includes bibliographical references and index.
    ISBN 0-295-98238-1 (alk. paper)
    1. Romanesque revival (Architecture)—Washington (State)—Seattle.
2. Architecture—Washington (State)—Seattle—19th century. 3. Architects—Washington (State)—Seattle—History—19th century. 4. Richardson, H. H. (Henry Hobson), 1838–1886—Influence. 5. Seattle (Wash.)—Buildings, structures, etc.
I. Andersen, Dennis Alan. II. Title.
NA735.S45 O270 2002
720'.979'77209034—dc21   2002018116

The paper used in this publication is acid-free and meets the minimum requirements of the American National Standard for Information Sciences—Permanence of Paper for Printed Library Materials, ANSI Z39.48-1984.

Illustration on p. i: Pioneer Square Historic District, Seattle; looking north on First Avenue South (originally Commercial Street) from South Washington. Photo by John Stamets, 2000.

Contents

Pioneer Square district,
with tideflats beyond, ca.
1907

*Manuscripts, Special
Collections, University
Archives Division, University
of Washington Libraries,
photo by A. C. Warner, 273*

Preface

Distant Corner: Seattle Architects and the Legacy of H. H. Richardson is a study of the architects and the architecture of a single city during a specific period of time. The city is Seattle. The time is the last two decades of the nineteenth century, with a primary focus on the years from 1889 to 1895, a time when the influence of the leading American architect Henry Hobson Richardson was at its height.

Seattle has, in recent decades, been ranked among America's most livable cities. How such rankings are determined is not always clear, but the city's attractive setting, the continuing vitality of its downtown and a wide variety of urban neighborhoods, a citywide network of parks, and the special character of such historic districts as Pioneer Square and Pike Place Market are factors often cited as contributing to the city's livability.

That Seattle should have achieved this kind of urban character seems all the more remarkable given its short history. In contrast to cities in the East, with histories stretching back several hundred years, Seattle is the result of incredibly rapid urban development that has taken place over little more than the last century. Although the city was founded in 1851, significant growth was delayed by a variety of factors, and as late as 1880 the census counted only 3,553 residents in this frontier community. However, largely as a result of the achievement of national rail connections, growth after 1880 was rapid, such that the census of 1890 counted a population of 42,000. By 1900 the population exceeded 80,000.

This population explosion was accompanied by dramatic physical change. On 6 June 1889, the urban core of Seattle was destroyed by fire, but within four years, substantial rebuilding was completed, with four-, five-, six-, and seven-story structures built of brick and stone, with interior frames of metal and heavy timber and details of terra-cotta and cast iron. In the same period, new cable car and streetcar lines fostered horizontal expansion and an urban pattern of tightly knit single-family residential neighborhoods. By 1895, construction had almost ceased because of the devastating effect of the national economic collapse. As a result of rapid growth and frenzied construction in a sharply limited time frame, Seattle offers a particularly condensed version of the architectural transformation of an American city in the late nineteenth century.

Our initial fascination with this early period grew from the formal character of the many surviving buildings and was enhanced by photographic documentation that offered a visual record of additional buildings that had been destroyed. However, as our interest deepened and we began to explore that period in greater detail, we discovered that the work that took place in Seattle did not fit easily into the familiar architectural narrative of the time. Further, although Seattle architects stated that they saw the works of H. H. Richardson and of architects in Chicago as models for their own projects, we discovered that design in Seattle could not simply be seen as derivative, but needed to be understood in its own terms. As a result, our study encompasses both a descriptive history of work in Seattle from 1880 to 1895, and offers a reconsideration of this entire period in American architectural history. In this context, we have focused on the specific challenges faced by architects in Seattle, particularly in rebuilding after the 6 June 1889 fire, and we have tried to discern how Seattle architects understood the American architecture of their own time and how they demonstrated that understanding through the designs they created. Thus, Seattle serves as a case study that sheds light on the complex interrelationships between urban development and technological and stylistic change in late-nineteenth-century architecture, as well as the influence of the key figure of H. H. Richardson.

Because the architectural history of Seattle has been the subject of limited analysis, this work has involved simultaneous efforts in both documentation and interpretation. One goal has been to develop a basic collection of accurate information about the buildings of the 1880s and 1890s in Seattle, while another goal has been to create an appropriate interpretive framework that reaches beyond formal architectural analysis toward a better understanding of the people who designed these buildings and the reasons they designed them as they did. Our efforts toward these goals have encountered unanticipated difficulties.

The volatility of architects' careers in most western cities, including Seattle, in the late nineteenth century seems to have been unparalleled in the East. Architects arrived from outside the Northwest and within a few months were able to win significant commissions. But their success was often fleeting, and some who were leaders in 1889 and 1890 saw their practices dissolve by 1892. The severity of the economic collapse after 1893 forced over two-thirds of the architects who had been in practice in Seattle in the early 1890s to depart by 1896. This high degree of transience means that primary source materials for these architects and their practices are scarce or nonexistent. Few documents survive from Seattle architects' practices of the pre-1900 era. While the most important evidence of these architects and their intentions remains the buildings themselves (and the photographic record of buildings that have disappeared), these alone are insufficient to create a complete picture of the period. Even the simple problem of attribution can be difficult. In this regard, we have depended to a large extent on contemporary publications to identify individual buildings and their architects. These publications include professional journals and local and regional periodicals and trade publications, but for the pre-1900 period the primary source for Seattle architecture is newspaper accounts. Fortunately, in the period before and after the 1889 Seattle fire, architects and their buildings were news (particularly because the buildings were physical evidence of the city's overcoming that calamity) and so were the frequent subjects of published reports. Such reports offer the added benefit of providing a sense of how the buildings were regarded at the time, but we have also had to recognize the limitations of local reporting with its hidden biases and frequent self-serving boosterism. Beyond the difficulty of attribution, the absence of drawings and similar records also makes it difficult to establish how these architects developed their designs. Here we have had to depend on the few cases where preliminary designs were published or where drawings do survive, and then we have tried to place these architects and their work within the context of the time and the city. Occasionally, design precedents in distant cities such as Chicago were mentioned in the press, and these reports provide an indication of specific influences addressed by Seattle designers.

An unexpected result of this study was the discovery of hidden linkages between Seattle in the late nineteenth century and in our own time, and the development of a deeper understanding of how the architecture and urban development of that period set a course for Seattle and left a legacy that continues to shape the city today. That legacy, we now believe, takes multiple forms. The most obvious consists of the surviving buildings, particularly the remarkable collection in the Pioneer Square Historic District at the south end of Seattle's downtown. However, we also discovered that the overall pattern of Seattle's urban form and the relationships that existed for most of the twentieth century, between the dispersed network of relatively small-scale urban institutions (such as schools and fire stations) and the tightly knit city neighborhoods, date from the 1880s and 1890s as well.

Our collaboration on this book began over fourteen years ago, soon after Ochsner moved to Seattle. Andersen had already been considering the idea of a book on Northwest architecture in the late nineteenth century for nearly a decade. His work began when he served on the staff of the Special Collections Division (now Manuscripts, Special Collections, University Archives Division) of the University of Washington Libraries. In the course of classifying and conserving architectural drawings, photographs, and ephemera, Andersen recognized the richness of the materials and began to imagine the possibility of a work on the subject. Working from nineteenth-century periodicals and other sources, he developed lists of architects and buildings and built a file of photographs and related information. His initial idea was a work on the influence of the Romanesque Revival on architecture in the Pacific Northwest and he developed a personal set of detailed notes on the period.

When Ochsner arrived in Seattle in 1987, he brought a familiarity with the work of H. H. Richardson from his own continuing research. Soon thereafter, when Ochsner expressed curiosity about the nineteenth-century architecture of Seattle, Andersen suggested collaborating on the further development of his project. Andersen subsequently reorganized information already collected in a consistent format, and also expanded his earlier explorations. Over the next several years Ochsner built up a second set of notes based on his own research and analysis. By 1990 it was becoming apparent that a book covering Seattle,

Tacoma, Spokane, and smaller cities in Washington might be too broad to be coherent, and Ochsner proposed that the book only address Seattle. Between 1991 and 1994, work on this project slowed as both Ochsner and Andersen were involved in the development of *Shaping Seattle Architecture: A Historical Guide to the Architects,* published by the University of Washington Press (with the assistance of AIA Seattle) in October 1994. The preparation of that book (the result of a collaborative effort with a six-person editorial board and twenty-five writers) uncovered substantial new information about the history of Seattle's architecture, and that information proved critical in the final development of the present work. In summer 1996, Ochsner wrote a complete draft manuscript. Revisions were carried out primarily by Ochsner between 1997 and 2001. In 1999, a number of colleagues reviewed the manuscript and their comments led to a substantial restructuring integrating material about the national context of American architecture more tightly into the chapters on Seattle. And, a year later, reports from external reviewers prompted further revisions. Although Ochsner remained the primary author, all changes were made in consultation with Andersen, so that the final product reflects additional input from both authors.

The general structure of this book moves from context to design and interpretation. Chapter 1 raises significant historiographic questions and sets the stage for our subject. Chapter 2 discusses how Seattle's distance from other metropolitan centers impacted its growth and describes the city's architecture and development prior to the 1889 fire. This chapter closes with the arrival of several architects whose careers developed primarily in the post-fire period. Chapter 3 addresses the technology, building types, and construction processes of the period after the 6 June 1889 fire. Chapter 4 deals with the influence of the architect H. H. Richardson and how it was received in Seattle; it also addresses the influence of the cities of Chicago and Minneapolis/St. Paul. Chapters 5 and 6 describe the new architecture created in Seattle between 1889 and 1895. They explore both the buildings of the new urban core and the development of a network of institutional and other buildings that established a framework for the expansion of the city. Chapter 7 examines the career of Seattle architect Willis Ritchie, whose practice was primarily oriented toward public buildings for communities across western Washington. Chapter 8 explores the dimensions of the collapse of the Seattle architectural profession after 1893; it also touches on the precipitous decline of the Romanesque Revival.

A number of ideas and hypotheses offered in this study challenge prevailing views found in Seattle and the Northwest. First, although the architecture of H. H. Richardson was influential during this period, and even though some of Seattle's architects claimed to be following Richardson's example, we are cautious about applying the term "Richardsonian Romanesque" to all their buildings. Unfortunately some local commentators have inappropriately lavished this term on almost any local building that includes semi-circular arches. We argue that before these buildings can be characterized as "Romanesque," we must reconsider both the architecture and the influence of H. H. Richardson, particularly in terms of how his work was understood and assessed in the years from 1885 to 1895 and how his work came to be known and understood in Seattle. Second, some commentators have argued that the pattern of Seattle's urban development dates from the period after 1900. We demonstrate that this pattern was created at least a decade earlier and must be credited to an earlier generation of Seattle civic leaders. Indeed, we argue that many of Seattle's urban institutions that came to fruition in the years after 1900 actually have their roots in the 1880s and 1890s.

In this book we have made certain choices relative to terminology and names. First, we use the terms "Romanesque" and "Romanesque Revival" to describe architecture in the period after the early 1880s that shows the direct or indirect influence of H. H. Richardson's own architecture. This architecture is sometimes known as "Richardsonian Romanesque," "Richardsonian Romanesque Revival," or simply "Richardsonian." We recognize that Richardson would probably not have approved of many of the works that we characterize as "Romanesque Revival," nor would architectural historians whose focus is European architecture of the ninth to the thirteenth centuries. However, the architects of this period clearly saw themselves as following Richardson's architecture, and often described their buildings as "Romanesque," so we have adopted this terminology for buildings with characteristic Romanesque features. Second, we have chosen to use late-nineteenth-century street names in describing the locations of buildings built in the period. Street names at the time were "Front Street," not First Avenue, "Commercial Street," rather than First Avenue South, and Second Street, Third Street, and so forth, rather than Second Avenue, Third Avenue, and so forth today; however, because today's Yesler Way came to have the name "Yesler Avenue" before the 1889 fire, we have used the name Yesler Avenue in all but chapter 2 (which addresses the pre-fire period), where the pre-fire name, "Mill Street," is used. In addition, today's Occidental Avenue South was identified as "South Second Street" in the late nineteenth century, and today's Second Avenue South was then "South Third Street." Because these names may occasionally cause confusion, we often also reference current (late-twentieth-century) names to clarify exact locations.

From the early days of research, this book has taken almost twenty years to produce. As a result, it has benefited from many types of assistance from multiple institutions and individuals. About 1989, Ochsner received funding support from the Graduate School Fund of the University of Washington that paid for travel to collections in Minnesota, Chicago, Washington, D.C., and Boston. In 1990, Ochsner received a summer stipend from the National Endowment for the Humanities that supported travel to Kansas as well as a return to Minnesota and Chicago. Both grants also supported the acquisition of a substantial number of photographs. For their generous support of publication, we are also grateful to the Graham Foundation and to Priscilla Bullitt Collins, Victoria Reed, and John Nesholm, as well as the Johnston-Hastings Endowment of the College of Architecture and Urban Planning of the University of Washington.

During the time this project was under way, the authors, either alone or in collaboration, produced a number of papers presented at conferences and articles that appeared in publications including *Journal of the Society of Architectural Historians, Pacific Northwest Quarterly,* and *Column 5* (student journal of the University of Washington Department of Architecture). Those papers and articles and the parts of this book that grew from them benefited greatly from the input of editors and reviewers including Maureen Meister, John Findlay, Carol Zabilsky, Kim McKaig, Tod Marder, Jay Henry, Robert Jay, and Jennifer Dee. Complete citations to all of these publications appear in the endnotes.

This book also benefited from those who read it in manuscript and made comments and suggestions, including Grant Hildebrand, David Rash, and the anonymous readers for the University of Washington Press. Sarah Wermiel provided specific assistance regarding fire resistant building technology. At various times assistance was received from students at the University of Washington, including W. Cory Crocker, Gretchen van Dusen, and Youngmin Han.

Finally, we wish to acknowledge the intellectual support we received from Margaret Henderson Floyd, whose own work on Longfellow, Alden, and Harlow reflected her interest in the reassessment of American architecture after Richardson. Over the course of the last decade, until her untimely death in 1997, Margaret frequently expressed her enthusiasm for this project and discussed with Ochsner the variety of understandings of Richardson's achievement in the 1880s and 1890s.

At various libraries and historical societies we thank the following: University of Washington Library, Manuscripts, Special Collections, University Archives Division, Richard Engeman, Kristin Kinsey, Carla Rickerson, Gary Menges, Karyl Winn, and Sandra Kroupa; Seattle Museum of History and Industry, Rick Caldwell, Carolyn Marr, and Howard Giske; Seattle School District Archives, Eleanor Toews; Puget Sound Branch, Washington State Archives, Greg Lange and Phil Stairs; City of Seattle Archives, Scott Cline; Northwest Museum of Arts and Culture, Spokane, Laura Arksey; Spokane Public Library, Nancy Compau; Washington State Historical Society, Tacoma, Edward Nolan; Northwest Architectural Archives, University of Minnesota, Alan Lathrop and Barbara Bezat; Winfield [Kansas] Historical Society, Joan Cales; Boston Public Library, Janice Chadbourne and Evelyn Lannon; California Historical Society, Wendy Walker; California State Library, Gary Kurutz; and in the offices of Jefferson County, Frank Gifford. We also were able to use the resources of the California State Library, University of California-Berkeley Bancroft Library, Minnesota Historical Society Library, Minneapolis Public Library, Chicago Art Institute Library, and materials held at Gladding, McBean, Inc. (with the assistance of Bill Wyatt).

Additional assistance of various kinds was received from Paul Clifford Larson, Gary Goss, Harold Kalman, Donald Luxton, Henry Matthews, Richard Longstreth, David Gebhard, Mark Hewitt, Leland Roth, Leonard Eaton, Meredith Clausen, Leonard Garfield, Maya Foty, Erin Doherty, Thomas Veith, and Ron Wright.

Jeffrey Karl Ochsner and *Dennis Alan Andersen*
June 2002

Distant Corner

Seattle Architects and the
Legacy of H. H. Richardson

1.1 Downtown Seattle
after the 6 June 1889 fire

*Manuscripts, Special
Collections, University
Archives Division, University
of Washington Libraries,
photo by John P. Soulé,
copied by Asahel Curtis,
36930*

I

Introduction

Seattle and Nineteenth-Century American Architecture

The architects of this city are taking their yearly vacation. J. W. Hetherington is in San Diego, Cal., E. H. Fisher is also in the Golden State, and Architect Parkinson also basks in her perennial sunlight. Architect Ritchie has gone East to visit, and half a dozen architect offices are locked up and no one knows where the bosses are.
—"Their Time of Rest: Architects Enjoying a Well Earned Holiday,"
Seattle Post-Intelligencer, 21 December 1889

In 1889, Seattle's rainy season began by late November. Construction became more difficult, and wet materials, slippery scaffolding, and cooling temperatures had combined with a shortage of materials to slow the pace of building. By December construction had all but halted. A few projects would be carried through the winter, but most were temporarily roofed over to await the return of better weather in the spring. On 22 November, the *Post-Intelligencer* had reported, "The architects' season is over for the year, and these practical artists are now, for the first time in many months, getting a chance to go out of their offices and take a look at the buildings which they have assisted in putting up."[1] And by December, the leading Seattle architects saw that construction had, indeed, slowed to such an extent that they could safely depart on their vacations.

On 6 June 1889, downtown Seattle burned to the ground. An area of more than thirty city blocks, virtually the city's entire business district and waterfront, was destroyed. (Fig. 1.1) Thankfully, there were few injuries, fewer deaths, and most of the city's residential districts remained untouched by fire.[2] Optimism prevailed. Seattle had been enjoying an economic boom, and the calamity of the fire proved only a temporary disaster. Within days a massive rebuilding campaign was under way. In the weeks and months that followed, the foundations of the modern city of Seattle were created at a feverish pace. Streets in the business core were widened, straightened, and regraded, utilities were improved, and the municipal government was largely reorganized. But the most visually significant evidence of the new Seattle was the new buildings. The fire had cleared away the city center of the 1880s. In its place rose a metropolitan center on the brink of the twentieth century.

On 1 January 1890, the *Post-Intelligencer,* in a special thirty-two-page edition, chronicled the economic, social, and cultural progress of Washington (which had just become a state in November) and highlighted the rebuilding of Seattle. According to the report, 3,465 new structures had been begun in the year; although most of these were residential structures located outside the burned area, within the fire limits some 256 new buildings were identified. For most of these, the city's professional architects had prepared construction documents—drawings and specifications to secure building permits and to provide instructions to contractors. It had indeed been a busy season.[3]

City directories for 1889 listed sixteen architecture firms in practice locally. Although other architects came to the city in the aftermath of the fire (the directories for 1890 reported more than twice this number of firms), the bulk of the commissions for new downtown business blocks went to those who had already established themselves, if only for six months or a year.[4] Not only was demand immense, but the pace of reconstruction pressed these architects day and night. Owners saw that a commercial advantage might be gained for the first buildings completed after the fire. There were frequent demands for immediate completion of drawings and specifications. Within a few weeks after the fire, the first permits for new buildings were issued, and the pace of construction appears to have been relentless, as almost daily announcements of new commercial blocks appeared in the newspapers through the summer and into the fall. And, because architects not only prepared the initial drawings, but also supervised construction and produced additional details and drawings, their work did not slow even after the pace of new commissions began to decline.

A visitor to Seattle in December 1889 would have seen an unfinished city. A few buildings had already been completed, among them a new resort hotel that had been rushed to completion, and a few other structures were being pushed through the winter, but for the most part, the construction of new business blocks had reached only the top of the first floor. These were temporarily roofed. In many cases, street-level retail spaces were already leased and occupied. Several of the largest business blocks, among them the Pioneer Building, the Burke Building, and the New York Building, had been announced and renderings had been displayed, but their construction would not even begin until spring 1890.

Beyond the commercial district, additional building was under way or about to begin. Seattle had opened two new school buildings in 1889; four additional schoolhouses had been designed, but the bidding climate was unfavorable because contractors were in such demand in the aftermath of the fire that school construction was put off until 1890. Similarly, designs for five new fire stations for the city's reorganized fire department had also been selected in late 1889 and would be built in the spring. And, a variety of other buildings, including hotels, churches, residences, and the like, were needed to respond to the pressure of the city's growth.

The significant buildings of the new Seattle were designed by a relatively small group of architects—William Boone, Elmer Fisher, Charles Saunders, Edwin Houghton, John Parkinson, and Willis Ritchie—most of whom had been in the city only a year or less. For most of them, this flurry of design activity would be the high point of their careers. Most would have continuing practices, but few would ever again produce so many buildings in so short a period

or do work of such significance. Indeed, the leading architect of the time, Elmer Fisher, was fated to descend from this pinnacle into obscurity in less than a decade. Still, in the six months between June and December 1889, these architects provided the framework for the emergent metropolis of the Northwest. Over the next two to four years they would extend that framework with additional designs and continuing construction supervision, but the basis for the new city of Seattle was a product of this very short but intense period of productivity. (Fig. 1.2)

The architects of late-nineteenth-century Seattle saw their work as different from that of earlier generations of the city's designers. One Seattle newspaper proclaimed the largest buildings to be equal to any on the West Coast while another said they were the "finest in the West."[5] Clearly, these buildings were seen as symbols of Seattle's cultural achievement and future promise. Not only were these buildings intended to respond to immediate needs, they were also addressed to succeeding generations of the city's residents. Today these works can be read as reflecting a complex conjunction of issues and forces, such as available technology and materials, local construction practice, client expectations and functional requirements, national design tendencies and indi-

1.2 Seattle in the 1890s, looking north on Front Street (Pioneer Building to the right)

Museum of History and Industry, Seattle Historical Society Collection, 801

vidual architects' personal knowledge and expertise, as well as civic and business leaders' aspirations for the future of their community. But to understand the designers and their buildings, it is necessary to turn back more than a century and to locate them in the context of their time and place.[6]

Contesting Traditional Narratives of Late-Nineteenth-Century American Architecture

When Seattle architects discussed the designs of the new buildings under construction in autumn 1889, they described them as "Romanesque" and specifically cited the example of the American architect Henry Hobson Richardson (1838–1886).[7] By the late 1880s, Richardson's example had come to dominate the thinking of American architects and his legacy was interpreted as an American revival of the Romanesque architecture of medieval Europe. The buildings of Seattle's commercial core, the result of the frenzied construction that took place in the three years after the fire, were described at the time as "Romanesque" or "modern Romanesque" and have since often been described as "Romanesque Revival" or "Richardsonian Romanesque," but these descriptions of the new Seattle architecture require re-examination, and assumptions about designers' sources and designers' intentions must be carefully reconsidered. Too often such labels mean that a work is never closely studied. Rather, the building is often only seen through the lens that the label is believed to imply.

Although architects in Seattle in 1889 did describe their buildings as "Romanesque," and did cite the example of H. H. Richardson, the evidence of the buildings suggests a more complex pedigree. Romanesque elements are present, but they sometimes seem to have been applied in highly inventive ways that may strike some as arbitrary or capricious. It might be tempting to argue that late-nineteenth-century Seattle architects were poor designers, but this fails to explain how or why these architects went about producing these designs. Others might characterize such buildings as "provincial," implying that they were poor copies by local practitioners of works in distant cities that they had never seen, but this, too, says little about the intentions of local designers. Further, it implies that the works and influence of a figure such as H. H. Richardson can be seen in only one way or that reinterpretations of his architecture in distant locations such as Seattle have no value unless they conform to accepted understandings of Richardson's achievement. In any case, such approaches do little to help understand the architecture actually built in Seattle after the 1889 fire.

Although Richardson's achievement forms one basis for evaluating design in the late nineteenth century, the work of architects practicing in the "Romanesque" mode in Seattle and elsewhere should be understood and evaluated in its own terms.[8] Richardsonian Romanesque architecture is often considered the first definably American mode of design. Its attraction for architects in Seattle, as in cities and towns across America, cannot be understood only in terms of imitation of a distant master. Rather, adoption of Romanesque design at a moment of rapid urbanization of American cities and towns must be evaluated in terms of its wide and ready applicability to a variety of emerging building types, its feasibility as an approach to fireproof or fire-resistive construction, and its image as an architecture emblematic of metropolitan development. Its adoption by a professionalizing architectural community can also be seen as a means by which a new professional class could differentiate themselves from the previous generation of nonprofessional contractor-builders. And, its specific character can only be understood in light of its general acceptance as a new mode within the context of American Victorian architectural practice. Architects in Seattle, as across America, defined the movement in terms of Richardson's work, but this must be understood in terms of their perceptions of Richardson's architecture, not in terms of how his architecture is interpreted today. This can present a very difficult challenge.

Today's understanding of H. H. Richardson has been shaped by our knowledge of later developments in architectural history and filtered by architectural historians whose interpretations reflect knowledge of later developments. Those interpretations have typically focused on some directions in Richardson's work, but have denigrated or excluded others. The work of architects influenced by Richardson, such as those in Seattle, whose work often does not fit the favored interpretations has also been effectively excluded. In fact, although H. H. Richardson, the progenitor of the "modern Romanesque," has been the subject of extensive study, the architects who were influenced by him have received, with few exceptions, little or no attention.[9] Virtually all of the studies of Richardson have framed his achievement in a way that emphasizes its uniqueness and sets him apart both from his apprentices and from all others, including those in Seattle, who may have attempted to continue the development of a "Richardsonian" mode of design. Indeed, this treatment of Richardson is a central component of the familiar narrative of American architecture from 1865 to 1914, a narrative constructed in the 1920s and 1930s—one that has only recently begun to be reconsidered. However, this familiar narrative must be challenged if Seattle architecture of the late nineteenth century is to be understood on its own terms and in its own time. In order to see the work of Seattle architects in the late nineteenth century clearly, the retroactive reframing of Richardson's achievement needs to be reconsidered.

The central narrative of late-nineteenth-century American architecture was largely constructed by Lewis Mumford and Henry-Russell Hitchcock, who sought in the 1920s and 1930s to find American roots for a modern architecture like that they had seen in Europe. In this narrative H. H. Richardson played a central role. Although Richardson's works and practice had been celebrated in his lifetime and his architecture was extensively published in the first few years after his death, the position he now occupies in the American pantheon derives largely from the assessment of his contributions initiated by Mumford and developed by Hitchcock. In his books *Sticks and Stones* (1924) and *The Brown Decades* (1931), Mumford presented Richardson from various perspectives, primarily as an "American romantic," but he also argued that Richardson was "the first architect of distinction in America who was ready to face the totality of modern life" and that his works pointed the way to a "new architecture."[10] Mumford's essays were soon overshadowed by Hitchcock's exhibition on Richardson at the Museum of Modern Art and his accompanying study, *The Architecture of H. H. Richardson and His Times*, published in 1936.[11] Hitchcock's book presented a detailed documentation and analysis of Richardson's buildings, placed them in a developmental chronology, and offered an explanatory framework that continues to shape how Richardson and his times are understood. The power of Hitchcock's work is reflected by its longevity: published in 1936, it was reissued in 1961 and appeared in paperback in 1966.[12] Until James F. O'Gorman's 1987 monograph *H. H. Richardson: Architectural Forms for an American Society*, it was the only full-length interpretive work on Richardson's architecture.[13]

But Hitchcock did not write independent of the currents of his own time. As a leading proponent of the Modern Movement in architecture as it has developed in Europe (and as co-curator of the seminal Museum of Modern Art exhibition on the International Style in 1929), Hitchcock approached Richardson through a specific frame of reference. Indeed, in his 1974 study, *H. H. Richardson and His Office: Selected Drawings*, O'Gorman argued that Hitchcock's underlying aim was "to establish Richardson as the father of the International Style."[14] In Hitchcock's framework, Richardson was seen as a proto-modern designer whose work moved from an undistinguished eclecticism based on his interpretation of contemporary European examples, to creative eclecticism based on the historical example of the Romanesque, to the brink of modern architecture through a process of simplification, elimination of extraneous ornament and historicizing detail, and a focus on the inherent quality of materials, particularly stone, to create an architecture of mass, gravity, and repose.[15]

On the basis of his assessment, Hitchcock focused on the inspiration and direction that Richardson offered to the young Chicago architect Louis Sullivan and claimed that his influence on Sullivan was Richardson's only significant legacy. Other understandings of Richardson's achievement (such as those in Seattle) may have flickered for a brief moment, but were seen by Hitchcock as failing to grasp the essential qualities of Richardson's work. Thus, Hitchcock characterized Richardson's influence on architects other than Sullivan as "almost meaningless."[16] O'Gorman's 1987 publication placed Richardson's work in a different context, suggesting the development of his architecture in an interpretive relationship to the American landscape, but O'Gorman's subsequent *Three American Architects: Richardson, Sullivan, and Wright, 1865–1915*, published in 1991, returned to the dominant narrative.[17] And, both works offered negative assessments of the other streams of architectural development, such as the Romanesque Revival, that can be traced back to Richardson. Thus, the architectural production of a city like Seattle in the period of the late 1880s and early 1890s simply has no place within the dominant narrative.

This narrative, although still dominant, has not gone unchallenged. In her 1994 publication, *Architecture After Richardson: Regionalism Before Modernism—Longfellow, Alden, and Harlow in Boston and Pittsburgh,* Margaret Henderson Floyd argued that O'Gorman's 1974 study of Richardson's drawings should be credited with opening the door to a re-evaluation because it focused on the production of Richardson's designs through the teamwork characteristic of an architect's office.[18] Floyd noted that Hitchcock was able to present Richardson as a lone proto-modern genius because he routinely credited the non-modern features of Richardson's buildings to the office staff and argued that there was an "almost total incapacity" on the part of Richardson's contemporaries and followers to understand his work.[19] Floyd pointed out, however, that Hitchcock made occasional mistakes in developing his narrative and he may at times even have misunderstood Richardson's intentions.[20] In this context, Floyd argued that the familiar linear narrative of late-nineteenth-century American architectural history should be replaced by a fan-shaped radial topology.[21] In Floyd's model, Richardson should be seen as a font of inspiration generating work in a variety of directions. Floyd's own research and writing traced one group of Richardson's apprentices. But the promise of Floyd's model is that it offers the possibility for a better accounting of the variety of Richardson's influence and recognition of the range of American architectural achievement of the period after 1865, including the architecture of Seattle.

A reconsideration of the years after 1865 will still find Richardson in a central role, but Hitchcock's interpretation of Richardson must be set aside because it precludes a full evaluation of American architectural achievement of the period. If the "Richardsonian Romanesque" architectural production in Seattle is to be understood, it must first be placed in the context of its own time. That context must be seen as architects of the period understood it, not in light of later directions that could not have been known at the time.[22]

Hitchcock's interpretation of Richardson and his time has remained influential at least partially because it appears to explain the subsequent history of the Romanesque Revival so well. The brevity of the flowering of the Romanesque as a national movement in the late 1880s and early 1890s might seem to prove that it must have been inherently flawed. It is easy to assume, therefore, that the avalanche of Romanesque architecture following Richardson's death must have been inferior.[23] The failure of Richardson's followers to understand his achievement (as explained by Hitchcock) meant that the American Romanesque was doomed to extinction. According to the standard narrative, these architects lacked Richardson's insight, produced little more than pastiche, and were overwhelmed by the academic classicism that soon overtook them. But this interpretation presents considerable difficulty when it is recognized that Hitchcock's model is framed in terms of emergent American Modernism after 1930, certainly not in terms that Richardson used to explain his own work or how it was received and understood by his contemporaries. To give fair consideration to buildings produced by Seattle architects after the 1889 fire—buildings that betray Richardson's influence—it is necessary to set aside historical narratives constructed more than forty years later and consider instead what Seattle architects would have understood of Richardson and his contemporaries as they were faced with creating a new city. This reframing becomes even more complex when it is recognized that Seattle architects would have understood Richardson's example not only through his own work, but also as filtered through the "Richardsonian" achievement elsewhere, especially in the cities of Chicago, Minneapolis, and St. Paul.

Unfortunately, the relative dearth of broadly based historical works on American architecture of the 1880s and 1890s poses a challenge to this reconsideration. Most studies of the period address a limited number of individual architects or just a few of the leading firms, typically in the East or Midwest. Perhaps because the dominant narrative has long devalued the post-Richardson Romanesque, architectural historians have largely ignored the full breadth of American architectural achievement in the years between 1885 and 1895. At the same time, it must be recognized that the breadth of the movement—Romanesque works were produced in virtually every city across the continent—combined with its brevity—Richardson died in 1886, the movement peaked in 1890, and was clearly in decline by 1892 (a period of just six years)—present almost insurmountable difficulties for the historian. As a result, there is but a single recent work on the American Romanesque, *The Spirit of H. H. Richardson on the Midland Prairies: Regional Transformations of an Architectural Style*, and it is a collection of focused essays.[24] Thus, in order to frame an analysis and interpretation of architecture in Seattle in the 1880s and 1890s, it is essential to reconsider the course of late-nineteenth-century American architecture, particularly as understood in the American West.

American Victorian Architecture Reconsidered

In reassessing the Romanesque episode in American architecture, we are also led to a more general reconsideration of American architecture from the 1860s to the 1890s. As long as Richardson was interpreted exclusively as a proto-modernist, the relationship between Richardson's example and American Victorian architecture in the late nineteenth century could be ignored. But if Richardson is considered in his time, then his work and influence must be recognized as transitional, both reflecting earlier tendencies as well as leading in new directions. The architecture he influenced, the Richardsonian Romanesque, must also be seen as one of the last phases of the American Victorian period in architecture, as well as one pointing in new directions. And, to understand how Richardson's example was received by most architects in the period, it is American Victorian architecture that must reconsidered.

Because Seattle's urban core was rebuilt after the June 1889 fire, examples of early Victorian modes such as Second Empire and Victorian Gothic do not exist. But, Seattle's late-nineteenth-century architecture still reflects many of the stylistic complexities and apparent contradictions that prevailed in American architecture in the thirty years after 1865. (Fig. 1.3) The buildings

of Seattle's nineteenth-century commercial core embody approaches that can be characterized as American Victorian, yet they also betray the influence of the Richardsonian Romanesque, a style Seattle's architects consciously sought to adopt.

Architecture created across the United States in the years between 1865 and 1895, broadly characterized as American Victorian architecture, still constitutes the fabric of many towns and is often found in older districts of larger cities. Although this architecture was eclectic in that it drew upon a variety of historical and contemporary sources, it also welcomed invention and experimentation, with results that varied widely from the inspired to the insipid. Often easily recognizable, American Victorian architecture nonetheless frequently eludes precise description or detailed analysis because of the array of elements drawn from diverse sources—Second Empire, Victorian Gothic, Renaissance Revival, Romanesque Revival, and others—found in these compositions, and because the architecture of this period was a complex amalgamation of influences that changed over these three decades.[25]

The apparent complexity of surface treatments of these structures has often led to a failure to appreciate their essential character. But it was their essential character that led the scholar Colin Rowe and the architect John Hejduk in 1957 to describe the Victorian buildings of the small town of Lockhart, Texas, as possessing "majestic seriousness," "intrinsic reasonableness," and "unsophisticated strength."[26] Rowe and Hejduk's 1957 *Architectural Record* article

1.3 Downtown Seattle, Second Street looking north from Cherry, July 1891, two years after the fire

Manuscripts, Special Collections, University Archives Division, University of Washington Libraries, photo by Frank LaRoche

"Lockhart, Texas" seems extraordinarily prescient in its celebration of both the historic urban plan and the late-nineteenth-century architecture of a small Texas courthouse town. At a time that embraced both Modernism and modernization, Rowe and Hejduk characterized Lockhart as "an exemplary urban success." While their appreciation embraced the spatial order of the town, their primary focus, architecture—"an interrupted staccato of distinctly assertive structures imposed upon the recessive background"—was described and illustrated: the jail was "brick and machiolated, partly Romanesque and partly Italianate," the courthouse "aggressive, bluff, and reasonably florid," a church "an ecclesiastical representative of the Richardsonian suburban world of the eighties, dating from 1898," a commercial building with "an awareness of the single volume, a sense of the horizontal, and a feeling for the significance of the structural bay," and another where, "subordinated to a controlling grid of stringcourses and pilasters, in simplified, almost abstracted, form, arches and all the acceptable components of a classical design are fused into a single statement of surprising intensity."

Rowe and Hejduk's discussion of the virtues of the Victorian architecture of a Texas town was exceptional in the 1950s and remains exceptional today. Scholars of American architectural history have generally avoided the subject, and American Victorian architecture has too frequently been contemptuously dismissed. While preservationists have embraced surviving nineteenth-century urban fabrics, they typically have been motivated primarily by sentimental attachment or broader urban design concerns and have not contributed a more precise analysis of this architecture. Instead, most accounts of late-nineteenth-century American architectural history have focused on stylistic directions imported from Europe (Second Empire, Victorian Gothic), on the careers of major figures such as H. H. Richardson, Frank Furness, and architects in Chicago, and on the work of the period *after* 1890. Indeed, the *full* development of architecture in America in the years from 1865 to 1895 has remained largely undescribed; a truly encompassing study of the period has yet to be written.

American Victorian architecture provided the context for architects, like those in Seattle, who adopted the Romanesque Revival. Because they had been trained as designers in the Victorian period, their approaches to the Romanesque frequently differed from Richardson's even as they copied his example. Indeed, because few American Victorian architects had had any formal training in architecture, their approaches to design differed markedly from the academically educated practitioners who came after them. Many Victorian practitioners were designer-builders who emerged from the construction trades and whose ideas of design reflected the influence of what they knew about construction and what they learned from builder publications, pattern books, and similar sources as well as buildings they had actually seen. The academically educated architects of the next generation, who sought to distance themselves from the earlier designer-builders, and to establish architecture as a profession distinct from construction, found much to dislike in the work of the earlier generation. Later generations of architects looked with disdain on the work of their Victorian

predecessors. We too often have inherited their prejudices and this has limited our ability to see, as Rowe and Hejduk did, the virtues in their work.

Late-nineteenth-century Seattle architects reflect the complexities of this
period as well. Although architects in Seattle in the 1880s and 1890s sought
to establish their architectural practices as fully professional, most had emerged
from the building trades, and therefore their approaches to design reflect what
they learned as builders working in the American Victorian modes. Most of
these architects approached the design process by combining aspects of the
traditional builder-designer background from which they had emerged and progressive professional directions, such as the Richardsonian Romanesque, that
they discovered primarily through the emerging professional press. The challenge to us is not to dismiss or sentimentalize their work, but instead to try to
understand it on its own terms.

Seattle as a Case Study

Because the city's downtown business district burned on 6 June 1889 and
was rebuilt over the next several years, the architecture of Seattle in this period

1.4 Pioneer Place Park,
Seattle, January 2001
Photo by John Stamets

presents a tightly focused episode in the history of American late-nineteenth-century architecture. In the late 1880s Richardson's influence was at its height. Seattle's economy had been booming, so the city's response to the catastrophe was an intense period of reconstruction that was slowed only by a national recession in 1891 and then was completely halted by the national depression after mid-1893. Seattle's architects produced their post-fire designs in an even more limited period. Although construction stretched over several years, most of the new buildings were permitted in late 1889; thus, the architects' design work was primarily concentrated in the six months after the fire. Seattle, therefore, presents a focused case study in the architecture of the late nineteenth century. And, a close examination of this episode may also serve to illuminate forces and issues broadly applicable to American architecture in the period after the death of H. H. Richardson, and may help to better explain the rise and fall of the Romanesque Revival.

No study can definitively explain why a particular architect designed an individual building in a particular way. Architects' design decisions have always been influenced by a multiplicity of factors, and design in 1890, as in 1990 or 2000, was the result of creative synthesis. But, we believe that the buildings of this period (particularly the collection of buildings standing in Seattle's Pioneer Square Historic District, as well as the few early buildings remaining elsewhere in the older parts of Seattle) can be better understood if seen in the context of their time and in terms of the choices that were available to the architects who designed them.[27] This cannot help but lead, in turn, to a more profound appreciation for the built environment of Seattle that exists today, and in turn for the architecture of American cities and towns which reflects the influence of H. H. Richardson and the achievements of America's late-Victorian designers. (Fig. 1.4)

II

Pre-Fire Seattle
Architects and Architecture

We have cast off our rough appearance and former stumpy condition and can no longer be nic-named [*sic*] "stump town," an appellation given us some two or three years ago by a correspondent of a California paper. Our appearance is our winning card, for from the water Seattle presents to the view of the weary traveler a beautiful city by the sea. . . . Her buildings are equal to any of a city her size both in size and beauty of design and in many instances rare taste being displayed.
—*Seattle Post-Intelligencer*, 27 April 1882

About 1870 a Portland land speculator predicted that somewhere between the Columbia River and the forty-ninth parallel there would rise a community that would become the "Queen City" of the Northwest and the gateway to the Orient.[1] At the time that city remained a distant dream, but the sense that a great metropolis must inevitably rise at the northern corner of the Pacific Coast of the United States permeated the early history of settlement and urban development in Washington, and especially on Puget Sound. This faith in future greatness spurred competition among early settlements, as it was believed that only a single city would eventually achieve this stature. It also led to the rather extravagant predictions that a city of the future on Puget Sound would someday equal or even surpass the largest cities in the East. Such predictions were, of course, typical of early western "boosterism," but even as late as the first decade of the twentieth century, Tacoma promotional publications were calling the city "another New York" and predicting that Tacoma was destined to become "one of the greatest industrial centers of the world."[2] Nonetheless, if the inevitability of metropolitan development was a shared faith of early residents of Puget Sound, so too was a feeling of frustration due to its continuing delay. Indeed, a sense of untapped potential due to physical isolation was a constant factor in shaping the early history of all of Washington.

Seattle: City of Promise

The subject of conflicting claims between Britain and the United States in the 1830s and 1840s, the land north of the Columbia River that was to become Washington State remained unsettled even as Oregon's rich Willamette Valley attracted covered-wagon pioneers from the East. By 1846, "Oregon fever" had drawn more than 10,000 people west, but the first party of Euro-American settlers arrived in the Puget Sound region only in 1845. The 1846 settlement of the United States–Canada boundary dispute extended the border along the forty-ninth parallel from the Rocky Mountains to the Strait of Georgia, but this reflected less the reality of existing settlement than the potential of future growth.

By the 1850s the ready supply of available timber along Puget Sound had begun to attract settlers, and a network of small towns sprang up. In mid-November 1851, a party led by David Denny formed a new settlement at Alki in what is now West Seattle, but lacking a protected deep-water anchorage they scouted other sites in the area and in February 1852 relocated to the east side of Elliott Bay. The name "Seattle," after the leader of one of the local native tribes, was adopted later that year. The community's initial economy was based on the export of raw logs primarily to San Francisco, but in March 1853, Henry Yesler (1810–1892) was enticed to build a steam-powered sawmill in the new community in return for a strip of land through the center of town. Yesler was born in Maryland, had worked in the lumber business in Ohio for over nineteen years, and arrived in Oregon in 1851. Yesler's mill was the first such steam-powered facility on Puget Sound, giving Seattle an economic advantage over other towns in the area. Yesler became a key figure in the development of the city, as business leader, in early government, and as a real estate developer.[3] (Fig. 2.1) The development of the waterfront with wharves, bunkers, and similar improvements followed Yesler's mill, and Seattle emerged as a center of local trade supported by the "mosquito fleet," a network of small supply ships traversing the sound.

Still, growth proceeded slowly, limited first by the Indian Wars of 1855–56 and thereafter by Puget Sound's remoteness and inaccessibility. Early settlement in Washington was concentrated in the southeast corner of the territory where farmland was readily available and the Columbia River provided a ready transportation corridor. In 1862 the population of Seattle was just 182; the nation's focus was on the Civil War, not on western development.

The belief in Seattle and Puget Sound's tremendous potential—that here was a vast land offering a favorable climate, a wealth of natural resources, and an opening to the Pacific trade—was sustained in the 1850s and 1860s by the hope that a northern transcontinental railroad would be constructed from the upper reaches of the Mississippi to the sound. Indeed, the history of Washington in the second half of the nineteenth century is largely focused on the fortunes of this transcontinental railroad, the Northern Pacific, which was regarded as the source of future progress.[4] Governor Marshall Moore's 1867 statement on the importance of a transcontinental line is representative of the hope that early settlers placed on the coming of rail connections: "We have seen that, in the short space of a few years, railroads have accomplished in our country what would, without them have been the work of centuries. They have made the broad prairies and boundless forests of the great West team with population and wealth—and caused mighty cities to spring up as if by magic."[5]

Although surveys for the northern transcontinental line had been initiated in the 1850s, and Abraham Lincoln had signed a bill on 2 July 1864, granting a charter to the Northern Pacific for a railroad from Lake Superior to Puget

2.1 Yesler's early building, southeast corner of Front and James Streets, 1859

Museum of History and Industry, Seattle Historical Society Collection, photo by E. A. Clark

Sound, the start of construction was delayed until 1870, by which time the transcontinental connection to California's San Francisco Bay was already complete. From the date of the Northern Pacific charter, however, every city and town on Puget Sound had proclaimed itself the logical choice as western terminus of the line. A visiting reporter in the early 1870s described this phenomenon as the "Terminus Disease."[6] Residents not only proclaimed the advantages of their particular location, but also faulted all of the others. The fundamental insecurity that arose from isolation was reinforced by the insecurity of competition—a city or town that achieved rail connections would be the site of factories, docks, business blocks, and new residences, while those that did not would stagnate and might even disappear. In an editorial titled "Now or Never" that appeared in the *Washington Standard,* an Olympia newspaper, in 1871, the writer argued, "The property holders of Olympia now have an opportunity offered to them that will never come again, and upon their determination depends the future of their town, whether it shall be a prosperous city . . . or a deserted village."[7]

While every city had an argument in its own favor, Seattle clearly saw itself as the inevitable choice for the terminus of the line. The early surveys had shown that Snoqualmie Pass, nearly due east of the city, was the lowest pass through the Cascades, the city was centrally located in the Puget Sound region, and the city's population of 1,107 in 1870 made it the largest of the competing Puget Sound communities. But in 1873, with the easternmost portions of the line already under construction, the Northern Pacific telegraphed, "We have located the terminus at Commencement Bay," thereby favoring the upstart competitor, Tacoma, because opportunities for land speculation were much greater. Seattle was bitterly disappointed.

This disappointment turned to anger and then to resolve, and, as railroad construction was delayed by depression during the 1870s, competition on Puget Sound grew more intense. Seattle continued to argue its case and then tried to

BIRD'S-EYE VIEW OF THE

CITY OF SEATTLE.

Puget Sound, Washington Territory, 1878.

2.2 Panoramic lithograph of Seattle (Eli Glover, del.), 1878

Manuscripts, Special Collections, University Archives Division, University of Washington Libraries, UW14531

build its own rail line, optimistically called the Seattle and Walla Walla (Walla Walla was the largest city in the territory at the time), east through the Cascades. Although in three years only sixteen miles were built, these gave Seattle access to coal fields south and east of Lake Washington, and by the late 1870s, the city was exporting coal to San Francisco by coastal steamer.[8] The city's economy continued to diversify. The population reached 3,553 in 1880. (Fig. 2.2)

A seemingly endless series of changes to management, policy, and direction, accompanied by frequent financial stringency, meant that the Northern Pacific connection was not achieved until 1884 after the railroad had come under the control of Henry Villard, and even then the route followed the Columbia River to Portland, Oregon, before turning north to Puget Sound. Still, the anticipation of this rail connection precipitated Seattle's first real estate and building boom in 1882–83; the 100,000 board-feet of lumber cut by Seattle mills in spring 1883 was completely consumed by local construction.[9] But in 1884, when Villard's transportation empire collapsed, development faded. Construction did not pick up again until 1886, when local entrepreneurs Daniel Gilman, Thomas Burke, and John Leary secured eastern funding for the Seattle, Lake Shore and Eastern Railroad, a line which extended around the north end of Lake Washington to reach coal and iron deposits east of Seattle as well as new stands of timber. In addition, the Northern Pacific was completed through Stampede Pass in the Cascade Mountains, finally allowing Puget Sound ports to compete on an equal basis with Portland after 1887.

Justification for the belief in a long-delayed future appeared in the 1880s once rail connections were realized to the East and then to California. The resulting boom was marked by a rapid rise in land values, commerce, population, and construction. In 1880 Seattle had only two banks with assets totaling about $300,000. By 1889 there were eight banks and several private banking concerns with assets exceeding $1,000,000.[10] Most of these were funded by eastern investors, reflecting their belief in the future of the city. In late 1889, Rudyard Kipling, then a twenty-four-year-old British journalist traveling in America, came to Puget Sound from California. Unconvinced about the future of the region, he nonetheless commented on the building boom, writing of "the raw new smell of fresh sawdust everywhere pervading the air."[11] Construction was news, and local newspapers and promotional publications enumerated the buildings under construction, the total amounts of investment, and similar facts and figures showing the rapid development that had followed the railroad lines.

The late 1880s were years of particular enmity between Seattle and Tacoma, each feeling that it should rightfully become the metropolis of the sound. From 1884 to 1889, the management of the Northern Pacific strongly favored Tacoma, even omitting Seattle from its maps and intermittently terminating all rail service to the city. A contemporary Tacoma school children's chant from the period after the Seattle fire, "Seattle, Seattle! Death rattle, Death rattle!" may convey some sense of the intense competition between these cities in the period.[12] But in mid-September 1889, James J. Hill announced the consolidation of various railroad lines to create the Great Northern with Seattle as its Pacific Coast terminus. This competition forced the Northern Pacific to announce the equalization of rail service between Seattle and Tacoma the following month.[13] Still, competition between Tacoma and Seattle remained intense through the next two decades until Seattle's ascendancy was no longer in question.

In spite of the efforts of the Northern Pacific and competition from Tacoma, Seattle developed rapidly in the later 1880s. In spring 1889, an assessor's report estimated that the city's population had reached 33,850; immigration continued and in 1890 the census counted a population of 42,837 in the city. Even the fire of 6 June 1889 did not slow the growth of Seattle, and the influx of laborers looking for work after the fire swelled the population. With growth at this pace, the architectural transformation of the city was inevitable. The 1889 fire provided an impetus for creating a modern city with the rebuilding of the commercial core, but the growth of Seattle was outward as well as upward, and the areas which emerged as Seattle's new residential neighborhoods in the early 1890s began to take the built form that they would have through the twentieth century. In many ways, the 1880s and 1890s became the defining decades for the character of urban Seattle.

The Victorian Context of Early Seattle Architecture

In the context of feverish boosterism and the intense competition among cities on Puget Sound, the three-dimensional physical fabric of a city took on an extraordinary importance. The architecture of a city was seen to be a representation of permanence, distinction, and metropolitan achievement. The conspicuous attention given by local and regional publications to new construction, civic improvement, and the progress of urban development clearly indicated the significance local leaders attached to the physical manifestations of urban preeminence. New water systems, electrification, street extensions, harbor improvements, streetcar lines, and residential subdivisions were widely reported as evidence of investment, permanence, and stability. Architectural work not only embodied these aspects but also, in the absence of other cultural measures, demonstrated a level of cultural achievement.[14]

The role of architecture as the hallmark of cultural ascendancy was recognized in the Northwest from an early date. Just the appearance of an "architect" in a city might be seen as signifying cultural development. As early as 1869, an Olympia paper made this clear:

> One of the most gratifying evidences of the march of civilization is the departure from the crude, unsightly structures characteristic of the new countries, and the adoption of models, with their elegant ornaments, which have become popular in old communities. The advent of Mr. R. A. Abbott, a skillful civic architect, whose advertisement will be found in another column, affords our people an opportunity now of obtaining designs and specifications for modern buildings with the embellishments and conveniences that a matured taste and use in the East have approved.[15]

The background of the thirty-five-year-old Mr. Abbott, a native of Vermont who had come to Olympia from Chicago, remains unknown, but he was probably a "contractor-builder"—a contractor who had some experience in design and who designed the buildings he constructed—who called himself an architect. In early Puget Sound communities, with fewer than a thousand residents, there simply was not enough demand to support an architect for long, if at all. Until the 1880s, most buildings in Washington were created by contractor-builders. Often itinerant, moving from town to town as opportunity presented itself, these contractor-builders usually based their designs on models they had learned as apprentices and buildings they had seen, supplemented by examples offered by pattern books and building manuals.

The early appearance of Seattle was unimpressive. Until the late 1870s the city was essentially built of wood, taking advantage of the local abundance of this resource. (Fig. 2.3) Structures were generally one or two stories, with gable roofs. Along Front Street (now First Avenue), the commercial center of the town, the predominant form was the false front, typical of many western communities. This architecture was generally utilitarian in character, with limited embellishment and detailing following the simpler forms of examples found in pattern books. The earliest exception was the building for Washington's Territorial University, erected in 1861. A two-story rectangular structure in a Classical Revival style with a portico supported by four two-story Ionic columns, this remained the town's most impressive structure for more than two decades.[16] (Fig. 2.4)

The restrained classicism of the Territorial University building was in marked contrast to most of the architecture built in Seattle in the 1870s and

2.3 View from Denny Hill, southeast toward downtown Seattle, 1878

Manuscripts, Special Collections, University Archives Division, University of Washington Libraries, photo by Peterson Brothers, copied by Asahel Curtis, UW 12054

2.4 John Pike, Washington Territorial University Building, 1861 (destroyed)

Manuscripts, Special Collections, University Archives Division, University of Washington Libraries, photo by Theodore Peiser, UW 12543

1880s which reflected the complexity of American architecture in the post–Civil War period. The emphasis was on an architecture of visual complexity and richness created by inventive applications of details and motifs drawn from a range of sources including English Victorian Gothic and French Second Empire, and occasionally Italianate and German, precedents. Initially the architecture of the period had drawn individually on these sources and applied motifs in an internally consistent pattern, creating American interpretations of contemporary European designs. However, by the mid-1870s, opportunities for experimentation allowed architects to create new works by combining details and motifs without concern for the historical boundaries of their sources. American Victorian architects were, therefore, not historicists, since they did not attempt to re-create the architecture of any particular historical period; rather they can be considered freely eclectic as they chose from and combined a wide variety of contemporary and historical features.[17] The result was an architecture of inventive articulation and visual richness that often demonstrated a preference for irregular profiles, strong contrasts, dynamic conjunctions, and layered and richly colored surfaces. The resulting designs can often be characterized as "picturesque eclectic," reflecting their layering of color, texture, pattern, and ornament.

The preference for roughness, irregularity, and surface texture derives in part from the "picturesque"—an aesthetic rooted in the late eighteenth and early nineteenth centuries. Developed initially by English landscape designers who were frustrated with the formal order of classical design, the principles of the picturesque were first defined by Uvalde Price, who wrote that the "picturesque" consisted of "the two . . . qualities of roughness and sudden variation, joined to that of irregularity."[18]

As in England, the picturesque was first introduced in the United States through landscape design and then was applied to rural architecture. Advocates of the picturesque such as Andrew Jackson Downing not only preferred irregular plans and silhouettes for country houses, but also objected to plain wall surfaces, arguing instead for texture and an emphasis on details and joinery—on porches, eaves, columns, moldings, and any other features that might add interest to the building surface. Downing wrote that such elements "confer the same kind of expression on a house that the eyes, eyebrows, lips, etc. do upon the human countenance."[19]

While these principles were first applied only to rural and suburban buildings, the widespread acceptance of the picturesque by the 1850s led to its transformation for use in urban settings. Although city street-wall architecture might not develop the overall irregularity of country houses, it could take on a significant picturesque character in detail through texture, with cornices, stringcourses, columns, pediments, moldings, rustication, and a high degree of polychromy. The picturesque appreciation which informed American architecture after 1850 did not dictate a particular style. Architects working in urban settings found that the Victorian Gothic and the Italianate, as well as the Second Empire and the round-arched German *Rundbogenstil*, might be developed or even combined in a picturesque way. And, even when a design was controlled by an overall symmetry as in most Second Empire and *Rundbogenstil* compositions, the potential for a richly modeled surface remained.

Downing's advocacy of Gothic as a style for residential architecture, and his attacks on classical design, prepared American architects for a general acceptance of the English Victorian Gothic. An even stronger impetus came from the writing of the English theorist and critic John Ruskin. Ruskin's *Seven Lamps of Architecture* published in 1849, and his *Stones of Venice* appearing two years later, gave the Gothic movement a stronger ethical imperative and, at the same

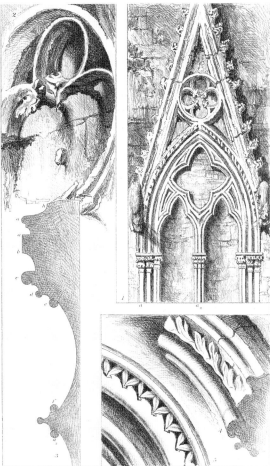

time, celebrated the polychromatic character of late Romanesque and Gothic architecture in northern Italy. Ruskin's primary focus was on detail and ornament. His books were illustrated with visually compelling sketches that achieved their effects by combining different elements, often from different sources, drawn at different scales. (Fig. 2.5) The dynamic character of these sometimes disjointed groupings found its way into the work of Victorian architects. American architects, who had already accepted picturesque ideals, readily adopted the High Victorian Gothic, and the immigration of a number of English Gothic revivalists reinforced this direction.[20] The influence of Victorian Gothic design was so widespread that Henry Van Brunt was to recall some years later, "The Gothic revival of that time was a universal cult among all English-speaking people."[21] (Fig. 2.6)

Victorian Gothic from England was only one of several sources that contributed to American Victorian architecture. The French Second Empire style, which had emerged with the rapid development of Paris after 1840, offered a richly detailed architecture often applied to public buildings. As realized in the additions to the Louvre completed in 1857, the style featured regularly or symmetrically disposed pavilions and high mansard roofs. Elevations were often animated grids formed by tiers of paired classical columns or pilasters sup-

2.5 Plates II (left) and X (right), from John Ruskin, *The Seven Lamps of Architecture*, 5th edition (1886)

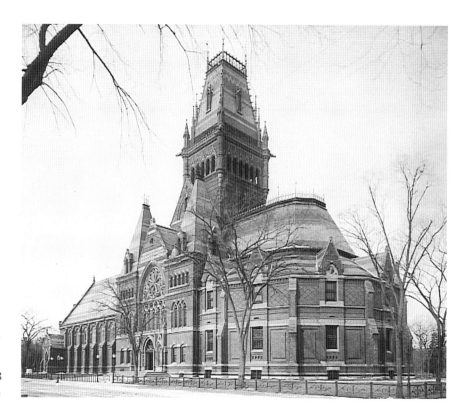

porting horizontal belt courses and rich sculptural detail which produced visually engaging patterns of light and shadow. The American adaptation of the
style was best exemplified by Boston City Hall, completed in 1865, which was
designed by Arthur Gilman and Gridley J. Bryant. (Fig. 2.7) This building apparently served as a prototype for Alfred B. Mullett, who as supervising architect
of the United States Treasury from 1865 to 1875 was responsible for the dissemination of Second Empire design through its application to federal government
buildings across the United States.[22]

Other sources also fed into the mixture that became American Victorian
design. The Italianate mode had originated as a picturesque style, vaguely
derived from Italian rural architecture. Initially applied to residential buildings, Italianate design featured low-pitched overhanging roofs with decorative
brackets, tall narrow windows with curved and decorated heads, and frequent
use of cupolas. Although Italianate design was applied only occasionally in urban
settings and slowly declined after 1870, Italianate details sometimes appeared
on American Victorian buildings. German precedents were also found in
American Victorian design drawn from the *Rundbogenstil*, a style characterized by floors treated as horizontal layers with repetitive round-arched elements.

By the 1870s, most American architects were working in multiple styles. For
example, both Victorian Gothic and Second Empire are reflected in H. H.
Richardson's early works. Victorian Gothic was most often applied for ecclesiastical, educational, and similar structures, while Second Empire was primarily applied to governmental and commercial work. In the mid-1870s,
architects had begun to combine elements drawn from French, English, Italian,

2.7 Gilman and Bryant,
Boston City Hall, Boston,
1861–65

*Library of Congress, Detroit
Publishing Company
Collection, LC-D4–19618*

and occasionally German sources into a rich and varied eclectic architecture where the individual detail was often emphasized at the expense of the whole. Within the framework of picturesque design, designers of the period produced an architecture that drew from a variety of classical, medieval, and contemporary sources to create works of vibrant texture, color, and ornament that would later be categorized as examples of "Victorian excess."[23]

The English Queen Anne movement, which emerged in the late 1870s, was generally absorbed within the preexisting framework of American Victorian design, producing its most dramatic impact on domestic architecture. Originating in the work of a group of English architects led by Richard Norman Shaw, the style initially appeared in the United States in H. H. Richardson's Sherman house, completed in Newport, Rhode Island, in 1876. The Queen Anne was most widely applied in American residential design where irregular shapes were typical, along with a wide variety of surface treatments loosely based on late-medieval models of the Elizabethan and Jacobean periods. The use of half-timbering and patterned masonry derived directly from Shaw and his contemporaries, while the use of patterned shingles and elaborate spindle-work were American adaptations. In its American urban applications the Queen Anne reemphasized picturesque compositional strategies and introduced patterned brickwork and free classical detail.

American Victorian architecture spread across the American West in the period after 1865. Although the nation's continental boundaries had been fixed by 1853, the settlement of most of the West waited for the end of the Civil War and the development of the transcontinental rail network. Thus, the post–Civil War period, when American architecture was at its most exuberant, was a time of sustained urban development and intense construction from the Midwest to the Pacific Coast. Illustrations of American Victorian design appearing in the new national architectural press after 1876 offer evidence of the wide range of individual virtuosity and dexterity of the nation's architects and builders.[24] Although the vast majority of illustrations in this period are from the East, examples of new work in the West appeared as well. In the larger western cities of San Francisco, Portland, Kansas City, Galveston, and Denver, a number of architects, often immigrants from the East or from abroad, produced surprisingly sophisticated works that would have fit easily in Philadelphia or New York or Boston. (Figs. 2.8, 2.9)

During these years two tendencies introduced a greater degree of order into Victorian architecture, according to Stephen Fox. First, after the mid-1850s, English architects, particularly G. E. Street, began to emphasize the structural and constructional rationality of Gothic architecture rather than its medieval associations and pictorial aspects. Interest in the structural basis of architecture was fostered in America when French theorist Eugene-Emmanuel Viollet-le-Duc's book, *Entretiens sur l'architecture*, was translated into English as *Discourses on Architecture* in the 1870s. Viollet-le-Duc had argued for a rational understanding of architecture in terms of the interaction of structure, environment, and culture. American architect and advocate of the Gothic, Leopold Eidlitz, whose 1881 book was titled *Nature and the Function of Art with Special Reference to Architecture*, also emphasized the structural and constructional logic of Gothic design. While most American designers of the period were unlikely to be aware of advanced architectural theory, it is evident that American Victorian buildings in the 1880s frequently featured what is best described as "constructive detail."[25] An implicit structural or constructional logic can be understood in the compositional grids formed by pilasters and belt courses as well as in the individual details on the exteriors of American Victorian buildings.

Second, at the same time as English Victorian architects sought to extend Victorian Gothic design to secular buildings, they also began to introduce classicizing tendencies, including the qualities of uniformity, symmetry, and repose, and even the horizontal lines that are usually associated with classical design.[26] This tendency, described by Charles Eastlake in his book *A History of the Gothic Revival*, published in 1872, brought an increased degree of order and regularity to Victorian architecture. These features became particularly apparent

2.8 Architect unidentified, Phelan Building, San Francisco, 1878–81 (destroyed)

California Historical Society, FN32362

2.9 Justus Krumbein, Kamm Building, Portland, Oregon, 1884 (destroyed)

Oregon Historical Society, OrHi 48801

in the commercial architecture of American urban centers in the late 1870s and 1880s. Eastlake also pointed to the influence of Viollet-le-Duc in the emerging preference for muscular elements such as thick flat pilasters and moldings that divided the facades of otherwise planar later Victorian buildings.

American Victorian design varied considerably in character and quality. Throughout the United States, trained architects accounted for only a small portion of what was built. Broad architectural training did not then exist, and most designers outside the large eastern cities began their careers as contractor-builders. Largely self-taught, these contractors-builders depended on their practical knowledge, on examples they had seen, and on pattern books and other popular design handbooks for plans, compositional schemes, and details.[27] In the smaller towns and cities as well as in many residential areas surrounding larger cities, contractor-builders acting as designers were responsible for virtually all design and construction. As with any large body of work, their creations varied widely. Clearly, economics was a significant factor. Where urban development had generated considerable wealth, as in San Francisco, a richly ornamented architecture could be produced. But this was the exception rather than the rule. In hundreds of smaller cities and towns such as Seattle, ostentatious ornament was too expensive, and the application of Victorian motifs and details such as pilasters, belt courses, cornices, and window heads was marked by practicality and economy even as expressiveness was sought.

The First Generation of Seattle Architects

Seattle's first practicing professional architect, Arthur Doyle (1819–1899), arrived in the city in 1871, coming from Denver.[28] His background included construction as well as design. With the small size of the community, his architectural production was limited to relatively few buildings executed in the prevailing Victorian modes. His Frauenthal Building (1876, destroyed) was a commercial block with a cast-iron facade, while his Martin Van Buren Stacy House (1883–84, destroyed), combined Italianate and Second Empire features. (Fig. 2.10) He was also designer of Squire's Opera House (1879–80, destroyed), the city's first theater, where President Rutherford Hayes spoke when he visited the city in 1880.[29] Nonetheless, some in Seattle turned to practitioners elsewhere for their architecturally ambitious projects. For example, Portland architects Warren Williams and Justus Krumbein designed the First Presbyterian Church (1876, destroyed), at Third and Madison, a wood frame structure with tall rounded windows and a square corner tower with Gothic finials.[30] (Fig. 2.11)

The form of Seattle in 1880 has been described as similar to a New England coastal town.[31] Although a large area of land had been platted, the community generally developed parallel to the shore, stretching about one and one-half miles from north to south, but less than a mile inland. The commercial focus of the community was the cluster of docks, wharves, and bunkers along the waterfront. The streets were aligned in regular grids, but these had been laid out parallel to the shore, resulting in awkward intersections, especially at Mill

2.10 Arthur Doyle, Martin Van Buren Stacy House, 1883–84 (destroyed)

Manuscripts, Special Collections, University Archives Division, University of Washington Libraries, photo by F. Jay Haynes

2.11 Warren Williams and Justus Krumbein, First Presbyterian Church, 1876 (destroyed)

Manuscripts, Special Collections, University Archives Division, University of Washington Libraries, photo by A. C. Warner, 191x

Street (now Yesler Way). The half-block offset between Front and Commercial (now First Avenue and First Avenue South) at Mill became a point of tremendous congestion as the community grew in the 1880s.

In 1882, the anticipated completion of the transcontinental railroad connection touched off the city's first building boom. A sense of the impending changes is evident in articles that appeared in the *Seattle Post-Intelligencer* heralding a "steady rise to greatness" and claiming "the experimental period in Seattle's history is past."[32] For the next eighteen months the paper routinely touted the new construction. Although wood had been virtually the city's only building material, the commercial core began to be transformed with the introduction of more substantial masonry structures. The opening of James McAllister's brickyard south of downtown in 1882 facilitated this development, and in May, when the paper reported on several new buildings it noted, "Three brick buildings will be in construction within half a block of each other—something never before known in these parts."[33] Institutional buildings such as churches and schools, however, remained of wood construction, as did residences.

In the early 1880s, Seattle's economic and transportation links were still oriented towards the south—via coastal steamer to Oregon and California and, after 1884, via the rail link to Portland. The cities to the south were the primary sources for materials and fabrications not available in Seattle. Foundries in San Francisco, for example, were the source of cast ironwork used in Seattle facades.[34] So it is not surprising that the primary models for the city's new construction were the Victorian buildings of Portland and San Francisco. However, Seattle buildings rarely approached the ornateness of those found in the leading Pacific Coast cities.

The promise of growth in the early 1880s prompted a new group of architects from Oregon and California to move to Seattle, including Donald MacKay, William Boone, Stephen Meany, and John Nestor. Information about these early architects is sparse, but in general they had similar backgrounds, lacking professional training and emerging from the building trades. For some their architectural careers were just an interlude, but for others, once they assumed the title of architect, they aspired to practice architecture on a continuing basis. These early practitioners generally came from rural or small town environments and had limited experience of cities other than San Francisco or Portland. They all had moved in pursuit of opportunity, so their individual decisions to come to Seattle generally fit within the pattern of their careers.

When Donald MacKay (1846–?1887) arrived in Seattle on 18 April 1882, he brought designs for a new hospital and remodeled church. He had been sent to the city at the behest of the Sisters of Providence, a Catholic religious order which, under the direction of their superior, Mother Joseph, was developing a network of schools, hospitals, and similar facilities across the Northwest.[35] An enigmatic figure, MacKay was born in Scotland, but by June 1880 he had arrived in Walla Walla where he worked as a contractor-builder. He is frequently confused with his namesake, Donald Mackay (1841–1924), contractor and longtime resident of Portland, Oregon.[36] MacKay came to Seattle as the architect for religious projects, but once in the city received several significant secular commissions.

When MacKay arrived, his drawings for Providence Hospital (1882–83, destroyed) were already complete, so the project was bid and the contract awarded in little more than a week. Initially only half of the design could be constructed, but additions in the later 1880s completed the symmetrical three-story composition. (Fig. 2.12) Detailing was restrained, but the mansard roof marked this as a Second Empire design, although the *Post-Intelligencer*

2.12 Donald MacKay,
Providence Hospital,
1882–83 (destroyed)

*Manuscripts, Special
Collections, University
Archives Division, University
of Washington Libraries,
photo by A. C. Warner, 289*

described it as "composite Italian."[37] MacKay's other initial project, also displayed within a few days of his arrival, was to enlarge Our Lady of Good Hope
Catholic Church (1882, destroyed). In this design the existing chapel dating
from 1869 was retained, but turned to serve as the transept of the new building. Built entirely of wood, on a steep site, the simple Gothic detailing of the
new building echoed the older one except at the more highly embellished
entrances.[38]

MacKay's design abilities evidently attracted notice because, on 6 May, the
Post-Intelligencer reported that he had been commissioned by Seattle entrepreneur John Collins (1835–1903) to design the Occidental Hotel (1882–84,
destroyed). Collins was an early Seattle political and business leader who
invested in railroads, mining, real estate, and other ventures.[39] The building
was located on one of the most prominent sites in the city, the narrow triangular parcel at the corner of James, Mill, and Front Streets in the heart of downtown. Initially announced as three stories and a basement, the building was
constructed to four stories including a mansarded attic level. Built of brick
faced with stucco, its facades were regularly gridded with a typical Victorian
pattern of pilasters and belt courses framing rectangular bay windows. (Fig.
2.13) The Second Empire style building was the finest hotel in the city from
its opening in 1884 until its destruction by the June 1889 fire.[40]

In August, MacKay, William Boone, and Joseph Sherwin (a leading architect from Portland) all submitted drawings for the new commercial block jointly
planned by Seattle pioneers Henry Yesler and John Leary, but it was Boone's
scheme, not MacKay's, that was selected.[41] Thereafter Boone surpassed
MacKay as the leading architect in Seattle, a position he would hold through
most of the 1880s. MacKay continued to supervise the projects he then had
under way, and he took on new work in 1883. His Holy Names Academy
(1883–84, destroyed), with its inventive combination of Second Empire,

Victorian Gothic, and Italianate features, was a prominent city landmark for many years, but MacKay's subsequent design career involved projects in Tacoma and Vancouver, and by 1884 he had moved to Portland.[42]

Of the Seattle architects of the early 1880s, William E. Boone (1830–1921) would have the longest active architectural career in the city, practicing into the early years of the twentieth century.[43] Born in western Pennsylvania on 3 September 1830 and raised in that state, he worked for several years in construction for a railroad company in Chicago, then moved to Minneapolis and probably became involved in design as well as construction about 1853. In 1859, he moved to California where he was for many years a contractor-builder initially in San Francisco and later in Oakland and nearby East Bay communities. He first came to Puget Sound in 1872, designing a number of small buildings in Olympia, and in 1873 he served as construction superintendent for the federal prison at McNeill Island, but returned to California upon its completion and continued to work as a contractor-builder. In 1881 Boone returned to the Northwest and for a time his practice alternated between Seattle and Tacoma.[44] From June 1883 to 1889 he practiced with George C. Meeker in the partnership Boone and Meeker, but Meeker is thought to have remained in Oakland, California, for most of this period.[45]

Boone already had several Seattle projects under way when his design was selected for the Yesler-Leary Building. He first advertised as an architect in the *Post-Intelligencer* in late April 1882, and his early 1882 projects included the Marshall Building (1882, destroyed) and the McNaught, Walker and Renton

2.14 William E. Boone/
Boone and Meeker,
Yesler-Leary Building,
1882–83 (destroyed)

*Manuscripts, Special
Collections, University
Archives Division, University
of Washington Libraries,
copy photo by Asahel Curtis,
6235*

Building (1882–83, destroyed), on Commercial Street, and the Boyd and Poncin
Store (1882, destroyed) on Front Street.[46] These were all two-story brick blocks
of relatively unexceptional design; the street fronts were faced in stucco and
divided by pilasters following Victorian convention, with cast-iron columns and
extensive glazing at the ground floor as appropriate for retail use. It was the
appearance of so many brick commercial structures that marked a decisive
shift in the character of downtown Seattle.

When Seattle pioneer business leaders Henry Yesler and John Leary
announced their selection of Boone's design for the Yesler-Leary Building
(1882–83, destroyed), the *Post-Intelligencer* described it as Seattle's finest
building and symbolic of the city's new metropolitan character.[47] (Fig. 2.14)
Like Henry Yesler, John Leary (1837–1905) had come to Seattle in connection with the lumber business. Admitted to the bar in 1871, Leary practiced
law until 1882, then served several terms on the city council and as Seattle's
mayor. He also invested in newspapers, railroads, and real estate.[48]

Occupying the acute angle at the intersection of Mill and Front Streets in
the center of downtown, the three-story Yesler-Leary Building with retail uses
at the ground floor and offices above, featured a mansard roof and tall octago-
nal cupola, and offered a prominent focus opposite the Occidental Hotel. The
building was constructed of brick faced with stucco; the first-floor columns and
projecting second- and third-floor bay windows were of cast iron. The design
was derived from the Phelan Block in San Francisco and featured a combination of Second Empire and Italianate detail. (See Fig. 2.8)

Although the *Post-Intelligencer* noted that several other brick commercial blocks were under consideration in summer and fall 1882, none proceeded into construction. Materials shortages, especially the difficulty of obtaining brick, limited building. Indeed, in late August the paper reported that the Methodist Church had waited two months for brick, but could wait no longer and would be constructed of wood. Other owners chose to wait until the building season in 1883.[49]

As the new building season began in March 1883, the *Post-Intelligencer* announced several new projects by Boone, including a proposed four-story addition to the Yesler-Leary Building (which itself was still under construction)—but this did not proceed beyond the drafting table. On 15 April, an article in the paper described still more commercial buildings under design in Boone's office, including the two-story C. P. Stone Block (1883, destroyed) on Front Street, and the three-story Schwabacher Building (1883, destroyed) on Commercial, both stucco-faced brick blocks with gridded facades and a mix of Victorian detail. Later in the year two additional commercial blocks of his design, the Wah Chong Building (1883, destroyed) on South Third, and the Squire Building (1883, destroyed), on South Second, also began construction; a shortage of brick caused the Squire Building to be constructed entirely of wood.[50] However, Boone's most significant Seattle project in 1883 was not a commercial block but the new residence for Henry Yesler.

The Henry Yesler House (1883–84, destroyed), occupying a full city block bounded by Third, Fourth, James, and Jefferson, was the largest residence in Seattle, measuring 80 by 120 feet at its extreme dimensions. Described as "Eastlake style," the three-story building was a highly irregular picturesque composition with a variety of bays and dormers.[51] Details included Victorian wood banding, Queen Anne patterned shingles, barge boards, and brackets, and Eastlake turned porch supports. (Fig. 2.15)

In 1884, as this early Seattle boom faded, Boone and Meeker continued as the leading commercial architects in the city, with projects including the three-story Seattle Safe Deposit Building (1884, destroyed) and Gordon Hardware Company Building (1884, destroyed), adjacent to each other on Front Street, which followed the general direction established in Boone's earlier work.[52] But, for the next two years, Boone and Meeker's practice increasingly focused on work in Tacoma. In July 1883 Boone won the commission for the Annie Wright Seminary (1883–84, destroyed), a private girls' school in that city, and following their success with this project Boone and Meeker received a series of Tacoma commercial and residential commissions.[53]

Although Boone was Seattle's leading architect in the early 1880s, his was not the only firm, and other architects received significant commissions. The city's largest building of the period, the Frye Opera House (1883–85, destroyed), was the work of John Nestor (1836–1912). Born in Ireland, Nestor came to the United States as a child. He initially practiced architecture in Indiana, and then in San Francisco, and in Portland after 1864.[54] He arrived in Seattle in

2.15 Boone and Meeker,
Henry Yesler House,
1883–84 (destroyed)

*Museum of History and
Industry, Wilse Collection,
88.33.1*

1883 and, because he had previous experience in theater design, soon received
the commission for the Frye Opera House. Although the theater opened in
December 1884, the building was not fully completed until the next year. This
four-story structure, located on Front Street between Madison and Marion, north
of the center of the commercial district, was particularly prominent when viewed
from the harbor. Measuring 120 feet square, the building included stores facing Front Street, with three floors of offices above. The theater, which could
seat more than one thousand, occupied half the site, with its entrance facing
Marion. Built of brick faced with stucco, the facades were detailed in a typical Victorian grid pattern, while the fourth floor featured an elaborate mansard
roof—a design the *Post-Intelligencer* described as "French street architecture."
(Fig. 2.16) At a cost of about $125,000, this was the most expensive building
constructed in the city at the time. The paper proclaimed the building's
significance: "The Frye Opera House stands unrivaled in the Pacific Northwest;
it is not excelled on the Pacific Coast; no city in the United States of less than
twice the size of Seattle can show its equal."[55]

Nestor was also involved in the most elaborate of Seattle's pre-fire churches,
the freely interpreted Gothic First Methodist Episcopal Church (1887–89,
destroyed), located at Third and Marion, although the original design was by
Portland architect William Stokes. Stokes was commissioned as architect for
the church in June 1887, and Nestor was employed as the local superintendent, but in August Stokes was let go and Nestor was responsible for many of
the final drawings.[56] The building was a highly articulated cruciform wood-

2.16 John Nestor, Frye
Opera House, 1883–85
(destroyed)

*Manuscripts, Special
Collections, University
Archives Division, University
of Washington Libraries,
photo by A. C. Warner, 294*

2.17 William Stokes/John
Nestor, First Methodist
Episcopal Church,
1887–89 (destroyed)

*Manuscripts, Special
Collections, University
Archives Division, University
of Washington Libraries,
photo by A. C. Warner, 97x*

2.18 Isaac Palmer,
Central School, 1882–83
(destroyed)

*Manuscripts, Special
Collections, University
Archives Division, University
of Washington Libraries,
photo by Theodore Peiser,
UW5041*

frame structure with an attached corner tower, including elaborate ornament, rose windows, and dramatic gable and tower profiles. (Fig. 2.17) The sanctuary interior featured the sloping floors and semi-circular seating arrangement which had become common for non-liturgical American Protestant churches in the late nineteenth century.

In the same years, Seattle also built its first two large school buildings.[57] The city's initial public schools had been two-room structures called "shack schools," but in the early 1880s after citizen agitation, voters approved funding for larger buildings. Although several proposals were submitted for the Central School (1882–83, destroyed) at Sixth and Madison, only the designer of the selected scheme, a contractor-builder, Isaac Palmer, was identified in the press.[58] The two-story wood structure, which could accommodate up to eight hundred students, was described by the *Post-Intelligencer* as "the largest [school] in Washington Territory."[59] Detailing was restrained, although the design was characterized as "Eastlake" due to the decorative treatment of the eaves and the entrance porch. (Fig. 2.18)

The continued growth of the city led the school district to proceed with a second large school building the next year. Designs were submitted in late June 1883 by Boone and Meeker, M. L. Keezer, and Donovan and Meany. The scheme by Donovan and Meany was selected on 29 June.[60] Stephen Meany had come to Seattle from San Jose, California, and had initially worked as a draftsman for William Boone. He later worked briefly for Donald MacKay and for Arthur Doyle. However, by mid-1883 he had formed a partnership with architect James P. Donovan, of whom little is known.[61] Their design for the North School, later known as Denny School (1883–84, destroyed), at Sixth and Wall, was a rectangular wood building with a hipped roof, gabled projections on each side, and a tall cupola. The detailing was Italianate, and the *Post-Intelligencer* described the building as based "on thoroughly scientific principles" and "hand-

2.19 Donovan and Meany,
Denny School, 1883–84
(destroyed)

*Manuscripts, Special
Collections, University
Archives Division, University
of Washington Libraries,
photo by A. C. Warner, 34*

some in the extreme."[62] (Fig. 2.19) The school district wished to build a third school south of Central, but the city's economic decline after 1883 meant construction could not be financed.

On 25 October 1883, Seattle papers reported the collapse of Northern Pacific stock, and by early November, the railroad was described as "retrenching." The building boom of the early 1880s came to an end, and Seattle's economy slumped. As a result, only a few new business blocks were commissioned in 1884. With the practice of Boone and Meeker increasingly focused elsewhere, it was Boone's former draftsman, Stephen Meany, who received the commissions for the Poncin Block (1884, destroyed) and the Kenney Block (1884–85, destroyed). These were three-story structures on opposite sides of Front Street. Meany generally followed the design of Boone's commercial buildings, with retail at ground level and offices above and with their stucco-faced brick fronts featuring Victorian detail; the Poncin Building was notable for its bay windows at the upper floors.[63]

Other notable buildings of the mid-1880s were residential structures. In addition to Arthur Doyle's Stacy House and William Boone's Yesler House, three large houses by architects from outside Seattle attracted attention. Designed by leading Portland architect Warren Williams, the James McNaught House (1883–84, destroyed) at the southeast corner of Fourth and Spring was a generally symmetrical two-story wood structure with a three-story central tower and a rich mix of Victorian detail.[64] (Fig. 2.20) The Morgan J. Carkeek House (1884–85, destroyed), on First Hill, was a gaunt three-story Queen Anne residence by the New York architects Palliser and Palliser, best known for their publication of several pattern books.[65] The largest house of the mid-

2.20 Warren Williams,
James McNaught House,
1883–84 (destroyed)

*Manuscripts, Special
Collections, University
Archives Division, University
of Washington Libraries,
photo by Boyd and Braas, 18*

1880s, and most significant residential structure in the city after the Yesler
mansion, was the George Kinnear House (1886–88, destroyed), by Kirby and
Randall of Syracuse. The picturesquely composed two-story Queen Anne house
with a profusion of gables and a prominent corner tower was, according to
David Rash, somewhat more elaborate than the published design, which lacked
the tower's distinctive attenuated roof capped with an onion dome.[66] (Fig. 2.21)
Located on the newly developing south slope of Queen Anne Hill, the house
cost a reported $25,000 and established the area as a fashionable residential
neighborhood.

The mid-1880s in Seattle were years of economic decline—a decline exac-
erbated by the policies of the new management of the Northern Pacific, which
promoted Tacoma at the expense of Seattle and in 1884 even terminated rail
service to the city. The financial stringency in Seattle grew so severe that, in
spring 1886, the school term ended a month early as the district ran out of
funds and could not pay the teachers. Architectural work lagged, few projects

2.21 Kirby and Randall, George Kinnear House, 1886–88 (destroyed)

Museum of History and Industry, Wilse Collection, 88.33.42

were mentioned in the local papers, and how Seattle's architects supported themselves in these years, if in fact they did, is not clear. Boone and Meeker, however, had fortunately secured one of the largest commissions of the time, the Washington Territorial Insane Asylum at Steilacoom (1886–87, destroyed), a massive institutional structure.[67]

The Late 1880s and a New Generation of Architects

When Seattle's economy rebounded in the late 1880s, the demand for architectural services initially grew slowly, as commercial space built from 1882 to 1884 had not been filled because of the weak economy. By 1887, however, construction began to pick up, and Boone and Meeker resumed their position as the leading architects in the city. By this time, however, the practice of building in brick finished with stucco for a monochromatic appearance had given way to a polychromatic architecture of brick and stone. In March 1887 the *Post-Intelligencer* reported on Boone and Meeker's design for the Toklas and Singerman Building (1887, destroyed) on Front at Columbia.[68] A three-story brick block, this featured a variety of Victorian detail like Boone's earlier projects, but now with a more varied color palette as a result of the contrast between the red brick walls and stone lintels, sills, belt courses, and other constructive details. (Fig. 2.22)

2.22 Boone and Meeker, Toklas & Singerman Building, 1887 (destroyed)

Manuscripts, Special Collections, University Archives Division, University of Washington Libraries, photo by A. C. Warner, 296

In September, Boone was also selected to supervise construction of the four-story Boston Block (1887–88, destroyed), at Second and Columbia, designed by the Boston firm Bradley, Winslow, and Witherall.[69] The first Seattle building with a passenger elevator, the Boston Block included stores at the first floor and three floors of office rooms above. The design was relatively plain with regularly gridded red brick facades facing the two streets.

Boone and Meeker also proceeded with the addition to the west side of the Yesler-Leary Building that had first been contemplated in 1883; identified as the Yesler Block (1887–88, destroyed), this was originally planned as four stories, but built to only three. Like the other buildings erected at this time, this addition was more colorful than the original Yesler-Leary Building as it was constructed of red brick with stone trim.[70] (Fig. 2.23)

In February and March 1889 the firm designed two more conventional brick commercial blocks, the I.O.O.F Building (1889) and the Phinney Building/ Carleton Block/Ramona Hotel (1889, destroyed). The Phinney Building was a four-story block begun in March that was bypassed by the fire in June and completed by December (under the name the Carleton Block). The I.O.O.F. Building (now the Barnes Building) was constructed on Front Street in Belltown,

Z.C.MILES,
STOVES, RANGES
& TIN-WARE.

g Brook LUMBER C
SHINGLES, FLOORING
&C.
ERS ORDERS FILLED.

YESLER AVE EAST FRO

559

2.23 Looking east on Yesler Avenue; on the left: Boone and Meeker, Yesler Block (Yesler-Leary addition), 1887–88 (destroyed)

Manuscripts, Special Collections, University Archives Division, University of Washington Libraries, photo by A. C. Warner

ten blocks north of the burned area; it is the only one of Boone's pre-fire Seattle structures that survives today.[71]

The preeminence of Boone and Meeker in the city was confirmed when their designs were selected for Seattle's first two brick school buildings. With the growth of the late 1880s the school-age population had far outstripped the capacity of the city's two large school buildings. By 1888 the district could finally proceed financially with needed construction and in early March called for proposals for South School, the building that had first been contemplated in 1883. On 2 April the district received six design submittals. A week later the six-year-old wood Central School burned to the ground. With competitive designs for South School in hand, the board selected two, one for South and the other to replace Central. Boone and Meeker had submitted two different designs and on 11 April, one day after the fire, the board selected both.[72] The two buildings had essentially the same floor plan, and both were constructed of brick with stone trim and walls divided by broad flat pilasters. South School (1888–89, destroyed) was completed as a symmetrical two-story building with a relatively low roof. (See Fig. 6.12) Central School (1888–89, destroyed), however, had a partial third floor, mansard roof, and asymmetrical towers. (See Fig. 6.11) Located at the crest of the slope just above downtown Seattle, Central School's dramatic profile was visible from many parts of the city.

Although Boone and Meeker continued to receive important commissions, their position was challenged in 1888 and 1889. William Boone would turn sixty in 1890, and his design sensibility was becoming dated. The explosive growth of Seattle was attracting younger architects to the city, and they, in turn, would eventually introduce new design approaches.

The architect who proved to be the most important of the new arrivals was Elmer H. Fisher (ca. 1840–1905), who came to Seattle in late 1887. Within little more than a year Fisher displaced Boone as the city's leading commercial architect. How he achieved this distinction is not altogether clear because there seems to have been little in his background to prepare him for this role. Much about Fisher's early life remains obscure, however, because the biographical information he provided after arriving in Seattle appears to have been largely fictitious. Like Boone, Fisher's background was in the building trades, and his initial Seattle architecture reflected American Victorian convention, but after the 1889 fire, Fisher would introduce Richardsonian elements into his work.

Elmer Fisher claimed to have been born in Edinburgh, Scotland, apparently about 1840.[73] He said he came to the United States at age seventeen, and he claimed to have entered the employ of an architect in Worcester, Massachusetts, and to have served in a Massachusetts regiment in the Civil War, but none of these claims are supported by surviving records.[74] His subsequent movements remain unknown until 1880, when he was listed in the city directory for Minneapolis as a clerk in several hardware and farm implement businesses. By 1884, Fisher had moved to Denver, where he was a partner in Corrin and Fisher, carpenters and builders.[75] Apparently the partnership did not last because Fisher soon moved to Butte, Montana; by early 1886 he had arrived in Victoria, British Columbia, the seat of government for the province and then its largest city.[76]

Fisher first advertised as an architect in the *Victoria Colonist* on 6 February 1886. Surprisingly, he almost immediately received commissions because, by 30 March, the *Colonist* reported that Fisher had awarded contracts for the construction of Spencer's Arcade (1886, destroyed), which was described as the "largest building in the Province."[77] Spencer's Arcade was a two-story commercial structure extending 240 feet from Government Street to Broad Street providing spaces for retail shops similar to arcades in Europe and in the eastern United States and Canada. The success of Spencer's Arcade, following quickly upon the death in late May of the prominent Victoria architect James P. Donovan, helped propel Fisher to the front rank of the architectural profession in the city.[78] Fisher was also apparently a social success in Victoria. In October the *Colonist* reported on the celebration of the opening of the Arcade and noted,

> A pleasing incident of the evening was the presentation to Mr. E. H. Fisher, the
> architect of the building, by the proprietor and contractors of the building of an
> appreciative address, accompanied by an elegant desk of solid walnut, . . . The recip-

2.24 Elmer H. Fisher,
Bank of British Columbia,
New Westminster, 1887
(destroyed)

*BC Archives, Province of
British Columbia, A-04619*

ient, though taken entirely by surprise, made a felicitous response, when the band
struck up "For he's a jolly good fellow."[79]

Even before the completion of Spencer's Arcade, Fisher's success was evident in the regular appearance, beginning in May, of his bid announcements
and awards on commercial and public buildings and residences in Victoria
and other British Columbia communities.[80] (Fig. 2.24) With the exception of
the commercial blocks, which were typically of brick, these were generally fairly
simple wood structures with restrained detail reflecting limited budgets. Barrett
and Liscombe, for example, describe Fisher's design in Nanaimo as a "crude
'Gothick' frame courthouse."[81]

In February 1887, Fisher advertised for bids for a two-story building at Port
Townsend on the Olympic Peninsula in Washington Territory.[82] This building,
the McCurdy Block (1887–88), which initiated Fisher's Washington career, was
typical of Fisher's commercial work at the time. Built of brick and heavy timber, this two-story business block featured a corner entrance marked by a high
pediment. The two street facades were divided into somewhat irregular bays,
topped by a prominent cornice, and enlivened by ornamental detail. During
the Port Townsend boom in 1889 and 1890 Fisher received three more commissions for commercial buildings in the city.[83] These three-story commercial
blocks were the James & Hastings Building (1888–89), the N. D. Hill Building
(1889), and the Hastings Building (1889–90), but it was the opportunities offered
in Seattle that drew Fisher away from Victoria.[84] (Fig. 2.25)

Fisher opened an office in Seattle in late 1887, but maintained a presence
in Victoria until 1889.[85] The first notice of his intent to practice in Seattle
appeared in the *Post-Intelligencer,* 17 November 1887, which reported that

2.25 Elmer H. Fisher,
Hastings Building, Port
Townsend, Washington,
1889–90 (altered)

*Jefferson County Historical
Society, 10.094*

Fisher and Goddard had decided to locate permanently in the city beginning
in December.[86] The paper went on: "Mr. Fisher is well known to most of our
readers, as many notices of his buildings at Port Townsend have found a place
in our columns. Mr. Fisher's reputation at Victoria, where his office is now
located, is second to none." On 7 December, an advertisement for Fisher and
Clark (not Goddard) appeared in the *Post-Intelligencer* and on 20 December,
the Victoria paper reported that Fisher had been commissioned to design a commercial block costing $175,000 in Seattle which was to be "the largest and
costliest edifice on the Pacific Coast north of San Francisco."[87] This large commercial block, the Colman Building, commissioned by John Collins, seems to
have been the immediate cause of Fisher's relocation. Fisher's Colman proposal displayed his typical compositional approach, dividing the block-long
facade into nine vertical bays. In detail the brick and stone exterior combined
Second Empire features—the expression of the end bays as pavilions and the
mansarded fourth floor—with typical Victorian detailing—recessed brick pan-

2.26 Fisher and Clark,
Colman Building project,
1887–88 (unbuilt)

*Museum of History and
Industry, Seattle Historical
Society Collection, 5169*

els, vertical incisions, horizontal banding, and a variety of arched window openings. (Fig. 2.26) However, Fisher's Colman design was not built and he was subsequently replaced by Stephen Meany as architect of the project.[88]

Nonetheless, Fisher did succeed in securing other commissions and his Seattle practice flourished in 1888 and early 1889. The Fisher and Clark partnership endured until mid-January 1889, but the role played by Clark was apparently minor. Thereafter Fisher practiced as a sole proprietor. The December 1887 *Colonist* article noted that Fisher already had another Seattle building costing $60,000 in design.[89] This was the (first) Korn Building (1887–89, destroyed), on Mill Street at Second Street, a building that repeated many of the features of Fisher's earlier work—corner entrance, molded brickwork, Victorian "constructive" ornament. Completed by early 1889, the building was destroyed in the fire just a few months later.

Five more Seattle buildings of Fisher's design were noted in the *Post-Intelligencer* in 1888 and the accelerating pace of his practice was indicated by the ten additional buildings reported between January and May 1889. Fisher's early Seattle commissions included a series of terrace houses, a few frame residences, an armory, and several commercial blocks, all displaying features similar to his Victoria designs. For example, the Scurry Terrace (1889, destroyed)

2.27 Elmer H. Fisher, Scurry Terrace, 1889 (destroyed)

Seattle: The Queen City (ca. May 1889); Manuscripts, Special Collections, University Archives Division, University of Washington Libraries, UW 12621

was a rectangular block of four three-story houses located at Third and James, completed in July 1889.[90] (Fig. 2.27) Fisher recessed portions of the 120-foot-long front facade to create symmetrically disposed pavilions, then punctuated these with a series of vertical bays, and detailed them with a mix of Victorian ornament.

However, some of Fisher's Seattle work suggested the exploration of new directions. The Gilmore and Kirkman Building (1888–90, destroyed), a large brick block on the west side of Front Street, which he began designing in mid-1888, reflects a tendency towards regularity and simplification. (Fig. 2.28) The east side of the building rose four stories above Front, but because of the fall of the site toward the water, the west side was seven stories in height. The building featured relatively restrained and consistent detail, giving it a greater coherence than found in his earlier structures. The facade was divided into regular bays featuring paired windows. Detail features included flat brickwork, recessed panels, and horizontal bands; the only exceptional element was the round corner turret, but even this was pulled almost completely into the mass of the building. Construction began in January 1889, and as this building was located north of the burned area, it was not destroyed in the June fire, but was completed in February 1890.[91] Nonetheless, Fisher did not achieve this degree of integration in most of his work. For example, his Austin A. Bell Building (1889–90, facade survives), a four-story brick structure begun in March 1889, offered an array of Victorian Gothic detail on a facade divided into four vertical bays of unequal widths. (Fig. 2.29) Located on Front Street in Belltown, north of the city center, this was also undamaged by the June fire and survived virtually intact until the late 1990s.[92]

Fisher's first years in Seattle seem to have been particularly charmed. He was among the architects who submitted proposals for the Denny Hotel, a large resort hotel project intended for Denny Hill just north of downtown Seattle.[93] The design selected was by New York architect Arthur B. Jennings, but the Denny Hotel Committee sent a letter, excerpted in the *Post-Intelligencer*, praising Fisher's proposal, which had placed second in the competition as it was too costly to build. The letter stated that the plans were "'the most perfect of any submitted to us.'" The paper added, "Mr. Fisher keeps four competent and skillful architects consistently employed at his office on James Street. His business however is so large that he cannot accept orders for ordinary residences, but confines himself to larger edifices."[94]

In January 1889, Fisher began work on the Pioneer Building, commissioned by Henry Yesler. That Fisher and not Boone (who had previously served as Yesler's architect) was selected for the Pioneer Building indicated his emergence as the leading architect in the city. However, the project was delayed and had not proceeded above the foundation at the time of the June 1889 fire. As a result, the design and construction of the Pioneer Building was part of the post-fire building boom.

Fisher's position as Seattle's leading architect was further confirmed in early 1889 when he was selected to design two buildings for Thomas Burke. These commissions, for the Burke Building and for Burke's New York Block, came

2.29 Elmer H. Fisher,
Austin Bell Building,
1889–90 (facade survives)

Washington Magazine 1
(October 1889)

from "Judge" Thomas Burke (1849–1925). Burke came to Seattle from Michigan in 1875. A practicing attorney, he invested in Seattle real estate, newspapers, streetcar lines, and railroads, and was arguably the city's most important civic and business leader in the late nineteenth and early twentieth centuries. Burke's impact on Seattle is best indicated by the title of his biography: *He Built Seattle.*[95] Burke's New York Block (1889, destroyed), at Third and Union, was a three-story structure that resembled Fisher's Gilmore and Kirkman Building.[96] (Fig. 2.30) Much more significant was the larger and more imposing Burke Building, announced in the *Post-Intelligencer* on 12 March 1889. Construction had proceeded only as far as the excavation at the time of the June fire, so the Burke Building, like the Pioneer Building, belongs to the post-fire period.[97]

After Fisher, the most important new Seattle architect was John Parkinson (1861–1935). An English immigrant who was initially trained as a carpenter and stair builder, Parkinson's path into an architectural career paralleled that of many other Seattle architects of the period. Nonetheless, it is clear that from early in his career Parkinson never saw himself as anything but a professional

2.30 Elmer H. Fisher,
Burke's New York Block,
1889 (destroyed)

*Museum of History and
Industry, Seattle Historical
Society Collection, photo by
Anders Wilse, 16759*

architect. In contrast, for example, to Fisher, whose emergence as an architect
followed over twenty years in construction and related trades, Parkinson
turned to architecture in his twenties and appears never thereafter to have considered any other career. Parkinson's approach to his projects appears to demonstrate his awareness, not just of local competitors, but of design directions
nationally. His desire to equal work being done elsewhere seems particularly
evident in his attention, from the very first, to the professional journals. After
1889, he was published more frequently in the national architectural press than
any other Northwest practitioner of the period.

John Parkinson was born in Scorton, Lancashire, in northwest England. In
his 1935 autobiography, *Incidents by the Way,* Parkinson reported that he pos-
sessed a natural ability to work with carpenter's tools as a boy and by age eight
he enjoyed drawing and painting.[98] About 1870, his father accepted a position as an engineer responsible for maintaining the steam engine at a new cotton mill being constructed in Bolton in Lancashire. After completing his
mandatory education at age thirteen, Parkinson was intermittently employed
for about two years, then entered into a six-year apprenticeship with a Bolton
contractor, through which he developed skills in carpentry and a working knowl-

edge of construction. In addition, for five consecutive winter sessions, Parkinson enrolled in classes at Bolton's Mechanic's Institute, where he gained a technical education that included aspects of building design as well as construction.[99] Parkinson wrote of his completion of the apprenticeship in 1882, "I could do anything in woodwork from rough carpentry to cabinet work, knew the construction of buildings from the foundation to the top of the highest finial, was a draftsman too, and an artist born, with confidence unlimited, and trained to endure."[100]

In March 1883, on hearing from a friend who had moved to Winnipeg, Parkinson decided to try the Canadian city for eighteen months. But his job building fences near Kildonan, just south of Winnipeg, lasted only two months, so Parkinson left Canada for Minneapolis, the nearest large city, where he worked as a stair builder until returning to Bolton in late November 1884. Disappointed with the prospects in England, Parkinson emigrated to California, arriving in San Francisco in March 1885. Two months later he took a position as a stair builder with a mill in Napa, where he worked for three and one-half years. Parkinson later wrote of his pride in the craft of stair building:

> Stair building, when circular or part circular stairs are used, is an art, and the expert must be an artist—also a finished mechanic with a practical knowledge of solid geometry. . . . Before any staircase was completed I would pass my hand over the entire length of the handrail to feel for any defect to be corrected before leaving it as a fit job. . . . it was a great joy to me as my own handiwork.[101]

Apparently impressed with Parkinson's abilities and his attention to craft, Solon Chapman, the president of the Bank of Napa, asked Parkinson to develop the architectural design for a new bank building. Parkinson's Bank of Napa (1888, destroyed) was a two-story brick block that drew on the conventions of the Victorian Italianate mode. The Napa *Register* described the building as "modern" in its 23 March 1888 announcement and noted, "The plans were drawn by John Parkinson, architect, who has given this style of architecture much study."[102] While the bank was under way, Parkinson apparently competed unsuccessfully for a high school building in Napa and a courthouse in Redding. The Bank of Napa was completed by late summer and in December 1888, Parkinson, having heard from friends of the many opportunities in Seattle, left Napa for the Northwest.[103]

Parkinson arrived in Seattle in early January 1889. He later wrote that, after failing to secure a position as a draftsman in an established Seattle architectural practice, he had no choice but to open his own office. By late February he was advertising as an architect in the *Post-Intelligencer*.[104] Just twenty-seven, Parkinson was one of the youngest architects in Seattle. He had almost no record of design or construction and he arrived with no personal connections to Seattle's business and civic leadership. As a result, he initially struggled in competition with more established figures such as Boone and Fisher. His first professional office was spartan: "With a pair of trestles, a detailing board, a couple of drawing boards, a cheap wood chair, stationery, paper, and the old box of drawing implements I had used at school in England, I was ready to begin upon any trusting client."[105]

About Parkinson's earliest Seattle project little is known. He later wrote that he was approached by a contractor, Weymouth Crowell, about a possible project designing residential flats for the Seattle business leader William R. Ballard. William Rankin Ballard (1847–1929) was born in Ohio but came to the Northwest in the 1850s. After a varied career, he was, by the 1880s, investing in real estate, banks, and street railway companies. In 1883, Ballard joined with John Leary and Thomas Burke to found the new town of Ballard (now part of Seattle), the venture for which he is best known.[106] Parkinson interviewed with Ballard and received the commission which was then built by Crowell. Although the project remains unknown, Parkinson's initial success as a Seattle architect proved important, as Ballard gave him several more commissions over the next few years.

Parkinson's first major successes came in Olympia, not Seattle. About March 1889 his design for the First National Bank, Olympia (1889, destroyed), was selected over several by more established firms in the region.[107] Parkinson's design was a conventional two-story mid-block commercial building. Its symmetrical facade (with a stone first story, a brick second story, and a central ornamental gable at the roof line) was unremarkable save for the two oriel bays at the second floor, a feature which may derive from commercial buildings he had known in England.[108]

In mid-March, before Parkinson had secured the Olympia Bank commission, he entered into a partnership with another architect, Cecil Evers, whose background remains unknown. Parkinson later wrote that the English-born Evers was the son of an architect, that he had been educated in France, that he had come to Seattle via Victoria and San Francisco, and that he was particularly adept at making watercolor presentation drawings.[109] Although he had been seeking a position as a draftsman, Parkinson offered him a partnership. Beginning on 12 March 1889, the firm advertised in the Seattle papers as Parkinson and Evers.

Winning the Olympia bank commission positioned the firm to compete for the design of the Olympia Hotel (1889, destroyed), a project they were awarded by early April. *West Shore*, a Portland-based periodical, published a line drawing of the design in April that showed a roughly symmetrical three-story building surrounded by a broad verandah and surmounted by a tall tower. The tower, the pavilion-like character of projecting gabled ends of the various wings, and detail features such as the smaller round turret with a high conical roof gave the design a strongly vertical emphasis, but when it was actually built, this effect was significantly reduced. Parkinson later wrote that the project exceeded the original budget of $60,000, but that construction went ahead nonetheless. As actually built, the strong horizontal lines of the porch and eaves, along with the continuous horizontal wood banding, tended to unify the composition. (Fig. 2.31) A later history offered this description:

2.31 Parkinson and Evers, Olympia Hotel, 1889 (destroyed)

Manuscripts, Special Collections, University Archives Division, University of Washington Libraries, photo by Rogers, UW 3957

Standing on a slight rise of ground overlooking the bay and beautiful surrounding country, the artistic lines of the structure are in themselves an architectural ornament, while the interior, which is the part most regarded by the critical traveler, is characterized by spacious elegance and the utmost regard for the comfort of the guests. . . . Its wide porches on the front and side and balconies above afford a superb opportunity to view the wonderful scenery, to get a comprehensive idea of the size and lay of the city, and to seize with one sweeping glance the beauties of the panorama outspread and hold them for one's own. . . . On the first floor is a grand hallway, topped with a roof of stained glass; in this hall is the large office, with entrances to the elevator, the stairway, the dining room and the parlors. . . . The rooms are furnished with all conveniences for the business public and those who desire luxury, and, in fact, the entire building seems to have been designed by a master hand.[110]

Parkinson's emergence as a leading architect in Seattle dates only from the period after the June 1889 fire. However, his first five months of practice were essential to his later success. Because he had arrived in January, he was one of the architects ready to offer services immediately after the calamity.

Although architects would flock to Seattle in the aftermath of the fire, few late arrivals would win major commissions. Of Seattle's leading architects in the immediate post-fire period only the firm of Saunders and Houghton and the individual architect Willis Ritchie had not established themselves in the city before June 1889. Charles Saunders's success would initially be built on his personal connection with William Bailey, one of Seattle's new real estate investors, making him a special case, and Ritchie's career would focus on insti-

2.32 West side of Front Street, looking north, ca. spring 1889

Manuscripts, Special Collections, University Archives Division, University of Washington Libraries, photo by A. C. Warner, UW5858

tutional buildings, not commercial construction. The architects who were already in Seattle, particularly Fisher, Boone, and Parkinson, would receive the largest number of important commissions in the post-fire boom.[111]

Seattle in early 1889 was a Victorian city. (Fig. 2.32) Its core reflected the complex crosscurrents of American architecture in the West in the 1880s. The cities that Seattle most resembled were Portland and San Francisco. The primary transportation links before the late 1880s had been to the south and those cities had provided examples of metropolitan development. But by 1889 this was changing: Rail connections to the East had changed the pattern of influences; the architects who arrived in the late 1880s had no connections to Portland or California; and the professional architectural press, based in Minneapolis, Chicago, and the East, was featuring the work of architects in the new Romanesque mode. All that was needed was a catalyst for a new architectural direction in Seattle.

III

The Fire and Its Aftermath

Technology, Construction, and Design

Have I told you anything about Seattle—the town that was burned out a few weeks ago when the insurance men at San Francisco took their losses with a grin? . . . In the heart of the business quarters there was a horrible black smudge, as though a Hand had come down and rubbed the place smooth. I know now what being wiped out means.

—Rudyard Kipling, *American Notes*, 1889

The time is not far distant when we will look upon yesterday's fire as an actual benefit to Seattle. . . . We will have a finer city within eighteen months. Seattle has sufficient capital and sufficient energy to do in eighteen months what other places could not do in years.

—Jacob Furth, quoted in *Seattle Post-Intelligencer*, 8 June 1889

The fire of June 6, 1889 was an appalling calamity. At one sweep it wiped out millions of dollars of property; but it wiped out also . . . frame structures and gave the opportunity for the construction in their stead of handsome, congruous, and convenient structures, a credit to the city and a durable monument to the enterprise of its citizens always best displayed, like Mark Twain's humor, under the most adverse circumstances.

—*Seattle Post-Intelligencer*, 1 January 1890

At the beginning of June 1889 Seattle was a city in transition. The city was growing rapidly as the influx of new residents generated an unprecedented demand for housing and the new cable car and streetcar lines were providing access to previously undeveloped areas, some more than three miles from downtown. The emerging commercial core presented a varied appearance. Wood frame structures surviving from the early decades of settlement adjoined the new commercial blocks of the 1880s. On the west side of Front Street, from Yesler to Columbia, stood the longest continuous row of new buildings, beginning with the Yesler-Leary Building and ending with the Toklas and Singerman Building. But this row faced a mix of old and new construction on the east side of Front, and in most areas of downtown the new brick structures were still surrounded by the survivors of the earlier period. Even some of the newer structures had been built of wood, either for economy or as a result of the frequent unavailability of brick. Streets that had seemed wide enough for a town of a few thousand were becoming overwhelmed with traffic, and the inconsistent plats north and south of Yesler Avenue had created constant congestion in the heart of the commercial core. Beneath the streets, the city was deteriorating.

3.1 Looking south on Front Street toward fire, 6 June 1889

Museum of History and Industry, Seattle Historical Society Collection, photo by William Boyd, 6395

The wood water mains and sewers that had seemed adequate for a population of fewer than a thousand were rotting away, and the low elevation of the city center caused severe problems at high tide.

About 2:30 P.M., on 6 June 1889, what was to become the Great Seattle Fire began in a cabinet shop in a wood frame building at the southwest corner of Front and Madison.[1] (Fig. 3.1) The wind was blowing from the northwest and the fire rapidly consumed the entire block. Firefighters hoped to contain it, but the fire jumped across Front Street to the Frye Opera House and from there it spread southward through the entire commercial core, consuming more than thirty downtown blocks. The inadequacy of the pipes meant that there was insufficient water to fight the fire; the many older frame buildings were easily consumed; and the wharves and docks also provided fuel for the flames. The fire spread primarily toward the south, but flammable buildings and elevated wood sidewalks also allowed the fire to spread north as far as University Street. North of James Street the fire was primarily contained at Second, but south of Yesler

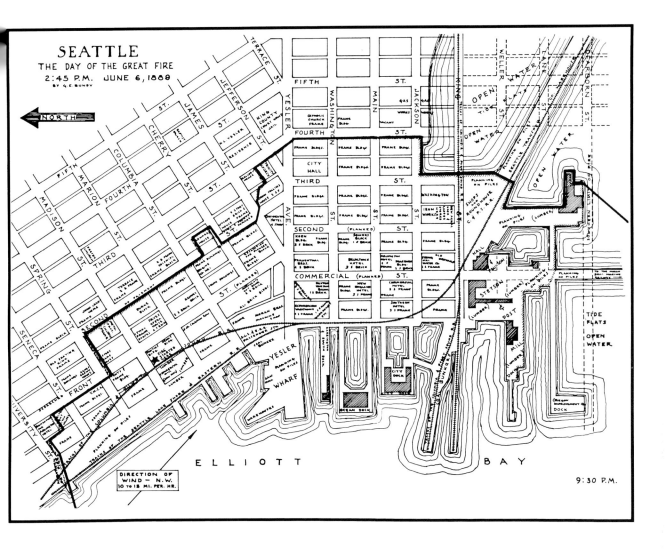

it spread east to Fourth (now Third). By morning on 7 June the fire had consumed 116 acres of the business center of the city. (Figs. 3.2, 3.3, 3.4) Although
some downtown frame apartment buildings and workingmen's hotels had been
destroyed, the residential areas of the city were otherwise largely untouched.
The large Victorian mansions survived, although several, including Henry
Yesler's house, nearly caught fire. All available evidence indicates that there
were very few immediate deaths from the fire and these were not widely
reported.[2] With little loss of life, the citizens were able to concentrate on the
task of rebuilding.

As Chicago demonstrated after its 1871 fire, a community with a growing
economy could rebound from such a disaster. At 11:00 A.M. on 7 June, Mayor
Robert Moran, the city's civic and business leaders, and almost 600 ordinary
citizens met at the Armory at Third and Union.[3] That Seattle would be rebuilt
was never in question. Rather, discussion centered on two issues: should brick
and stone construction for the new buildings be mandatory; and should the commercial core be replatted? On these questions there was a clear consensus. A
resolution was passed that wood buildings should not be allowed within the

3.2 Map of Seattle fire
area, 7 June 1889, as
drawn by former Seattle
Fire Chief Harry Bring-
hurst, redrawn by Seattle
Fire Department Lieuten-
ant George Bundy, 1964

Seattle Fire Department
Centennial Commemorative,
1889–1989 *(Seattle: Taylor
Publishing, 1989), 38*

commercial district. The only concern had been the cost of brick and stone construction, but the bankers present pledged that funds would be available. Those present also agreed that the streets should be widened and Front and Commercial Streets should be linked by cutting the corner of Henry Yesler's property (the site of the destroyed Yesler-Leary Building); this would also create a new triangular Public Square, later renamed Pioneer Place. And it was proposed that the grades in the low areas should be raised in order to improve drainage. Although these resolutions were not binding, the city council met that evening and began to take necessary statutory action. In order that the city could continue to operate, tents were approved as a temporary expedient, and within a few days stores and restaurants re-opened under canvas. The council also learned that eastern capitalists would invest in reconstruction of the city only if wood buildings were not allowed in the commercial district, so the resolution for brick and stone was immediately accepted, and work began on the necessary ordinances.[4] Within a few days the fire came to be seen as an opportunity to modernize the city. In addition to requiring masonry construction in the burned areas and widening and linking the downtown streets and raising the grades, over the next several months the city acted to improve the downtown water and sewer systems, to implement a modern building permitting and inspection process, and to establish a permanent fire department. Many of these ideas

had actually been proposed in the year before the fire, but it was the fire that made it possible to implement them all at one time.[5] The matters affecting reconstruction were completed in a remarkably short time: on 22 June, under the headline "The Replat Consummated," the *Post-Intelligencer* reported on council's consideration of the replat, the new street grades, and the proposal for the new water system.[6] On 30 June the replat was approved (although Henry Yesler initially balked) and the other questions were addressed in sequence thereafter.

Maintaining confidence and demonstrating that the city's future was unaffected were matters of critical concern during the bleak period after the fire. Seattle was only one of many western cities seeking eastern investment, and the effort by the Northern Pacific to foster the growth of Tacoma and suppress that of Seattle continued unabated.[7]

Evidence of commitment to rebuilding the city was, therefore, extraordinarily important, both to convince local owners to proceed and to entice eastern investors to lend money at favorable rates. Fortunately insurance covered many of the losses and notices began appearing in the newspapers within a few days inviting the insured to present their claims.[8] Once it was apparent the city would modernize, outside investment flowed in to finance the new construction. Still, in the face of uncertainty, the newspapers took every opportunity to tout the

3.4 Ruins after the fire, looking north toward the Boston Building, standing just outside the burned area

Museum of History and Industry, Seattle Historical Society Collection, photo by John Soulé, 10277

rebuilding of the city. On 8 June, reporting on the citizens meeting, the *Post-Intelligencer* headlined "Full of Hope A New Seattle Will Arise." The paper also editorialized, suggesting that owners who could not afford to rebuild should sell to those who could.[9] In succeeding days and weeks, almost every issue of the paper reported on progress toward the new city. Initially these reports were general, addressing the issues of streets and grades and the broad commitment to modernization. But soon the reports became more focused, emphasizing specific buildings that were in design, about to proceed into construction, or already under way. As early as 15 June, the *Post-Intelligencer* reported that Elmer Fisher was already at work on designs for several new projects, and on 19 June the paper claimed "Architect Boone has completed plans. . . ." Subsequent headlines show the paper's focus: on 20 June, "The List Grows"; on 21 June, "With One Accord"; on 24 June, "Falling in Line"; on 30 June, "Onward in Solid Phalanx"; on 2 July, "Making a Solid City." For the next few years every new building was a major story in the news.

The transformation of Seattle in the aftermath of the fire became the basis for the understanding of the calamity primarily not as a destructive event, but rather as a regenerative one.[10] The absence of loss of life facilitated this reconsideration, and the city's success in moving to implement public improvements as well as the burgeoning level of private construction all provided the basis for a narrative of rebirth. On 26 June, the *Post-Intelligencer* published a supplement to its regular edition, with the headline "Seattle's Future Assured" with the subhead "The Great Holocaust Not Altogether an Unmixed Evil: Benefits of the Fire." From this point the reconstruction after the fire began to be seen as providing the basis for modern Seattle.[11]

Meeting the Danger: Fire-Resistive Construction

The danger of fire is almost as old as the history of cities. Although cities in antiquity were generally less vulnerable to fire as a result of limited use of wood in construction, with the growth of cities and the increasing use of wood, conflagration became an ever-present concern. Although only a few general fires, such as the London fire in 1666 and the Chicago fire in 1871, are widely remembered, fire was a frequent occurrence in urban centers before the twentieth century.[12] In nineteenth-century America, the rapid growth of cities, the widespread use of wood, the lack of building codes, and the limited capabilities of early (usually volunteer) fire departments made urban areas particularly vulnerable to fire. In Washington alone, fire destroyed the business districts of Seattle, Ellensburg, and Spokane in summer 1889.

The danger of fire in the commercial cores of American cities was not completely solved until the late 1880s when the system of the complete iron or steel frame protected by terra-cotta fireproofing was perfected in Chicago and elsewhere. Developments in this direction were first noted in Seattle in July 1883 when a *Post-Intelligencer* report titled "Better Buildings" discussed East Coast trends in construction including use of brick and stone enclosures, iron framing, and terra-cotta and plaster fireproofing.[13] By the mid-1880s, widely used builders' manuals such as Frank Kidder's *Architects and Builders Pocketbook* (1885) were illustrating "fireproof construction" involving the use of masonry load-bearing walls and iron or steel floor beams with terra-cotta protection.[14] However, this fireproof technology was more expensive than building in masonry and wood, and the materials needed for this kind of construction were not readily available in the Puget Sound region. Even if this fireproof technology had proved feasible and affordable (it was neither), its adoption would have delayed rebuilding. As a result, this construction method with masonry partitions and an iron or steel and terra-cotta floor system was used only for major public buildings where protection of public records required the best fireproof technology available.[15] Seattle would not see a fully iron- or steel-framed high-rise commercial structure until 1903 when the Alaska Building began construction.

Seattle architects and builders turned instead toward an approach that has been called "mill construction," "slow-burning," or, sometimes, "semi-fireproof" (and which today may also be described as "fire-resistive"). As discussed by Sara Wermiel, the technique of "mill construction" was developed in New England in the early nineteenth century for textile mills where fire hazards were severe.[16] The leading advocate of this approach, Edward Atkinson, who became president of the Boston Manufacturers Mutual Fire Insurance Company in 1878, promoted the system, which he named "slow-burning construction," through reports, pamphlets, and articles in the professional and popular press.[17] As described by Atkinson, the complete system included the use of masonry walls for fire containment, oversized wood structural members (including plank floors) that, in a fire, would char but not burn through, enclosures for stairs and other vertical spaces, and standpipes and sprinklers. Builder's guides, such as Kidder's *Architects and Builders Pocketbook*, began to include descriptions of the elements of slow-burning construction in the 1880s, and it continued to appear in texts on architecture into the twentieth century, for example *A Treatise on Architecture and Building Construction* published by the International Correspondence Schools (ICS) beginning in 1899.[18] (Fig. 3.5) Kidder's description is a good summary of the masonry and heavy timber elements of the slow-burning system:

> The *desideratum* in this mode of construction is to have a building whose outside walls shall be built of masonry (generally of brick) concentrated in piers and buttresses with only a thin wall containing the windows between, and the floors and roof of which shall be constructed of large timber, covered with a plank of suitable thickness; the girders being supported between the walls by wooden posts.[19]

Although initially used in mills and factories, slow-burning construction was applied much more widely in the late nineteenth century as it was an affordable technology, within the capabilities of most contractors, and it allowed the use of readily available materials, primarily brick and heavy timber. However, as Wermiel notes, designers had little guidance in the adaptation of slow-burning

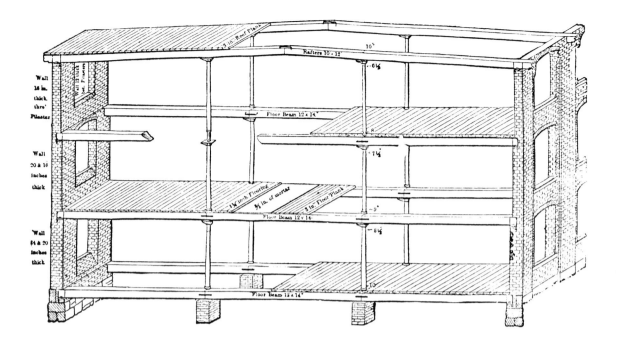

3.5 Cross-section diagram of mill construction

Frank Eugene Kidder, Architects and Builders Pocketbook (New York: John Wiley & Sons, 1885), 378

construction to nonindustrial buildings, and, as a result, some buildings characterized as "slow-burning" were actually imperfect examples of the system.[20] Designers often readily embraced the elements of masonry and heavy timber, but omitted the shaft and stair enclosures and fire suppression equipment typically found in mills.[21]

The slow-burning construction system was based on the use of heavy timber posts and individual girders spaced 8 to 10 feet on center, with thick floor planks spanning between the girders. While this system worked in textile mills where loads were usually only 60 pounds per square foot (psf), in urban buildings loads could be much higher—some warehouses in Seattle were designed for loads as high as 500 psf! These loads necessitated a more elaborate system of floor framing, usually involving heavy timber girders in one direction and heavy timber beams as close as 12 or 18 inches on center in the other. Some do not consider this approach true slow-burning construction; Wermiel has recently described this as "warehouse construction" to contrast it with "mill construction."[22]

The masonry and heavy timber elements of warehouse construction were capable of considerable variation depending upon the building types to which they were applied. As initially developed, mill construction generally involved the use of wood throughout, including, for example, wood impost blocks where beams crossed over posts and wood pegs to tie the system together. By the 1880s and 1890s, iron and steel anchors, post caps, and similar elements were often used to reinforce the joints; these connections were typically bolted. For example, a system of iron connecting elements patented by the Goetz-Mitchell Company of Indiana was in common use and was featured in some texts, as these elements could be copied by any foundry on payment of a fee.[23] Even where iron or steel anchors and caps were not used, ties and straps were typical by the 1880s and 1890s as a way of providing continuity throughout the wood frame and between the frame and the masonry walls. But some argued that the use of metal anchors and straps was incorrect—that in true slow-burning construction, beams which burned through should be allowed to fall freely so that the collapse of a floor would not also pull down the adjacent walls. The slow-burning construction system was based on the use of heavy timber posts and beams, but designers of urban buildings sometimes substituted a frame of cast-iron columns, and girders might be iron or steel as well. Exterior walls were of masonry, either brick or stone. Kidder discussed the use of masonry piers with thinner walls between (as typically applied in the New England mills), but continuous thicker walls were also sometimes used as in the well-known Marshall Field Wholesale Store in Chicago, by H. H. Richardson, an example cited by Atkinson in a *Century Magazine* article in 1889.[24] Floor beams and joists were usually set in pockets in the exterior and interior masonry walls. (Fig. 3.6) Where additional bearing was desirable, the masonry wall would be corbeled out to provide a deeper pocket or a shelf on which the beams could sit. Corbeling was advocated as a fire stop which would prevent the spread of flames from one story to another and was said to make the walls stronger because the floor beams would not extend as far into the depth of the wall.[25] (Figs. 3.7, 3.8)

By 1889, slow-burning construction had been in development for half a century and had been adapted for buildings in urban settings for nearly a decade. Although the complete slow-burning system was no doubt imperfectly understood by Seattle architects, the elements of masonry and heavy timber warehouse construction could easily be applied in rebuilding the city. Masonry walls and heavy timber framing and floors had the advantage of broad flexibility. Given the wood which was available from the old growth of Puget Sound forests, the size of members could be increased to accommodate taller buildings or wider spans. Ceiling heights could also be varied. In some cases, cast iron and wood would be combined—lower floors might be constructed with cast-iron columns, while upper floors would still involve the use of wood. Thus, Seattle designers turned to this approach in the reconstruction of Seattle's downtown.

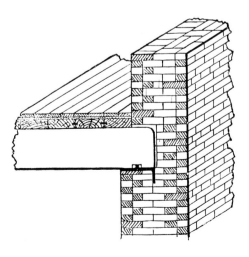

3.6 Framing floor joists into load-bearing masonry walls

Frank Eugene Kidder, Architects and Builders Pocketbook (New York: John Wiley & Sons, 1885), 379

The decision to rebuild Seattle's core in brick and stone was endorsed immediately after the fire. A 20 June *Post-Intelligencer* article, titled "Reducing the Fire Hazard: How Seattle's Buildings Should be Constructed," reported the comments of Francis H. Porter, the "chief of the fire underwriters inspection bureau of San Francisco," who was visiting Seattle building owners and architects. Porter described himself as an advocate of slow-burning construction, which he indicated was preferred by the fire insurance companies. He not only noted the use of masonry and heavy timber but also emphasized aspects such as the need for shaft and stair enclosures and draft-stopping between floors. He also stated that the city should have a building code and construction inspection system.[26]

The city was already at work on new regulations for building. An ordinance said to be based on those of the cities of Kansas City and San Francisco was introduced at council on 27 June, and was approved on 1 July.[27] The full text of the forty-four sections of the ordinance was carried in the *Post-Intelligencer* on 5 July. As approved, the ordinance was a compromise—it offered detailed requirements for the thickness and construction of walls, but made only limited mention of the framing and construction of floors. There were no requirements for stair or shaft enclosures (although passenger-elevator hoistways were to have smoke-proof enclosures). Although standpipes were required in all buildings of more than three stories, other fire suppression equipment such as sprinklers was not mentioned. Fireproof construction was not required for any building.

Within the city's commercial district (identified as the "fire limits"), sections of the ordinance addressed both fire safety and structural stability. Inside the fire limits walls were to be constructed of masonry. Foundations were required to extend at least 4 feet below grade. Walls were to be a minimum of 12 inches thick, but the lower walls of tall buildings increased in thickness depending upon height. Thus, for a five-story building, the basement walls must be 24 inches

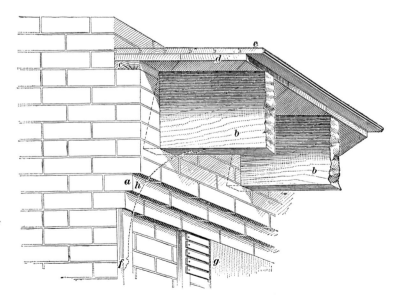

3.7 Corbeling masonry wall for better support of floor beams

International Correspondence Schools, A Treatise on Architecture and Building Construction *(Scranton, Penn: Colliery Engineer Co., 1899), 2: 131*

thick, the first story 21 inches, the second through fourth stories 16 inches and the top story just 12 inches. A six-story building required 21-inch walls at the first and second stories, 16-inch walls at the third through fifth stories, and 12-inch walls at the sixth story. The construction of the walls was also specified with header courses at regular intervals. Masonry "division walls" to prevent the spread of fires in larger buildings were required and could be spaced no farther apart than 66 feet; multiple arched openings of a limited size could be provided through the division walls. For spans longer than 27 feet, intermediate columns of iron, steel, or heavy timber were required. The ordinance also specified the use of metal anchors to tie floor beams to the walls to reduce the chance of collapse. (The result was a stiffer building, but this did not allow the beams to fall free in a fire—a significant difference from the approach often advocated by the fire insurance companies.) The design of openings in the required masonry walls was also regulated: all window and door openings were to be spanned by brick or stone arches or have horizontal stone or metal lintels; the size and detailing of each of these elements were specified. Other sections of the ordinance prohibited wood cornices, limited the size of bay windows, specified that partywalls must extend above roofs, and required fireproof roofing materials.[28]

When slow-burning construction was initially developed, it provided a solution to design of large free-standing mills and factories. It proved adaptable to city centers because of the typical condition of partywall construction. In the nineteenth century it was common for adjoining urban buildings to share one partywall (rather than each having a structurally independent wall, as is typical today). For the interior lots on any block, the partywalls, shared with the adjacent buildings, would be completely solid, providing both a complete fire

3.8 Framing in J.M. Frink Building, Seattle, 1890–92

Photo by John Stamets, 2000

separation and also a continuous bearing wall to support the floor beams. In partywall conditions, the first building constructed would necessarily have walls of the thickness required by the ordinance, but the second building constructed would often add only one or more brick layers against the existing wall—an amount sufficient with additional corbeling to provide bearing for the second set of floor beams. The typical layout of Seattle's post-fire commercial buildings clearly reflects the impact of the ordinance. A general pattern appeared in which partywalls between buildings and division walls within buildings extended from the primary streetfront to the alley. Where the walls were spaced farther apart than 27 feet, one or more intermediate rows of columns was introduced, almost always paralleling the walls. Beams (usually 12 to 24 inches on center) would span from the girder that ran across these columns to the walls.In this configuration, the front wall at the street and the back wall at the alley typically did not carry significant floor loads because the floor beams framed into the partywalls. Therefore, the street and alley walls could have large areas of windows which would be necessary to bring abundant natural light into the interior. On corner lots the structure would become more complex. Some floor framing would be carried by a street wall with windows; the window openings might be limited by the need to provide adequate bearing area for the floor loads.

The major post-fire blocks typically occupied more than one downtown lot. Buildings occupying two lots were typically 120 feet wide. As downtown lots were also about 100 to 110 feet in depth, these large blocks required internal masonry firewalls since the ordinance required such walls to be no more than 66 feet apart. Designers of Seattle's new large business blocks incorporated these "division walls" extending from the street to the alley (thereby compartmentalizing the buildings internally to limit the spread of fire).

Even though Seattle designers rarely embraced the full slow-burning system, they sometimes tried to enhance the fire-resistance of masonry and heavy timber construction. First, the ready availability of old-growth fir in the Puget Sound region meant that the recommended sizes of columns, girders, and beams could be increased. For a three-story building, Kidder had recommended nine-inch round columns at the first story, eight-inch columns at the second story, and seven-inch columns at the third. The ICS *Treatise* illustrated a two-story building with columns ten inches square at the first story and nine inches square at the second.[29] In Seattle, buildings occasionally had columns this small, but larger columns were often used, as anticipated loads were higher; for some warehouses wood columns at the lower floors exceeded eighteen inches square and girders were more than twenty inches deep. When Francis Porter, representing the insurance underwriters, visited Seattle, he had advocated "wire lath plaster" for elevator and stair enclosures, and this recommendation was incorporated into a few Seattle buildings. And, the heavy timbers could also be protected by enclosure with fire-resistant masonry or plaster. Although this was rarely done in Seattle, in at least one case, the New York Building, the cast-iron columns were enclosed in brick, and the underside of the wood floor fram-

3.9 View north along
Second Street from
James, mid-1890s. The
impact of Seattle's new
building ordinance is
reflected in the masonry
structures with no bay
windows and minimal
projecting cornices.

*Manuscripts, Special Collec-
tions, University Archives
Division, University of
Washington Libraries; photo
by Frank LaRoche, 2128*

ing was surfaced in plaster; the building featured fire-resistant stair and elevator enclosures as well. Advertisements in the 1890s proclaimed it Seattle's
most "fireproof" commercial office building (although it did not meet the standards of true fireproof construction since it was built of combustible materials).

The relative ornamental restraint of Seattle buildings after the fire was fostered, at least in part, by the new building ordinance. (Fig. 3.9) The elaborate
wood cornices of pre-fire construction were not allowed and bay windows, typical in pre-fire buildings, were limited in size.[30] Along with the requirement
for masonry construction, the ordinance presented a challenge to Seattle's
designers: to find an appropriate architectural solution within these constraints
to the design of a masonry commercial architecture. In this context, the turn to
the Romanesque Revival may have been less a stylistic decision than simply
the logical outcome of a search for an aesthetic approach which could guide
design under the new constraints.

The adoption of masonry and heavy timber construction as standard in Seattle
was heralded on 4 July 1889, in a *Post-Intelligencer* article headlined "New
Fireproof City," although the article actually described several new buildings,
not the new building ordinance.[31] Yet the city was not "fireproof" and few if
any buildings were close to the standard that Atkinson had advocated for slow-

burning construction. Thus, on 1 January 1892, when Seattle's newly appointed Board of Fire Commissioners issued their first annual report, they were highly critical of the new downtown buildings, which they called "hastily constructed with no thought of being fire-proof or even of slow-burning construction."[32] They noted aspects such as open elevators and stairways, and also suggested that fires could spread from one building to another across the 16-foot alleys in the downtown area.

Still, Seattle was a safer city in 1892 than it had been before June 1889. The many light, wood frame downtown buildings, left from the early years of the city, were gone. A new professional fire department had been created. And the new building ordinance requiring masonry construction may not have prevented fires, but it did mean that future fires would be contained. The success of the new measures became fully evident on 27 June 1892, when a blaze destroyed a substantial portion of the interior and Commercial Street front of the Schwabacher Building, just south of Yesler. This fire caused a loss of over $425,000 in damage to the structure and its contents, but did not spread to any adjacent buildings.[33] Fire remained a danger in Seattle, as in all cities, but after 1889, it was a danger that was more contained and controlled.[34]

Building Types in the New Business Core

The second half of the nineteenth century saw the transformation and differentiation of building types. Structures such as offices, warehouses, and stores were not generally recognized as distinct types of buildings until the 1870s and 1880s, and even urban hotels and apartment buildings show resemblances to office buildings in the 1880s and 1890s. By 1920, each of these kinds of buildings would be fully recognized as a distinct type, but in the years around 1890 their individual evolutionary directions were not fully apparent. Thus, the buildings of Seattle's new downtown reflected an intermediate state, showing some, but not all, of the features that would distinguish these types as they matured.

The office building emerged in the post–Civil War period with the growth of American business organizations and their clerical staffs. As a distinct type, office buildings in significant numbers first appeared in London in the 1840s and in New York after 1865. Although early office buildings were most often built by insurance companies primarily for their own growing bureaucracies, construction of buildings to be leased to individual tenants soon followed. As Sarah Bradford Landau and Carl W. Condit note in *Rise of the New York Skyscraper, 1865–1913*, the New York City building code recognized office buildings as a distinct type only in 1875, and warehouses in 1882. Prior to that all of these buildings were simply classified as "1st class stores and storehouses."[35] The Seattle building ordinance adopted in 1889 did not identify office buildings as a type, mentioning only "stores, warehouses, hotels, shops and manufactories," as well as "churches, theaters, machine shops and foundries."[36]

Even though these types were becoming distinct in the late nineteenth century, the evolution of office buildings and warehouses occurred in parallel. In 1904, architectural critic Russell Sturgis identified the warehouse as a building serving the "rougher kind of business enterprise" that primarily involved shipping, receiving, and storage of goods. He noted that its floors are "to a great extent left open in great 'lofts'." This kind of building he differentiated from the office building, which was devoted "primarily to offices where professional men sit quietly or clerks pursue their daily task."[37] But warehouses typically devoted some of the floor area at the front of the building to offices for the managers and bookkeepers. Those warehouses, like H. H. Richardson's Marshall Field Wholesale Store, that served the wholesale trade (traveling salesmen) also needed space to receive customers and to display samples. The architectural evolution of the office building and the warehouse was clearly interrelated. Richardson's Field Store directly influenced the commercial buildings of Burnham and Root and Adler and Sullivan, both office blocks and warehouses, and in turn the Chicago architects' work influenced others, including the architects of Seattle.

By 1889, however, the office building and the warehouse were clearly different in three aspects. First, the office building was divided into office rooms; the warehouse was primarily undivided floor space. Second, because it was designed for human occupancy, the office building was controlled by the need to provide adequate natural light—this required either exterior light courts or interior atria or light wells; the warehouse was constructed to achieve the largest area of floor space for storage of goods. Third, as storage space, the warehouse required greater structural strength.

In September and November 1892, Dankmar Adler published essays in *Engineering Magazine* discussing the design of office buildings.[38] Although he focused on the new steel-framed skyscrapers, his comments on office layouts are indicative of the issues faced by all designers of office buildings about 1890. According to Adler, key issues for attracting the best class of tenants were the availability of natural light and fresh air in every office. Adequate light depended on planning so that no workspace should be "at a greater distance than twenty-five feet from the source of light," and he argued that in many cases the limit was twenty feet or even less. Adler therefore calculated that the office building should be a maximum of sixty-five feet between the outer walls, and it was often better if this depth were only forty feet or less. In Adler's discussion, these dimensions could be achieved on urban sites only with the use of rear light courts or interior light wells.

At Seattle's northern latitude, designers faced even greater pressure to provide adequate access to natural light. Two solutions appeared in Seattle office buildings built after the fire. In parallel with Adler's recommendation, where sites were sufficiently large, office blocks were often designed with sizable exterior rear light courts. Thus, a building such as Elmer Fisher's Burke Building, which appeared almost as a square block to the street, was actually U-shaped, surrounding a light court facing the alley. The second solution was to shape the building around one or more interior courts or atria roofed with skylights. Such a solution was applied by Fisher at the Pioneer Building.

The steel-framed office buildings that emerged from Chicago and New York in the 1890s typically were designed to allow for flexibility in the office layout to accommodate a variety of tenants. Those buildings, and office construction since then, have generally been designed with non-structural interior partitions between offices so they might be repositioned as needed. However, in Seattle in 1889, office partitions were most commonly constructed with the idea that they were permanent. In part this was fostered by the building ordinance that required that partitions be carried up completely to the underside of the floor above. Thus, a tenant would usually rent one or more "office rooms" from a layout that had already been determined. For example, drawings of the Pioneer Building show an office room layout on every floor and this is the arrangement still found in the building today. The drawings also indicate that the building's interior metal frame extends only through the fifth floor; the office partitions on the sixth floor not only divide the office rooms but also provide the structural support for the roof. In early November 1889, the *Post-Intelligencer* reported that "over 3000 office rooms" were included in the buildings under construction in Seattle, and that many of these were already leased.[39]

Although office structures were built on parcels of varying size, shape, and location in downtown Seattle after the fire, corner sites were preferred for the largest and most prestigious business buildings. A corner site, particularly one that was nearly square in shape, allowed a large and impressive building with two major street facades. These sites were open on three sides (the two streets plus the rear alley), allowing designers to maximize the exterior perimeter and, therefore, the number of office spaces with direct access to light and air. All of the major post-fire office blocks in Seattle, including the Pioneer Building, Bailey Building, Burke Building, New York Building, Seattle National Bank, and others, were located on prime corner sites. (Fig. 3.10)

The ground floors of the new office blocks were designed to be leased for retail stores. Bank tenants preferred the corner location, and banks frequently featured an entrance that turned the corner. Ground floors were designed with large areas of glazing to maximize the exposure of the retailers, but banks preferred larger wall areas and smaller (usually arched) windows. In some cases, as at the Pioneer Building, these business blocks were designed with a raised first floor and a partially exposed basement to allow two floors of retail shops with access to the sidewalk.[40] Many new buildings on corner sites north of Yesler, where the east-west streets sloped significantly, included retail spaces on two levels, with entrances to the different levels on different sides of the building.

In the late nineteenth century, warehouses developed largely in conjunction with the system of wholesale supply that was directly connected initially with water-borne shipping and subsequently with the growth of the national railroad network. As Leonard Eaton has discussed, wholesalers supplied small town retailers, traveling salesmen, and farmers from warehouses located in cities that served as railroad "gateways."[41] Cities such as St. Paul, Omaha, and Winnipeg

3.10 Elmer H. Fisher,
Burke Building, at corner
of Front and Marion,
1889–91 (destroyed)

*Museum of History and
Industry, Wilse Collection,
88.33.448*

developed as major wholesaling centers with warehouse districts because they were locations from which railroad lines provided for convenient distribution across the West. (Figs. 3.11, 3.12) To a somewhat lesser extent, similar patterns of distribution developed from the West Coast eastward, and cities such as Oakland and Portland saw the construction of warehouses to serve the wholesale trade. In Washington, the policies of the Northern Pacific Railroad in the 1880s and 1890s favored Tacoma, and it was that city that developed a rail-related warehouse district.[42] Seattle, however, became the center of shipping on Puget Sound, and many goods that arrived on Seattle's wharves and docks were subsequently transported on the small vessels of the "mosquito fleet" to other Puget Sound communities. Thus, Seattle also saw the construction of warehouses and wholesale stores, but a concentrated rail-related warehouse district was slower to develop; most of Seattle's warehouses and wholesale stores were adjacent to or no more than a block or two from the waterfront.

In the late 1880s and early 1890s, Seattle's commercial district centered along Commercial and Front (now First South and First) was primarily composed of office blocks, stores, and hotels. A retail district would gradually coalesce to the north of Yesler, while wholesale businesses were more common to the south. Some wholesale businesses located east of Commercial and warehouses were built closer to the waterfront along West Street (now Western

3.11 Orff and Orff, Mutual Block (later Janney & Semple warehouse), St. Paul, Minnesota, 1887–88. A published example of a "gateway city" warehouse, possibly known to Seattle architects who had visited St. Paul

Northwestern Architect 6/9 (Sept. 1888). Minneapolis Public Library, Minneapolis Collection, M0435

3.12 Eckel and Van Brunt, Richardson, Roberts, Byrne and Co. Wholesale Drygoods House project, St. Joseph, Missouri, 1892. An example of a published rendering of a "gateway city" warehouse

Inland Architect 19/4 (May 1892); courtesy Trustees of the Boston Public Library

Avenue), but this was not always true. For example, the Schwabacher Building constructed immediately after the fire facing Commercial and Yesler was a wholesale dry goods store; when the Schwabacher Company built the State Building on South Second Street (now Occidental Avenue South), that building was a warehouse intended primarily for storage, described in the press of the time as strong enough for loads of five hundred pounds per square foot.[43]

The spaces designed for retail and wholesale businesses were similar in several ways. Both were primarily undifferentiated "loft" spaces. Without the requirements for natural light that office blocks demanded, stores and warehouses could fill their sites completely. A major difference between retail and wholesale operations was interior finishes; retail store interiors were usually much more completely finished throughout, whereas a high level of finish in wholesale businesses was usually limited to display and sample rooms, front offices, and other spaces which typically received customers. In addition, the exterior embellishment of retail stores was sometimes more elaborate. But the exterior appearance of wholesale stores and warehouses was not ignored. These exteriors had the symbolic purpose of conveying stability and strength, so their designs often embodied a sense of solidity and gravity.[44]

In addition to office blocks, stores, and warehouses, Seattle's new commercial core included a number of hotels. As a building type, the hotel traces its origins to public lodging places constructed in the Middle Ages, but the modern hotel with private rooms, public spaces, toilet and bathing facilities, and related services originated only in the early nineteenth century.[45] By the late nineteenth century, large numbers of hotels were found in American cities serving a wide variety of travelers as well as permanent residents. Indeed, long-term hotel residents very likely outnumbered visitors. Reports of construction after the Seattle fire sometimes referred to the "lodging rooms" then under construction. This term suggests the ambiguity of the term "hotel" at that time; some buildings then described as hotels would today be identified as "lodging houses." As noted by Paul Groth in *Living Downtown: The History of Residential Hotels in the United States,* in the nineteenth and early twentieth centuries, hotel living was a common phenomenon, especially in the developing cities in the West. Hotel accommodations were highly stratified, serving every economic class from the well-to-do to transient laborers. Groth notes that the hotels serving different groups were less typologically differentiated before 1900. Regarding San Francisco, he noted, "In 1880, half the rooms in the city's rooming houses occupied the upper floors of fairly undifferentiated commercial structures."[46] In Seattle, in the years immediately after the fire, the large transient population of workers and the rapid growth of the city due to immigration created a high demand for lodging rooms of all kinds that led to a situation in which most of the city's lodging rooms would be found on the upper floors of the new commercial blocks.

Hotel development serving tourists and traveling businessmen often followed railroads, which were a primary source of customers. In some cases, railroad owners would also develop fashionable hotels themselves; for example, Henry Villard had initiated development of hotels designed by McKim, Mead, and White in Portland and Tacoma.[47] The Occidental was the most fashionable hotel in Seattle before the fire. The growth in demand in the late 1880s prompted the owner John Collins to expand the building in 1887–88; his architect, Otto Kleemann of Portland, followed MacKay's original design. But this was only one of a number of hotels of all kinds in the city; most of these were destroyed in the fire, although some smaller hotels did survive outside the burned area.[48]

After the fire, the demand for hotel space at all economic levels was immense and one of the first projects undertaken was the construction of the large wood Rainier Hotel on Fifth between Columbia and Marion.[49] This was called a "summer hotel" and today would be considered a resort hotel. John Collins rebuilt the fashionable Occidental Hotel.[50] (Fig. 3.13) The construction of the rather grand Denny Hotel, on Denny Hill north of downtown, began in 1888 and was not affected by the fire. However, the project was continually delayed by serious financial difficulties and was not completed until after the turn of the century, so it played no role in meeting post-fire demand for hotel space.[51] Other hotel buildings serving travelers, such as the New England Hotel, were also constructed. Many commercial blocks included hotel spaces (probably more appropriately termed "rooming houses"), such as the Terry-Denny Building that housed the Northern Hotel, the Olympic Building that had at least one floor of hotel rooms, the Marshall-Walker Building, that was later partially occupied by the Globe Hotel, and others.

In 1894, the Butler Block, originally designed by Parkinson and Evers as an office block, was converted to a fashionable hotel. Such a conversion was feasible because the arrangement of the office rooms then typical in a commercial office block was close enough in character to the arrangement of lodging rooms in a hotel. In fact, when the *Post-Intelligencer* reported the Butler Block conversion, it indicated that the Butler Hotel would open little more than a month or so after the office tenants vacated the building (although the actual conversion apparently took longer)![52] In office buildings at the time many of the office rooms included wash basins; toilet rooms were located at the end of a corridor on each floor. The arrangement then typical in many hotels was not significantly different—individual rooms had wash basins, but toilets were shared. Rooms with bathtubs needed to be added on each floor accessible from the corridors, but this could be done with the conversion of one or more office rooms.[53]

The difference between a residential hotel or rooming house and an apartment building in late-nineteenth-century Seattle was primarily a matter of name and not of planning and design. A few structures identified as apartment buildings were constructed in the period, but for the most part, these were outside the new commercial core. Within the commercial core, residential buildings were typically identified as hotels, even if they primarily served permanent residents. The best known example of an apartment building was Elmer Fisher's Austin A. Bell Building, located in Belltown, about ten blocks north of the commercial core. When the project was announced, it was described in the *Seattle Times*

3.13 Stephen Meany,
Occidental Hotel (later
Seattle Hotel), 1889–90
(destroyed). One of the
first fashionable travelers'
hotels erected after the
fire

*Museum of History and
Industry, PEMCO Webster
and Stevens Collection,
83.10.7324*

as containing sixty-five apartments.[54] The design, however, appears remarkably similar to that of Fisher's Pioneer Building. The use of a skylit atrium to
bring light to the interior and the layout of the apartment rooms appears to fore-
shadow Fisher's approach to the Pioneer Building project. (Figs. 3.14, 3.15)
Indeed, without the evidence of the newspaper account, the Bell Building might
have been mistakenly identified as an office block, the designs match so closely.[55]

    The urban core that emerged in Seattle after the fire was focused on com-
merce. Its components were office buildings with ground floor retail stores,
wholesale stores or warehouses, and hotels. Other construction also took
place, including residences and institutional buildings, but this was located
outside the commercial core. In Seattle's boom years in the late nineteenth century the construction of office blocks, stores, warehouses, and hotels was seen
as the primary measure of the city's recovery after the fire.

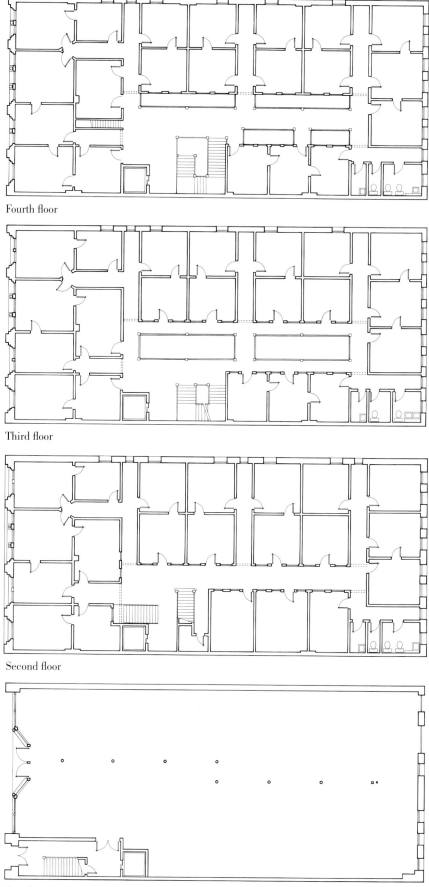

3.14 Elmer H. Fisher,
Austin A. Bell Building,
1889–90 (destroyed);
floor plans

*Measured drawings by Peter
Anderson, Barbara Bussetti,
Erin Doherty, Amy Scarfone,
Jacqueline Smith, Margaret
Stanton, Kirsten Wild;
presentation drawings by
Youngmin Han*

Fourth floor

Third floor

Second floor

First floor

3.15 Austin A. Bell Building,
interior atrium view from fourth
floor (destroyed). Although
covered over by the time this
photo was taken, the skylights
originally provided natural light
to interior apartment rooms by
means of relights along the sides
of the three-story atrium.

Photo by John Stamets, 1996

Building in Seattle after the Fire

The process of construction is largely a matter of scheduling and coordination—bringing the appropriate people, the proper tools, and the necessary materials to the construction site at the time they are needed. Although buildings were less complex in the nineteenth century than they are today, construction still involved a complicated sequence of activities that could be disrupted at any point. Although the pressure to erect the new buildings after the fire was intense, the pace of construction was limited by factors which were beyond the control of any individual architect, contractor, or owner.

The nineteenth century was the last period in which the technology of construction was based almost exclusively on manual labor. Simple machines such as block and tackle and primitive hand-operated cranes had been in use since Roman antiquity. In the 1830s steam power was first applied to construction with the invention of the steam shovel, and steam-powered hoists were first used in Philadelphia in the 1850s. However, the use of steam-powered equipment was limited because costs remained prohibitive, especially in the relatively low-cost labor market of the late nineteenth century. Landau and Condit report that steam equipment did not become typical on New York City construction sites until about 1890.[56] In Seattle this would not occur until 1900. In 1889 buildings in Seattle were erected largely through basic manual labor, although hand-operated devices such as cranes and hoists were routinely employed.

Although Seattle buildings in 1889 had interior heavy timber or metal frames, the exterior walls were load bearing. The separation between frame and cladding typically found in technologically modern construction had not yet occurred. As a result, construction proceeded incrementally, one floor at a time. In twentieth-century "curtain wall" construction, the structural frame is erected first and then the cladding which forms the enclosure is applied, but for Seattle buildings in the late nineteenth century the exterior walls were both structure and enclosure. The interior frame could be constructed only as rapidly as the masonry walls. The beams for each floor could be placed only when the masonry which would carry them had reached that level. Thus, the pace of the masonry construction generally governed the rate at which the entire project could proceed. (Figs. 3.16, 3.17, 3.18)

Although Seattle's ordinances provided for both brick and stone construction, brick was the primary material in use after the 1889 fire. Stone was typically used for foundations and for basement walls because of the porosity of brick and the problem of seepage and deterioration if brick was placed in constant contact with damp materials. South of Yesler the water table was high and elsewhere the frequent rains meant that soils tended to remain damp for long periods. Above grade, stone was used primarily for embellishment (as on the first floors of major office blocks). The only large office block built after the fire with facades completely of stone was the Bailey Building, and even that had brick walls facing the alley and adjacent property.

These materials came from a variety of sources. Stone was not available in

3.16 Reconstruction after the 1889 fire, view south from Second Street about October 1889. The partially completed first floor of the Butler Block, facing Second Street, is to the right of center; the tents in the center of the image provide temporary enclosure for retail businesses while reconstruction takes place.

Museum of History and Industry, Seattle Historical Society Collection, photo by Frank LaRoche

3.17 Reconstruction after the 1889 fire, view east on Yesler Avenue. The completed Korn Building is to the right; the still under construction Occidental Hotel is to the left.

Museum of History and Industry, Seattle Historical Society Collection, photo by F. Jay Haynes

3.18 Reconstruction after the 1889 fire, view north on Front Street. The construction of the Pioneer Building is to the right; the completed Starr-Boyd Building is to the left; the future Pioneer Place Park is covered with construction debris.

Museum of History and Industry, Seattle Historical Society Collection, 13472

Seattle but was most often obtained from three other locations on Puget Sound: Tenino and Wilkeson stones were quarried near Olympia; Chuckanut stone was quarried south of Fairhaven (now Bellingham).[57] Stone was typically cut to appropriately sized blocks at the quarry and then transported to Seattle by barge. The final trim was done as part of the construction process in Seattle. Occasionally, special stone, such as the red sandstone on the Seattle National Bank Building, would be imported by rail from outside the region. Brick was available from local brickyards although demand soon outstripped supply. Brick was also shipped to Seattle from elsewhere on the sound and occasionally special brick, of a quality better than that available locally, would be shipped by rail from outside the region. Wood was readily available from Seattle's sawmills and from sawmills in other Puget Sound ports, as well as along the rail lines in the interior. Architectural terra-cotta was not produced in quantity in Seattle until 1898; in 1889 terra-cotta was typically ordered from manufacturers outside the region, most often the Gladding, McBean Company of central California.[58] This material could be shipped via rail or coastal steamer. Some cast iron was produced locally but larger cast iron elements and steel beams were often purchased from suppliers outside the region, typically in Portland or San Francisco.

In the months after the fire, the key issue for construction was the availability of these building materials. The pace and scale of construction meant that demand would have outrun supply under any circumstances, but the destruction of most of the wharves meant that in the first weeks after the fire the deliveries of materials from elsewhere on the sound were delayed simply because they could not be unloaded. Initially only a few small wharves were usable, and the first reconstruction that was undertaken was the rebuilding of the docks. Within a week after the fire the Yesler dock had been repaired to the extent that it could be used for passengers and light freight, but it was several weeks to a month before the major wharves would near completion, and in late June the *Post-Intelligencer* was still reporting on the difficulties of transporting materials into Seattle.[59]

Once the docks were rebuilt and the problems of receiving materials were overcome, the demand for materials still outpaced supply. Three million board feet of lumber had been ordered in the first three weeks after the fire, and mills from Tacoma to Snohomish were unable to keep up with the demand. As buildings began to proceed above the ground, the demand for brick could not be met. Brickyards tended to supply their best customers, and contractors were often required to order lots with a minimum of a half million bricks. In early July, the *Post-Intelligencer* reported that all the brickyards in the area were busy but were keeping up with demand.[60] By mid-August, however, the newspaper headlines read "Building Materials Scarce" and "Famine of the Builders," and suppliers were indicating that their total production expected before the end of the building season had already been sold.[61] In November, shortages of iron were reported to be causing additional delays in projects such as the Occidental Hotel and the Colman Block.[62] As a result, several projects which did not begin construction until August were able to proceed only as far as their foundations, and others were barely begun before 1890.

Only a few of the smaller business blocks were completed in 1889. By October the winter rains had begun. The brick of the new masonry walls had to be completely dry both before and immediately after walls were laid up in order for the mortar to set properly. In 1889 it was rarely feasible for contractors to provide shelters over their construction sites such that bricklaying could continue in the rain. Further, because brickyards in Puget Sound did not have large sheltered areas for brick making, their production slowed or stopped. Thus, on 1 October, the *Post-Intelligencer* headlined, "No More New Brick" and reported that the capacity of Puget Sound brickyards was exhausted and production for the year was drawing to a close.[63] In October and November newspaper articles about the new buildings expressed concern about the weather. On 15 October, a headline read "Praying for No Rain"; by early November construction was described as "A Race with the Weather" and a subhead noted "Temporary Roofs Are the Fashion."[64]

Only those buildings that were weathertight by late 1889 saw continuing construction through the winter months. Interior finish work could continue once a building was closed in, but if this point had not been reached, little could be done. However, because construction was floor-by-floor, a building that had reached at least to the second floor or above could be temporarily roofed over so that the first floor spaces could be finished and leased; this was done in many cases. The building season in 1890 began in March and extended until November. Supply was more regularized in 1890 and few shortages developed. Many of the new downtown office blocks were completed that year, although nearly all of the largest blocks, including the Pioneer Building, Burke Building, New York Building, and others, were not finished until 1891 or even 1892.[65]

In the first month after the fire, Seattle was flooded with building tradesmen seeking employment. Although there had initially been a concern that laborers would try to charge exorbitant prices for their services, a surplus of workers rapidly developed. By 6 July the *Post-Intelligencer* was reporting that there were far too many carpenters in Seattle for the available work.[66] The decision that the commercial core would be rebuilt in fire-resistive brick and stone construction had meant that the need for carpenters was limited. Skilled tradesmen, particularly stone and brick masons, were in demand, but the pace of reconstruction was not sufficient to absorb the hundreds of laborers who had migrated to the city seeking work, some from as far away as New England.

The Role of the Architects

The fire presented an unprecedented opportunity for Seattle's architects. The demand for new buildings was immense. With the newly implemented building ordinance and permit process, sufficient drawings to demonstrate that the new structures would meet the new requirements were necessary before construction could proceed. Only a few architects had not suffered losses in the fire. Parkinson and Evers were among the lucky ones. They had lowered their drafting tables, drawings, and equipment through a window when they thought the Boston Block would be destroyed; once that building was saved, they were able to take on new work immediately.[67] Most architects did not fare so well as they had had their offices in buildings in the burned district. Still, within a few days many architects were advertising in the newspapers that they had reestablished themselves and were ready to meet the demand for new buildings. Elmer Fisher, for example, advertised on 23 June that he had taken space in the Scurry terrace houses (a project of his own design), and that he had four capable draftsmen ready to undertake new projects.[68] A few days after the fire Fisher was also described as the fortunate owner of a safe which had survived the fire; the drawings and records he had stored in the safe were intact.[69] The rapidity with which architects were able to find space and take on work also reflects the relative simplicity of an architect's office in the period. (Fig. 3.19)

In the absence of written records and with the survival of only a few drawings from the period, it is almost impossible to describe the full design and construction process exactly. The few records that do survive suggest only a general outline. As is generally true today, public building commissions were offered through an open process that any architect might enter. In late-nineteenth-century Seattle, this usually involved the production of a design proposal to

meet the client's requirements (or program) within an established budget. The client would then select among the competing proposals the one which most closely met the requirements and the budget. Private commercial commissions were seldom secured in this way because an open process was not required. In many cases, owners simply turned to architects with whom they had already had experience. This seems to have been common in post-fire Seattle—those owners who had lost buildings in the fire turned for replacements to the architects who had designed their pre-fire buildings. Thus, William Boone designed the pre-fire Wah Chong Building and also its post-fire replacement; Elmer Fisher designed both the first (pre-fire) and second (post-fire) Korn Buildings.[70] Stephen Meany was already designing the Colman Building for John Collins when the fire destroyed the Occidental Hotel; by 18 June, Collins had selected Meany to design the new Occidental.[71] Henry Yesler gave a series of post-fire commissions to Elmer Fisher. And once an architect such as Fisher had secured a number of significant commissions, other owners might select him just on the basis of reputation. It was for these reasons that John Parkinson later complained that most of the large commissions after the fire went to the already established architects.[72] Occasionally, a private client might seek multiple designs from which to select a preferred scheme, but this was less common, especially given the demand for new buildings in the immediate post-fire period.

In the typical late-nineteenth-century design process, the architect would explore design directions and alternatives through a series of design sketches

3.19 Architect Albert Wickersham in his office, late 1890s

Museum of History and Industry, Seattle Historical Society Collection, 15547

before settling on a particular design solution. Preliminary sketches were often the basis for larger design studies and explorations as the architect sought to develop the three-dimensional scheme that best fit the client's needs and the specific site context. Once the direction of the design was settled, presentation drawings were usually prepared for client approval (or in a competitive process, for submission for client review and architect selection). These drawings usually included plans, elevations, and sections, all drawn to scale, as well as representational views such as perspectives. (Today an architect might also use models to explore design ideas and to present design schemes, but models were never mentioned in any of the newspaper reports or surviving records of the time and were apparently seldom used by Seattle architects in the nineteenth century.) In post-fire Seattle, particularly for the first buildings, the early part of the design process was apparently truncated. A client might approve a scheme based on a very limited set of drawings, perhaps a single plan and street elevation, and the project would then be pushed along as rapidly as possible. Surviving drawings do indicate, however, that the larger business blocks, such as the Burke Building, did proceed through a series of design studies before a scheme was fully resolved.

Once the design was accepted, or required only minor modifications, the architect would prepare the construction drawings (sometimes called "working drawings") and the specifications from which a contractor could actually erect the building. Construction drawings and specifications provide the instructions in written and graphic forms that describe the building that the client wants built. Drawings and specifications are sometimes referred to as "contract documents" because they become part of the legal agreement (the contract for construction) between the owner and the contractor. As a result of Seattle's new building ordinance after the fire, these drawings and specifications were reviewed by the city for conformance with the building requirements before a permit would be issued and they provided the basis for subsequent inspections of the project by city building inspectors.

In the 1880s and 1890s, it was common for the architect to prepare drawings all through the construction process, usually only as they were needed on the job. Most of these later drawings were details showing specific design features such as window and door trim, interior and exterior finishes, and other individual features and decorative elements. In order to secure a building permit and begin construction on a foundation, only an overall set of plans, sections, elevations, and the like, were required. These were typically the drawings the architect would prepare first in order to get the project under way. The other drawings would follow as necessary over the course of construction. A small commercial block might require fewer than forty sheets of drawings, but for a large commercial block the full set of drawings might easily fill 80 to 100 sheets. The surviving set of drawings of the Pioneer Building by Elmer Fisher includes over 100 sheets. In addition, the architect would prepare drawings to order building elements, for example cast iron and terra-cotta, from manufacturers and fabricators.[73] (Figs. 3.20, 3.21)

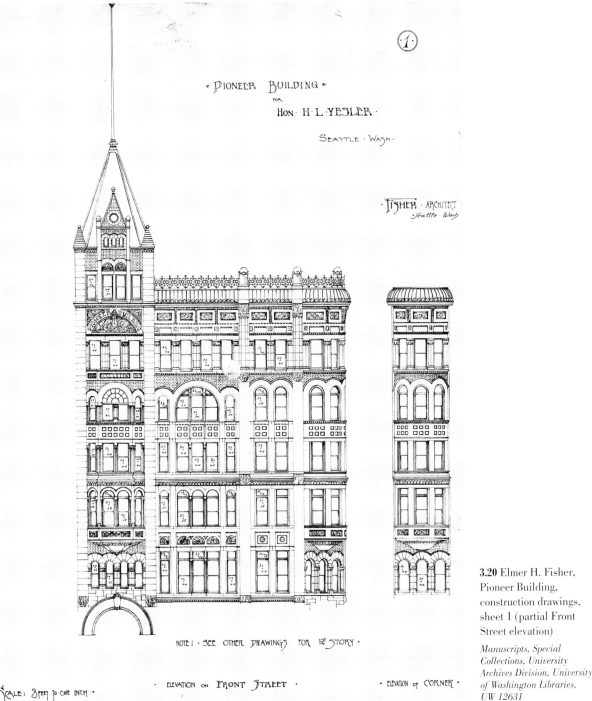

· PIONEER BUILDING ·

FOR

HON· H·L·YESLER·

SEATTLE · WASH ·

·FISHER · ARCHITECT

Seattle · Wash

NOTE: · SEE OTHER DRAWINGS FOR 1ST STORY ·

· SCALE: 8 FEET TO ONE INCH ·

· ELEVATION ON FRONT STREET ·

· ELEVATION OF CORNER ·

3.20 Elmer H. Fisher, Pioneer Building, construction drawings, sheet 1 (partial Front Street elevation)

Manuscripts, Special Collections, University Archives Division, University of Washington Libraries, UW 12631

Once construction began, the architect was typically involved in supervising construction to see that the building was built in accordance with the contract documents. This would typically involve review of samples of materials provided by the contractor, regular visits to the project, production of the additional detail drawings as required at each stage of the construction process, and verification of the contractor's invoices to the owner.

An individual architect practicing alone might have been able to carry out

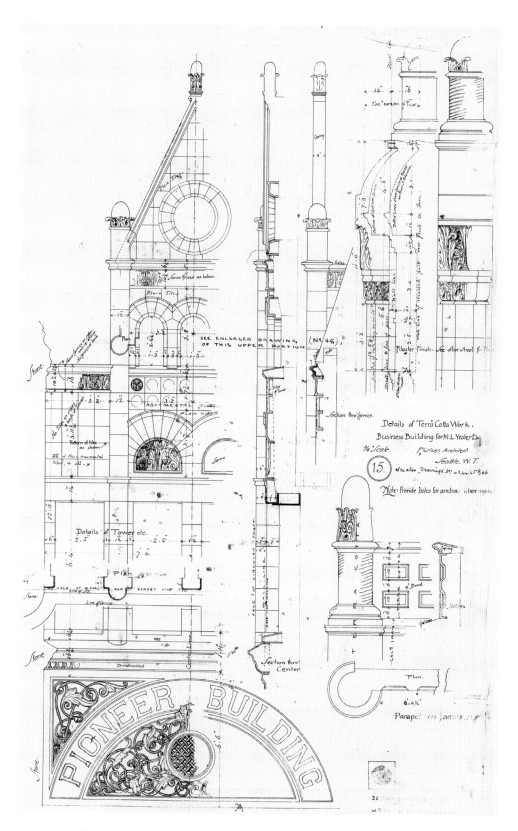

3.21 Elmer H. Fisher, Pioneer Building, construction drawings, sheet 15 (terra-cotta details)

Manuscripts, Special Collections,
University Archives Division,
University of Washington Libraries,
UW 12633

all of these tasks for small projects, but those architects who secured commercial commissions in the post-fire boom depended on the members of their office staffs. Seattle's architectural offices did not grow very large, usually consisting of the owner or owners and one or two draftsmen. For a brief time after the fire Elmer Fisher's office grew to employ as many as six draftsmen, but this was unusual and could not be sustained after 1890. The owner or partners were generally responsible for securing commissions, generating design ideas, and directing and participating in preparation of drawings and specifications; the draftsmen prepared the large number of necessary drawings. Some of their work was simple copying. In the late nineteenth century, construction drawings were usually prepared on construction paper or linen one set at a time. Drawings sent to the job site were most often originals or hand-made copies; although blueprinting was available, it was not yet widely used in construction.[74] But it would be a mistake to suggest that draftsmen performed no other function but copying. In a practice such as Fisher's, which was overwhelmed with commissions, many responsibilities must have been delegated. Indeed, the variety of designs produced by any single office of the time may partially reflect the influence of different draftsmen in the design process. Their involvement in drawing preparation also served to prepare the draftsmen to supervise during construction, although in some offices supervision might be the responsibility of the person with the most construction experience. The involvement of draftsmen in all phases of these projects also prepared them eventually to undertake their own independent practices.[75]

Architectural firms could remain small, yet design and supervise the large buildings built after the fire because the character of construction remained technologically traditional. Although the new commercial buildings typically featured internal heavy timber or metal frames, load-bearing masonry provided the primary support. During the post-fire period, Seattle architects did not need to address the demands of modern structural engineering. The separation of the frame from the exterior cladding and the independent design of the two was not an issue for Seattle architects before 1900. The enormous complexity that the new structural technology added to the architectural design of buildings— the requirements for engineering the design of steel or concrete frames and the design and detailing of independent cladding systems—emerged as problems in architectural practice in Seattle only in the twentieth century.

Because the post-fire buildings were constructed on the basis of experience and generally accepted approaches to structural design, some decisions could be made during the construction process. As the post-fire boom peaked in 1889 and 1890, several owners enlarged their buildings by increasing the number of floors. The Burke Building was originally intended as a five-story building but a floor was added once construction was begun. The Bailey Building was initially proposed as four stories, but was finally built as six.[76] In general, these increases in height were achieved just by thickening the walls and increasing the dimensions of the interior wood or metal columns. This is not to say that the architects of the post-fire period would not have benefited from improved engineering knowledge. For example, the structural bearing capacity of the old growth timber made it especially suitable for columns, but the designers of the period apparently did not fully understand that when used for horizontal girders or beams, the degree of bending was dependent upon depth. Thus, some buildings from the period show sagging and uneven floors where heavy loads bear in the middle of the spans of some of these framing elements. Similarly, understanding of soils and foundation design was not always adequate. In the area south of Yesler, where the early pioneer community had been built, the land had initially been tidal flats, and subsequent layers of fill included trash, sawdust, and the like; inadequate bearing soils resulted in uneven settlement and wall cracks which can sometimes be found in the surviving post-fire buildings today. And several buildings collapsed during construction. The Kline and Rosenberg Building, on Washington between Commercial and South Second, designed by Towle and Wilcox, collapsed in April 1890, apparently due to an old sawdust pocket.[77] The Brodeck and Schlesinger Building, on Washington between Third and Fourth, designed by Stephen Meany, began construction in March 1890; by late May the walls were approaching the second floor when the foundation suddenly gave way and the building collapsed. These architects' reputations undoubtedly suffered as a result.[78]

Mechanical and electrical systems, and other building technologies, were also relatively unsophisticated in Seattle buildings in the post-fire period, although this was just beginning to change. While indoor plumbing was a typical feature of commercial and institutional buildings by the 1880s, heating and lighting remained relatively primitive. Heating systems were bid independently for most buildings in Seattle in the 1880s and 1890s and their design remained the responsibility of the bidder. By the late 1880s, electric lighting was becoming common in nonresidential construction. Nonetheless, it was still enough of a novelty that in 1892 when the Seattle Theater opened, the widespread use of electric lighting was considered among the most notable features of the design.[79] Because electrification of American cities began only in the last years of the 1880s and many problems of city-wide electrical distribution had not been solved, Seattle business blocks built after the fire typically provided their own power generation. For example, the Pioneer Building was planned with electric lighting throughout and an "electric light plant" in the basement. Institutional buildings constructed outside the urban core faced similar requirements. Both the Seattle Seminary building, completed in 1893, and Denny Hall at the University of Washington, completed in 1894, were equipped with electric lights but depended initially on their own power generation.[80] (Rapid progress would be made in urban electrification in the 1890s, and this practice disappeared thereafter.) Although the architect would frequently position the lights and select the fixtures (whether gas or electric), the design of the gas or electric system was usually the responsibility of the contractor or supplier at that time; this would change early in the twentieth century. The first Seattle office building with a passenger elevator, the Boston Block, had only been completed in 1888, but all the new commercial blocks constructed after the fire included elevators; again, the technical aspects of their design were left to the suppliers and contractors.[81] Finally, the multiplicity of materials and the complexities of modern detailing—dealing with water penetration, sealants, damp-proofing, insulation, prefabricated building elements and assemblies, construction joints, and the like—were simply not issues for architects in practice before 1900.[82] Indeed, it is often forgotten that the comfort levels that clients now expect to be routinely provided would have been considered luxurious less than a century ago.

After the fire, Seattle architects faced immediate pressure to generate the designs to rebuild the city's commercial core. Although these architects faced a large number of commissions, often at a scale their work had not previously approached, the materials and methods of construction were familiar to them. Their work preceded the technological transformation of building and the corresponding emergence of multiple specialized technical disciplines within the design field, so these architects were not required to deal with the number of consultants and the level of coordination of structural, mechanical, electrical, and specialty services that in the twentieth century have become part of every project. (The importance of the architect's role as coordinator of the project team as well as lead designer has emerged only with the increasing sophistication of building.) Still, the architects of the period were not alone in the creation of the new city. The architectural firms involved participation by multiple individuals, and the buildings were the creations of the owners who commissioned them, the architects who designed them, and the contractors who built them.

IV

The Architectural Context
The Influence of Richardson and the Romanesque Revival

Seattle's new buildings are rising on every hand and the public is for the first time getting an idea of the appearance of the exteriors. . . . It is a fact, however, that, in rebuilding, Seattle business men have looked more toward making strong buildings than fancy, and have preferred to put their money into extra stories rather than into a profusion of ornament. . . . Almost all of the buildings are of the Romanesque style of architecture, while the heavy, ponderous, unsightly and inflammable cornice has disappeared entirely. . . . Seattle's architects have followed the example of Mr. Richardson, the great architect of America, in his modifications of the Romanesque style and have applied it faithfully to the requirements of the present time.

—unidentified architect, probably Elmer Fisher, quoted in
Seattle Post-Intelligencer, 19 October 1889

When Seattle architects turned to the example of H. H. Richardson in 1889, they joined with their contemporaries across the continent in attempting to continue the architectural movement they understood Richardson to have initiated. Richardson's architectural achievement was the work of just two decades, but he was seen as personally having redirected the course of American architecture. When he died on 27 April 1886, Richardson was just forty-seven years of age and his influence was growing. Whether it was that Richardson's death had "extinguished envy" as the critic Montgomery Schuyler later suggested, or whether it was simply that the overwhelming sense of loss had created an urgency to carry on and complete the architectural project that Richardson had begun, the Romanesque Revival soon became the dominant tendency in design from Boston to Seattle.[1]

Speaking on 5 March 1887, less than a year after Richardson's death, John Wellborn Root, the leading Chicago architect, summarized his view of the state of American architecture:

Nowhere today do we find academic productions in Neo-Grec so common a decade since; nowhere those pseudo Gothic designs to whose production were consecrated the talents of Burges and Street and Scott. In high stays, and crisp, unyielding ruffs, Queen Anne has taken coach and driven off, and now only the rumble of her distant wheels, and the lingering perfume of her lavender remain; the neo-Jacobean has lost its royal state; the Dutch have come to London, and, like William of Orange, hold silent sway in Cadogan Square; here in America the present vogue is a style called "Romanesque."[2]

Root's description of the Romanesque as a "vogue" was to prove more accurate than he could imagine given its rapid rise and subsequent decline, but his statement also serves to frame the context of American Victorian architecture within which Richardson's contribution was received. Although this level of flourish was beyond his typical literary style, Root offers a sense of why architects found the Romanesque so attractive in the late 1880s: Not only did it offer a simple lithic style applicable to a wide range of settings and building types, it also offered a level of coherence that contrasted sharply with the wide diversity that had dominated American architecture after the Civil War. Implicit in Root's statement was also the belief that the elemental qualities of the Romanesque could be seen in contrast to the more agitated ornamental aspects of the prevailing Victorian modes. And, as the term "vogue" indicates, Richardson's example was not the sole representative of the Romanesque. Rather, many architects were contributing to the development of the mode, and seen from Seattle, the production of architects in the Midwest, like Root, would prove particularly influential.

Root's statement must be interpreted with care as his suggestion of a clear succession—that is, that the earlier Victorian modes had disappeared to be replaced by Romanesque—is only partly true. The idea that architectural development is merely the replacement of one mode by another must be regarded as much too simplified. Rather, architectural history might better be understood as a "palimpsest"—that is, as a surface written on more than once, the previous inscriptions imperfectly erased and therefore visible to influence later inscriptions. Architects in the 1880s may have turned to the new Richardsonian mode, but how can architects erase completely what they already know? A new mode is usually interpreted through an architect's previous experience; therefore, new designs will often reflect both architects' earlier experiences and their attempts to incorporate the new direction. At any point in time, the variety of expression will show a range of interpretations reflecting an architecture in transition—an architecture that balances and accommodates continuity and change.[3] Thus, the "Richardsonian" or "Romanesque" production of the 1880s and 1890s reflects, in part, the varied circumstances of the American Victorian architecture that preceded it. Some progressive architects may have pushed the new design in the direction of modernity while others sought academic regularity, but the Romanesque Revival work of most contemporary architects, such as those in Seattle, is best understood as framed by the American Victorian architecture they already knew. (Fig. 4.1)

The Rise of H. H. Richardson

Although the architectural achievement of H. H. Richardson was widely recognized during his lifetime, it was not until after his death that the full impact of Richardson's career was felt by his contemporaries. Nonetheless, the exact nature of Richardson's achievement has remained elusive. Richardson wrote little to explain his architecture, apparently preferring his buildings to speak

4.1 Elmer H. Fisher,
Pioneer Building, Seattle,
1889–91

*Manuscripts, Special
Collections, University
Archives Division, University
of Washington Libraries,
photo by Frank LaRoche,
1009*

for themselves. As a result, his work has always been subject to varying interpretations.[4]

Richardson's early career was largely unknown to most architects who followed his example. Although he opened his practice in 1866, his national fame
dates from a decade later, beginning with the completion of Boston's Trinity
Church in 1877. The architects who followed his example responded to his
mature works, and knew little of the sources of the design synthesis these
reflected. Richardson's earliest works had drawn on contemporary English and
French precedents and reflected his effort to accommodate the architectural
principles he had learned at the Ecole des Beaux-Arts in Paris in light of the
realities of Victorian eclecticism in post–Civil War America. Early in his career,
Richardson's works appeared little different from those of his contemporaries,
but by 1870, he had begun to explore the Romanesque in works such as Brattle
Square Church, Boston (1869–73). (Fig. 4.2) Richardson's free adaptations of
the Romanesque, executed in monochromatic stone with round-arched features,
included New York State Hospital, Buffalo (1869–80), Hampden County
Courthouse, Springfield, Massachusetts (1871–74), and unbuilt projects such
as Trinity Church, Buffalo (ca. 1871–72). However, the emerging direction of
Richardson's career would not have been widely known outside New York and

4.2 Gambrill and Richardson, Brattle Square Church, Boston, 1869–73 (First Baptist Church)

American Architect and Building News 43 (24 March 1894)

New England. Although drawings of some of his projects appeared in the early 1870s in the new architectural periodicals *The New York Sketchbook of Architecture* and *The Architectural Sketchbook*, these were short-lived ventures with limited circulation. But Richardson's mature career coincided with the first decade of the Boston-based *American Architect and Building News*, the first successful national architectural journal, started in 1876.[5] *American Architect* was the primary vehicle through which Richardson's work was to become nationally known.

In 1872, Richardson won the commission for Trinity Church, Boston. Constructed between April 1874 and February 1877, this building marked Richardson's emergence as a leading American architect; it also can be considered the true beginning of Richardsonian Romanesque architecture. (Fig. 4.3) Richardson wrote of the architecture as one of "grandeur and repose," but

the free use of historical sources, described by Richardson in the dedication
program as a "free rendering of the French Romanesque," and the picturesque
characteristics of the composition allowed many of Richardson's contemporaries to see the building as pointing to a new direction within the framework
of Victorian design.[6]

Trinity Church brought Richardson broad recognition. On its completion in
1877, Trinity Church was considered one of the finest examples of American
architecture, attracting attention in the popular press as well as in the architectural journals.[7] In 1885 it was named first in the survey of the "ten best
buildings in the United States" by *American Architect and Building News.*[8] A
cultural as well as an architectural monument, Trinity Church was one of the
buildings American architects would cite as a source for their designs over the
next two decades.

Richardson's mature career moved in several directions. Although Trinity
became one of the buildings for which he was best known, he built only two
small churches over the rest of his career. Instead, as his practice expanded,
Richardson addressed a wide variety of secular building types, including

libraries, railroad stations, university buildings, commercial blocks, and city halls and courthouses.[9]

Since the 1930s, historians of Modernism have emphasized the tendency towards simplification evident in some of Richardson's mature designs, exemplified by Sever Hall at Harvard (1878–80), a classroom building set within the context of the older architecture of Harvard Yard. Richardson's response was a straightforward rectangle of brick with a hipped roof. (Fig. 4.4) Built with a limited budget, Richardson's design for Sever used only the simplest elements—two half-round bays on each long elevation—and details—panels of carved brick at key locations and molded brick at the windows and doors—but combined these to achieve a design that his biographer, Mariana Griswold Van Rensselaer, described as "neither monotonous nor restless" with "rich effect produced with so little aid from decoration."[10]

In contrast to Sever, Richardson's contemporaries saw his Oakes Ames Memorial Hall, North Easton (1879–81), as evidence of his continuing picturesque experimentation within the framework of the Romanesque. (Fig. 4.5) Designed as a meeting hall, the building is a rectangle in plan and features a loggia at the ground floor, an engaged tower at one corner and a hipped roof with multiple dormers. The lower floor of granite is approached by a stair which grows out of the rocky landscape, the second story is built of brick, and the north-facing dormer is half-timbered.[11]

The variety of the messages that architects of the 1880s could take from Richardson's work is reflected in these two buildings. Both Sever Hall and Oakes

4.4 H. H. Richardson, Sever Hall, Harvard University, Cambridge, Massachusetts 1878–80

American Architect and Building News 24 (3 Nov. 1888); courtesy Trustees of the Boston Public Library

4.5 H. H. Richardson,
Oakes Ames Memorial
Hall, North Easton,
Massachusetts 1879–81

American Architect and
Building News *13 (19 May
1883); courtesy Trustees of
the Boston Public Library*

4.6 H. H. Richardson,
Austin Hall, Harvard
University, 1881–84

American Architect and
Building News *17 (28 Mar.
1885); Columbia University,
Avery Architectural and Fine
Arts Library*

Ames Memorial Hall were considered among Richardson's finest designs, as both appeared on the list of the ten best American buildings that *American Architect and Building News* published in 1885, but their differences are quite marked—for example, the symmetrical balance of Sever as opposed to the picturesque asymmetries of Ames, and the unity of materials and spareness of detail at Sever as opposed to the variety of materials and mix of detail at Ames.

After 1880, Richardson's professional success was reflected in the expanded scope of his practice, when he was besieged with commissions. Several, including Austin Hall, Harvard (1881–84), Billings Library, University of Vermont, Burlington (1883–86), and the unbuilt project for the All Saints Episcopal Cathedral, Albany (1882–83), display continuing use of Romanesque ornament or picturesque compositional strategies and contributed to the contemporary perception of Richardson's work as a wide-ranging and freely interpretive version of the Romanesque.[12] (Fig. 4.6)

The spread of Richardson's reputation, and with it the spread of Richardsonian architecture, was enhanced by the geographic expansion of his practice after 1883. In his last years Richardson was responsible for houses in Washington, D.C., Buffalo, Chicago, and St. Louis and for major civic and commercial structures in Pittsburgh, Cincinnati, and Chicago. Two of these commissions, the Allegheny County Courthouse and Jail, Pittsburgh (1883–88), and the Marshall Field Wholesale Store, Chicago (1885–87, destroyed), are buildings of which Richardson was particularly proud, although neither had been completed at his death. Richardson's Allegheny design was selected in a competition in early 1884. The courthouse is a symmetrical four-story structure surrounding a courtyard. (Fig. 4.7) The chief exterior feature is the tower, which appears to grow directly out of the base of the building. The resulting silhouette captivated Richardson's followers in succeeding years. Romanesque detail was limited to the entry arches and a few other key points, but still served to animate the design. Richardson's competition brief explained his project:

> A free treatment of the Romanesque has been followed, throughout, as a style especially adapted to the requirements of a large civic building; for while it maintains great dignity together with a strong sense of solidity, it lends itself at the same time most readily to the requirements of utility, especially in the matter of light.[13]

Richardson recognized the significance of his Pittsburgh buildings; he called his earlier work "pygmy things" in comparison.[14] Widely publicized, the Allegheny Courthouse provided a model for the many Richardsonian courthouses, city halls, and other public structures of the next few years, including buildings in Washington State.[15] Leading architectural critic Montgomery Schuyler, writing in 1911, still praised the design: "Richardson did nothing, in civil architecture at least, more significant than this group. . . . This group is one of the chief ornaments of Pittsburgh. It would be among the chief ornaments of any American city fortunate enough to possess it."[16] Along with Trinity Church, the Allegheny County Buildings were those most frequently cited as models for inspiring a generation of Richardsonian architects.

4.7 H. H. Richardson,
Allegheny County
Courthouse, Pittsburgh,
1883–88

*Architectural Record 1/2
(Oct.–Dec. 1891)*

Richardson provided a direction for commercial architecture in the Marshall
Field Wholesale Store. (Fig. 4.8) Here Richardson's design moved toward simplification and elimination of historical detail, a direction that would serve the primarily utilitarian requirements of commercial construction.[17] The virtues of
the building were celebrated in Van Rensselaer's biography:

> The whole effect depends upon the structure of the walls themselves. No building
> could more frankly express its purpose or be more self-denying in the use of orna-
> ment. Yet the most elaborately massed, diversified and decorated structure could
> not be more truly a design; and its prime virtues of a solidity commensurate with
> its elevation and dignity equal to its bulk are secured in such way that even a high
> degree of beauty is not wanting.[18]

The design inspired a generation of Chicago architects, but unlike Richardson's other large work it was not published in *American Architect and Building*

News, although it did appear in the Chicago-based *Inland Architect* in 1888.[19]

Although later denigrated by historians of Modernism, the Chamber of Commerce Building, Cincinnati (1885–88, destroyed), was recognized in the late 1880s as one of Richardson's major late works. (Fig. 4.9) The widely publicized competition drew entries from architects in Boston, New York, Chicago, Buffalo, and Cincinnati. Richardson's winning design housed a complex mixed-use program including commercial activities at the ground floor, an exchange hall with a forty-eight-foot ceiling height at the second floor, and three stories of offices above. Although the fenestration pattern responded to the varied uses, prominent corner towers with conical roofs and the tall hipped roof served to unify the design and gave it a strongly vertical expression. In her biography of Richardson, Van Rensselaer commented on the difficulty of the project and wrote of its "expressional clearness" and "the beauty of the exterior treatment." The Chamber of Commerce was published in multiple illustrations in *American Architect and Building News, Inland Architect*, and *Architectural Record*.[20]

Richardson's last commercial building, the Ames Building, Harrison Avenue, Boston (1886–87, destroyed), housing the J. H. Pray and Sons Store, has been recognized as offering a surprisingly advanced solution for the commercial building. (Fig. 4.10) Instead of several stacked arcades, the design features a simply detailed vertically continuous arcade with narrow brick piers and broad windows.[21] Although the Harrison Avenue design can be seen as a development of his earlier work, it also suggests the influence of Chicago architects

4.9 H. H. Richardson, Chamber of Commerce Building, Cincinnati, 1885–88 (destroyed)

Architectural Record 1/2 (Oct.–Dec. 1891)

Burnham and Root, whose new work Richardson had seen when he visited the city in 1885.[22] Just as Richardson would continue to influence Chicago architects, he also may have learned from them and the direction in which their work was proceeding—a direction that contributed to the development of Richardsonian Romanesque design in the late 1880s, especially in the American West.

When *American Architect and Building News* published its 1885 survey of the best buildings in the United States, a large number of Richardson's late works, including the Allegheny Courthouse, Field Store, and Cincinnati Chamber of Commerce, were incomplete. His selected buildings, Trinity Church, Sever Hall at Harvard, Albany City Hall, Oakes Ames Memorial Hall, and the New York State Capitol, were a mixed group which represent some of the different directions within Richardson's production. An evolutionary trend toward simplicity and restraint that twentieth-century critics would find in Richardson's work cannot be discerned from these designs. Indeed, these five suggest that contemporaries understood Richardson's own architecture not as a univalent approach, but rather as a set of interrelated but varied directions.[23] Richardson's late works also displayed similar variation. The Field Store would

be celebrated for its "proto-modern" character in the 1930s, but the Allegheny County Buildings received much more publicity in the 1880s. Modern historians would express a preference for the Allegheny County Jail, but it was the courthouse that attracted the most attention at the time and the most imitators. And, the widely published Cincinnati Chamber of Commerce would have been seen as demonstrating Richardson's continuing use of Romanesque precedent.

The discussion of Richardson's work in the popular press also presented his achievement as multivalent. The leading critic Mariana Griswold Van Rensselaer prominently featured Richardson's buildings in her series of articles, "Recent Architecture in America," in *Century Magazine* from 1884 to 1886. These articles included almost every type of building Richardson had designed, and the only buildings Van Rensselaer questioned were his masonry houses. In an article on public buildings, she noted the picturesqueness of Ames Hall and contrasted this with the order and symmetry of Sever, but she did so within a context that recognized such differences as appropriate given the setting and program for each design.[24] Late-nineteenth-century architects, including those in Seattle, looking at Richardson's work in publication, both professional and popular, would never have seen a single design direction. As a result, in subsequent years the Romanesque Revival interlude in American architecture would develop along multiple lines derived from Richardson's works.

Richardson was plagued by ill health most of his life and on 1 May 1886, *American Architect and Building News* reported his death just a few days before, noting both his remarkable career and its impact on American architects: "Few of us, perhaps, and least of all himself, have realized how conspicuous he was in the profession in this country, yet from Maine to Texas there is probably not an office in which Mr. Richardson's work, past and to come, was not an inexhaustible subject of discussion and source of inspiration."[25] This obituary also suggested that the quality of the work of a "younger generation" of architects was largely due to Richardson's example. The *Inland Architect* obituary noted that Richardson's efforts had provided the basis for an American style of architecture: "No other architect has done so much toward the development of a style as Mr. Richardson, his work bearing the boldness of the Romanesque and the oriental lightness of the Byzantine, . . . it may be because he selected that style of itself most adaptable to our needs, or it may have been the genius of the man, that has done so much toward forming a basis for an American architecture."[26] The recognition that Richardson had been America's foremost architect, and that the profession had suffered an irreparable loss, permeates all of his obituaries, both in the professional and the popular press.[27] In turn, Richardson's premature death freed architects to contribute to the further development of the movement Richardson was understood to have initiated.

The spread of Romanesque Revival design was fostered by the extensive publication of Richardson's work.[28] Van Rensselaer's biography appeared in 1888, just two years after his death, but as only 500 copies were printed, it was not widely available and the architectural journals proved more important in sharing examples of his designs. Particularly influential was *American Architect and Building News* which published illustrations of Richardson's buildings as late as 1895.[29] In fact, more images appeared in the first years after his death than had appeared previously.[30] And, the way in which *American Architect* published Richardson's work in the late 1880s and early 1890s accentuated the perception of multiple directions encompassed within his system of design. Among the buildings included were Brattle Square Church, Trinity Church, town libraries in Woburn, North Easton, Quincy and Malden, Ames Memorial Hall, Sever and Austin Halls at Harvard, Albany City Hall, Cincinnati Chamber of Commerce, Allegheny County Courthouse and Jail, and several of his masonry houses. (Figs. 4.11, 4.12) Images were not published in chronological order, and the apparent randomness of their sequence emphasized the diversity of Richardson's work.[31] The impact of the varied images of Richardson's work was heightened because, at his request, his buildings appeared only in photographs, not drawings.[32] The journal even noted its role in promoting Richardson's influence within American architecture: "every issue of ours with one of his designs was studied in a thousand offices and imitated in hundreds."[33]

Inland Architect, the Chicago-based publication widely distributed in the Midwest and Far West, including Seattle, also carried images of Richardson's buildings, but only those outside New England. The Marshall Field Store was presented in a single view in October 1888. In 1889, the Cincinnati Chamber

4.11 H. H. Richardson, Crane Library, Quincy, Massachusetts, 1880–82

American Architect and Building News *13 (30 June 1883); Columbia University, Avery Architectural and Fine Arts Library*

4.12 H. H. Richardson, City Hall, Albany, New York, 1880–83

American Architect and Building News *26 (13 July 1889); courtesy Trustees of the Boston Public Library*

of Commerce received four images and the Allegheny County Courthouse received six. *Inland Architect* also carried images of six of Richardson's masonry houses.[34]

It is essential to recognize that Richardson was not seen in isolation from the other architects of his time. Historians have tended to study Richardson in isolation in order to focus on his career and trace his development, but there are two problems with this approach. First, other than a few close personal acquaintances, architects of Richardson's time knew far less about the development of Richardson's career and the sequence of his buildings than is known today. Second, although isolation of Richardson's work by architectural historians has enabled the study of his career, this isolation is an artificial one that interferes with seeing Richardson in context. Architects of Richardson's time, such as those in Seattle, undoubtedly saw Richardson as a great architect, but they did not see him in isolation. Instead, they saw his projects as part of a continuum of contemporary work. Between 1876 and 1895, Richardson was well-published with forty-two illustrations appearing in *American Architect and Building News*. But, in that same period, *American Architect* published well over 3,500 illustrations, so Richardson's work was only about 1.2 percent of the total.[35]

Romanesque Revival Architecture

One aspect of Richardson's work that made it such a good source for architects in the late nineteenth century was the variety of building types it appeared to encompass. The 1880s and 1890s were a period of rapid city building in the West and urban expansion in the East. The growth of cities in the period was accompanied by an increasing variety of building types requiring architectural design. Richardson was one of the earliest architects to respond to the new building types—for example, the small-town library or the large urban business block.[36] To architects of his generation, faced with a bewildering array of new building types, Richardson's architecture seemed to offer a clear architectural system that could be applied to most of the tasks they faced. And, the variety of Richardson's buildings offered a range of examples of solutions to the building tasks faced by architects in an urbanizing America.

For business blocks in the burgeoning cities, Richardson's examples were the Ames Stores on Harrison Avenue and on Bedford Street, both published in *American Architect*, and the Marshall Field Store, published in *Inland Architect*. Many cities at the time, including Seattle, were adopting new fire ordinances requiring masonry construction in their urban cores. Architects in Seattle, as in other cities, turned to the Richardsonian Romanesque to solve the problem of the architectural character of the new fire-resistive business buildings, as well as to create an image of metropolitan achievement. (Fig. 4.13) After the highly ornamented surface treatments that had been typical in the United States in the 1870s and 1880s, Richardson's design approach demon-

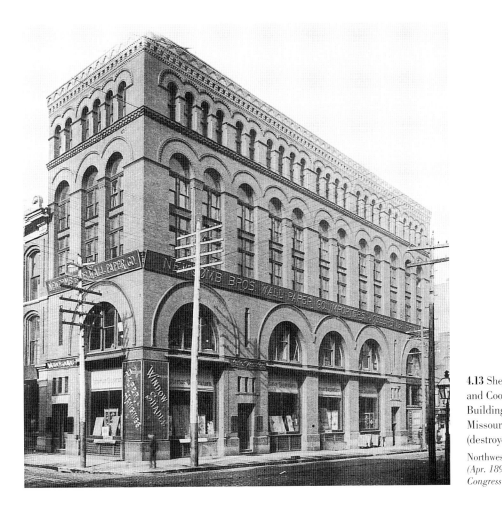

4.13 Shepley, Rutan and Coolidge, Newcomb Building, St. Louis, Missouri, 1887–89 (destroyed)

Northwestern Architect *8/4 (Apr. 1890)*, *Library of Congress*

strated how to achieve a powerful architectural image of strength and stability without an elaborate decorative treatment.

For large public buildings, the preferred example was the widely published Allegheny County Courthouse and occasionally the Albany City Hall or Oakes Ames Hall. For example, an 1892 article on the design of city halls in *Engineering Magazine* cited Richardson's Albany and North Easton buildings as models, and illustrated several other Richardsonian examples.[37] The 1880s and 1890s were a time of significant investment in new public buildings across the United States—particularly county courthouses. Fireproof construction for storage of permanent public records was often the major issue and masonry buildings were the answer. Richardson's work frequently provided the model for the new masonry construction. The Pierce County Courthouse in Tacoma (1890–93, destroyed), for example, showed a particularly knowledgeable application of the Richardsonian Romanesque vocabulary. (Fig. 4.14)

Urban and suburban growth in the East and Midwest also required new public buildings on a smaller scale—new libraries, schools, railroad stations, and similar structures. Here Richardson's smaller public buildings provided good examples. His series of suburban libraries had been published in *American*

4.14 Proctor and
Dennis, Pierce County
Courthouse, Tacoma,
Washington, 1890–93
(destroyed)

*Manuscripts, Special
Collections, University
Archives Division, University
of Washington Libraries,
photo by Asahel Curtis, 8679*

4.15 Van Brunt and Howe,
Rindge Public Library,
Cambridge, Massachu-
setts, 1887–89

*Inland Architect, 16 (Jan.
1890); courtesy Trustees of
the Boston Public Library*

Architect as had Sever and Austin Halls at Harvard. As the public library movement continued to develop, many architects designed small masonry libraries with simplified Romanesque details.[38] (Fig. 4.15) Other public buildings received similar treatments, and Richardson's Harvard buildings proved suitable models for schools at all levels. Similarly, Richardson's churches, primarily Trinity Church, but occasionally his earlier church buildings, offered precedents for new religious construction.[39]

Richardson was less influential in the design of residential architecture. His masonry residences offered useful models for houses for the wealthy only in the very largest metropolitan centers such as Boston, New York, Washington, Pittsburgh, Detroit, Chicago, Minneapolis, St. Paul and St. Louis.[40] Almost everywhere else, residential construction remained wood frame and the Queen Anne and "modern colonial" (now shingle style) modes were common, but neither was considered "Richardsonian" in the same way as was the masonry Romanesque Revival.

By the mid-to-late 1880s, the published Richardson designs were supplemented by many more office blocks and public and institutional structures by other architects working in the Romanesque mode. As American architects began to draw upon the precedents Richardson had established and submitted their own work for publication, the pages of the professional journals were filled with Richardsonian examples. Photographs of Richardson's buildings continued to be published into the 1890s, but many more Romanesque Revival buildings not by Richardson were also published, providing many more examples of the applicability of Richardson's design approach to the multiple building types that architects faced in the last decades of the nineteenth century.

A second reason why Richardson's work appeared accessible was that it seemed so open to interpretation. Richardson rarely wrote about his work, and he never addressed his design ideas in the general circulation architectural press.[41] This contrasts markedly with other American architectural leaders, such as John Root, Louis Sullivan, and Frank Lloyd Wright, who were prolific writers; they provided frameworks through which to see their work. Because Richardson offered so little published commentary on his own work, architects in his time were able to "project" their own interpretations onto it.[42] What Richardson's contemporaries found in his work, whether reading the architectural journals or, in some cases, actually visiting the buildings themselves, depended on what they brought to it. Those trained in the Victorian modes perceived in Richardson what they already knew. Those with academic backgrounds saw Richardson through that framework. The diverse directions of Richardson's works illustrated in publications allowed each architect to see Richardson in a different way. The result is the wide variety of directions in the "Richardsonian" Romanesque work of the years 1886 to 1893. The number of buildings produced in the period is extraordinarily large, but a few examples of the applications of the Richardsonian Romanesque architectural system will show how widely varied were contemporary architects' understandings of Richardson.

4.16 Long and Kees,
Masonic Temple,
Minneapolis, Minnesota,
1887–89

*Long and Kees Papers,
Northwest Architectural
Archives, University of
Minnesota Libraries,
Minneapolis*

The Masonic Temple, Minneapolis (1887–89), by the local firm Long and
Kees, was one of the business blocks erected as part of that city's building
boom in the 1880s. (Fig. 4.16) In May 1890, a critic writing in the Chicago-
based *Building Budget* characterized this building as "a pitiful display of mon-
grel Romanesque" and "one mass of detail from top to bottom."[43] The Masonic
Temple building was among the larger commercial structures built in Minneapolis, but it was treated less as a coherent block and more as a series of horizontal layers and vertical bays (making it completely unlike Richardson's
Marshall Field Store). The expression, particularly of the end elevation, shows
the continuing influence of the late-Victorian tendency to grid facades and to
treat a large block as a series of adjacent vertical pavilions. The variety of detail
drawn from almost every period in architectural history was intended as an
expression of the Masonic Order, but its irregular character and lack of integral relationship to the overall design clearly links this to the Victorian modes.

The building is perhaps best described as late-Victorian with a Romanesque vocabulary and an overlay of picturesque sculptural detail.[44] Elmer Fisher's post-fire buildings show similar tendencies, although economics limited embellishment in Seattle. Fisher continued to follow Victorian convention, designing gridded facades with pilasters and belt courses and treating larger blocks as a series of adjacent vertical pavilions, even as he adopted Richardsonian Romanesque details as at the Pioneer Building.

Architects who knew Richardson's work first-hand also produced varying interpretations. One example is the Newton Center Baptist Church (1887–89) by John Lyman Faxon.[45] (Fig. 4.17) Faxon apparently saw Richardson as a picturesque eclectic architect. Faxon's design strategy was to assemble a series of related masses—an approach he would have seen in Richardson's designs for the Woburn Library and Trinity Church. Faxon's work is clearly not as sophisticated or well-integrated as Richardson's, but this building was well-enough regarded at the time that a photograph appeared in *Inland Architect*.[46] A similar example is Arthur Vinal's Boston Water Works building in Chestnut Hill (1887–88), which O'Gorman described as "picturesque Romanesque."[47] (Fig. 4.18) This building was published in multiple views in *Northwestern Architect* in 1889.[48] In turn, examples like these very likely influenced the picturesque Romanesque compositional strategies adopted by Willis Ritchie for public projects in Washington State.

The Cambridge City Hall, Cambridge (1888–89), by Longfellow, Alden, and Harlow shows a more strongly disciplined, academic approach. A drawing of the competition-winning design appeared in *American Architect* in July 1888.

4.17 John Lyman Faxon, Newton Center Baptist Church, Newton, Massachusetts, 1887–89

American Buildings, Selections 3, *pl. 26, image from* Inland Architect *13/4 (April 1889), Columbia University, Avery Architectural and Fine Arts Library*

4.18 Arthur Vinal, Boston Water Works, Chestnut Hill, Newton, Massachusetts, 1887–88

Northwestern Architect 7/2 (Feb. 1889); Library of Congress

Alexander W. Longfellow, who had been educated at the Ecole des Beaux-Arts, had emerged as one of Richardson's chief assistants in the early 1880s before initiating this partnership in early 1886.[49] Given Longfellow's education the stronger academic direction with clear symmetries and studied proportions evident in the Cambridge City Hall is not surprising.[50] (Fig. 4.19) Ultimately, for Longfellow, the academic eclectic approach underlying Richardson's design method was to prove much more important than its Richardsonian language.

Although these are only a few examples, they show that Richardson's work appeared to offer a diversity of design directions. The architects of the time, including those in Seattle, saw Richardson through their own eyes, projected on his work their own interpretations, and produced a variety of kinds of works that they thought were following Richardson's example—and they were, each in his own way.

As the critic Montgomery Schuyler noted, Richardsonian architecture independent of Richardson had barely begun at Richardson's death in April 1886. Only a few architects had already started designing Richardsonian buildings. Among the more prominent of the early "Richardsonians" was Henry Van Brunt (1832–1903), whose pedigree included Harvard and study of architecture in the atelier of Richard Morris Hunt.[51] His Boston-based practice with William R. Ware had produced work in a variety of modes including Victorian Gothic and Queen Anne, but for the design of the Public Library, Topeka, Kansas (1881–83, destroyed), Van Brunt created a building clearly derived from Richardson's example. (Fig. 4.20) One of the first identifiably Romanesque buildings west of the Mississippi, the Topeka Library was a simple volumetric composition built of rock-faced native limestone with round arched openings and cut sandstone trim generally following Richardson's example.[52] Van Brunt's sub-

ACCEPTED·DESIGN·FOR
CAMBRIDGE·CITY·HALL

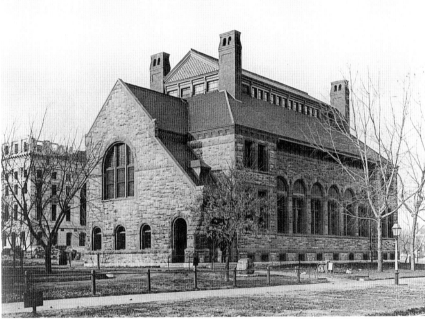

4.19 Longfellow, Alden,
and Harlow, City Hall,
Cambridge, Massachu-
setts, 1888–89

American Architect and
Building News *24 (28 July
1888); courtesy Trustees of
the Boston Public Library*

4.20 Henry Van Brunt,
Topeka Public Library,
Topeka, Kansas,
1881–83 (destroyed)

The Capital City *(1888),
Kansas State Historical
Society, FK2.S5T.761*10*

sequent buildings (with Frank Howe, his partner after 1882), including libraries
in East Saginaw, Michigan, and Cambridge and Dedham, Massachusetts, and
railroad stations in Ogden, Utah, and Cheyenne, Wyoming, all dating from the
1880s, reflect his adoption of the Richardsonian Romanesque approach.
Because Van Brunt and Howe's buildings were frequently published in *American
Architect* and *Building News,* his work offered an example to others that the use
of the Romanesque mode was not restricted only to H. H. Richardson.[53]

Van Brunt is important because his influence was not just confined to his
practice. As an essayist and critic, Van Brunt expressed his admiration for

Richardson early and often, and after the mid-1880s was a consistent advocate of Richardson's style as the basis for a national American architecture. In March 1886, he praised Richardson's "revival" of the Romanesque in an essay in *Atlantic Monthly* and cited the style's advantages as "an early and uncorrupted type" with "apparently unexhausted capabilities."[54] In his November 1886 tribute to Richardson in *Atlantic Monthly* Van Brunt reiterated the promise of Richardsonian architecture, and he continued to emphasize its potential in subsequent articles.[55] Van Brunt's 1889 *Atlantic Monthly* article on architecture in the West ended with a brief discussion of Richardson and cited his influence as the most positive for architecture in the American West.[56] Van Brunt's articles, which interpreted the historical Romanesque as a transitional style, presented Richardson's architecture as a new beginning, not simply a revival. The Richardsonian mode was thereby opened to experimentation and innovation, an attitude which was a further impetus to the varied character of the Romanesque designs produced thereafter. A similar theory of the incompleteness or "arrested development" of the historical Romanesque, and, therefore, its openness to further evolution in an American context, was also advanced by the critic Montgomery Schuyler.[57]

The Boston-based partnership Peabody and Stearns had also produced some work in a Romanesque vocabulary as early as 1882. Among their most important works was the R. H. White Wholesale Store, Boston (1882–83, destroyed), that featured expanses of plain masonry and arcaded fenestration. The building appeared in *American Architect and Building News* in September 1883, and was one source for Richardson's design for the Ames Store on Harrison Avenue.[58] (Fig. 4.21)

Still, it was not until Richardson's death that the mode began to be widely adopted. Initially it was the work of Richardson's former apprentices that showed the potential variety of interpretations of his achievements. After Richardson's death, his practice was carried on by the partnership Shepley, Rutan, and Coolidge.[59] Because almost twenty commissions were unfinished including major works such as the Allegheny County Buildings and the Field Store, the first task of the reorganized firm was to complete this work. Simultaneously they began to accept new commissions. Shepley, Rutan, and Coolidge generally followed the conventions of Richardson's mature designs as they took on new commercial and institutional projects. For example, their F. L. Ames Building, Boston (1889–91), followed Richardson's earlier commercial commissions for the Ames family, and the Public Library, New London, Connecticut (1889–1890), is composed of elements that recall Richardson's series of libraries.[60]

Shepley, Rutan, and Coolidge furthered the geographic expansion of the practice that Richardson had begun. By 1889 the firm had its own projects in Chicago, St. Louis, New Orleans, and California. Their most important commission in St. Louis, where they had opened a branch office, was the Lionberger Warehouse (1887–88, destroyed), a seven-story block with rock-faced walls and great arched bays that echoed Richardson's Field Store. (Fig. 4.22) Other commercial work in the city followed. Their New Orleans project, the Howard

4.21 Peabody and Stearns, R. H. White Wholesale Store, Boston, 1882

American Architect and Building News *14 (15 Sept. 1883); courtesy Trustees of the Boston Public Library*

4.22 Shepley, Rutan, and Coolidge, Lionberger Wholesale Warehouse, St. Louis, 1887–88 (destroyed)

Architectural Record *1/2 (Oct.–Dec. 1891)*

Memorial Library (1887–89), was an enlarged version of Richardson's unsuccessful project for East Saginaw. The firm's major commission on the West Coast was the design of the new Stanford University that adapted precedents from Richardson's works to create a regionally responsive architecture.[61]

Shepley, Rutan, and Coolidge's continuation of Richardson's practice received wide attention in the architectural press. Between 1886 and 1893, their work appeared almost as frequently in *American Architect and Building News* as Richardson's had in previous years, although more frequently in drawings than in photographs.[62] When Montgomery Schuyler wrote a lengthy article on the Romanesque Revival in America for *Architectural Record*, their works were singled out for detailed discussion.[63] The ability of Shepley, Rutan, and Coolidge to practice in the Richardsonian mode without Richardson's presence was most likely seen by other professionals as further confirmation that Richardsonian design was available to any practitioner. And the geographic reach of their practice brought built examples to cities in the West, further aiding the spread of the Romanesque Revival.

Although Longfellow, Alden, and Harlow were not Richardson's direct heirs, they, too, benefited from his legacy, as both Longfellow and Alden had worked in Richardson's office until early 1886. With offices in both Boston and Pittsburgh, they were able to secure important commissions in both New England and Pennsylvania.[64] After Richardson's death, other apprentices also opened their own firms and initially produced Richardsonian work. While some remained in Boston, forming firms such as Andrews, Jacques, and Rantoul, others moved west; for example, Harry Jones carried the Richardsonian legacy to Minneapolis and Edward Cameron brought it to St. Louis.

Training in Richardson's office was not necessary to use the Richardsonian system. George B. Post, among the leaders in the design of office buildings in New York, was responsible for several essays on the mode, notably the *New York Times* Building (1888–89), that appeared in *Architectural Record*, and the Union Trust Building (1889–90, destroyed), that appeared in both *Architectural Record* and *American Architect*.[65] (Fig. 4.23) In fact, a wide range of eastern and midwestern firms were practicing in the Romanesque Revival mode by the late 1880s and receiving exposure in the architectural press.

The spread of the Richardsonian Romanesque mode was also fostered by the Office of the Supervising Architect of the United States Treasury. Responsible for the design of all federal buildings across the United States, including post offices, custom houses, and federal courthouses, the supervising architects were never leaders in design, but could be influential through the broad reach of the Office.[66] When Mifflin E. Bell became supervising architect in 1884, he directed the Office away from the Victorian modes that had typified his predecessors' projects and toward Richardsonian design. These federal buildings were frequently published in *American Architect*; the number of these illustrations indicates their impact. For example, between April and September 1886, fifteen different federal projects for cities from Maine to Georgia and Michigan to Texas appeared. The Post Office and Courthouse for

4.23 George B. Post, Union Trust Building, New York (1888–90, destroyed)

Architectural Record *1/1* *(July–Sept. 1891)*

San Antonio (1887–89, destroyed) is a typical example. (Fig. 4.24) Although the style was described as "modified Moresque," the design reads as a picturesque composition in a Richardsonian vocabulary; one source for the tower was Richardson's Brattle Square Church.[67] The supervising architects continued to produce Romanesque designs into the mid-1890s, including that for the U.S. Custom House and Post Office, Port Townsend, Washington (1885–93).[68] (Fig. 4.25)

The impact of this publicity was such that by the late 1880s and early 1890s, *American Architect, Inland Architect, Northwestern Architect,* and other journals were receiving and publishing illustrations of Richardsonian buildings from architects in locations including Maine, Massachusetts, New York, Illinois, Ohio, Michigan, Kansas, Texas, Wisconsin, Minnesota, Colorado, Washington, and other states. The peak years for the publication of Richardsonian designs in *American Architect* were 1889 and 1890, just as Seattle was rebuilding after the 6 June 1889 fire. After that the number of illustrated Richardsonian designs began to decline, although this did not become fully evident until 1892.

The role of the architectural press in disseminating the Richardsonian mode

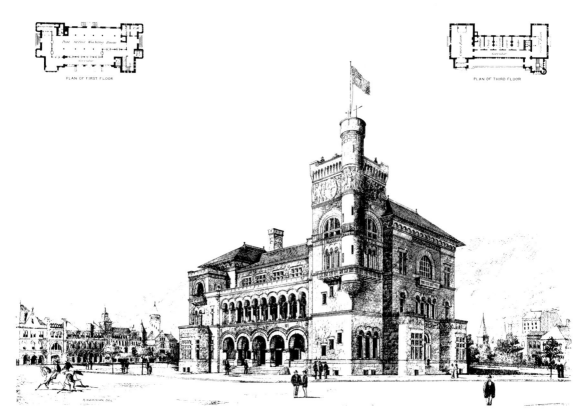

4.24 Mifflin E. Bell,
Supervising Architect
of the Office of the
Treasury, Post Office
and Courthouse, San
Antonio, Texas, 1887–89
(destroyed)

American Architect and
Building News *22 (13 Apr.
1887); courtesy Trustees of
the Boston Public Library*

4.25 Mifflin E. Bell and
successors, Supervising
Architect of the Office
of the Treasury, Custom
House and Post Office,
Port Townsend,
Washington, 1885–93

*Jefferson County Historical
Society, Port Townsend*

deserves additional emphasis.[69] Early architectural publications often presented illustrations with only the name of the project, its location, and the name of the architect and no critical analysis. As formal architectural education was just being initiated in the United States, most architects in the 1880s were trained as apprentices, were largely self-taught, or emerged from the building trades. As a result, they lacked an education in any abstract system of architectural ideas and they seldom would have had the opportunity for architectural discourse. Because most architects' design approaches were based on examples of built work, they were particularly dependent on published images. The new professional architectural periodicals were the best source of contemporary models, especially in a period of changing architectural styles. Based in Boston, where Richardson had practiced, but with a national circulation, *American Architect and Building News* proved especially powerful in presenting examples of Richardsonian Romanesque designs to a national audience. Chicago-based *Inland Architect* and Minneapolis-based *Northwestern Architect* played similar roles, particularly for architects in the West. All three of these journals were received by architects in Seattle in the late 1880s and early 1890s.[70]

That the architects of this period worked primarily from examples, and by a design method that involved a freely inventive eclecticism, helps to explain the persistence of Victorian approaches to composition throughout the decade of Richardsonian design. Many architects, even those who knew Richardson's work first-hand, produced Richardsonian designs that were picturesque assemblies of disparate elements executed in Richardsonian Romanesque rather than Victorian Gothic materials and details. The tendency to develop Romanesque buildings as picturesque compositions was common across the United States; the juxtaposition of asymmetrically placed towers and similar elements with relatively simple rectilinear blocks or otherwise symmetrical compositions indicates the continuing influence of the picturesque aesthetic.

The picturesque tendency was also fostered by the way in which buildings were typically illustrated. Although Richardson had tried to limit publication of his work to photographs, most images in the architectural journals before the mid-1890s were pen-and-ink perspective renderings, frequently drawn freehand by skilled delineators. As noted by Eileen Michels, this presentation technique was best suited to picturesque asymmetrical compositions and its use reinforced the continuing influence of picturesque approaches to design.[71]

Another characteristic of Victorian design that marked Richardsonian works was an insistent verticality. Although many of Richardson's own later works, such as the railroad stations and libraries, had moved in the direction of horizontality and a stronger relationship to the ground, widely published designs such as Trinity Church, Cincinnati Chamber of Commerce, and Allegheny Courthouse included strongly vertical elements and could be interpreted by contemporary architects as falling within a Victorian compositional framework. As a result many Romanesque designs were marked by a prominent treatment of vertical elements.[72] For example, the leading Kansas firm, Proudfoot

and Bird did work described by Richard Longstreth as employing ". . . a more-or-less Richardsonian vocabulary, while maintaining the High Victorian penchant for agitated vertical masses."[73] Examples included their Garfield University, Wichita (1886–88), and Wichita City Hall (1890–92), buildings probably known by Willis Ritchie who came to Seattle from Kansas. (Figs. 4.26, 4.27) A verticalizing approach is also evident in the Pierce County Courthouse, Tacoma (1890–93, destroyed); a watercolor appeared in *Northwestern Architect* in 1890.[74] The Los Angeles County Courthouse, Los Angeles (1886–91, destroyed), by Curlett, Eisen, and Cuthbertson showed a similar vertical emphasis; it was published in *Architectural Record* in 1891.[75] (Fig. 4.28) This tendency was not only found in the West. R. H. Robertson's unbuilt project for the *New York World* headquarters, New York, was both picturesquely composed and strongly vertical; published in *American Architect and Building News* in February 1889, this served as the model for C. B. Seaton's Richardsonian design for the Review Publishing Company Building, Spokane (1890–91).[76] (Fig. 4.29)

The ready adaptability of Richardsonian design to virtually any building problem assured its spread. The prominent place given to Richardsonian design in the architectural press provided models for architects across the country. Many practitioners were able to command the eclectic Richardsonian Romanesque and produce well-detailed, well-integrated public, institutional, and commercial structures. Some architects worked within a generally Victorian compositional framework and produced works that exhibit the compositional complexity and ornamental richness of Victorian architecture, but used Richardsonian Romanesque details and motifs. Others in the Southwest and California even developed the mode in a regional direction integrating the Romanesque with Spanish forms and motifs. Of course, Romanesque Revival design could easily

4.27 Proudfoot and Bird, City Hall, Wichita, Kansas, 1890–92

*Kansas State Historical Society, Topeka, FK2.S3W.1C*1*

4.28 Curlett, Eisen, and Cuthbertson, Los Angeles County Courthouse, Los Angeles, 1886–91 (destroyed)

Architectural Record 1/1 (July–Sept. 1891)

4.29 Chauncey B. Seaton,
Review Publishing Company
Building, Spokane,
Washington, 1890–91

Northwest Museum of Arts and
Culture/Eastern Washington
State Historical Society, Spokane,
L95–6.23

devolve into pastiche. Montgomery Schuyler noted this particularly in regard to residential architecture: "In city houses throughout the country the influence of Richardson has been perhaps even more marked than in any other class of buildings, but in most cases has operated by the unprofitable method of direct imitation, and has consisted in fastening 'features' from his work upon buildings of inconsistent physiognomies or no physiognomies at all."[77]

By 1889, when Seattle architects faced the problem of designing the new Seattle, the Romanesque Revival had become the leading national architectural style. In 1891 Schuyler could write, "Such an array of buildings in so many different kinds, some admirable, many suggestive and nearly all in some degree interesting, constitutes at once an impressive demonstration of the extent to which the Romanesque revival has already gone, and a promise that in the future it may go further and fare better."[78]

The Influence of Chicago

When Seattle architects looked for examples of the "modern Romanesque," they particularly looked to new buildings in Chicago. In contrast to Boston, Chicago was seen as a western city; its extraordinarily rapid growth as a commercial center in the nineteenth century provided a model that cities such as Seattle sought to emulate. And, the successful reconstruction after the 1871 Chicago Fire was especially meaningful in Seattle after its own 6 June 1889 calamity.

Of Seattle's leading architects in the late 1880s, only Charles Saunders, and later Warren Skillings, had come from the Boston area and were likely to have visited a large number of Richardson's works. But several Seattle architects made visits to Chicago, as did some of their clients, so they would have seen the many new commercial blocks by Chicago architects, as well as Richardson's Marshall Field Store. By 1889, the fame of Chicago architects was sufficient so that Judge Burke, Elmer Fisher's client, pointed to the example of the Rookery office building by Chicago architects Burnham and Root, and the following year Seattle's business leaders turned to Chicago's Adler and Sullivan for the design of the new Seattle Opera House.[79]

Today, design that is characterized as Romanesque Revival is often thought to derive entirely from the example of H. H. Richardson and his successors; however, the emergence of similar work in Chicago cannot be traced entirely to Richardson's influence alone. The growth of Chicago and the development of a commercial architecture related to Richardson's work reflect a convergence which proved particularly significant for the spread of the Romanesque mode in the American West.

Although he saw himself as independent of Richardson, John Wellborn Root, the primary design partner in the prominent Chicago firm of Burnham and Root, was clearly aware of and influenced by the direction of Richardson's work in the 1880s.[80] Burnham and Root produced a wide variety of buildings in their eighteen-year partnership, but the firm was particularly recognized for its contributions to the design of urban business structures. The evolution of Root's commercial office blocks can be traced independently of Richardson's career, but their work was clearly complementary. Because Richardson was responsible for comparatively few commercial commissions, Root's development of a commercial architecture that freely interpreted the Romanesque led many contemporaries to see Root, like Richardson, as a key contributor to the development of the "modern Romanesque." Root's obituary by Henry Van Brunt emphasized this aspect:

> [It] was his fortune to contribute to the development of this great Americo-Romanesque experiment nearly or quite as much as Richardson did. This latter introduced the revival, and, through the unexampled vigor of his personality, had already led it to an interesting point of development when his career was interrupted by death; the former [Root] carried it still further toward the point of its establishment as the characteristic architectural expression of American civilization. The latter conferred upon it power, the former variety.[81]

Burnham and Root's initial success as architects for Chicago's business blocks was based on their structural solutions, their functional planning, and their control of costs, as well as their three-dimensional architectural design. Unlike Richardson, Root had not had the advantage of architectural schooling, but, educated as an engineer, came to explore design within the experimental tradition that informed nineteenth-century engineering. Root was initially driven to the simplification of design by the investors who took a direct interest in the design of their buildings. Within a few years Root, learning from Richardson's example and from his own experiments, often emphasized simplification and order in his work.

Although Root's awareness of Richardson may be indicated by some features in Root's designs in the early 1880s, Donald Hoffman suggests that by 1883–84, Root's buildings show that he was learning more from Richardson than just details.[82] Burnham and Root's Atchinson, Topeka, and Santa Fe Railroad Building, Topeka, Kansas (1883–84, destroyed), was a relatively unified four-story block with windows grouped under a series of regular (but segmented, not Romanesque) arches and a well-delineated stone base. The Insurance Exchange Building, Chicago (1884–85, destroyed), shows similar considerations in a ten-story structure. A red brick block on a stone base, the Insurance Exchange impressed contemporaries with its refined brick detailing. (Fig. 4.30) The tourelles at the entrance and on the corner recall those that Richardson had used at the Trinity Church tower, and the grouping of the windows from the sixth to ninth floors under a regular round-arched arcade was the first use of this Richardsonian motif in Root's work. Cut and molded brick and occasional matching terra-cotta enlivened the elevations, yet all were subsumed within the block conceived as a whole. The Insurance Exchange became one model for commercial buildings across the West in the next few years following its publication in a photograph in *Inland Architect* in July 1885.[83]

Although not all of Burnham and Root's designs were as successful as the

4.30 Burnham and Root, Insurance Exchange Building, Chicago, 1884–85 (destroyed)

Inland Architect 5/6 (July 1885); courtesy Trustees of the Boston Public Library

Insurance Exchange, their commercial office structures in this period do show that Root had learned from Richardson how to develop designs displaying a high degree of order and coherence. Root's McCormick Harvesting Machine Company building, Chicago (1884–86, destroyed), is recognized as the project that may have influenced Richardson. (Fig. 4.31) In this structure Root unified four office floors under a broad arcade, separately delineating only the base and attic—the pattern found in Richardson's only slightly later Ames Store on Harrison Avenue in Boston, although both Root and Richardson may have been influenced by the White Store in Boston by Peabody and Stearns.[84] And, for the Art Institute, Chicago (1885–87), an institutional structure, Root turned to a strongly Richardsonian treatment. (Fig. 4.32) Constructed of stone, this featured windows at the second and third stories grouped under broad arches

4.31 Burnham and Root, McCormick Harvesting Company Building, Chicago, 1884–86 (destroyed)

Chicago Historical Society, ICHi-01026

to form arcades in the two principal elevations. In addition to the lithic treatment, the entry arch and dormers were elements directly echoing Richardson's work. Schuyler praised this building in *Harper's Monthly* in 1891 for its simple clear composition, describing it as "admirable" and noting its "sobriety and moderation."[85]

Nonetheless, Root experimented with a variety of sources; and in his career, he never did fully settle on the applicability of an architecture based on the massive character of the Romanesque as Richardson did.[86] Still, Richardsonian motifs, such as arcaded window walls, continued to appear in Burnham and Root's designs in the mid-to-late 1880s even as the firm explored other directions. Their masterpiece of the period was the Rookery, Chicago (1885–88), a block-square office building, which attracted national attention. (Fig. 4.33) The coherence of the block and the order of the elevations owe much to Richardson, the detailing somewhat less—at the time it was described as "Moresque."[87] The elevations were composed of several levels of arcades divided by continuous belt courses. The two lower floors were rusticated stone, but with a maximum amount of glass; the upper floors were of brick with well-matched terra-cotta. The front entrance was marked by an arch of rusticated stone centered in a slightly projecting bay. The exterior elevations and details of the Rookery were immediately influential after *Inland Architect* published a drawing and photographs of the structure in July 1888.[88]

4.32 Burnham and Root,
Art Institute, Chicago,
Illinois, 1885–87
(destroyed)

Architectural Record *1/3*
(*Jan.–Mar. 1892*)

Unlike Richardson, who rarely wrote about his architecture, Root was quite prolific, speaking in Chicago and publishing in the Chicago-based *Inland Architect*. In these writings, Root made explicit his search for repose and refinement in his buildings; he also, unconsciously perhaps, may have displayed his debt to Richardson. For example, in an essay on the question of architectural style Root noted the possibilities of the simple masonry wall: "The value of plain surfaces in every building is not to be overestimated. Strive for them, and when the fates place at your disposal a good generous sweep of masonry, accept it frankly" for "very successful buildings have the quality of temperance."[89] Root's paper on the design of the office building delivered at the Art Institute and published in *Inland Architect* in June 1890 emphasized the practical and planning aspects of this type of design, but he also commented on the buildings' architectural character: "In them should be carried out the ideas of modern business life—simplicity, stability, breadth, dignity . . . they by their mass and proportion convey in some large elemental sense an idea of the great,

4.33 Burnham and Root,
Rookery Building,
Chicago, 1885–88

*Chicago Historical Society,
ICHi-26160, photo by
J. Taylor*

stable and conserving forces of modern civilization."[90] In this, Root's understanding of and contribution to the Richardsonian idiom are made explicit. His
most important explorations of Richardsonian design centered around its via-
bility for commercial construction.

Root's influence also grew as the geographic scope of the Burnham and Root
practice extended beyond Chicago. In the late 1880s, the firm was responsible for buildings from Cleveland to the Pacific Coast. The firm did several buildings in Kansas City, among which the best known was the Exchange Building
(1886–88, destroyed), that was won in a widely publicized competition. The
San Francisco Chronicle Building (1887–90, destroyed) was the firm's first
project on the Pacific Coast; and two years later, the firm undertook two projects
in Tacoma: the Fidelity Trust Company Building (1889–91, destroyed) and the
Pacific National Bank Building (1889–91). Almost without ornament, both
buildings were crisply cut rectilinear blocks of brick. The Fidelity Trust Com-

4.34 Burnham and Root,
Fidelity Trust Company,
Tacoma, Washington,
1889–91 (destroyed)
Tacoma Public Library

pany, the larger building, featured an H-shaped plan; the primary elevation
was designed as a continuous arcade of windows and featured an arched entry.
(Fig. 4.34) The smaller Pacific National Bank Building received a similar treatment.[91]

In the 1880s, *American Architect and Building News* only occasionally published projects by the leading Chicago architects. No doubt this was due to
competition from *Inland Architect*, with its official relationship with the Western
Association of Architects.[92] Burnham and Root's work was, therefore, less well-
known in the East, but was frequently brought to the attention of architects in
the Midwest and West. *Inland Architect*'s frequent publication of Root's essays
as well as the firm's buildings served to disseminate Root's approach to commercial design. Thus, the Romanesque mode in the East was primarily dependent on Richardson's example, but in the central and western states, Root's
influence played a significant role as well in shaping the form of Romanesque
Revival design. Architects in the West had both Richardson's and Root's works
as available models.

Other leading architects practicing in a Romanesque Revival mode in Chicago
were also featured in the pages of *Inland Architect*, including Henry Ives Cobb,
Solon S. Beman, and Adler and Sullivan. Among these Adler and Sullivan
emerged as the most prominent. Louis Sullivan is, of course, most often recognized for his contributions to the design of the tall building, but his work
included a Richardsonian phase in the late 1880s, and his contemporaries would
have perceived some of his published projects as further extending Richardson's approach. As has been well-demonstrated by William Jordy and others,

Sullivan's "Richardsonian" work generally developed as a reaction to Richardson's Marshall Field Store.[93] The importance of Richardson's example was first evident in Adler and Sullivan's Auditorium, Chicago (1886–90), which drew national attention upon its completion. (Fig. 4.35) A virtual city in itself with its theater, office building, hotel, restaurants, and other facilities, this filled an entire city block. Its exterior treatment was completely revised by Sullivan once he had seen Richardson's Field design. The pattern of arcades and fenestration was drawn directly from the Field Store, but modified to fit the larger scale and specific requirements of the Auditorium project. It was the success of the Auditorium that led Seattle business leaders to turn to Adler and Sullivan for the design of the Seattle Opera House in 1890.

Jordy's analysis has shown that Sullivan's fascination with the Field Store lasted until 1890. Multiple Adler and Sullivan buildings, including the Walker Warehouse, Chicago (1888–89, destroyed), the Dooly Block, Salt Lake City (1890–91, destroyed), and the Kehilath Anshe Ma'ariv Synagogue, Chicago (1890–91), responded to the Field Store through direct borrowing and recomposition of various elements to produce new designs. Like the Auditorium, the Walker Warehouse design was presented in a perspective drawing in *Inland Architect*.[94] (Fig. 4.36)

The Chicago examples proved particularly important in Seattle because they offered usable models for commercial construction. Richardson's direct influence was most important in public and institutional work, but the influence of Chicago was more than equal to Richardson for commercial construction because Richardson had had such a limited commercial practice. Indeed, the difference between Root and Richardson reflects the changing mix of architectural commissions that faced the profession in the 1880s and 1890s. Richardson, like most well-educated architects of his generation, was initially involved primarily with commissions for churches and educational and other institutional buildings, and with residences for the wealthy. Commercial work was not ignored, but it was a lesser part of his practice before 1876. The early years of Richardson's practice paralleled the typical pre–Civil War practices of leading American architects. In the post–Civil War period, the rapid development of industrial and commercial organizations had been partially slowed by the depression of the 1870s, but commercial clients emerged in the 1880s with rising profits and higher aspirations. Their burgeoning business organizations required new structures to house growing clerical and professional staffs and a new class of independently practicing professionals in business, law, accounting, and similar fields also sought office space. Commercial clients became increasingly attractive to architects. Such clients typically sought economical but nonetheless impressive designs for their buildings. Richardson's later works, such as the Field Store in Chicago and Ames Store on Harrison Avenue in Boston, exemplified this direction. In the West, the business districts of rapidly developing cities were largely composed of new commercial structures and their character was the focus of substantial attention. Chicago, as a transportation hub, was the first of this kind of city to emerge, and Burnham and Root were

4.35 Adler and Sullivan,
Auditorium, Chicago,
1886–90

*Museum of Modern Art,
New York*

4.36 Adler and Sullivan,
Ryerson Wholesale Store/
Walker Warehouse,
Chicago, 1888–89
(destroyed)

Inland Architect *13/4 (Apr.
1889); courtesy Trustees of
the Boston Public Library*

the first Chicago architects whose reputation was built on their commercial designs. Adler and Sullivan had initially built their reputation on theater design, but by 1890, commercial office blocks had become their most important commissions as well. In the land and building boom that lasted until 1893, cities and towns across the West replaced their early frame buildings with substantial brick and stone commercial structures. Largely without architectural traditions, cities like Seattle looked not just to the East but also to Chicago and other new cities in the Midwest. In the example of Chicago, it was Root and Sullivan, as well as Richardson, who offered models for the new commercial architecture—models that showed an architecture that was well designed but nonetheless straightforward, imposing but not overly ostentatious. This kind of architecture was exactly appropriate to rebuilding downtown Seattle in the post-fire period.

The Example of Minneapolis and St. Paul

Although the Chicago of Burnham and Root and Adler and Sullivan was recognized as the leading city in the Midwest for architectural design from an early date, the character of Minneapolis and St. Paul drew attention in the late 1880s and early 1890s, as well. When Montgomery Schuyler profiled "architecture in the West" for *Harper's Magazine* in 1891, he featured work in Minneapolis and St. Paul in addition to Chicago.[95] Because the Minnesota cities saw such significant growth after 1880, they became important centers of Richardsonian Romanesque design.[96] Describing Minneapolis, Schuyler said it had "risen like an exhalation."

Minneapolis and St. Paul architects were influenced both directly by Richardson and by work in Chicago, and Romanesque Revival buildings began to appear after 1885; by the late 1880s, the most successful Minneapolis firm working in the Romanesque Revival mode was Long and Kees.[97] Their best commercial block was the Lumber Exchange, Minneapolis (1885–88, altered).[98] With a two-story base of granite and eight floors of sandstone, this was then the tallest building in the city. (Fig. 4.37) Long and Kees appear to have drawn compositional strategies from Root's Chicago designs, especially the Insurance Exchange and the Rookery. Although the continuous expression of the horizontal sills contradicts the vertical continuity of the openings and the use of oriel bays could be questioned, Schuyler still characterized the building as "very respectable."[99]

Two of the largest Romanesque Revival commercial blocks in Minneapolis, the Globe (Printing Company) Building (1888–89, destroyed) and the Northwest Guaranty Loan Building (1888–90, destroyed), were by Milwaukee architect E. Townsend Mix, who opened a Minneapolis office in 1888. (Fig. 4.38) However, both buildings displayed irregular treatments with picturesque corner towers and strongly vertical emphasis indicating that Mix, who had been in practice since the mid-1850s, addressed the Romanesque mode within the Victorian compositional framework of his earlier work.[100]

4.37 Long and Kees,
Lumber Exchange,
Minneapolis, 1885–88
(altered)
*Minnesota Historical Society,
MH5.9MP3.1L*

The building generally recognized as the finest Richardsonian Romanesque commercial structure in Minneapolis was by Harry Jones, who had studied at MIT from 1881 to 1882 and is thought to have worked for Richardson in 1883. His National Bank of Commerce (1888, destroyed) drew on the example of Richardson's Marshall Field Store and other advanced designs of the mid-1880s. (Fig. 4.39) Jones's building was a relatively simple stone block with broadly arcaded facades. Jones followed Richardson's Field example in his use of segmented arches at the ground floor and smaller rectangular windows at the attic story. The recessed bay at the entrance was not from Richardson, but Schuyler praised the design, writing "the architecture is but the expression of the structure" and several photographs were published in *Northwestern Architect*.[101]

Long and Kees also proved adept as institutional designers. The firm's Minneapolis Public Library (1886–89, destroyed) was a compact three-story composition with large windows to create a well-lit interior. (Fig. 4.40) The

4.38 E. Townsend Mix,
Northwest Guaranty Loan
Building, Minneapolis,
1888–90 (destroyed)

*Minnesota Historical Society,
Mh5.9MP3.1M*

main entrance derived from Richardson's unbuilt project for the YMA Library
in Buffalo, published in *American Architect and Building News* in 1886. Long
and Kees achieved their most significant work when they won the competition
for the Minneapolis City Hall and Hennepin County Courthouse (1888–1905),
commonly called the Municipal Building, with a design directly modeled on
Richardson's Allegheny County Courthouse. (Fig. 4.41) Like Richardson's building, the Long and Kees design was a rock-faced masonry block organized around
a central courtyard featuring a prominent tower at the center of the main facade.
The building was both more open and more volumetrically complex than
Richardson's, but nonetheless this is considered one of the finest buildings ever
inspired by his example. The library was illustrated in *Northwestern Architect*,
and the Municipal Building appeared there and in *American Architect*, as well.[102]

St. Paul did not experience the same rapidity of growth as Minneapolis, so

4.39 Harry Jones, National Bank of Commerce, Minneapolis, 1888 (destroyed)

Northwestern Architect 7/5 (May 1889), Library of Congress

4.40 Long and Kees, Minneapolis Public Library, Minneapolis, 1886–89 (destroyed)

Northwestern Architect 8/8 (Aug. 1890), Library of Congress

4.41 Long and Kees,
Minneapolis City Hall
and Hennepin County
Courthouse, Minneapolis,
1888–1905

*Minnesota Historical Society,
MH5.9MP8*

4.42 J. Walter Stevens,
Noyes-Cutler Warehouse,
St. Paul, 1886–87
(altered)

*Minnesota Historical Society,
MR2.9SP3.1N*

4.43 Willcox and Johnston, Laurel Terrace (Riley Row), St. Paul, 1884

Northwestern Architect 6/6 (June 1888), Minnesota Historical Society

there were fewer opportunities for Richardsonian commercial structures.[103] The leading Richardsonian designer in the city was J. Walter Stevens, whose West Publishing Company building (1885–87, destroyed) showed arcaded windows reflecting the influence of both Richardson and Root; two small renderings appeared in *American Architect* in 1887.[104] His Noyes-Cutler Warehouse (1886–87, altered) was a six-story brick block with crisply incised openings and a generally Richardsonian character.[105] (Fig. 4.42) The ground-floor arches anticipate a similar feature on Adler and Sullivan's Ryerson Building/Walker Warehouse in Chicago. The building was illustrated by the Noyes-Cutler Company in their advertisements and was therefore widely known. Schuyler's *Harper's* article featured only two of the city's commercial blocks, the Pioneer Building (1888–89) by S. S. Beman of Chicago, a simple rectangular brick block with a two-story stone base and Richardsonian detail, and the Bank of Minnesota (1887) by the local firm Willcox and Johnston, which Schuyler described as "a well-proportioned and well-divided piece of masonry."

The Romanesque Revival was applied to some residential buildings in both cities. St. Paul was the site of several Richardsonian Romanesque rowhouse projects. The Laurel Terrace (1884), frequently called the "Riley Row" by Willcox and Johnston, published in *Northwestern Architect*, showed a mix of Queen Anne influences along with the Richardsonian round-arched vocabulary.[106] (Fig. 4.43) The premier residential street in the region, Summit Avenue in St. Paul, could boast several notable Romanesque designs including the massive James J. Hill House (1887–91) by Peabody and Stearns, but most of the houses reflected Queen Anne tendencies.[107]

L·S·BUFFINGTON ARCHITECT
MINNEAPOLIS MINN·1887·

4.44 LeRoy S. Buffington (Harvey Ellis, del.), Pillsbury Hall, University of Minnesota, Minneapolis, 1887–90

American Architect and Building News 23 (21 Jan. 1888); Library of Congress

One of the leading delineators of the period, Harvey Ellis, worked first in St. Paul and then in Minneapolis between 1886 and 1890.[108] The pen-and-ink perspective renderings he produced of commercial, residential, and institutional designs by J. Walter Stevens, LeRoy Buffington, and Orff and Orff were appreciated both for their imaginative explorations of the Romanesque mode and for their artistry as drawings.[109] (Fig. 4.44) The frequent appearance of Ellis's drawings in the architectural journals no doubt drew increased attention to the two cities' architectural achievements.

The impact of the new work in Minneapolis and St. Paul was particularly enhanced by its dissemination through the Minneapolis-based architectural journal *Northwestern Architect and Improvement Record,* first published in November 1882. Unlike *American Architect* and *Inland Architect,* it did not survive the national economic depression of the mid-1890s and has, therefore, been largely forgotten, but it was probably the journal of most importance to Seattle architects. *Northwestern Architect* remained in publication through twelve volumes to 1894, absorbing the Chicago-based *Building Budget* in January 1891 (when the name changed to *Northwestern Architect and Building Budget*). After mid-1894 it passed through a bewildering series of name changes and mergers.[110] *Northwestern Architect* carried illustrations of the new work in Minneapolis and St. Paul as well as buildings in Chicago, Detroit, St. Louis, and other cities, and after 1888, in the Pacific Northwest.[111] Among the individuals and practices whose work was included were not only Long and Kees, Willcox and Johnston, J. Walter Stevens and Harry Jones, but also Shepley, Rutan, and Coolidge, Burnham and Root, and Adler and Sullivan.

Although the growth of Minneapolis and St. Paul slowed in the late 1880s, their development attracted wide attention in the West. Located at the eastern terminus of the Northern Pacific Railroad (and subsequently the Great Northern), the two cities served as "gateways" to the upper Midwest, northern plains, and Pacific Northwest.[112] The railroads provided a direct economic link to the cities of the Pacific Northwest including Seattle, and throughout the northern tier of states, Minneapolis and St. Paul provided models for urban architecture that were nearly as powerful at the time as those found in Chicago and points east. Some might argue that the work in Minneapolis only occasionally equaled that in Chicago or the East, but nonetheless, the example of the Twin Cities was a visible demonstration for architects in Seattle of the applicability of the Romanesque language to the creation of a burgeoning metropolitan center.

For the Pacific Northwest, the connection to Minneapolis and St. Paul went beyond the obvious transportation and communication linkages.[113] Just as many of the settlers who came to the Pacific Northwest passed through Minneapolis and St. Paul, a number of architects who became prominent in Washington had once lived in the Twin Cities. Among them were Seattle's William Boone, Elmer Fisher, John Parkinson, William Willcox, and Arthur Chamberlin.[114]

Richardson's Influence Received

The Romanesque Revival mode was never a unified or singular tendency, but always encompassed a variety of directions. Even Richardson's own work was seen by contemporaries as offering multiple points of departure since a single evolutionary direction in Richardson's work was never evident from illustrations in the architectural journals. After Richardson's premature death, the contributions of others, particularly those in Chicago and in Minneapolis and St. Paul, were seen from Seattle as extending the range of the design approach Richardson was thought to have begun, the "modern Romanesque." As a result, for architects in Seattle, distant from Richardson's office and from the bulk of his work, the Richardsonian Romanesque or Romanesque Revival was open to a variety of responses. In fact, how Seattle architects used the Romanesque mode often depended on the background each brought from early experience in building and design. (Fig. 4.45)

When Seattle architects adopted elements of Romanesque Revival design for their new commercial and institutional buildings, they did so in the context of the changes and challenges they faced. In particular, in the aftermath of the June 1889 fire, they faced the demand for an up-to-date architecture that could prevent another such tragedy. With the city's new building ordinance, masonry construction was mandated in the commercial core and many of the decorative elements of the older Victorian modes such as elaborate cornices became illegal, and other features, although not prohibited, were also viewed as fire hazards. In contrast, the Romanesque mode provided a system for organizing a solid and impressive modern architecture of fire-resistive masonry construction and it was to this mode that Seattle architects turned.

Nonetheless, the post-fire buildings of Seattle frequently confound our

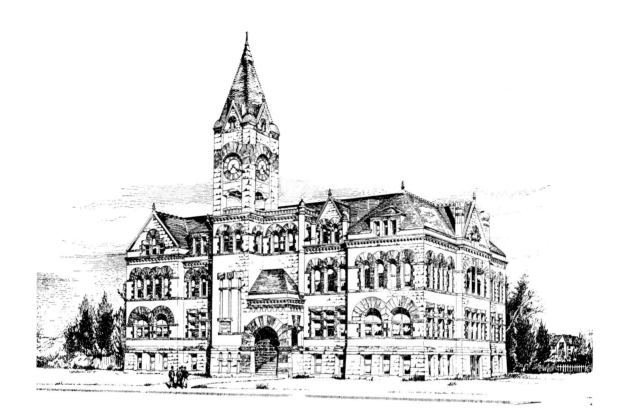

4.45 Willis A. Ritchie, (D. J. Patterson, del.), Whatcom County Courthouse, Whatcom (Bellingham), Washington 1889–91 (destroyed) Ritchie's public building designs often reflect the continuing influence of the picturesque within the Romanesque mode.

Northwestern Architect 9/5 (May 1891).

expectations. The Richardsonian or Romanesque system is sometimes applied inconsistently and works which are pure examples of the mode are actually few in number. Romanesque elements were sometimes applied with a very non-Richardsonian capriciousness or even arbitrariness. Further, clear and direct relationships between building plans and elevations often are not evident. Commercial buildings often display apparently regular bay systems on their facades (and may even show a knowledgeable response to the commercial architecture of Chicago, Minneapolis, or Boston), but internally the structure may not be aligned with these bays and the interior organization may appear unrelated to the exterior. Given the inconsistencies, yet recognizing that these architects claimed to be following Richardson's example, how is their work to be understood?

The architects of this period in Seattle rarely wrote or spoke about their buildings, their design processes, or their design ideas. They never explained why or how they made their particular design choices. The only architect who published anything about his career was John Parkinson, and his later reflections were largely anecdotal, speaking of design only in terms of its "soundness" and "practicality."[115]

Other than a few late arrivals from the East and Midwest, the Seattle architects of the 1880s and early 1890s had typically begun working either as builders or as designers of relatively simple structures primarily of wood in smaller towns and cities. Over little more than a decade, they faced rapid change in building types and clients, in technology and construction, and in the structure of their own emerging profession. Their success in dealing with the pressures they faced is evident in the buildings they designed. But even as these designers adapted to change, they could not fully leave their backgrounds behind. To understand the designs created by Seattle's late-nineteenth-century architects, it is necessary to consider the approaches they had first learned as builders.

Victorian design has been characterized as the "art of assemblage."[116] Clearly the freely inventive eclecticism of Victorian designers allowed them to draw on a variety of sources to create their new designs. The design method by which they did this can be best described as a traditional one of manipulation of relatively concrete images through decomposing or disassembling known models and then recomposing or reassembling them to create new designs. As described by Thomas Hubka, this design method can be directly contrasted with the approach taken by academically educated practitioners. The academically educated designer typically proceeds according to abstract concepts and generalized ordering principles which can be conceived without attachment to specific concrete images.[117]

The architects who began practicing professionally in Seattle in the 1880s had not had access to professional architectural schooling, and therefore had never been exposed to the idea of architectural design as a process beginning with generalized ordering principles or abstract concepts. Even those who had learned architecture through apprenticeship generally learned design as a practical discipline. Therefore, it can be argued that their design method remained traditional, at least in part, in that they created new designs by decomposition and recomposition of existing models or available images.

By the late 1880s, Seattle practitioners were following and publishing in a variety of national professional architectural journals. But, none of these Seattle architects who were reading these journals in the 1880s had received an academic education in architecture. Nor did any Seattle architects bring experience in leading architectural offices where practice was governed by principles derived from academic training. Thus, although Richardson had had the advantage of an architectural education that involved the learning of abstract compositional methods and generalized principles for design, this understanding was not available to Seattle architects who only knew Richardsonian work from the array of interpretations of the Romanesque Revival that filled the pages of the professional architectural journals.[118] These images provided a wide range of source material that could be applied within a method of decomposition and recomposition.

This approach to design as an "art of assemblage" can be found in the works of virtually every architect in Seattle in the post-fire period, but may be most easily exemplified in the buildings by the most prolific of Seattle's post-fire designers, Elmer Fisher. Fisher's early commercial works reflect his learning of a fairly typical mid-nineteenth-century Victorian compositional approach with banded facades divided by flat pilasters and belt courses accented by a variety of ornament. Fisher also frequently alternated slightly setback and projecting bays such that his buildings appeared to take the form of a series of nar-

4.46 Elmer H. Fisher,
Sullivan Building, Seattle,
1889–90 (destroyed).
Fisher described this
as "of the Romanesque
order of architecture
with ornaments in the
Renaissance style."
Northwestern Architect 8/9
(Sep. 1890).

row vertical pavilions. Fisher's post-fire Seattle business blocks reflect his solutions to the requirements of fire-resistive construction and the needs of his commercial clients as well as his response to new developments in architectural design, primarily the ascendancy of the Richardsonian Romanesque mode. Fisher's post-fire work did employ Romanesque elements, but his overall compositional method did not emulate Richardson's. Rather, Fisher continued to demonstrate his traditional Victorian strategy of dividing building facades into vertically articulated pavilions often with vertical and horizontal banding creating a gridded effect; arched windows, half-round entry arches, colonettes, and other conspicuously Romanesque Revival features appear in his work, but his earlier compositional framework remains. Fisher's method seems to follow that of a traditional designer working within "a small set of rules that define the limits within which he can modify the concept according to his taste and talent and the taste and pocketbook of his clientele."[119] Fisher's sources changed to the progressive imagery of the Romanesque mode as illustrated in the architectural press; his compositional process remained a traditional Victorian one. (Fig. 4.46)

A similar argument can be made about works by other Seattle architects in the period. Some, such as John Parkinson, may have done better at transcending the limitations of their training, but none really ever learned an approach to design based on abstract principles.[120] (Fig. 4.47)

4.47 John Parkinson and
J.B. Hamme (J. Anderson,
del.), Chamber of
Commerce Building
competition project,
Portland, Oregon, 1890

American Architect and
Building News *29 (20 Sep.
1890)*

It is not possible to state with complete certainty how most architects in most cities applied the Romanesque Revival. However, the rapid spread of the Romanesque can only reflect its broad acceptance by architects whose experience and practice had been in the Victorian modes and whose working methods, therefore, embodied aspects of both traditional and progressive tendencies in varying proportions. In turn, this suggests another reason why the architecture that Richardson inspired was so varied.

To understand how Richardson's influence was received and then applied by architects in Seattle—and possibly elsewhere—is to see that influence embodied in a complex set of forces that were no doubt never fully recognized by those whose work they shaped. Such an understanding of Richardson's influence speaks much more directly about how change in architecture actually occurs and how architects in any period struggle to do innovative work. For his contemporaries, Richardson was an architect who worked within and clearly mastered the tendencies of his time, and who occasionally transcended them. His work was complex and at times even contradictory. His work occasionally pushed toward new possibilities in architecture, and these possibilities provided inspiration and direction for the architects of his time whatever their backgrounds, including the architects of Seattle after the 6 June 1889 fire.

V

The New Commercial Core
Architecture for a Metropolitan Center, 1889–1895

There is no sort of comparison in point of quality and general character of the buildings destroyed and those which have taken their places. In the stead of low wooden ranges, unsightly, cramped in spaces, and much exposed to the danger of fire, we have massive blocks of brick, stone and iron constructed upon the best models of modern architectural science.

—*Seattle Post-Intelligencer*, 6 June 1890

The demand was made of the architects of Seattle that the new city should be more stately and beautiful than the old one; that the structures should be more substantial, more perfect in their appointments, more elegant in their appearance than any which had heretofore adorned the young metropolis of the Northwest; and how well the architects of Seattle have fulfilled these conditions must be apparent to the most unobservant of mankind.

—*Northwestern Real Estate and Building Review*, May 1891

Once the rebuilding of Seattle's commercial core was assured, design and construction went forward at an extraordinary pace. Owners and investors sought to gain an advantage by pushing their projects forward so that they might be the first to offer new space for business tenants. The architects were pressed to finish sufficient drawings to secure the building permits necessary to begin construction.[1] The initial designs, therefore, generally reflected each architect's pre-fire predilections. Design tendencies that had been evident in their pre-fire work were often repeated in their earliest post-fire projects. In the larger business blocks, which took longer to design, and in the later work, early post-fire directions were often reconsidered and an increased sophistication sometimes appeared. The post-fire buildings of Seattle have been routinely characterized as Romanesque Revival in local accounts, yet although there were a large number of Richardson-influenced designs, the projects actually encompassed a wider American Victorian vocabulary.[2]

Elmer Fisher and the New Commercial Architecture, 1889

In the months leading up to the fire, Fisher's emergence as Seattle's leading designer had been confirmed by his selection as the architect for the Pioneer Building and the Burke Building, two major projects by Seattle's leading entrepreneurs.[3] However, neither of those projects had proceeded beyond the early stages at the time of the fire, and both appear to have been at least partially reconsidered in summer 1889. The Pioneer Building was delayed until September, and when it did proceed, the site was nearly twice the size initially intended. Similarly, a drawing for the Burke Building was published in May, but the structure actually erected was both taller and architecturally more coherent than the published design; it, too, must have been revised. Although these buildings might be considered the first of Fisher's post-fire commissions, both were delayed and it is appropriate to turn to his early post-fire work first.

Fisher was the most prolific post-fire architect; he received commissions from so many of Seattle's civic and business leaders that he can be credited with almost half of the major downtown office blocks erected between 1889 and 1891. Just nine days after the fire, in a 15 June article headlined "Building Anew—Healing the Wounds of the Fire," Fisher was prominently listed as the architect for the new Haller, Kline and Rosenberg, and Sullivan buildings.[4] Thereafter, his name appeared once or twice in almost every published list of new building announcements.

Among the first of Fisher's post-fire commissions was the three-story Korn Building (1889, altered) to replace his earlier block destroyed in the fire. The building was announced as a two-story structure on 18 June, but on 1 August the *Post-Intelligencer* reported that the building would be increased to three stories.[5] Completed in October, the building housed retail tenants at the ground floor and twenty-six office rooms at the second and third floors. A comparison of the new Korn Building and the old shows how Fisher's approach to design had developed over the previous year. While the new Korn design was similar in plan to the old, the elevations of the brick block, reflecting the impact of the new fire ordinance as well as Fisher's new awareness of Romanesque Revival design, were much flatter and featured round arches over grouped windows. (Fig. 5.1) Still, Fisher's Victorian compositional approach was evident in the emphasis placed on the corner bays and the raised cornice over the corner entrance.

The hybrid nature of Fisher's approach to design was particularly evident in the Sullivan Building (1889–90, destroyed), a mid-block four-story structure on the east side of Front Street between Columbia and Cherry. A notice regarding the project had been published in April 1889; on 15 June the *Post-Intelligencer* reported that the project was proceeding, and construction, which began in July 1889, was completed by January 1891 at a cost of $150,000.[6] The project is likely transitional—given its size, and the rapidity with which it went forward, the design cannot have been changed very significantly after the fire. The treatment of the three office floors, with round arches and piers of pressed brick, was not strongly supported visually by the cast-iron columns and broad areas of glazing of the first floor storefronts. (Fig. 5.2) This treatment was structurally feasible because the floors were framed into the partywalls and supported on interior columns and girders so the front facade carried only its own weight. Fisher was, nonetheless, evidently pleased with this design for he submitted a perspective for publication in *Northwestern Architect*, where it appeared in September 1890.[7] (See Fig. 4.46) In Fisher's familiar Victorian

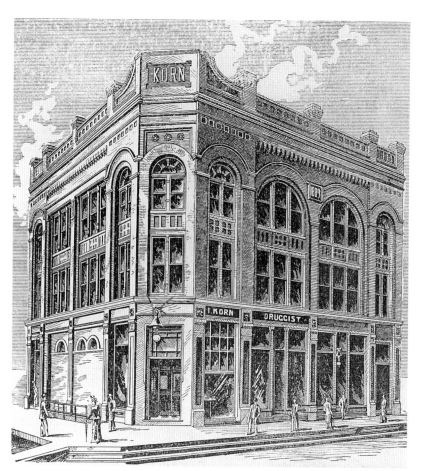

5.1 Elmer H. Fisher, Korn Building, 1889 (altered)

Seattle Illustrated
(ca. 1890), Manuscripts,
Special Collections,
University Archives, University
of Washington Libraries,
UW 12619

compositional approach, a symmetrical "classical" design was developed by treating the central entrance bay as a tower and the two end bays as individual pavilions. The treatment was not entirely arbitrary, but reflected internal divisions and the structural bay system of the building. The mix of vocabularies—the Romanesque round arches and the distorted classical ornament—may seem strange, but this was a deliberate design decision as explained in the *Post-Intelligencer* in October 1889. The paper quoted the unnamed architect, most likely Fisher:

> There is the Sullivan Building. It is of the Romanesque order of architecture with ornaments in the Renaissance style. It will be one of the best of its class in the city. Its ornaments will be of pressed zinc and terra cotta. Pressed zinc is cheaper than terra cotta or stone and its effect is almost as fine. Perhaps more work will be put on the Sullivan front than on any other building in the city.[8]

Among the most eccentric of Fisher's post-fire buildings was the Starr-Boyd Building (1889–90, destroyed), begun shortly after the fire and completed by May 1890. This four-story block was commissioned by the owners of two small adjacent lots, who decided to combine their properties to make a roughly trapezoidal site. The asymmetrically composed facade facing the new Public Square (later renamed Pioneer Place) was executed in brick trimmed with stone and

terra-cotta and was described by the *Seattle Times* in August 1889 as "after the beautiful Moorish style."[9] (Fig. 5.3) The juxtapositions of classical, Romanesque, and other ornament made this the most agitated building of Fisher's post-fire career.

In contrast, Fisher's designs for the Haller Building and the Lebanon Building seem almost quiet. The Haller Building (1889–90, destroyed) at Second and Columbia was commissioned shortly after the fire and was completed by September 1890.[10] A five-story brick block, this housed a bank and stores on the first floor and sixty office rooms on the upper four floors. (Fig. 5.4) The Haller Building showed Fisher's familiar architectural treatment, emphasizing the corner bays by altering the window pattern, enlarging the piers, and raising the cornice line. The windows were grouped under arches and the detailing was comparatively restrained. The *Seattle Times* described this as "a splendid combination of architectural beauty and solidity." The Lebanon Building (1889–91, destroyed) was commissioned in July 1889 for the northeast corner of South Second (now Occidental) and Main.[11] This six-story commercial block was completed by February 1891; one tenant was the Occidental Hotel (one or more floors of lodging rooms, not to be confused with the free-standing Occidental Hotel building commissioned to Stephen Meany by John Collins).

5.2 Elmer H. Fisher, Sullivan Building, 1889–90 (destroyed)

Manuscripts, Special Collections, University Archives Division, University of Washington Libraries, photo by Asahel Curtis, 20595

5.3 Elmer H. Fisher,
Starr-Boyd Building,
1889–90 (destroyed)

*Manuscripts, Special
Collections, University
Archives Division, University
of Washington Libraries,
photo by Asahel Curtis, 90*

5.4 Elmer H. Fisher,
Haller Building,
1889–90 (destroyed)

*Museum of History and
Industry, PEMCO Webster
and Stevens Collection,
83.10.7089.1*

5.5 Elmer H. Fisher,
Lebanon Building,
1889–91 (destroyed)

*Manuscripts, Special
Collections, University
Archives Division, University
of Washington Libraries,
photo by Asahel Curtis, 5686*

Again, Fisher emphasized the corner bays and gave the entrance bay expression as a tower. (Fig. 5.5)

In both the Haller and Lebanon buildings, the cage-like quality of the exterior wall and the extent of the glazed area are clearly apparent in surviving photographs. In these buildings, Fisher's detailing of the openings varied, but a generally regular bay system and a relatively open wall expression were required in order to maximize the level of natural light. Here, as in all of Fisher's larger post-fire commercial blocks, he worked within the framework of his less than perfect understanding of the Romanesque Revival, but he was forced by the requirements of daylighting to reduce the exterior wall surfaces to a minimum and to maximize the fenestration. Because both the Haller and Lebanon buildings occupied corner sites, the two exterior facades carried their own weight plus some interior floor loads, but Fisher still opened up the exterior walls to the greatest extent feasible.

The pressure to increase natural illumination is also reflected in some of Fisher's smaller buildings. One example was the New England Hotel (1889–90, altered). Its site, at Commercial and Main, was first considered for a business block, and the commission was initially awarded to Stephen Meany and then to Comstock and Troetsche, but by late July 1889 Fisher had received the commission to design a three-story hotel with retail at the ground level.[12] (Fig. 5.6) The brick structure with relatively regular fenestration, continuously arcaded street fronts, and terra-cotta trim was completed by the following May. The treatment of the cornice was nearly identical to Fisher's Korn Building. (The building survives today, but has lost its cornice; as a result its originally Romanesque character is not readily apparent.)

Occasionally Fisher's work moved towards greater simplicity as exemplified by the four-story Schwabacher Building (1889–90, altered), commissioned in July 1889 and completed about a year later for one of the city's leading wholesalers.[13] Schwabacher Brothers, grocery wholesalers distributing goods across Washington and north to Alaska, had been in business in Seattle since 1869 on this site. Fisher's Schwabacher Building occupied an L-shaped parcel fronting on both Commercial (now First South) and Yesler and presented two narrow brick fronts (the two ends of the L) for architectural development. Fisher organized the windows on each street within a trio of arches extending the full height of the facade (only the Yesler Avenue front survives in its original condition).[14] (Fig. 5.7) Perhaps Fisher felt the simpler treatment was appropriate because this building housed a wholesale store, with offices, sample rooms, and storefronts on the ground floor, and storage above.[15]

Fisher's extraordinary productivity in the months after the fire became apparent as the pace of building slowed in late 1889. He was able to take a four-week vacation in California, but returned to Seattle on 31 December. On 1 January 1890, the *Post-Intelligencer* published a story devoted entirely to Fisher's work, titled "Two and a Half Millions: Architect Fisher's List of Buildings for the Past Year," and subtitled "A Record Never Before Assembled by Any Architect in Seattle—His Many Fine Buildings."[16] Similar to most articles about the rebuilding, this was primarily a listing of work accomplished in 1889; thirty-three new structures (twenty-seven were commercial blocks) were identified as his "principal buildings in Seattle" and it was stated that he also had work in Port Townsend, Ellensburg, Yakima, and other cities. The opening paragraphs praised Fisher's capabilities:

> Architect E. H. Fisher has probably expended more thought and devoted more study to the proper rebuilding of the city from an artistic and economic view than any other man. Mr. Fisher and his group of assistants have executed during the past year, the plans for over two and a half millions of dollars worth of buildings in Seattle, and several hundred thousand dollars worth in Port Townsend, Ellensburg, Yakima, and other places. It is to Mr. Fisher's good taste and knowledge of correct and symmetrical architecture that the credit is largely due for the beauty and strength of the new buildings which have been built and are being built at the present time.

5.6 Elmer H. Fisher, New England Hotel, 1889–90 (altered)

Museum of History and Industry, PEMCO Webster and Stevens Collection, 83.10.7368

5.7 Elmer H. Fisher, Schwabacher Building, 1889–90 (altered)

Manuscripts, Special Collections, University Archives Division, University of Washington Libraries, UW 2270

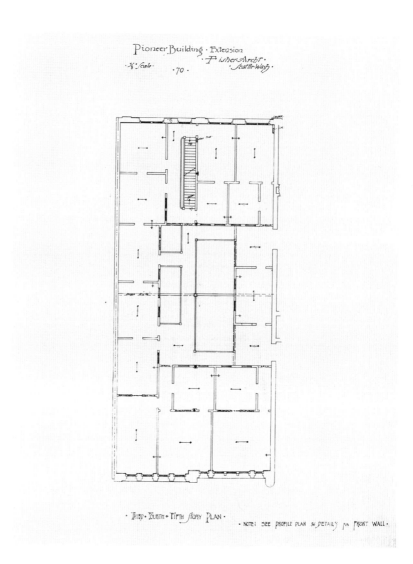

· Third· Fourth· Fifth Story Plan ·

· NOTE: SEE PROFILE PLAN & DETAILS for FRONT WALL ·

5.8a Elmer H. Fisher, Pioneer Building, 1889–91; construction drawings, sheet 70 (north portion of plan of third, fourth, and fifth floors)

Manuscripts, Special Collections, University Archives Division, University of Washington Libraries, UW23133Z

It cannot be determined how deeply Fisher was actually involved in the design of many of his buildings. Prior to the fire Fisher had had sufficient work in his office to assemble a force of four draftsmen.[17] In the months after the fire, the volume of work in Fisher's office must have forced him to rely even more heavily on his draftsmen, and the occasional variations in the character of the work may reflect the abilities of the different members of his staff who produced the drawings for these projects. Still, for his two most important projects, the Pioneer Building and the Burke Building, Fisher was fully involved.

The Pioneer Building

From the beginning, Henry Yesler intended the Pioneer Building (1889–91, altered), located in the heart of Seattle's business district, to be one of the most significant business blocks in the Northwest. In September 1888, Yesler refused an offer of $143,000 for his corner lot at Front and James, indicating instead that he intended construction of a four-story brick block, and Fisher began work on the design early in 1889.[18] But a story in the *Post-Intelligencer*

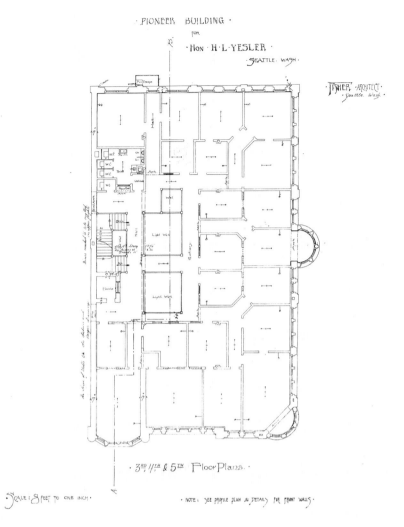

· PIONEER BUILDING ·

FOR

· HON · H · L · YESLER ·

· SEATTLE · WASH ·

FISHER · ARCHITECT
· Seattle · Wash ·

· 3ᴿᴰ, 4ᵀᴴ & 5ᵀᴴ Floor Plans ·

SCALE: 8 FEET TO ONE INCH ·

· NOTE: SEE PROFILE PLAN & DETAILS FOR FRONT WALLS ·

5.8b Elmer H. Fisher,
Pioneer Building,
1889–91; construction
drawings, sheet 10 (south
portion of plan of third,
fourth, and fifth floors)

*Manuscripts, Special
Collections, University
Archives Division, University
of Washington Libraries,
UW21332Z*

in late February, in which "Pioneer Building" was first announced as the name of the proposed structure, also reported that further work had been delayed; bids for construction were received in April, but the project did not proceed and little had been done before the fire.[19]

Because Yesler initially resisted the decision by the city to cut the corner of his property on the opposite side of Front, he did not proceed with any building projects for several months after the fire. By September work was under way on the Pioneer Building basement, but it was not until early October that Yesler announced his intention to proceed with the project, stating, "The Pioneer Building is a hobby of mine and when it is completed you will have to travel a great many miles to find its superior."[20] Because construction began so late in the year, little could be done before the rainy season and the project was not completed until early 1891.[21]

Although the building appears today as a symmetrically composed block, measuring 115 by 111 feet, the 94-foot-tall structure was designed in two distinct phases. (Figs. 5.8a, b) When the project was initially discussed in January 1889, Yesler announced that only the southern portion, measuring just

5.9 Pioneer Building

Manuscripts, Special Collections, University Archives Division, University of Washington Libraries, UW8813

67 feet wide, would be built in the first year. Thus, surviving drawings show that Fisher initially designed an asymmetrical block.[22] The tower which marks the center of west front of the building was at first to have been its northwest corner. After the fire and Yesler's delay, the entire project eventually filled the full width of the site at 115 feet. Fisher designed the north portion of the building to balance the south portion which had been intended as its first phase.

The exterior walls of the six-story structure are Bellingham Bay gray sandstone at the ground floor and red brick at the upper floors, with the exception of the two stone pilasters which extended up the full height of the building to the tower over the main entrance. (Fig. 5.9) The spandrel panels and other ornamental details are of terra-cotta. The three projecting bays—the curved bays at the corner and at the center of the James Street facade and the angular bay at the center of the Front Street facade—are of cast iron detailed to match the terra-cotta. Fisher's Victorian compositional conventions are evident as the two

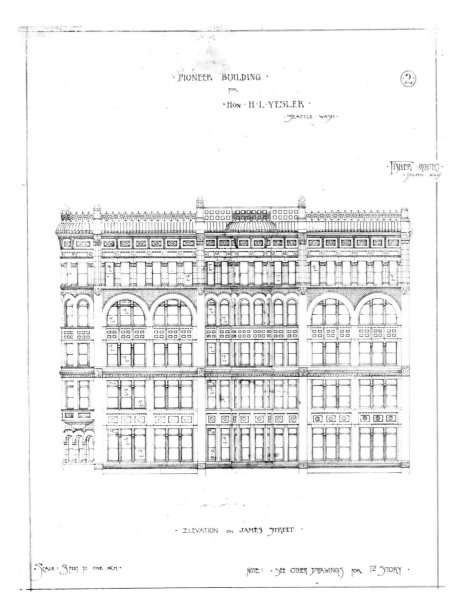

5.10 Pioneer Building, construction drawings, sheet 2 (James Street elevation, second to sixth floors)

Manuscripts, Special Collections, University Archives Division, University of Washington Libraries UW12632

street facades are divided into vertically expressed bays, and individual details such as the stone pilasters and the central tower (later removed) reinforced this vertical emphasis. (Fig. 5.10)

The detailing of the building, however, shows Fisher's growing awareness of Richardsonian Romanesque design. Within the individual bays, Fisher grouped several floors of windows under arches. Where windows are not grouped in this way, they are often individually arched forming continuous arcades. Overall, the detailing of the facades, though varied, is comparatively restrained and the excessive modeling of the wall surface with ornament offering highly contrasting colors, textures, and forms, typical of some of his pre-fire work, is generally absent. At the sixth floor, the row of windows separated by colonettes is clearly similar to features that appear in Richardson's own work. The relatively restrained cornice reflects the limitations of the new fire ordinance and may also show awareness of recent commercial work in Chicago. The most obvious

5.11 Pioneer Building, entrance

Photo by John Stamets, 2000

influence from Romanesque Revival work is found in the arched entrances at the corner and at the center of the front. (Fig. 5.11) The center entrance features a broad arch, supported on each side by four grouped polished granite columns, while that at the corner, which was the entrance to the Puget Sound National Bank, is slightly narrower and is supported by only three polished granite columns on each side. The stone between the store windows at the ground floor was laid up in alternating broad and narrow courses (a feature found in some of Richardson's late work). The most curious and unexplained feature of the exterior is the treatment of the pair of stone pilasters. Each stone piece is crudely cut in a rounded form. Rather than reading primarily as continuous columns, these read as stacks of individually rusticated elements.[23]

The interior arrangement of the Pioneer Building reflects the two phases of its design. The building is divided by a brick firewall the runs from front to back just north of the main entrance. At each floor arched openings connect the two parts of the building. Each half of the building is planned around a tight central skylit atrium which extends from the second floor to the roof. (Fig. 5.12) A double rank of office rooms fills the space between the balconies and the exterior wall so that every office receives light either from the outside through

5.12 Pioneer Building,
atrium

Photo by John Stamets, 2001

windows or from the skylit atrium through relights. Cast-iron columns and steel
girders are the primary structure from the basement to the sixth floor; the sixth-
floor partitions and the roof are entirely wood frame. The steel beams support
wood floor joists, and this floor structure frames into the brick and stone exterior bearing walls. The cast-iron columns are enclosed by wood, but the steel
beams have always been visible where they cross the interior atria. The ground
floor provided space for two banks and several other stores. A barber shop and
additional stores in the basement were also accessible from the street. The office
floors were divided into 185 office rooms. The finishes of the entrance lobby
were tile and the offices were select cedar.

At a cost of over $250,000, the Pioneer Building was, from the first, con-
sidered one of Seattle's finest business blocks. Even during construction it was
described as "a monument of architectural beauty and magnificence."[24] Upon
completion, the building was seen as an expression of Henry Yesler's role in
the building of Seattle: "The building is an outgrowth of Mr. H. L. Yesler's

laudable ambition to erect on the site of early struggles in business, a structure that would rival in point of magnificence, any business building, not only in Seattle, but in the State of Washington, and the result is a credit to the progressive pioneer's public spirit and enterprise."[25] Its significance as an anchor of post-fire Seattle was especially enhanced by its position forming one side of the new Public Square (now Pioneer Place). The Pioneer Building is also revealing of Fisher's limitations as a Romanesque Revival designer. The overall compositional framework of the Pioneer Building is still a Victorian one. Romanesque motifs were adopted and the facade detailing was simplified, but this new language was still applied to a Victorian structure. This criticism must be tempered, however, by a recognition that the Pioneer Building was one of the very finest buildings built in Seattle in the nineteenth century, and it would certainly rank among the best buildings on the Pacific Coast in the late 1880s and early 1890s.

The Burke Building

If the Pioneer Building can be said to have marked Fisher's emergence at the forefront of Seattle architects in 1889, this position was confirmed when he received commissions from Thomas Burke. The smaller of these, Burke's New York Block, was located north of the fire zone, and although under construction in June 1889, it was undamaged by the fire.[26] The more significant commission was the Burke Building (1889–91, destroyed) which Fisher had received in late February or early March.[27] Located on a quarter-block site at the corner of Second and Marion Streets, the building is evidence of the spread of Seattle's business district northward in the late 1880s. Unlike Yesler, who, as far as can be determined, was not particularly knowledgeable or interested in architecture, Burke (who was later one of the instigators of the Seattle Opera House project) took an active interest in the design as well as construction aspects of his building. Surviving correspondence between Fisher and Burke, as well as occasional references in Burke's letters to others, indicates Burke's involvement in details such as the color and quality of terra-cotta and the choice of appropriate roofing materials. In addition, there are references in Burke's letters to the quality of terra-cotta used in Chicago, suggesting that he was aware in more than a general way of the new commercial architecture of that city. Indeed, even in the first announcement of the building in March 1889, it was compared to the Rookery.[28] (See Fig. 4.32) Thus, it seems clear that Burke pushed Fisher in regard to specific aspects of the design. And, because the Burke Building was under design in mid-1889, when the Pioneer Building was delayed, it may be that some of the design improvements found in the Pioneer Building resulted from Fisher's experience with the Burke Building. Although it had been announced in the *Post-Intelligencer* on 12 March 1889, only the excavations were completed before the June fire. Construction was not restarted until August, and must have extended for at least the next eighteen months. The building was described as "almost completed" in March 1891.[29]

5.13 Elmer H. Fisher,
Burke Building, 1889–91
(destroyed); initial scheme,
early 1889

Seattle: The Queen City
(ca. May 1889); Manuscripts,
Special Collections,
University Archives Division,
University of Washington
Libraries

The completed Burke Building was a generally symmetrical six-story block
measuring 120 by 108 feet. Like the Rookery, the Burke Building was planned
around an open court, but given the smaller size of the Seattle site, only a quarter of a city block, the Burke court lacked the expansiveness of the Chicago
building. Because the site was smaller, the Burke Building plan was U-shaped
and the court was open on one side. (Figs. 5.14a, b) The Burke Building also
did not have space equivalent to the Rookery's expansive lobby.

Because surviving drawings show several stages in the design of the project,
it is possible to trace the evolution of Fisher's scheme. A perspective published
about May 1889 shows Fisher's early idea for the building.[30] (Fig. 5.13) The
front of the five-story block is shown divided into five distinct bays along Second
Street, with the central bay expressed as a six-story tower with a high peaked
roof and the end bays pushed slightly forward to read as pavilions. The facade

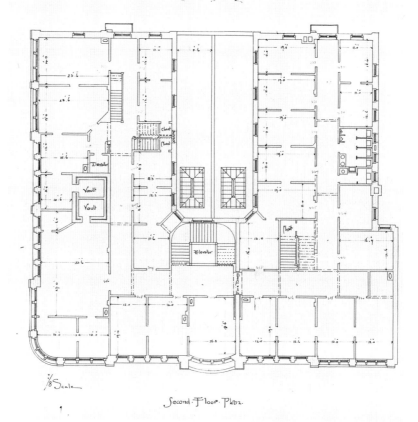

-The Burke Building-
-Seattle Wash.-

Second Floor Plan.

⅛ Scale

5.14a Burke Building; second floor plan

Northwest Museum of Arts and Culture/Eastern Washington State Historical Society, Spokane

5.14b Burke Building; first floor plan

Northwest Museum of Arts and Culture/Eastern Washington State Historical Society, Spokane

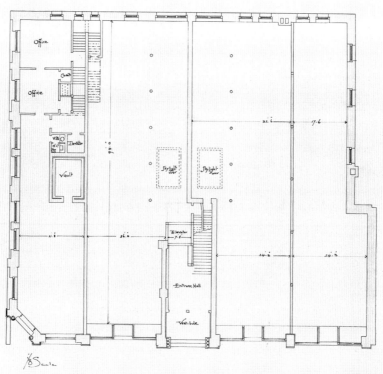

-The Burke Building-
-Seattle Wash.-

First Floor Plan

⅛ Scale

5.15 Burke Building,
intermediate scheme

Northwestern Architect 8/6
(June 1890), Minnesota
Historical Society

curved to turn the corner so that the Second Street front seamlessly extended
along Marion. While the arches at the entrances and over the third-floor windows may reflect Chicago commercial building practice, the overall character
of the detailing remained Victorian with features such as frieze bands, recessed
panels, distorted classical details, and an exaggerated cornice.

By August 1889, however, the Burke design had been modified and most of
these Victorian details eliminated. The announcement in the *Seattle Times* that
construction would resume was accompanied by an illustration that was a
reduced version of the perspective rendering of the building published in
Northwestern Architect a year later.[31] (Fig. 5.15) From these drawings it is clear
that the overall organization of the five-story building remained the same, but
the detailing had been simplified. The stepping of the facade was largely eliminated so that although the pavilion-like character of the end bays remained,
it was significantly reduced; the peaked roof of the tower had disappeared. In
this phase, windows at the second, third, and fourth floors were grouped under
arches providing a vertical coherence not previously present. The brick and
stone detailing were more elemental, and specific features, such as the slight
bow of the windows above the entrance, the terra-cotta details at the spandrels,
and the treatment of the cornice, reflected an awareness of the Rookery and
other contemporary Chicago work. While the initial scheme had shown consid-

erable use of stone, in this drawing the primary material was brick with stone only at the first floor and pilasters at the front entrance bay (similar to those on the Pioneer Building).

Surviving plans and elevations show a five-story structure. Therefore, it does not appear that Burke decided to add an extra floor to the building until construction had actually commenced. Reflecting the optimism of the period the building was completed as a six-story structure. (Fig. 5.16) As constructed, the Burke Building shows further reduction of extraneous detail. The stone pilasters were eliminated; the facades were further flattened, reducing, but not completely eliminating, the independent reading of the end bays; the cornice was simplified; and decorative metalwork at the roofline was omitted. Burke's correspondence shows that he was particularly concerned that the color of the terra-cotta exactly match that of the brick, even writing this into his contract with the supplier, Gladding, McBean. An initial sample of terra-cotta that was not close enough in color to the brick was rejected.[32] Surviving color images of the building show that a monochromatic appearance was achieved, with the result that the building presented a level of coherence unmatched by most work in Seattle at the time. Only the ground floor of stone was strongly differentiated. The Romanesque entry arch may reflect Richardson's direct influence, but otherwise the commercial architecture of Chicago provided the precedents. In particular, the design of the central bay of the main facade was clearly derived from the Rookery.

The interior of the Burke Building similarly reflected Burke's architectural interests. The U-shaped block with central light court featured a structure like that of the Pioneer Building, with cast-iron columns supporting steel girders framing into the load-bearing exterior walls and carrying wood floor joists. The Commercial National Bank was located at the corner of the ground floor and the building provided space for three stores facing Second. A lower floor was accessible from Marion; the basement was accessible from the alley. The public spaces at the first two floors were finished in oak, and redwood was used throughout the office floors.

The Burke Building, like the Pioneer Building, was regarded as one of the most significant buildings of the new Seattle. In early reports it was described as "a building of [the] most handsome features of the modern styles of architecture."[33] Later descriptions were similar: "The magnificent Burke Building, one of the finest office blocks in the Northwest, is almost completed. . . . Nothing but the best of everything has been used in any part of this building."[34]

The clear evolution of the Burke Building and the surviving correspondence indicate that Fisher was strongly influenced by Burke in developing this design. It was Burke who had suggested the Rookery as a model and it is clear that Burke was involved in approving every detail of the project. It was his prodding, apparently over the course of almost two years from initiation of design to completion of construction, that brought the Burke Building to this level of refinement. Fisher's achievement in the Burke Building was remarkable. Here, at the age of fifty, with limited professional training as an architect, Fisher came as close as he ever would to transcending the conventions of his Victorian background. Whether he fully understood his achievement seems unlikely because the Burke Building remained exceptional in his work.

William Boone and the New York Building

William Boone had designed over half of the prominent buildings destroyed by the fire, but by 1889 his position as the city's leading architect had been taken by Elmer Fisher. The rapidity with which his many buildings had been consumed may have led some clients to question his knowledge of the new fire-resistive technology. Further, as architects such as Fisher, Saunders, and Parkinson began to present their new designs, Boone's highly embellished Victorian work must have appeared dated. In 1889 Boone was nearing sixty. He had learned design from trade literature, pattern books, and examples he had seen, particularly the Victorian architecture of San Francisco and Oakland, but new design directions were to be found in the new professional architectural press and not in familiar builders' literature. It is notable that among the leading post-fire architects in Seattle, Boone was the only one whose work was never published in an architectural journal. He did eventually become a leader in the effort to professionalize architectural practice in Seattle, but his work after the fire remained conspicuously Victorian until some of the new buildings by others provided clues as to the new direction of progressive design.

Most of Boone's initial post-fire commercial commissions came from clients for whom he had previously designed projects. The Wah Chong Building (1889, destroyed), a replacement for his earlier Wah Chong structure which the conflagration had destroyed, was announced just twelve days after the fire. (Fig. 5.17) Completed by early December, this three-story brick block housed the Phoenix Hotel, which provided lodging for single working men, on the upper two floors and retail stores at ground level.[35] The design was drily Victorian; the windows were irregularly spaced and embellishment was minimal except for a slightly corbeled cornice and central pediment at the front facade. Boone's other early post-fire work was similarly *retardataire*.[36]

Boone's first large post-fire commission was the Dexter Horton Building (1889, destroyed) at the northwest corner of Third and Cherry. One of the most rapidly constructed buildings of the time, this was completed by 23 October, little more than three months after excavation began. The *Post-Intelligencer* reported that construction of the "largest [building] roofed since the fire" had taken just seventy-one days, and noted that Boone had been especially "clever" at obtaining the necessary materials, including over one million bricks.[37] This building was the project of local business leader Dexter Horton (1825–1904), an early Seattle pioneer who had opened the city's first bank in 1870.[38] The Dexter Horton Building was nearly square, measuring 120 by 126 feet. (Fig. 5.18) It was five stories tall with 126 office rooms on the second to fourth floors and stores at street level facing Third. Additional stores in the basement opened to Cherry and to the alley. The brick facades were divided vertically by flat pilasters and horizontally by beltcourses creating a layered rectangular grid with windows in groups of two or three. The detailing echoed pre-fire construction in Seattle, but its consistency and restraint lent an overall coherence only somewhat countered by the irregularity of the grid. The overall treatment may reflect the influence of the Boston Block which was nearby. For Boone the design was a step away from High Victorian agitation and toward a more straightforward approach to design.

The *Post-Intelligencer* report on the completion of the Dexter Horton Building also mentioned Horton's intention to begin construction in spring 1890 on an even larger structure fronting on Cherry and Second to complement the completed building. This second building was initially called the "Seattle Block," but by 1892 it had been renamed the "New York Building" (1889–92, destroyed), the name by which it was known throughout its history.[39] The New York Building was one of the most powerful expressions of the new architecture in post-fire Seattle. It was also among the most technologically advanced of the new buildings. The structure is exceptional in Boone's career and one might be inclined to doubt his authorship of the project, but a description in the *Post-Intelligencer* on 9 October 1889 indicates that this was Boone's work.[40]

Although designed in 1889, construction of the New York Building was delayed because the site was occupied by businesses operating in tents after the fire. When excavations began in July 1890, it was reported that Boone had "had the plans completed for some time." However, as late as March 1891, the

5.17 William Boone, Wah Chong Building, 1889 (destroyed)

Museum of History and Industry, PEMCO Webster and Stevens Collection, 83.10.8470

5.18 William Boone, Dexter Horton Building (Occidental Building), 1889 (destroyed)

Manuscripts, Special Collections, University Archives Division, University of Washington Libraries, photo by Asahel Curtis, 5301

5.19 William Boone/ Boone and Willcox, New York Building, 1889–1892 (destroyed), preliminary scheme

Northwestern Real Estate & Building Review *1/2* *(Mar.–Apr. 1891); Manuscripts, Special Collections, University Archives Division, University of Washington Libraries, UW18319*

project was barely above the street; as *Northwestern Real Estate and Building Review* reported, "a large force of stonemasons is now at work laying the massive stone columns and walls of the first story."[41] These delays allowed the building's design to be simplified. Boone visited Chicago in January and February 1890, and minor changes might have resulted from that trip. However, the October 1889 newspaper report included a relatively clear description including the two-and-one-half-story rock-faced stone base, a projecting entrance bay, the vertical piers and arches forming arcades on both street facades, and a different treatment of the top floor and cornice. Still, a drawing in the March 1891 *Northwestern Real Estate and Building Review* shows a full-height entrance bay projecting from the six-and-one-half-story volume of the building (echoing Fisher's Burke Building design) and a top floor with plain rectangular windows and detailing similar to other buildings by Boone in 1890 and 1891.[42] (Fig. 5.19) As finally realized, the New York Building was constructed to seven-and-one-half stories in height (not the initially reported six and one-half), and the arches topping the piers were brick, not stone as first described. The special treatment of the entrance bay extended only to the second floor so that the four-story brick arcades were continuous on both street facades. And the top floor was much more delicately detailed. (Fig. 5.20) These changes enhanced the strength and coherence of the result. Construction was finally completed in early April 1892.[43]

Credit for the final design of the New York Building is generally given to the firm of Boone and Willcox. In December 1890, while the building was under construction, Boone formed a partnership with William Willcox, who had come to Seattle from St. Paul, Minnesota.[44] Because construction proceeded so slowly, Willcox may have contributed to the final design resolution even though the

initial conceptualization of the building appears to have been Boone's alone.

The New York Building filled a quarter-block site at the northeast corner of Second and Cherry measuring 120 by 108 feet. The building was characterized from the first as "massive" and this evident solidity set it off from virtually all of its Seattle contemporaries. The design was clearly conceived as a coherent block. Extraneous detail was reduced to a minimum. Above the two-and-one-half-story rusticated stone base rose five floors of brick, with limited stone trim at the cornice. The nine bays on Second and eight bays on Cherry were all treated consistently and the regular bay spacing carried through all floors. A single break occurred at the entrance where the second floor is marked by slightly projecting fenestration. The most remarkable feature of the design was the continuous arcade from the third to the sixth floors on the two street elevations. The continuous vertical piers and recessed spandrels gave a strong vertical expression which clearly recalled the Ames Building on Harrison Avenue in Boston by Richardson, and the work of Burnham and Root, but appears to have been an original reinterpretation of tendencies evident in those

5.20 New York Building

Manuscripts, Special Collections, University Archives Division, University of Washington Libraries, UW4164

designs. Only the spindly colonettes and somewhat fussy detailing at the seventh floor varied from the otherwise consistent treatment.

From the first, the New York Building was also notable for incorporating the most advanced fire-resistive construction of any of the commercial structures built in Seattle before 1895. The interior framing was iron and steel throughout and the columns and girders were all encased in brick. The floors were said to be of slow-burning wood construction, and these were protected by ceilings on every floor of plaster with metal lath.[45]

The New York Building was regarded as one of the most impressive buildings of Seattle. While under construction it was reported that it would be "one of the largest and most substantial buildings in the city."[46] The interiors, however, received less notice; on 2 April 1892, a week before the building was complete, the *Post-Intelligencer* described the building only as "elegantly furnished inside" and noted the building included "two high speed elevators."

The sources for the New York Building's advanced Romanesque design were found primarily in Chicago. The New York Building was Boone's largest post-fire commercial structure. Surprisingly, given Boone's authorship, the New York Building represented one of the best Seattle interpretations of Richardsonian Romanesque design. Unlike Fisher, who seems never to have freed himself fully from Victorian conventions, Boone here appears to have transcended the limitations of his background to create a building that incorporated and extended the best design tendencies of the time. In its simplicity, stateliness, and repose, the New York Building ranked with the best of Seattle architecture until its demolition in 1922.[47]

Saunders and Houghton and the Patronage of William Bailey

The Seattle business community's openness to outside investors was never more evident than in the welcome extended to William Elder Bailey (1860–1925). The son of Charles L. Bailey, a leading iron and steel manufacturer in Pennsylvania, William Bailey visited Seattle on an extended vacation to the West in 1888–89.[48] Impressed by the city's prospects, he invested in local property, then went on to California. On learning of the 6 June fire, Bailey immediately returned to Seattle to join in the rebuilding. He brought access to eastern capital and invested in real estate, business ventures, newspapers, and railroads. Some of his ventures were his own, but others were in partnership with other Seattle business leaders such as Thomas Burke.

Bailey commissioned his projects to the architect Charles Willard Saunders (1857–1935), whom he evidently met in southern California and invited to join him in Seattle. Saunders first advertised as an architect in the *Post-Intelligencer* on 28 June 1889.[49] His first project was announced at the beginning of July. Saunders is the only example of an architect who arrived in Seattle after the fire and secured significant commercial commissions, a result of his unique connection to William Bailey.

Relatively little is known about the early life of Charles Saunders, who came from an old Massachusetts family.[50] He was raised in Cambridge, Massachusetts, and worked as a clerk and then in the lumber business in Boston in the early 1880s. Where he learned architecture is unknown.[51] In 1882 he married Mary Channing of Providence, Rhode Island, and by 1886 they had moved to Pasadena, California, where in 1884 his father-in-law had built a house thought to have been designed by the couple. They opened a joint architectural practice in Pasadena, but only one additional project, a house for themselves, is known.[52] Neither the partnership nor the marriage survived and Saunders moved to Seattle alone in June 1889.

In September 1889, Saunders formed the partnership Saunders and Houghton with Edwin Walker Houghton (1856–1927), very likely because the press of architectural work had become too great for Saunders to handle alone. In addition, Houghton brought experience in the technical and construction side of architecture, which would have been especially useful as projects proceeded into construction. Houghton was born in Hampshire, England, 5 August 1856, into a family of architects and quantity surveyors. He apparently gained his architectural training in Chelsea and in the London practice of his brother, Thomas M. Houghton, probably in the mid-to-late 1870s.[53] About 1884 Edwin Houghton immigrated with his family to western Texas near El Paso where they attempted farming for nearly four years. Unsuccessful in this venture they continued west to Pasadena, California, where Houghton first practiced architecture independently and where he may have met Saunders. In early 1889, the Houghton family moved north to Port Townsend and by September they arrived in Seattle where Houghton joined Saunders.[54] The joint firm advertised in the *Post-Intelligencer* on 18 September. The initial built work of Saunders and Houghton had first come to Charles Saunders so the early designs were clearly his alone. After Houghton joined the firm their work became more varied and in the absence of records, credit for individual projects is difficult to assign.[55]

William Bailey's confidence in the future of Seattle was nowhere more evident than in his creation of the Washington Territory Investment Company, of which he assumed the presidency. Established within the first months after the fire, and capitalized at $50,000, this company was involved in investments, real estate transactions, and insurance, and offered full services for non-residents who might wish to invest in Northwest property.[56] Saunders was evidently at work on the commission for the Washington Territory Investment Company Building (1889–90, destroyed) in June and July, because excavation had been completed and brick work was beginning when the project was described by the *Post-Intelligencer* on 7 August. The building was reported as "up one story" in December, and was completed in mid-1890.[57] A three-story structure initially planned for a lot measuring 60 by 96 feet at the northwest corner of Second and Cherry, this was enlarged in late August when the adjacent parcel was acquired so that the final design measured 60 by 108. The walls were brick with stone trim; the internal structure was cast-iron columns supporting wood floors. The enlarged design provided space for the *Post-Intelligencer* presses in the basement and editorial offices upstairs. The first floor was occupied by

stores; Investment Company offices and leasable space occupied the remainder of the upper floors. The two street facades were divided into bays by flat
brick pilasters with incised vertical grooves. Triangular pediments extended
above the cornice at the two entry bays and the entrances were marked by heavy
stone columns and entablatures. The windows arranged under two-story half-
round arches reflected Romanesque influence, but overall the exterior design
was governed primarily by Victorian convention. (Fig. 5.21)

The lack of sophistication of the Washington Territory Investment Company
Building seems surprising when compared to Saunders's other early project
for William Bailey, the Bailey Building (1889–92), which stood just across
Cherry on a site that William Bailey had purchased as an investment during
his initial visit to Seattle in January 1889.[58] The building was first mentioned on
4 July, when the *Post-Intelligencer* reported it was to be a four-story brick block
and Saunders was said to be well along in preparing drawings.[59] However,
just ten days later, when the elevations were complete and "on exhibition," the
building had grown to five stories and the "imposing structure" was described
in terms of "firmness, massiveness, elegance and architectural simplicity."[60]
Then, on 5 October, the paper reported that new drawings were being prepared
for the project because it would now be six stories; however, the design was
essentially the same as the five-story scheme. By early November construction
was proceeding, although only the foundations were completed before the
December rains. In April 1890, the *Post-Intelligencer* reported that the facades

5.22 Charles Saunders, Saunders and Houghton (A. B. Chamberlin, del.), Bailey Building, 1889–92

The Graphic *(3 Oct. 1891)*

would be entirely of Tenino stone and that the first floor would be completed within five weeks. Thereafter, the project was repeatedly delayed; tenants moved into the partially completed building in August 1890 and in September 1891, and construction was finally finished in March 1892.[61] Because of the lengthy construction sequence, it is not possible to be certain exactly when all the design features were finalized. A rendering of the building, possibly drawn in 1890 (but not published in the Chicago publication *The Graphic* until October 1891), showed an overhanging cornice, possibly of wood or metal, but this was eliminated when the building was constructed.[62] (Fig. 5.22) It was reported in March 1891 that the stone cornice was being lifted into place and that completion was planned for the anniversary of the fire in June, but the building was not actually completed until a nearly year later.[63] In addition, confusion about the building has arisen because during construction the project was most often identified as the Harrisburg Building, and less frequently as the Bailey Building.[64] (In the early twentieth century it came to be called the Railway Exchange Building, further adding to the confusion.)

From the first, Bailey intended that this building, which was to cost $200,000, would be one of the finest of Seattle's new business blocks. It was the only one of the city's large new buildings that featured facades entirely of stone. (Fig. 5.23) The architecture was surprisingly advanced, bearing few traces of

5.23 Bailey Building

Victorian design convention, but sharing instead an affinity to forward-looking contemporary work in Chicago. Measuring 120 by 108 feet, the Bailey Building was 92 feet tall, with rock-faced Tenino sandstone on the two street facades, and brick walls on the other two sides. The minimization of extraneous detail emphasized the coherence of the rectilinear block. The windows and other openings were square cut with straight lines. However, the bay arrangement was not symmetrical on either facade but reflected the interior divisions of the building. On Second Street, around a narrow entrance bay, three bays with paired windows were balanced by two wider bays with groups of three windows. The Cherry Street facade featured an off-center entrance and an unbalanced arrangement of unequal bays. The very slight recessed treatment of each bay from the third to fifth floor was a residual Victorian motif. (Fig. 5.24) Continuous horizontal moldings at the third and the sixth floors divided the block into three zones; these can be interpreted as structurally expressive as they correspond to the levels at which the exterior wall thickness was required to change by the new building ordinance. The second through sixth floors were divided into offices. Framing was cast-iron columns with steel girders supporting wood beams and floors. Carved stone ornament was located primarily at the two entrances and at the cornice.

The Bailey Building was regarded as among the finest buildings in Seattle on its completion. In March 1891, the building was described as "imposing" and on completion a year later it was headlined as a "Symphony in Stone."[65] The care taken in the construction of the building was also noted: "Mr. Houghton in talking about the building said it was very carefully constructed. . . . Mr. Houghton is an English architect, and believes that the slowly built structure is the best constructed one. Therefore, he built the Bailey Building slowly, surely, strongly and well."[66] Although the Bailey Building never attracted the attention given to the Pioneer Building or the Burke Building, it was among the most architecturally advanced structures constructed in the city at this time. The simplicity of this block and, in particular, the absence of varied surface decoration contrasted with almost all other buildings in the city. Also notable was absence of Richardsonian Romanesque arches. The Bailey Building vaguely recalls one or two elements of Richardson's Marshall Field Store, but it is closer to buildings that had appeared in the architectural press (and that were derived from the Field Store), such as Shepley, Rutan, and Coolidge's Lionberger Warehouse, St. Louis, or Harry Jones's National Bank of Commerce, Minneapolis. (See Figs. 4.22, 4.39) However, the most intriguing relationship may be to Adler and Sullivan's buildings of the mid-to-late 1880s that employed rock-faced masonry and square-cut windows.[67]

In addition to these projects, William Bailey was also a leader of the effort to create a "summer hotel" and may have directed the commission to Saunders. After the fire one of the problems in Seattle was a lack of hotel space.

5.25 Charles Saunders,
Saunders and Houghton,
Rainier Hotel, 1889
(destroyed)

*Manuscripts, Special
Collections, University
Archives Division, University
of Washington Libraries,
photo by Frank LaRoche, 20*

Rooms were needed immediately, but the new downtown hotel projects would
not be completed until 1890 or later. At a citizens' meeting on 20 July, Thomas
Burke, William Bailey, and Thomas Ewing formed a committee to promote the
hotel project which was characterized as "of the type of those at fashionable
watering-places."[68] Ewing, like Bailey and Burke, was deeply involved in
Seattle real estate and development, especially in West Seattle.[69] The projected
hotel was to be constructed on a sloping site bounded by Fifth, Sixth, Marion,
and Columbia, overlooking downtown. A week later, the *Post-Intelligencer*
reported the selection of the "modern colonial" design by Charles Saunders
for the new Rainier Hotel (1889, destroyed). Planned and built at an extraordinary speed, at a cost of $35,000, the building opened on 11 November, and
reportedly housed more than two hundred guests in the first week.[70] The four-
story, U-shaped building included common rooms, a dining room, and similar
spaces at the first floor and fifty rooms on each of the three floors above. (Fig.
5.25) The hotel was finished in wood siding described as "channel rustic" with
shingles at the upper floor and gambrel roof; it measured 176 feet along the
west-facing elevation and was wrapped by a 21-foot-wide verandah with views
of downtown and Puget Sound. Although generally symmetrical in design, its
selectively placed windows and asymmetrically disposed tower reflected a
residual picturesque tendency. The simple forms, horizontal lines, and absence
of skeletal articulation all show the influence of the shingled structures—then
called "modern colonial"—that were frequently published in the architectural
press in the 1880s.[71] Saunders's knowledge of the style was evident in the

5.26 Saunders and
Houghton (A. B.
Chamberlin, del.),
Manhattan Building
project, 1889–90 (unbuilt)

Northwestern Architect 8/11
(Nov. 1890); Minnesota
Historical Society

houses he and his wife had designed in Pasadena, and he was very likely familiar with some of the resort hotels proposed for the West that had seen recent
publication.[72]

Saunders received one final commercial commission from William Bailey,
the Manhattan Building (1889), a four-story brick commercial structure
intended for a quarter block site at Second and Union to cost $50,000.
Although excavations were reported to be nearing completion on 2 November,
and $10,000 had apparently been spent by June 1890, the building was never
finished.[73] The design is known from two surviving drawings, including one
published in *Northwestern Architect* in November 1890. (Fig. 5.26) Both show
a four-story stucco-faced block featuring an off-center entrance bay with a loggia. Why the building was not completed is not known, but Bailey may have
been over-extended financially.

Having established a reputation with the projects for William Bailey,
Saunders and Houghton began to receive a variety of commissions from other
clients. The most important commercial structures were two very different business blocks, the Olympic Building (1889–91, destroyed) and the Terry-Denny
Building (1889–91). Standing at the southeast corner of the intersection of
Yesler and Commercial, the Olympic Building occupied a prominent position
on the south side of the new Public Square. Announced as the Starr-Colman
Block on 5 October, and completed about a year later, the project was a four-
story commercial block with stores at the first floor and offices and a hotel
above.[74] The first floor piers were rock-faced stone, but the brick walls of the
second through fourth floors were faced in stucco detailed with attenuated classical motifs. A circular bay turned the corner. (Fig. 5.27) The Terry-Denny
Building, on the west side of Commercial, was also announced in October 1889,
and was completed mid 1891.[75] A five-story commercial structure occupying
a mid-block site, this was U-shaped in plan surrounding a narrow central court

and required two additional light wells at each partywall to provide minimal light and ventilation. The building housed the Northern Hotel on its upper floors. The Terry-Denny Building was constructed of flat red brick with stone trim and featured a variety of arches, ornamented terra-cotta spandrel panels, and a high cornice. The most prominent element was the central bay with an arched entry displaying distorted classical detail. The facade might be read as a Victorian interpretation of a Renaissance palazzo and may reflect Houghton's knowledge of English commercial construction.[76] (Fig. 5.28) A comparison of the Bailey Building, Olympic Building, and Terry-Denny Building indicates the wide variation found in the designs produced by Saunders and Houghton that may have arisen from differences in the design temperaments of the two partners. But since the operation of Saunders and Houghton's office is unknown, the individual responsibilities for these projects and the different roles the partners may have played in the production of these designs are also unknown.[77]

John Parkinson's Commercial Buildings, 1889–1890

Because the Boston Block came through the 6 June fire unscathed, Parkinson and Evers were well prepared to take on new commissions. In his 1935 autobiography Parkinson wrote, "Here was an opportunity for young architects and we appreciated the situation thoroughly. We found, however, that the old and well known architects there were favored, getting practically all of the work despite our efforts to get some of it."[78] The record of the post-fire period lends credence to Parkinson's complaint; in the first year after the fire Parkinson and Evers received only a few commercial projects, and two of these were evidently won on a competitive basis. Still, they did win two large commercial blocks on quarter-block sites and these helped establish Parkinson's reputation as one of the leading architects of the period.

On 3 July, the *Post-Intelligencer* reported that Parkinson and Evers were "completing plans for a big brick building to be built for Mr. Guy C. Phinney and Mr. Daniel Jones on the northwest corner of Second and James."[79] The building was subsequently named the Butler Block. Guy Phinney (1852–1893), the primary developer of the project, was involved in banking, insurance, and real estate in Seattle.[80] Daniel Jones, who held a minority interest, was a developer of residential real estate in the neighborhoods near Lake Union.[81] Parkinson later wrote that he heard of this opportunity through an acquaintance and was able to secure an interview with Phinney, whom he described as a colorful character: "a typical frontiersman, a big rough looking fellow with dark eyes, bushy black whiskers, carried a gun in both hip pockets and could manage to put a cuss word in every second word."[82] According to Parkinson, Phinney agreed to consider his proposal if he could come up with something in twenty-four hours. Apparently Parkinson met Phinney's requirements because his design was accepted. The 3 July article described the project in detail and construction proceeded at a rapid pace. In late July, Phinney was in San Francisco ordering steel; by the beginning of August work was proceeding on the foundation.

5.27 Saunders and Houghton, Olympic Building, 1889–91 (destroyed)

Museum of History and Industry, Wilse Collection, 88.33.46

5.28 Saunders and Houghton, Terry-Denny Building, 1889–91

Museum of History and Industry, Wilse Collection, 88.33.209

5.29 Parkinson and Evers, Butler Block, 1889–90 (destroyed, partial facade survives)

Manuscripts, Special Collections, University Archives Division, University of Washington Libraries, photo by Boyd & Braas, UW 8297

Construction was completed by October 1890 at a cost of about $180,000.[83]

The Butler Block (1889–90, destroyed/partial facade survives) was a prominent five-story brick structure on the corner of Second and James near the center of Seattle's rebuilding downtown. (Fig. 5.29) Designed and built as a commercial office building, this had four floors of offices, and stores on the first floor facing Second and in the basement facing James. The rectangular block filled its 120- by 108-foot site, with a plan organized around a central skylit light court. The building can be characterized as echoing the form of an Italian Renaissance palazzo. The exterior elevations featured alternating wide and narrow courses of stone at the first floor and four stories of brick above. The brick block was divided symmetrically into bays by flat pilasters and horizontally by stone bands. Although the detailing of the openings varied, these variations were sufficiently restrained such that the overall continuity of the block is the primary impression. An early perspective of the design that appeared in *Washington Magazine* in December 1889 emphasized the vertical divisions of the facades and showed a cupola above the central bay, but this element was omitted in the final project and the vertical emphasis was less pronounced as a result of the continuous stone bands at the second and third floors.[84] The Butler Block was remarkably unified, especially in contrast to the work of Elmer

5.30 Butler Block, entrance

Photo by John Stamets, 2001

Fisher, but it did not show any overt Richardsonian Romanesque elements, except the round granite arch at the building entrance.[85] (Fig. 5.30)

On 2 April 1890, the *Post-Intelligencer* reported that William Ballard would build a brick block for eastern capitalists on lots he had just acquired at the corner of Second South (now Occidental) and Yesler. Later that day Ballard announced the formation of the Seattle National Bank.[86] Ballard then invited competitive designs for the bank's building from Seattle architects. Although Parkinson had previously done work for Ballard, it was by no means certain that he would receive the project as Ballard had also given commissions to others.[87] On 23 April, the paper reported that a dozen architects had submitted designs; the selection of the scheme by Parkinson and Evers was announced on 29 April. Construction proceeded thereafter, reaching completion in 1892.[88]

Parkinson and Evers's Seattle National Bank Building (1890–92) is a six-story office block measuring 120 by 111 feet, organized around a light court. The ground floor provided rooms at the corner for the bank and stores facing Yesler and Second. The second floor included large offices and storage. The upper four floors were devoted to offices. The architectural treatment reflects Parkinson's development as a designer. The 30 April article described the project: "The exterior of the building will be Romanesque in style and nothing but pressed brick, stone, and terra-cotta will be used. The corner will be rounded and the whole building will present as fine an appearance as any other

5.31 Parkinson and
Evers/John Parkinson,
Seattle National Bank
Building (Interurban
Building), 1890–92

*Manuscripts, Special
Collections, University
Archives Division, University
of Washington Libraries,
photo by Frank LaRoche,
1082*

building in the Northwest."[89] (Fig. 5.31) The design shows the influence of
the publication of Richardsonian Romanesque commercial architecture, and
also reflects Parkinson's continuing move away from Victorian convention. The
Romanesque treatment, particularly the continuous arcade at the first two floors,
was among the most sophisticated interpretations of the mode in Seattle. The
design may show the influence of Richardson's Ames Store on Bedford Street
in Boston or some of the later published work by Shepley, Rutan, and Coolidge.
The decision to use Colorado red sandstone at the base, rather than the locally
available stone which was generally light gray, added to the coherence of the
design. The horizontal division above the second floor corresponded to the pro-
grammatic difference between the two lower floors and those above. This horizontal division and that above the fifth floor also corresponded to the points
where the wall thicknesses changed as required by the building ordinance. Only
the horizontal division above the third floor appears to have been purely a compositional choice. The primary entrance to the building was located in the center of the Yesler elevation; the entry to the bank was on the corner.

5.32 Seattle National
Bank Building,
entrance

Inland Architect *23/2*
(March 1894), courtesy
Trustees of the Boston
Public Library

Ballard and the investors intended the Seattle National Bank Building to be one of the finest business blocks in the city. Parkinson's awareness of the quality of the design is evident in that he sought its publication in the professional architectural press almost immediately. A pen-and-ink rendering of the building appeared in *American Architect and Building News* on 5 July 1890. A photograph of the bank entrance appeared in *Inland Architect* in 1894. (Fig. 5.32) Both the rendering and the photograph were published only in Parkinson's name as his partnership with Cecil Evers was terminated at the beginning of June 1890. Parkinson retained this project and has always been credited with the design.[90] The Seattle National Bank Building was the second large block that Parkinson, the youngest of the city's commercial architects, had successfully produced. With this design he clearly demonstrated that he was ready to take on additional projects of this scale.

Other Commercial Blocks in 1890: Boone and Fisher

The primary focus of Seattle's leading architects in 1890 was the continuing construction of buildings begun the previous year. Although a few projects were completed in 1889, most had been left incomplete when the rains began and were awaiting the new building season. By March 1890, construction resumed and completion of the new buildings went rapidly forward. The material shortages and delivery problems of the previous year were largely resolved, although some materials, such as stone, were still occasionally in short supply. The newspapers continued to report on the new structures, although, unlike 1889, most articles focused on the progress of construction already under way rather than announcements of new projects. Most of the smaller projects were completed in 1890, but many of the larger ones remained unfinished until the following year. Thus, on 11 August 1890, a *Post-Intelligencer* article titled "Not All Work Done" reported that only about half of the new buildings had been finished. Important new commercial blocks continued to be announced, although the pace was much less frenzied than the previous year. Parkinson's Seattle National Bank Building was one of the first of the new projects of 1890. Boone and Fisher also received new large business commissions in Seattle.[91]

William Boone's Marshall-Walker Building (1890–91, altered), one of his more important post-fire works, was announced in the *Post-Intelligencer* on 16 May. Located at the corner of Commercial and Main, this commercial block was designed to serve the wholesale trade. Construction began in June and the building was completed in spring 1891 for about $125,000.[92] The Marshall-Walker Building was a four-story rectangular stone and brick block measuring about 110 by 120 feet developed jointly by the two owners. The building was divided at the center by a brick wall, but appeared unified from the street. Designed for wholesale stores, the building was framed in heavy timber sized for the loads anticipated from the storage of dry goods. The exterior expression seemed *retardataire* in comparison to Boone's New York Building of the previous year. (Fig. 5.33) The upper floors of brick were divided into regular bays by flat pilasters. The two corner bays were more substantial in appearance, giving the building an expression of strength and solidity. Each provided for a separate entrance to each owner's half of the building. The terra-cotta panels and round-arched windows in these bays indicate Boone's continuing awareness of Romanesque motifs, but the gridded wall treatment of the Marshall-Walker Building still recalls Boone's earlier Victorian designs.[93]

Elmer Fisher began 1890 in an enviable position. Work already under construction would keep his office busy with administrative and supervisory tasks through the entire year. At the same time, the office would be called upon to prepare additional detail drawings for many of the ongoing projects. New work also came into Fisher's office, but the pace of new projects could never equal those received in 1889, and few projects approached the scale of the Pioneer Building or the Burke Building.

On 30 May 1890, a *Post-Intelligencer* story with the headline "Yesler Will Build" reported that Henry Yesler would construct new structures on his parcels (vacant since the fire) bordering Pioneer Place, the city's new Public Square at Yesler and Front. Fisher was at work on the buildings in June because they were included in an article about the success of his firm that appeared in the paper late that month.[94] Located on adjacent corners across from the Pioneer Building, these commissions gave Fisher the opportunity to create a unique

architectural ensemble. The Bank of Commerce (1890–91, altered) was located at the southwest corner of the intersection of Yesler and Commercial on a lot measuring only 24 by 70 feet.[95] Fisher's design was described as a five-story block of which only the first two floors would initially be built. (Fig. 5.34) The exterior treatment featured piers of heavily rusticated sandstone. The two-story arches and massive scale of the piers produced a solidity not found among most of the other new commercial buildings. The rugged stone gave the building a primitive rustic feeling (and seems almost to recall the size and shape of logs). The treatment echoed the detailing of the stone pilasters on Fisher's Pioneer Building across the Square.

The second commission was the Yesler Building (1890–91, altered), at the northwest corner of Front and Yesler (the building known since 1895 as the Mutual Life Building). From the first, Yesler intended this as a multi-story block to complement the scale, materials, and detailing of the Pioneer Building. A description of the Yesler Building was published in March 1891: "The first story is of Salt Lake red sandstone with carved stone capitals and trimmings. Above the first story the walls will be of cream-colored brick, with red stone trimmings. When completed the building will present one of the most showy exteriors in Seattle. Its design is semi-Romanesque, with two red tile-covered towers on the broad eastern front."[96] The ground floor stonework featured the same rounded rough-hewn texture as the Bank of Commerce across Yesler.

5.33 William Boone, Marshall-Walker Building, 1890–91 (altered)

Manuscripts, Special Collections, University Archives Division, University of Washington Libraries, photo by Asahel Curtis, 1064

5.34 Elmer H. Fisher,
Bank of Commerce,
1890–91 (altered)

*Manuscripts, Special
Collections, University
Archives Division, University
of Washington Libraries,
photo by Asahel Curtis, 4090*

One small drawing, subsequently published in *Pacific Mason*, shows Fisher's initial proposal for the six-story Yesler Building.[97] (Fig. 5.35) The design reflected Fisher's continuing tendency to conceive of large buildings not as unified blocks, but as grouped vertical pavilions. The facade presents a mix of detail that reflects the continued influence of Fisher's Victorian background in his design approach. Whether Fisher might have simplified this design if it had gone forward is unknown. Only the first floor of the project was completed before it was temporarily roofed in March 1891. (Fig. 5.36) Construction did not proceed due to the economic stringency of that year, and when construction did resume in 1892, the design was not by Fisher.[98]

At the same time, Fisher created a building of much more unified design. The State Building (1890–91), at the southeast corner of Main and South Second (now Occidental), was commissioned by Schwabacher Brothers about June. By September the building was under way and it was completed by May 1891.[99] Built to serve Schwabacher Brothers' wholesale dry goods business which was expanding beyond their building on Commercial, this was a simple four-story brick block with cast-iron columns at the first floor and sandstone trim, measuring 111 by 120 feet. Only the central entry bay on each street front received independent expression as a pavilion. (Fig. 5.37) The design derived in part

5.35 Elmer H. Fisher, Yesler Building, 1890–91, initial design

Pacific Mason 2/6 (June 1896); Manuscripts, Special Collections, University Archives Division, University of Washington Libraries

5.36 View looking south on Commercial Street (now First Avenue South), 1891; incomplete Yesler Building is visible to the right.

Manuscripts, Special Collections, University Archives Division, University of Washington Libraries, photo by Boyd & Braas, 145

5.37 Elmer H. Fisher,
State Building, 1890–91

*Museum of History and
Industry, PEMCO Webster
and Stevens Collection,
83.10.7374.1*

from the perspective illustration of the Ryerson Wholesale Store, by Adler and
Sullivan, published in *Inland Architect* in April 1889.[100] (See Fig. 4.36) Although
Fisher's building was smaller in scale, it duplicated the pairs of arches, the
groups of four windows, and the stepped detail along the edges of the arches
in the published drawing. Because the State Building was built as a wholesale
warehouse, the interior structure was substantial, with cast-iron columns, steel
beams, and heavy timber floor joists. The design was notable among Fisher's
later buildings, but the newspaper reports of the building focused more on the
strength of its floors, reportedly capable of supporting loads of 500 pounds per
square foot, rather than on the architectural character of the project.[101]

An Opera House for Seattle

Through the course of 1890 downtown Seattle was transformed. Although
construction had been initiated in 1889, it was 1890 before most of the new
buildings began to reach their full size. The new commercial core began to fill
out and by early 1891 much of the explosion of post-fire construction had been
completed. It was becoming clear that the former commercial core had
expanded both up and out. The Pioneer Building and the New York Building
at seven stories were among the tallest new structures, but several others were
reaching six stories and most of the new buildings in the commercial core would

SEATTLE OPERA HOUSE BUILDING
SEATTLE. WASHINGTON
ADLER AND SULLIVAN ARCHITECTS
• CHICAGO ILLS

5.38 Adler and Sullivan,
Seattle Opera House
project, 1890 (unbuilt)

Inland Architect *16/8 (Jan.
1891)*

rise to at least three or four. Similarly the commercial center had previously
been focused around the intersection of Yesler, Commercial, and Front, but now
it stretched north almost to Pike, and north of Yesler it was even beginning to
spread east of Second. There were still vacant sites in the business district;
many of these would be filled in over the next several years. But the evidence
of the fire had largely disappeared and in its place stood a new urban center.

In early 1891 a Chicago printer published a panoramic "bird's eye view" of
Seattle, subtitled "Eighteen Months After the Great Fire." (See Fig. 6.1) The
lithograph presented an aerial view of the new city drawn from the southwest
and centered on the rebuilt commercial core. In the custom of the time, to allow
the view to remain up-to-date for a few years, the artist actually looked into the
future. Projects incomplete in December 1890 when the view was drawn, including the Bailey Building, New York Building, Yesler Building, and others, were
nonetheless shown as finished. Several projects which were planned but
unbuilt were also drawn in. One of these projects was a new Seattle Opera House.
(Fig. 5.38) In late 1890, confidence in the Seattle Opera House project was
running high, but the building never actually proceeded beyond its foundation. The Opera House was one victim of the worsening economy of late 1890
and early 1891—a period of economic troubles which drew the first phase of
Seattle's post-fire construction to a close.

Although the reconstruction of Seattle's commercial core was centered on the building of new business blocks for offices, stores, and hotels, interest also developed in the building of new places of entertainment. The Frye Opera House had been destroyed by the 6 June fire, and on 18 July 1889, a replacement building by John Nestor was reported in the *Post-Intelligencer*, but as the rebuilding proceeded and the scale of the new commercial district began to be evident, Seattle's business leaders began to aspire to symbols of metropolitan achievement. One of these symbols was a new grand opera house.

The Opera House was first discussed in early October 1889.[102] Business leaders Thomas Burke, William Bailey, and Thomas Ewing, who had successfully promoted the Rainier Hotel, were the primary instigators of the project. Articles of incorporation for the Seattle Operahouse Company (the first of three corporations created to build the Opera House) were filed on 4 December 1889. According to published reports, the company was created "to build an opera-house and to equip and manage the same, and to build and conduct a hotel and restaurant in connection with the theatre, or otherwise; to purchase and acquire real estate and to borrow money." The capital stock authorized totaled $250,000 to be sold in 2,500 shares at $100 each.[103] The trustees of the corporation were Burke, Bailey, Ewing, John Leary, and Amos Brown. The two most involved were Burke, who served as president for the corporation, and Bailey, who served as secretary. Burke acted for the corporation in matters of design and construction, and all correspondence with the architects was carried out in his name.[104]

The papers did not mention the Opera House again until May 1890, probably because Burke and Bailey were deeply involved in their own building projects. On 25 May the *Post-Intelligencer* reported that negotiations had been concluded for a quarter-block site, measuring 180 feet by 108 feet, at the corner of Second and University. According to Bailey, site preparation was to begin by June, with some portions of the building ready by winter and the rest completed the following spring at a total cost of $200,000.[105] No architect was mentioned in this report. A report on 19 June indicated that work had begun on the site. Occupants of the property had been notified to move. An existing residence on the site was demolished and some grading work was evidently carried out by the beginning of August.[106]

From the first, the Opera House trustees were willing to look beyond Seattle for an architect. A brief announcement in the 15 November 1889 issue of *California Architect and Building News* reported that an open national competition would soon be announced for the project.[107] However by mid-1890, Burke was in touch with Chicago architects Adler and Sullivan. Burke had already shown a personal knowledge of Burnham and Root's architecture in Chicago in his correspondence with Elmer Fisher regarding the Burke Building, so he would also have known the work of Adler and Sullivan. The fame of Adler and Sullivan's Chicago Auditorium, which opened 9 December 1889, was also a contributing factor.[108] Not only did the Auditorium establish Adler and Sullivan as leading architects in the field of theater design, but the building also incorporated a hotel, restaurants, and retail shops, features which the Seattle investors sought. In addition, Adler and Sullivan's practice was already expanding into the West and the Pueblo (Colorado) Opera House, a project similar in scale to Seattle's, that had been commissioned in 1888, was nearing completion in mid-1890.[109]

By late July 1890, Adler and Sullivan were evidently under contract because Louis Sullivan traveled to Seattle in early August. Sullivan stayed the night of 2 August in Spokane Falls (now Spokane) and telegraphed Burke of his arrival in Seattle on 3 August and of his intention to see Burke the following day.[110] Sullivan met with the trustees for several hours daily from 4 to 8 August. He also exhibited photographs of the Chicago Auditorium and spoke to the newspapers. Asked about Seattle, he stated: "It's very much like Chicago. I can emphatically say that I like Seattle very much. It resembles Chicago in the bustle and activity on the streets. I was prepared to see a pretty lively town, but the reality passes any expectations and you really have a Chicago on a small scale. Your people go about with a 'get-there-or-bust' air which is peculiar to Chicago."[111] Asked about Seattle architecture, he said the city had "some very fine buildings" and "some worthless ones." On 9 August Sullivan left Seattle. In a lengthy article about the design, the *Post-Intelligencer* stated: "The plans of the new theater were finally decided upon . . . yesterday. The cost of the building will be $325,000, and it will be the finest theater west of the Rocky Mountains."[112] The paper described the scheme at length, indicating that the auditorium and stage measuring 130 feet by 72 feet, with a seating capacity between 1,200 and 1,250, would be toward the interior of the block and a five-story business building would occupy the street frontage. Above the entrance facing Second Street, a tower would rise to a height of 170 feet with an observation platform at the top. The exterior would be stone and the sloped roof Spanish tile. The interior was characterized as "a dream of artistic beauty." Sullivan was quoted as saying the building might be constructed in sixteen months once the drawings were complete. The trustees indicated that excavation of the site would begin immediately.

On 16 August, the *Telegraph* reported,

> Within six weeks Architect Sullivan who planned the celebrated Auditorium of Chicago will have completed the designs of the grand new Seattle Operahouse, which is to be built by a stock company under the supervision of W. E. Bailey. It will be one of the most important structures in the West. Laborers are at present engaged in excavating and grading the site at the southeast corner of Second and University streets and the foundation will be laid during the first part of September. The estimated cost is $325,000. The structure will be built of gray stone and will be 180 feet long, 108 feet deep and five stories high. It will compare favorably in size and splendor with the finest theatres of the large cities in the East.[113]

From Seattle, Sullivan went on to visit the firm's projects in Salt Lake City and Pueblo, so his trip was not completed until late that month. On 28 August he wrote to Burke of his return to Chicago and the initiation of work on preliminary plans. Other correspondence concerning the size of the property fol-

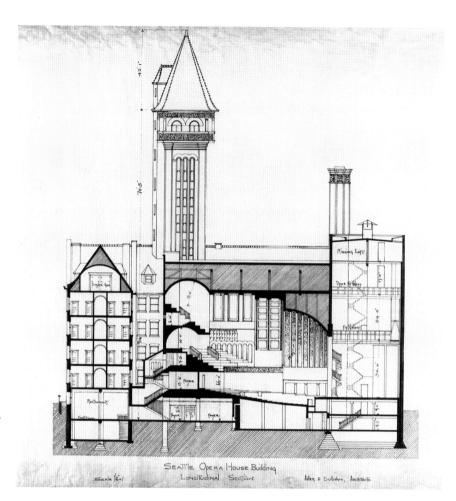

5.39 Seattle Opera House, section

University of Minnesota Libraries, Northwest Architectural Archives, St. Paul, Minnesota

lowed in September.[114] On 13 September, Burke released a letter and telegram from Adler and Sullivan for publication. The letter, dated 8 September, reported that plans had "pretty well matured." Adler and Sullivan indicated a decision to proceed directly to working drawings on the Opera House while awaiting Burke's comments on the rest of the design. The paper further reported, "It is our present belief that within ten days our Mr. Rebb [meaning Bebb] will leave for Seattle carrying sufficient with him to make a start on the operahouse part." The telegram, dated 13 September, indicated that floor plans would be sent the following day.[115]

Precisely what plans were sent is unknown, although it seems likely that they were similar to a set of five preliminary design drawings now held by the Northwest Architectural Archives of the University of Minnesota. These drawings include floor plans for the first, second, fourth, and sixth floors, as well as a longitudinal section.[116] (Figs. 5.39, 5.40) The rapidity with which these plans were produced may be accounted for by the degree to which the scheme was resolved while Sullivan was in Seattle and the similarity of the design to that of the Pueblo Opera House. In both schemes, the auditorium was placed against the interior corner of the site and the commercial uses occupied the zone along the street fronts. Minor differences resulted from the smaller site and sloping

5.40a,b,c Seattle Opera
House, plans

*University of Minnesota
Libraries, Northwest
Architectural Archives,
St. Paul, Minnesota*

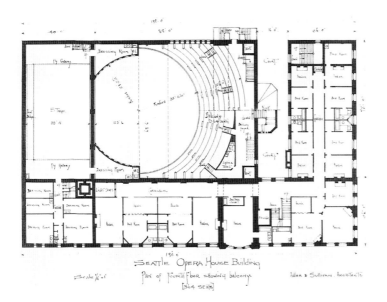

Fourth floor

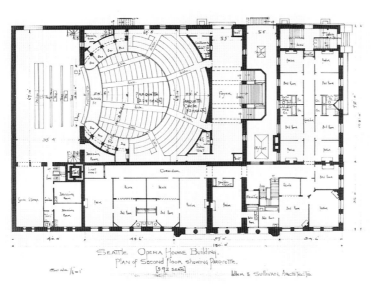

Second floor

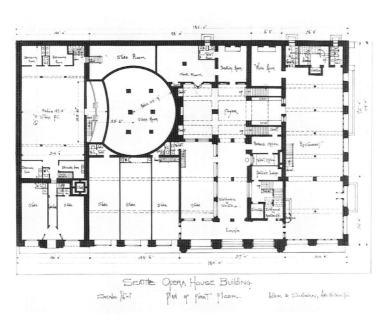

First floor

grades in Seattle. In addition, the Seattle plans proposed 1,256 seats in contrast to the 993 provided at the Pueblo Opera House.

By 11 October 1890, Adler and Sullivan's building superintendent had arrived in Seattle. Charles Herbert Bebb (1858–1942), whose background was in engineering and fireproofing design, had been hired by Adler and Sullivan near the end of the Chicago Auditorium construction as a superintending architect and soon rose to the position of Chief Superintendent.[117] Bebb was described in the *Telegraph* as "a comparatively young man of pleasing appearance and excellent address." The article went on to quote Bebb at length about the Opera House:

'The building will be as substantial and elegant as money can make it. It will have all the modern improvements . . . and will be equal to any theatre in the country. Our firm has long been especially employed in theatre construction, and the Seattle Operahouse obtains the benefits of the results of their large experience. It will have a seating capacity of 1200 people, and will be the best ventilated and heated house in the country, while we know that its acoustic properties will be perfect.

'The stage and stage-fittings will have the most recent improvements, the seating will be commodious, the foyers large and inviting and as to exits, if possible need should arise, the 1200 people can vacate the building in two minutes so numerous and so well-arranged are the doors and passages.

'The apartments house, which will occupy the other portion of the building, will be so separated from the theatre hall by the formation of the walls that even if it were possible that the hotel should be destroyed by fire, the theatre might be saved.

'The stone face of the building will be massive and imposing. The tower, 250 feet high, with its observatory of great scope, will be one of the features of the building. The cost will be about $250,000.'[118]

Work on the foundations began the following week, but construction never proceeded beyond the excavations. The 15 November failure of Baring Brothers and Company, the great British financial house, halted construction. In 1890, a variety of economic factors led European investors to begin withdrawing funds from the United States. This in turn led to a severe tightening of the American money market, and by the fall of 1890 interest rates rose to extraordinary levels (at times credit was virtually suspended), which had already begun to delay some projects in Seattle. The announcement of the Baring failure shattered confidence, led to a decline in stock prices, and drove some businesses into bankruptcy. The American economy did not really recover until August 1891 when exports of American crops following poor harvests in Europe led to an improved situation.[119]

The Opera House project began without full funding in place. Although the project would be unable to proceed, this was not immediately apparent. Charles Bebb remained in Seattle through mid-December, but finally returned to Chicago.[120] Adler and Sullivan submitted drawings for publication in expectation that construction would proceed. These appeared in *Inland Architect* in January 1891.[121] Subsequent correspondence between Burke and Adler and Sullivan evidently dealt with payment on invoices, and the full architectural fee of $7,500 was paid in May.[122] Burke continued to seek financing, but by late spring it was evident that the project would not go forward. Bebb continued to correspond with Burke, and as late as 1892 expressed hope that the Opera House might be built, but it was not to be.[123] Later biographers of Louis Sullivan described the project as one of the "office tragedies" of 1890.[124] The termination of the project was also a loss for Seattle.

Commercial Architecture after the Panic of 1890

The economic stringency of 1890–91 not only ended plans for a large opera house, but also slowed all post-fire commercial construction. Seattle, like other rapidly building cities in the American West, was dependent on investment from the East and from Europe. When, as a result of financial difficulties elsewhere, European investors began to sell off their American securities in 1890, interest rates rose and money became tight. The West felt the effects most strongly because the region was dependent on a continuing flow of outside investment. With high interest rates and a loss of confidence, borrowing proved impossible and construction gradually came to a halt. Projects under way were finished if financing was already in place; other projects were temporarily delayed; and still others could not even begin construction because credit was unavailable. Early 1891 was a slow time for architects and contractors. Unlike 1889 and 1890, no optimism was expressed about the coming building season. On 2 April the *Post-Intelligencer* called attention to the relative absence of building and noted that almost all the new projects in Seattle were residences.[125] Construction continued on many of the large post-fire business blocks that were still unfinished. Some structures, however, such as Henry Yesler's new block, were temporarily roofed over and construction on these did not resume until the economy improved.

In March 1892 Thomas Burke predicted "better times." He indicated that money would soon be available from European investors and he also argued that the completion of the Great Northern Railroad would boost Seattle's economy.[126] But the value of new construction in 1892 continued to decline. In January 1893, the *Post-Intelligencer* reported that over $13 million worth of new construction had been put into place since the fire. But over $10 million of this had been spent in 1889 and 1890, and just over $3 million in 1891 and 1892.[127]

At the same time, a noticeable shift occurred in the architectural character of the new buildings. First, although the economic stringency of late 1890 and early 1891 was lessened thereafter, the impact of the recession continued to be felt in architecture and construction. The buildings of the years 1891 to 1894 never approached the same scale as the largest projects of the immediate post-fire period. Further, the buildings of these years generally showed more restrained embellishment, as the impact of the financial problems required more economical buildings. Second, the beginning of the decline of the Richardsonian Romanesque mode began to be apparent. Many buildings built from 1891 to 1894 were lighter in color than the earlier buildings as light-colored stone and white and buff brick began to be commonly used. The buildings in Seattle appear to be part of a general tendency toward lighter buildings that developed in American architecture at this time. The number of Romanesque designs that appeared in American architectural magazines had peaked in 1889 and 1890 and declined thereafter. The initial development of academic eclecticism emphasized classicizing designs and these became more common in the professional journals. The highly classical buildings of the 1893 World's Columbian Exposition began to be published in the architectural press in 1892, and these too were influential. Fine Richardsonian Romanesque buildings continued to be built, but the mix of projects reflected the changing direction of American architectural design.

The economic uncertainty and lack of new work placed severe pressure on Seattle's architectural offices. Firms that a year or two before had been unable to keep up with the flow of new commissions now faced the prospect of little or no work. As a result, the years after 1890 were marked by a shake-up in many of Seattle's architectural practices. When construction did resume in 1891, the landscape of the architectural profession of the city had changed.

A shift in the leadership of the architectural community in Seattle became inevitable when Elmer Fisher decided to retire. Fisher's practice had been in slow decline for nearly a year. Although he had received several major commissions in 1890, the State Building for Schwabacher Brothers was his last large building. In May 1891, the local publication *Northwestern Real Estate and Building Review* celebrated Fisher's achievements in an article titled "Fifty-Four Buildings Designed in 18 Months by One Man," and characterized him as one of the "architects of the highest attainments in their profession."[128] Although the article claimed that Fisher was involved in the design of "a great many more" structures, most of the work that had been under way was finished and few new buildings were actually on the drawing board. His name last appeared in the practicing architects' listing in the *Post-Intelligencer* on 10 August 1891. Fisher had invested in Seattle property himself, as the developer of the Abbott Hotel (1889–90, destroyed) at Third and Pike and the Fisher Building (1890, destroyed) on South Second between Washington and Main, and was a partner in a company that distributed steam to downtown office blocks.[129] (Fig. 5.41) In the next city directory he listed no occupation, only his residence, but advertising at the time identified him as "Proprietor, Abbott Hotel."

Fisher's practice passed into control of his draftsman, Emil DeNeuf (d. 1915). About DeNeuf's background nothing has been discovered. He had arrived in Seattle in 1889 and worked thereafter in Fisher's office. His name began to appear in the architects' listing in the newspaper on 1 September 1891, just a

few weeks after Fisher's listing ended. DeNeuf never achieved the preeminent position that had been held by Fisher, but when Henry Yesler decided to proceed with his unfinished building on the west side of Pioneer Place, he did turn to Fisher's successor.[130]

On 24 April 1892, the *Post-Intelligencer* announced that two additional floors would be added to the Yesler Building. DeNeuf was responsible for redesigning the project so that two floors could be added immediately and three more when the economy allowed. But, once the second and third floors were nearly complete in early September, Yesler decided to proceed with the final three floors as well. The project was incomplete at Yesler's death on 16 December, but was pushed to completion by 31 July 1893. In 1895 the building was sold to the Mutual Life Insurance Company, acquiring the name by which it is known today.[131]

As completed by DeNeuf, the Yesler Building (1889, 1892–93, altered) was a symmetrical six-story business block measuring 100 feet along Front and only 51 feet along Yesler. The first floor and basement were divided into retail shops with a bank at the primary corner. A centrally located arched entrance led to the stairs and elevator to the five office floors. The first floor, designed by Fisher, was heavily rusticated red sandstone; the five upper floors by DeNeuf were a pale yellow brick, with flush stone trim. (Figs. 5.42, 5.43) The rather florid detail intended by Fisher was omitted in favor of a more restrained treatment. Fisher's design divided the building into five clearly expressed bays, but DeNeuf retained only the slight projection of the two corner bays. The omission of the central bay and the division of the building by horizontal bands

5.41 Elmer H. Fisher, Abbott Hotel, 1889–90 (destroyed)

Manuscripts, Special Collections, University Archives Division, University of Washington Libraries, photo by Anders Wilse, UW4663

5.42 Elmer H. Fisher/Emil DeNeuf, Yesler Building (Mutual Life Building), 1890, 1892–93 (altered)

Museum of History and Industry, Seattle Historical Society Collection, 12422

5.43 Yesler Building, detail (altered)

Manuscripts, Special Collections, University Archives Division, University of Washington Libraries, photo by Asahel Curtis, 4100

above the third and fifth floors gave it a much more unified design than Fisher's initial scheme. (The division at the third floor reflects the intended two-stage sequence of construction.) However, the two corner bays still extended above the cornice, resulting in an odd appearance.[132] The source for DeNeuf's design may have been the Richardson, Roberts, Byrne, and Co. warehouse by Eckel and Van Brunt that appeared in *Inland Architect* in May 1892. (See Fig. 3.12)

DeNeuf's other commercial projects were nearby.[133] His Lowman and Hanford Building (1892, altered), facing Pioneer Place, was designed as a seven-story office block, but initially only four floors were built. (Fig. 5.44) The project was begun in April 1892 and completed the following September.[134] The relatively plain exterior was constructed of light orange brick from St. Louis. DeNeuf was also responsible for the redesign of the Schwabacher Building after it was partially destroyed by fire in June 1892. Schwabacher Brothers suffered a reported loss of $425,000, and for the next year was headquartered in the State Building. When the company finally decided to rebuild in February 1893, it was decided to restore the original facade by Fisher facing Yesler, but facing Commercial, where the fire had been more severe, DeNeuf created a new

facade in cream-colored brick.[135] The new fourth floor featured three groups
of round-arched windows with detailing now drawn from Renaissance rather
than Romanesque sources. (Fig. 5.45) The fire was important as well in that it
was limited to a single building and demonstrated the success of the building
code adopted in 1889.

The year 1891 also witnessed the break-up of the Saunders and Houghton
partnership. The firm had not secured major downtown commercial commissions after 1889. They were successful in winning some institutional buildings
and residences, as well as several projects in other Washington communities,
but the economic recession left them in a difficult position. William Bailey,
their most important commercial client, suffered financial reverses and was
slow to pay architectural fees due to the firm. In mid-September 1891, when
the partnership was dissolved, Saunders returned to Massachusetts for several
months.[136] Houghton took over the practice and completed projects such as
the Bailey Building that were still under construction. Bailey's financial problems continued and in June 1892 Houghton sued Bailey for unpaid fees for
work on the Bailey Building.[137] Saunders returned to Seattle in 1892, but the

partnership was not resumed. With one exception, neither Saunders nor Houghton played a significant role as an architect of new commercial structures between 1891 and 1894.

The sole exception was the new Seattle Theater and Rainier Club (1892, destroyed) that Charles Saunders designed after his return to Seattle. Once it became clear that Adler and Sullivan's Seattle Opera House project was unlikely to proceed, several groups made theater proposals.[138] On 12 April 1892, the Seattle Theater Company announced plans for a new theater on a site measuring 120 by 120 feet at the northeast corner of Third and Cherry. Within ten days it was explained that the site would be shared by a new building for the Rainier Club, and that both would be designed by Saunders. Construction of the joint project began in June and the theater opened 5 December.[139] The four-story theater block, which had little need of natural light, was positioned at the back of the site away from Third, with the lobby facing Cherry. The three-story Rainier Club occupied the entire Third Street frontage with the exception of the first floor at the corner which was the primary theater entrance. Saunders's building was constructed of a light-colored pressed brick and the restrained detailing was classical in character. (Figs. 5.46, 5.47)

Fisher's retirement and the dissolution of the Saunders and Houghton partnership might have presented the opportunity for John Parkinson or William Boone to assume a leadership position in the continuing rebuilding of downtown, but the relatively small number of commissions limited their actual impact,

5.46 Charles Saunders, Seattle Theater and Rainier Club, 1892 (destroyed)

Manuscripts, Special Collections, University Archives Division, University of Washington Libraries, photo by Hester, 10070

and both architects played more significant roles as designers of institutional buildings outside the commercial core. The difficulties these architects encountered also reflected the challenging circumstances of the years after 1890.

William Boone attempted to strengthen his practice by forming the partnership Boone and Willcox with William H. Willcox (1832–1929) in December 1890.[140] Willcox brought more than thirty years experience in architecture to the new firm. Born and raised in Brooklyn, he first practiced architecture in New York in the 1850s and during the Civil War drew maps for the Union army. By 1871 he was working in Chicago, and after 1873 he was again heading his own architectural practice and developing a specialty in church design. About 1879, Willcox won the commission for the Nebraska State House in Lincoln and he practiced in Nebraska for several years while superintending the state capitol construction. Although the Nebraska State House was not completed until 1888, Willcox moved to St. Paul, Minnesota, in 1882, where he again rapidly achieved success designing churches, institutional buildings, and residences. In 1886, Willcox formed a partnership with a younger architect, Clarence Johnston, who had attended MIT for one year, and Willcox and Johnson soon became prominent practicing in a Richardsonian Romanesque mode. By 1890, however, the partnership was dissolved and Willcox soon moved to Seattle.[141]

Willcox brought a wide-ranging background in architecture, although his primary focus had been institutional rather than commercial structures, and he clearly played a role in the diversification of Boone's practice. In February 1891, when the Minnesota-based *Northwest Magazine* presented the rebuilding and growth of Seattle, Boone and Willcox was the only architectural firm promi-

nently featured. Their profile, titled "Leading Seattle Architects," cited the achievements of each individually and then featured their joint practice as "beyond doubt the strongest architectural firm on the Pacific Coast."[142]

Appropriately, the first major project of Boone and Willcox was the new building of the Plymouth Congregational Church (1891–92, destroyed), located at Third and University, announced in March 1891.[143] (See Fig. 6.33) But Boone and Willcox proved less successful in their commercial work. After it became clear that the Adler and Sullivan Opera House project would not go forward, Henry Yesler and D. K. Baxter commissioned Boone and Willcox to design an opera house to be sited at Yesler and South Fourth (now Third). In May 1891, the *Post-Intelligencer* reported that the $250,000 project, incorporating an opera house, music hall, and hotel, would begin immediately. Although the site was cleared and excavations were begun, no construction ever took place.[144] A decade later the site remained vacant. Boone and Willcox also designed a mid-block commercial building for Cyrus Walker (one of Boone's clients for the Marshall-Walker Building) on South Second (now Occidental) adjacent to the Korn Building. Although a four-story brick and stone structure was described in the newspaper, only the first story of the Walker Building (1891–92) was constructed.[145] Boone and Willcox's one successful large commercial commission was the J. M. Frink Building (also known as the Washington Iron Works Building and later as the Washington Shoe Building) (1891–92, altered), a massive four-story wholesale warehouse of plainly detailed red brick at the southeast corner of South Second (now Occidental) and Jackson.[146] (Fig. 5.48)

5.48 Boone and Willcox, J. M. Frink Building, (Washington Iron Works Building; Washington Shoe Building), 1891–92 (altered)

Manuscripts, Special Collections, University Archives Division, University of Washington Libraries, photo by Asahel Curtis, 19584

John Parkinson's later commercial buildings were located on Front Street at the north end of the expanding downtown area. Beginning in spring 1892, he was responsible for two two-story brick blocks for J. G. Kenyon, one at the corner of Front and Madison, completed in October 1892, and one on the east side of Front at Seneca. The second building was intended as a six-story structure, but never went beyond the first floor as Kenyon died on 22 December, and the Panic of 1893 brought construction to a close.[147] More significant were Parkinson's two buildings on the west side of Front north of Seneca. The first, the Seattle Athletic Club Building (1892–93, destroyed), was a building which Parkinson developed himself. Like Elmer Fisher, Parkinson had begun to invest in Seattle property. He acquired the site at the northwest corner of Front and Seneca in early November 1892 and his projected business block was reported in the *Post-Intelligencer* on 4 November.[148] Because of the difference in elevation between Front Street and Post Alley, the building was seven stories tall, but only four floors above Front Street. (Fig. 5.49) The Seattle Athletic Club leased the three floors below Front and these were constructed with a natatorium at the Post Alley level, a gymnasium on the next two floors, and other athletic club rooms including a billiard room, reading room, and locker rooms. The floor opening on Front included retail stores, and the space above was leased as offices. The building was completed by August 1893, at a cost of $65,000.[149]

In February 1893, while the Athletic Club Building was under construction, the Dobson and Denton Building (1893, destroyed), which occupied the lot between the Athletic Club and the Gilmore and Kirkman Building/Arlington Hotel (by Elmer Fisher), was announced.[150] Also by Parkinson, this structure filled in the only empty space on the block such that a complete street-wall stretched from Seneca to University along the west side of Front. (Fig. 5.50) Completed in October 1893, this new block was leased to the Arlington Hotel and provided additional hotel rooms and support spaces. The Athletic Club Building, the Dobson and Denton Building, and both buildings for J. G. Kenyon were heavy timber construction with exterior walls of light-colored sandstone and white pressed brick. The horizontal divisions on the front street facades of the Athletic Club and the Dobson and Denton Building corresponded to the points where the wall thickness changed in accordance with the building ordinance. The detailing was classical in character and shows some similarities to the detailing of Saunders's Seattle Theater.

The lower level of demand for architectural services after 1890 provided few openings for any new firms to emerge, but several new architects saw fleeting success and designed commercial work of particularly notable quality. Albert Wickersham, who had come to Seattle in 1889 as supervising architect for the Denny Hotel, was in independent practice by 1892.[151] He designed the Dexter Horton Bank (1892, now Maynard Building), located at the northwest corner of Commercial and Washington.[152] This five-story block of Bellingham Bay sandstone and St. Louis buff-colored pressed brick was praised by Sally Woodbridge and Roger Montgomery: "The most sophisticated of the Chicago School buildings in the area, it is true to the Sullivanesque principle of weav-

5.49 John Parkinson,
Seattle Athletic Club
Building, 1892–93
(destroyed)

*Manuscripts, Special
Collections, University
Archives Division, University
of Washington Libraries,
photo by Asahel Curtis, 1031*

5.50 John Parkinson,
Dobson & Denton Build-
ing (Arlington Hotel
Annex), 1893 (destroyed)

*Manuscripts, Special
Collections, University
Archives Division, University
of Washington Libraries,
photo by Asahel Curtis, 1080*

5.51 Albert Wickersham, Dexter Horton Bank (Maynard Building), 1892

Museum of History and Industry, PEMCO Webster and Stevens Collection, 83.10.7086

ing spandrel and pier to create a refined and structurally expressive design."[153] (Fig. 5.51) Certainly this was among the most knowledgeable of the Seattle interpretations of the Romanesque mode as developed by commercial architects in Chicago, but it would appear to be related most directly to the work of Burnham and Root. (For example, see Fig. 4.30.) Still, even with this success, Wickersham did not win other significant commissions.

Similarly, Arthur Bishop Chamberlin (1865–1933), who had worked in Seattle as a draftsman since 1890, initiated his independent practice at this time. Chamberlin had worked as a draftsman for Long and Kees in Minneapolis and developed his drawing skills under the tutelage of Harvey Ellis, the leading architectural delineator. Chamberlin arrived in Seattle in 1890 and over the next three years worked first for Saunders and Houghton, then for John Parkinson, and briefly for William Boone. His skills as a delineator in pen and ink were particularly noteworthy as he was responsible for well over half of the illustrations of Seattle buildings that appeared in *American Architect* and *Northwestern Architect* between 1890 and 1894.[154] In June 1893, Chamberlin was selected as architect for John Collins's new project, the Collins Building (1893–94), located at the southeast corner of Second and James. Construction

5.52 Arthur Bishop
Chamberlin, Collins
Building, 1893–94

*Museum of History and
Industry, Seattle Historical
Society Collection, 17357*

proceeded rapidly and the building was mostly completed by the fall.[155] A five-story block, measuring 80 by 108 feet, this provided space for stores facing Second and offices above. After May 1894, the city's growing library occupied the top floor. The interior was divided into two unequal portions by a fire wall and a column grid of cast iron and heavy timber that did not align with the exterior bay system. Notable for the quality of its brickwork, the Collins Building read as a coherent block with restrained detail, its fenestration arranged under a regular arcade of five bays on Second and seven on James. (Fig. 5.52) The first floor was of stone; the classically detailed cast-iron columns at the Second Street storefronts seem the only discordant note. The design shows the clear influence of Burnham and Root's Fidelity Trust Company Building in Tacoma (see Fig. 4.33), and more distantly of Adler and Sullivan's Walker Warehouse. Unfortunately, like Wickersham, Chamberlin won few other commercial commissions.

The firm of Skillings and Corner enjoyed slightly more success in 1893 and 1894. Warren Porter Skillings (1860–1939) was born and raised in Portland, Maine, and had attended Bowdoin College from 1877 to 1880. He was employed as an architectural draftsman in the Boston area from the early 1880s until

1889, then moved to Seattle soon after the fire. He served as supervising architect on the California Block (1889–90, destroyed), at the corner of Front and Columbia, by the San Francisco architects Copeland and Pierce, but otherwise his early Seattle projects were primarily residences.[156] By late 1891 he began to receive a few commercial commissions such as the Dearborn Building (1891–92, destroyed) on South Third (now Second Avenue South).[157] Skillings's work began to attract more attention after his design was selected in early 1892 for the Washington State pavilion at the Chicago World's Columbian Exposition.[158] In September 1892 he formed a partnership with James N. Corner (1862–1919), who had just come to Seattle from his native Boston.[158] Skillings and Corner were finalists in the British Columbia Provincial Parliament Buildings competition in early 1893, and thereafter they began to secure more significant commercial commissions in Seattle.[160]

In mid-January 1893, the *Post-Intelligencer* reported that Skillings and Corner were at work on a new Watson Squire Building (1893, destroyed), a relatively plain three-story brick block located at the northwest corner of Main and South Third (now Second Avenue South).[161] This provided space for stores at the ground level and a hotel on the upper floors. They were also selected as designers of the Coal, Lumber, and Mineral Palace (1893, destroyed), a temporary exhibition pavilion that opened in early July in Pioneer Place.[162] This was erected as part of the city's celebration of the opening of the Great Northern Railroad line to Seattle in 1893. However, their more significant contributions to the city were the Union Trust Block and the Rialto. The Union Trust Block (1893), located at the southwest corner of Main and South Second (now Occidental), was a four-story wholesale business block, described in the *Post-Intelligencer* as "Italian Renaissance" in style, announced in mid-March.[163] Built at a cost of $100,000, and completed the following October, this featured the use of heavy timber construction throughout in anticipation of the floor loads required for wholesale business use. The walls of white brick and the classical detailing may reflect Corner's input as his recent arrival in Seattle likely meant he brought direct experience of the new eclectic architecture in the East. (Fig. 5.53)

The last large commercial project by Skillings and Corner was the Rialto (1893–94, destroyed), a venture by Boston investor Herman Chapin. Initially identified as the Arcade Building, this retail block stretched 240 feet along the west side of Second between Madison and Spring. The cost, including the site, was $325,000. The Rialto, intended solely for retail stores, rose two stories above Second; the floor below Second was at the level of the alley, and an additional basement was included. When the building opened in March 1894, it was called a "Palace of Trade" and advertised "Forty Stores Under One Roof."[164] The building was constructed of brick faced with stucco, but the most conspicuous feature was the continuous cast iron and plate glass first floor for show windows along the sidewalk. (Fig. 5.54) The Rialto was part of the creation of the city's first fashionable shopping district. At the same time, John Leary and Cyrus Walker erected a temporary block-long building, just one story

5.53 Skillings and Corner,
Union Trust Block, 1893

*Museum of History and
Industry, Wilse Collection,
88.33.78*

high and forty-five feet wide, for retail stores on the opposite side of Second;
designed by William Boone (whose partnership with William Willcox ended
in June 1892) and costing less than $18,000, this opened in September
1893.[165]

The shift to retail construction reflects the impact of over-building in the
commercial office market in Seattle. As early as July 1889, the *Post-Intelligencer*
had reported rumors "that if the brick buildings now projected are erected, it
will be difficult to rent the offices and lodging rooms they will contain."[166]
Although the paper responded by characterizing this as a "great fallacy," after
the business slow-down in 1891, offices had proved more difficult to lease. The
financial difficulties of William Bailey have already been noted, but others were
facing problems as well. Lenders foreclosed on the Seattle National Bank
Building on 18 March 1893, two months before the string of bank failures that
triggered the Panic of 1893.[167] On 17 April in an article discussing the new
retail store projects, the *Post-Intelligencer* noted that owners now believed
that big office blocks would not pay, but that stores would be successful.[168]

In early April 1893, the paper looked forward to "very bright prospects" for
construction in Seattle for the year.[169] But just a month later, headlines began
to focus on major bank failures across the United States. Articles on bank runs
began appearing on 10 May, and almost every day for the next week the paper

5.54 Skillings and Corner, Rialto (Frederick and Nelson Building), 1893–94 (destroyed)

Manuscripts, Special Collections, University Archives Division, University of Washington Libraries, photo by Asahel Curtis, 34144

carried stories of bank failures in cities including Chicago, Milwaukee, Minneapolis, Denver, Indianapolis, and New York.[170] By 17 May the term "business crisis" was being used to describe the condition of the national economy, and through the following month articles on "business troubles" continued to appear; the next month the paper used the phrase "hard times."[171] By July, the impact of the economic slump on commercial construction in Seattle began to be felt. On 17 July 1893, Edwin Houghton summarized the situation the city's architects were facing. He indicated that construction under way would be completed, but new commercial buildings would have to wait for the economy to improve.[171] In fact, it would be more than five years before commercial construction would resume in Seattle.

VI

A City of Neighborhoods
The Network of Public Institutions, 1889–1895

We have had saloon booms, and real estate booms, and now, for God's sake, let's have a school boom.
— Judge J. R. Lewis, Chairman of Seattle School Board, 14 January 1882

Building in Seattle after June 1889 encompassed much more than the commercial core. Although downtown reconstruction after the fire was the primary focus of attention, the city grew outward into areas which had previously been unsettled, and began to develop the residential neighborhood patterns that would shape the form of Seattle through the first half of the twentieth century. As the city grew, residents supported the creation of the network of public institutions that promoted that pattern of neighborhood development.

The urban form of Seattle was influenced by multiple factors, chief among them topography and transportation. The Denny Party had relocated the new community to the shore of Elliott Bay in 1852 because a protected deep water anchorage was available relatively close to shore. As the city grew in the nineteenth century, the city center remained in the general area of the initial settlement and the heart of the new community after the 1889 fire was the new Public Square, later named Pioneer Place, at the intersection of Front/Commercial and Yesler. The waterfront was looked upon as an appropriate place for wharves and docks, sawmills, canneries, and similar facilities. Sawmills developed not only along Elliott Bay but also on Lake Union and Lake Washington. The relatively level land close to the water also became the location of railroads and related industrial development. As the city spread out in the 1880s and 1890s, residential neighborhoods climbed the hills, both to get away from the lower level industrial areas and associated sewage and drainage problems and to take advantage of the views. The topography of the city led, therefore, to the development of a pattern of individual residential areas that ringed the city's commercial core including such neighborhoods as First Hill, Denny Hill, Queen Anne, and West Seattle. (Fig. 6.1)

The other primary influence on urban form was transportation. Because Seattle's population had grown slowly until the 1880s, the city's expanding urban development was influenced from the first by the pattern of horse car, cable car, and streetcar lines. Cities which developed before the 1870s generally showed a compact urban form because they were "pedestrian cities"—most people moved about the city on foot. But cities began to spread out when horse

car lines provided improved public transport. Seattle's first horse car lines began service in 1884, and the construction of cable car lines, particularly appropriate in Seattle because of the city's hills, began in 1887, with service from downtown to Lake Washington on Yesler and Jackson first offered on 27 September 1888. Cable car construction from downtown to Lake Washington along Madison followed in 1890. Other cable car lines were developed along Front Street and James Street. The conversion of the city's horse car lines to electrified streetcar lines was initiated in 1891, and by the end of the decade, residential neighborhoods were expanding north to Green Lake, east to Lake Washington, south to Beacon Hill and the Rainier Valley, and across Elliott Bay to West Seattle. These streetcar and cable car lines made substantial tracts of undeveloped property accessible, and a pattern of single-family "streetcar suburbs" (which are now Seattle's urban neighborhoods) followed. Linear retail and commercial development generally paralleled the streetcar lines, giving each residential district a "neighborhood commercial center," although this pattern did not fully develop until the first decades of the twentieth century, and residential development took place in the adjacent areas. As a result, although Seattle did see some rowhouse construction, most residential construction was in the form of single-family houses, even in the late nineteenth century.

From 1885 to 1895, Seattle was hard-pressed to keep pace with urban growth, both as a result of immigration and as a result of physical expansion through

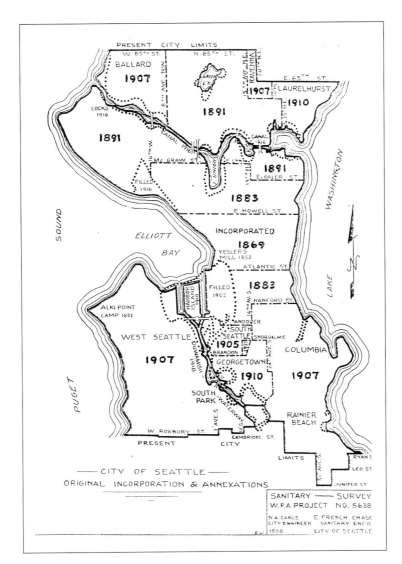

6.2 Annexation map showing growth of Seattle to 1938

Manuscripts, Special Collections, University Archives Division, University of Washington Libraries, UW4105

annexation. The initial city boundaries were at Howell Street on the north and Atlantic on the south, but in 1869 Seattle annexed areas north as far as McGraw and south as far as Andover. In 1891 the city limits expanded toward the north again, taking in all of Queen Anne and Magnolia and reaching as far as 85th Street north of Green Lake. (Fig. 6.2)

In this period, the city's population surged. In 1885 the city assessor's office had numbered the city's population at less than 10,000, but the 1890 census counted over 42,000 residents, and the assessor estimated the population in 1891 at 50,000 and in 1892 at 58,000.[1] In 1900 the census would tabulate over 82,000 residents in the city.

The rapid growth of Seattle exerted constant pressure on city leaders to expand a network of public institutions that had not even existed a decade before. The city's permanent fire department was created in late 1889 after the 6 June fire. By the next year five fire stations were being built in the city but residents in outlying neighborhoods were soon petitioning for more, even as city finances were increasingly strapped after 1891. Similarly, as late as 1888, the city had had only two large school buildings, but by the mid-1890s there would be more than ten large buildings in use. In the same period the state university relocated away from downtown, and proposals were made for an urban park system.[2]

Seattle's new public institutional buildings were generally built to meet the functional requirements of a particular use—for example, schools required classrooms and related instructional spaces as necessary for the educational program. However, beyond their basic functions, these public buildings played at least two other roles. For residents in the neighborhoods in which they were built, public buildings, especially schools, often played a significant role in establishing or strengthening neighborhood identity. At the same time, each building represented an emerging institutional system. New public buildings were important, therefore, to city leaders and citizens as manifestations of the growth of the metropolitan services provided by the city, and to individual neighborhoods as reflections of community character. Although usually simple in design, such buildings often featured symbolic elements (or even a degree of monumentality) that demonstrated their significance in the eyes of the general public as well as civic officials.

The design challenges faced by Seattle's architects in shaping the city's new institutional structures and residential architecture were different from those that guided their work in the commercial core. The city's new fire ordinance had few provisions limiting construction outside the downtown fire district. The material most readily available for construction in Seattle was wood, and other than foundations and basements, it could be used for almost every part of any building. Wood construction was much more affordable than masonry, so Seattle's new residences were almost all built of wood. The level of wealth simply did not yet exist in Seattle to build a street comparable to Prairie Avenue in Chicago or Summit Avenue in St. Paul. A few Seattle houses were built of brick or stone in the early 1890s, but these were truly exceptional. The same proved true of private institutions such as churches; although a few masonry structures were built, most new churches were built of wood. Public institutional buildings might also be built of wood. While the new fire department headquarters was a masonry structure, the other fire stations were wood frame. The Seattle School District oscillated back and forth between building in wood and building in brick.

With a broader range of construction materials available for Seattle's new institutional and residential buildings, Richardson's example and the Romanesque Revival, particularly as it had appeared in publication, provided few clear models for this architecture. Further, even if Seattle residents had been able to afford a masonry residential architecture, the appropriateness of Richardson's example would likely still have been in question. Even Van Rensselaer had commented unfavorably in her biography of Richardson on his urban residences, suggesting that most were inappropriately monumental, a point she also made in *Century Magazine*.[3] And, none of the other architects who were well published in the professional press of the period seemed to offer a coherent direction for wood construction. Although the emerging academic and the Arts and Crafts movements would both eventually offer a framework appropriate to residential design, neither had achieved ascendancy in Seattle by the boom years of the early 1890s. Thus, while the Richardsonian Romanesque offered Seattle's leading architects possible solutions for rebuilding the downtown core, the design tendencies these same architects applied in the outlying areas were much more diverse. In fact, the difficulties these architects had in addressing a non-masonry architecture indicates the limitations of Richardson's influence and the shortcomings of the Romanesque Revival as a national style.

The earlier Victorian modes, popular in Seattle until the early 1880s, had not entirely disappeared, but most projects by Seattle architects in the late 1880s and early 1890s presented stylistic directions including Queen Anne, both in its half-timbered and free classic versions, shingled "modern colonial" (now called "shingle-style"), and more literal use of historical, generally classical, detail. These modes were not perceived as distinct, but rather tended to blend at their edges; for example, a shingled Queen Anne work would not have been seen as radically different from a freely composed "modern colonial" design. The different combinations reflected the continuing tendency of architects trained in the Victorian period to experiment with multiple motifs and details.

In general, the leading architects in Seattle's neighborhood construction were those who were also leaders in the reconstruction of downtown. William Boone, Saunders and Houghton, and John Parkinson all played important roles in the creation of the new network of public institutional buildings. The one exception was Elmer Fisher. Although successful as a commercial architect, he proved unable to secure public building commissions, and he limited his residential practice to a few select clients. While these architects all demonstrated some mastery of Romanesque Revival commercial design, their institutional and residential work presents a much more uneven picture. While it is difficult to generalize, John Parkinson, who had experience in carpentry, proved a master of the Queen Anne, but experimented in other styles as well. The shingled buildings by Charles Saunders, who had come from New England, were Seattle's most knowledgeable interpretations of the "modern colonial"; but he, too, did not restrict himself to a single design approach.

Protecting the City from Fire

The difficulties faced by Seattle's architects in finding an appropriate mode of design for wood structures are evident in the seven new fire stations that were erected by the city between 1890 and 1895. Only the new headquarters building involved substantial masonry construction, and even there only the round-arched doors might be said to suggest Richardson's influence. The other six fire stations were similar to large houses and they reflected the then popular modes of Queen Anne, modern colonial, and, after the economic collapse, a very restrained classicism.

The decision by the Seattle city council to create a permanent "paid department" to fight fires can be seen as part of the general movement in late-nine-

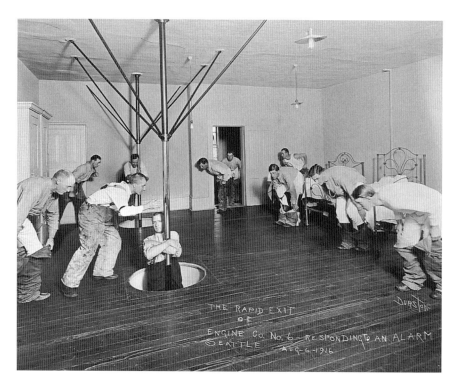

teenth-century cities toward the professionalization of fire fighting. The earlier
volunteer fire companies were seen as no longer capable of dealing with the
scale of fires that could erupt in the burgeoning urban centers. Professional
paid fire departments were created in St. Louis in 1857, in Baltimore in 1858,
in Boston in 1860, and in Philadelphia in 1871; New York created the first
full-time paid department in 1865.[4]

Ironically, Seattle's first fire station was destroyed in the June 1889 fire.
Seattle's first successful volunteer fire-fighting company had been formed in
1876, and in 1884 the city had moved to create an official fire department.[5]
But the 1880s were a period of dispute concerning fire fighting in the city. Some
argued that the city's water system was inadequate for fighting fires, others suggested there was inadequate equipment, and still others noted that the members of the department were demoralized. In 1888 the city council approved
salaries for drivers and engineers, but this included fewer than ten of the city's
approximately 380 firemen. In the first months after the June 1889 fire, debate
erupted over who was responsible for letting the fire get out of control, and
what steps should be taken to deal with such fires in the future. By August,
however, the management of the department had changed hands and the city
had approved purchase of several new fire engines as well as construction of
the city's first fireboat. Action was also taken to improve the municipal water
system. On 12 October, the *Post-Intelligencer* heralded the council's action,
which finally created a fully paid fire department, with the headline "Protection
at Last."[6] On 28 October, the council chose a new fire chief, and a week later
announced five new fire station sites for which designs would soon be invited
from Seattle's architects.[7]

6.4 Charles Saunders,
Engine House Number 6,
first floor; firefighters
responding to an alarm

*Museum of History and
Industry, Seattle Historical
Society Collection, 7841;
photographed 7 Aug. 1916*

Although Seattle's fire stations were of various sizes, they all accommodated similar programs and conformed to the general functional arrangement that had emerged as typical for American fire station construction in the post–Civil War period.[8] (Figs. 6.3, 6.4) The ground floor was typically given over to the storage of fire apparatus and the stabling and care of horses. The engine or apparatus room was placed at the front with equipment aligned with the entrance doors facing the street. Horse stalls, feeding troughs, and a harness or tack room were also provided. The upper floor primarily provided domestic quarters for the fire fighters. Quarters were typically plain, with the bunk room taking up most of the space. Officers often had separate rooms, and the rest of the floor might include a sitting room and feed storage, but these last spaces could also be on the first floor. In addition, by the 1880s, fire stations were beginning to include an array of unique equipment such as the firepole, which had been invented in 1878. Finally, most fire stations included a tower, primarily intended for hose drying, but also usually the location of a bell or siren and offering a lookout over the city. Of course, the tower also served a symbolic purpose, identifying the building as a civic structure and providing an opportunity for embellishment that the otherwise utilitarian program did not encourage.

The variations of scale and design among Seattle's fire stations reflected the differences in the equipment and fire companies that each was intended to house. The 29 October announcement of the new Seattle fire stations identified the five sites and provided a general description of the city's needs. More specifics were reported on 31 October.[9] The official request for design submittals was published on 5 November, and on 21 November, the *Post-Intelligencer* reported, "Half of the architects in the city are working on plans of a model fire engine house to be put up on Columbia Street."[10] Their designs were reviewed by the city council's Fire and Water Committee on 25 November and three firms were selected as designers for the five stations: Saunders and Houghton, Willis A. Ritchie, and Charles A. Alexander. Construction bids were let in early December. However, the poor bidding climate in 1889 and the winter rainy season delayed the buildings and construction contracts were not signed until February 1890. Three fire stations were completed in July and one in August, but the new headquarters was not finished until October.

Saunders and Houghton received the biggest prize, the $20,000 Fire Department Headquarters Building (1889–90, destroyed) located on Columbia between Sixth and Seventh.[11] The department headquarters was a three-story brick and stone structure of symmetrical design except for an offset tower. (Fig. 6.5) The ground floor provided four apparatus bays facing Columbia with space for vehicles including a hook and ladder truck, a hose wagon, a chemical engine (later a steam engine), and the fire chief's carriage, plus quarters for stabling and care of the horses. The second floor included a bunk room for three fire companies, plus other rooms for the city fire chief, chief engineer, and other necessary offices. The third floor served as an assembly room. The nearly square building had a hipped roof broken by a single dormer and the tower. The stone basement walls were carried up four feet above the first floor, providing a legible base for the red brick walls above. The symmetrical front facade featured four ten-foot-wide arched openings at the ground floor and a slightly projecting bay at the center of the second floor extending up to the third-floor dormer. The corbeled brick bands at the second floor and below the roof, the horizontal lines of the stone base and the eaves, and the generally horizontal proportions tied this to the ground. The one vertical exception was the tower, located near the back corner on the Sixth Street side of the building; thirteen feet square at the base, this rose to a height of 70 feet. The design seems unusually disciplined, with the offset tower the only element displaying the residual influence of the picturesque.

Saunders and Houghton also designed Engine House Number 2 (1889–90, destroyed) at the northeast corner of Third and Pine.[12] This two-story rectangular structure faced Pine Street and backed into the slope of Denny Hill. (Fig. 6.6) The two first-floor apparatus bays were designed for a steam engine and a hose wagon, with stable spaces for four horses behind. The second floor provided space adequate for sixteen men plus fire department offices. The wood building was clad in horizontal siding on the first floor and shingles above. The front composition featured arched openings of different sizes and a bulging round hose tower rising out of the second floor. This asymmetrical composition was somewhat tempered by horizontal bands and the slight overhang of the hipped roof. The building no doubt reflected Saunders's knowledge of the shingled "modern colonial" from his years in Massachusetts, and is similar in character to his design for the Rainier Hotel.

Willis A. Ritchie, whose background is discussed in detail in the next chapter, also won two fire station commissions. Although he had only arrived in

Seattle in July 1889. Ritchie's previous design experience in Kansas included
city buildings with provisions for fire fighters and their equipment. His first
Seattle fire station was Engine House Number 4 (1889–90, destroyed) at the
northeast corner of Fourth and Battery.[13] This building had three apparatus
bays, designed to house a steam engine, a hose wagon, and a hook and ladder
truck on the ground floor, with quarters for the firemen and offices on the second floor. The building was approximately square with a hipped roof. Clad in
horizontal siding at the ground floor and shingles above, this was similar to the
Saunders and Houghton design for Engine House Number 2, but Ritchie's odd

6.7 Willis A Ritchie,
Engine House Number 4,
1889–90 (destroyed)

*Museum of History and
Industry, Wilse Collection,
88.33.85*

juxtaposition of several different dormers, a tapered corner tower, and a central triangular gable was much more overtly picturesque. (Fig. 6.7)

Ritchie's second fire station was Chemical Engine House Number 2 (1889–90, destroyed), located on a triangular site at Terrace, 11th, and Broadway.[14] Designed for a new chemical engine company, the building was described as "three-sided," but was actually trapezoidal in plan. The two-story structure with a hipped roof was clad in shingles at the lower floor and horizontal siding above. The front elevation, with a round tower rising at one second-floor corner intersecting a partial gable, was even more irregular than Ritchie's building at Fourth and Battery. (Fig. 6.8) Both of Ritchie's fire stations reflect his untutored approach to the Queen Anne.

Engine House Number 3, (1889–1890, destroyed) on Main Street between South Seventh and South Eighth, was designed by Charles A. Alexander, who was primarily a residential architect.[15] This, his first identified Seattle project, was a two-story rectangular building designed to house a steam engine, a hose wagon, horses, and the associated company of fire fighters. His shingled structure featured a gabled roof that extended down to the second floor, an intersecting cross-gable and an offset tower. (Fig. 6.9)

Although Ritchie and Alexander had won fire station commissions, it was Charles Saunders who established a permanent relationship with the fire department. In 1894 the department turned to Saunders again for two additional buildings.[16] In this case Saunders provided one design which the fire department used for Engine House Number 6 (1893–94, destroyed), on Yesler Avenue at Taylor (now South 23rd), and Engine House Number 7 (1893–95, destroyed),

6.8 Willis A. Ritchie, Chemical Engine House Number 2, 1889–90 (destroyed)

Twentieth Century Souvenir of the Fire Department of Seattle *(1901)*.

6.9 Charles A. Alexander, Engine House Number 3, 1889–90 (destroyed)

Museum of History and Industry, Wilse Collection, 88.33.123

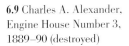

at Harrison and North 15th. Each of these buildings housed a steam engine and a hose wagon, four horses, and a company of eight fire fighters. Each was a simple rectangle with a hipped roof and a tower at the back corner. (Fig. 6.10) Clad in horizontal siding with white trim, the symmetry and discipline reflect both the budget limitations and the classical design tendencies of the mid-1890s.[17]

Engine House Number 7 was the last substantial fire station the city could afford to build and equip before 1901.[18] While fire protection could not be extended to all areas of the city, the basis for the department's growth and development after the turn of the century had been established. These buildings were visible evidence of the increasing role of city government as Seattle grew to metropolitan status.

Providing for Education

The characteristic form of the urban public school building was established early in the nineteenth century as laws requiring school attendance, at least through the elementary grades, became common in eastern states. In the 1830s, treatises had been published describing school architecture, and advocating classrooms with high ceilings and large windows for adequate air circulation, ventilation, and natural light, and an individual desk for every student. Classroom size became standardized at about 25 by 35 feet by the 1840s, and by the time of the Civil War, the essential program and form of the public school building had been formulated: a building housing a series of uniform classrooms and a few ancillary facilities necessary for the instructional program.[19] After 1900, expanding programs and extracurricular activities led to the incorporation of additional specialized spaces, particularly at the high school level, but otherwise, until the late 1930s, these buildings provided remarkably consistent settings for the education of multiple generations of American school-age children.[20] Schools also reinforced neighborhood identity to a greater extent than most other institutional buildings. And, of course, each new school building represented one component of an emerging city school system. The buildings were usually designed as relatively simple blocks, but almost always featured symbolic elements such as towers and/or ornamented cupolas and might strive for monumentality as an expression of their importance in the community.

In Seattle, the pattern of school development has been characterized by recent scholars as one of "many small neighborhood grade schools (instead of fewer large ones)."[21] The relationship of this pattern of small neighborhood schools to the overall pattern of Seattle's development as a city of strong neighborhood identification has been widely recognized. Although often credited to the period between 1900 and 1920, this pattern actually took shape earlier, in the years between 1880 and 1900. Schools were important in establishing and stabilizing the new residential neighborhoods in the emerging city. Just as fire stations symbolized a commitment to the community's physical permanence, schools represented an investment in the future generations of Seattle's citizens.[22]

With the rapid development of Seattle in the late nineteenth and early twentieth centuries, the history of school design and construction was always one of continuing pressure to expand facilities, both to provide new schools in outlying areas and to offer adequate classroom space in densifying older neighborhoods. In the 1880s and 1890s, Seattle School District Number 1 could never keep up with the growth of the school-age population; every time a new school opened, it was soon filled beyond its capacity.

It was not until February 1888 that the territorial legislature passed a law allowing school districts to issue bonds for school construction if approved by the voters.[23] This became the typical mechanism for funding school construction during the boom years of 1888 to 1893; its first tangible result was the long-delayed South School. In April 1888 the district accepted the design proposals of Boone and Meeker, for the new school and also for a replacement for the Central School which had been destroyed by fire.[24] The decision whether to build these new buildings of wood or brick was actually placed on the ballot for the construction bonds. When Seattle voters approved the bonds and brick for both schools on 8 May 1888, the *Post-Intelligencer* characterized the response as a "new departure in public buildings" and stated that the vote reflected "the intelligence, liberality and public spirit" of the citizens.[25] South School opened in February 1889; the larger Central School was not ready until September. (Figs. 6.11, 6.12) The South School opened with little fanfare, but the new Central School was the subject of a detailed report in the *Post-Intelligencer* on 15 October, which described it as a "splendid structure."[26] Neither school displayed any Richardsonian influence; instead both reflected Boone's experience in the Victorian modes.

Even before these buildings were completed, however, the district had embarked on a new building program in response to Seattle's continuing growth. The June 1889 fire that destroyed the city's business core had not damaged any school buildings; overcrowding was the impetus. Indeed, in August 1889 the superintendent of schools reported, "the number of pupils in our schools has almost doubled in a single year."[27]

Although the school board discussed the need for additional schools as early

as February 1889, it was not until August that architects were invited to submit designs. Boone and Meeker's use of identical floor plans for Central and South Schools demonstrated that a single basic design could generate different buildings, so the board invited architectural submissions for an eight-room wood-frame school design that would be the basis for four buildings of similar size.[28] On 30 August the board accepted plans prepared by Charles Saunders, who envisioned roughly square two-story frame structures with full basements. Each floor was to have four classrooms plus closets and teachers' rooms. The designs, characterized as "old English modified," specified that the exterior of the lower floor would be "channel rustic" (horizontal siding) and the second floor "halved timber," apparently an interpretation of the half-timbered version of the Queen Anne mode.[29] Saunders estimated the cost of each school at $14,000, but the bids for all four totaled nearly $72,000. No doubt the construction boom after the 6 June fire created a difficult bidding climate.[30] Construction was postponed to 1890.[31]

Nonetheless, the board continued to discuss the proposed eight-room school buildings. On 27 January, Saunders and Houghton apparently presented alternative exteriors because the next day, the *Post-Intelligencer* reported: "The four schoolhouses will . . . be ready for occupancy next fall. The elevations have been selected and two of them will be Colonial, one Queen Anne and one original."[32] Over this period the board also gave these schools their permanent names: Minor, Mercer, Rainier, and Columbia.[33] Three of these schools opened in September, but Rainier was delayed until January 1891.[34]

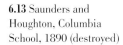

6.12 Boone and Meeker, South School, 1888–89 (destroyed)

Manuscripts, Special Collections, University Archives Division, University of Washington Libraries, photo by Asahel Curtis, 4329

6.13 Saunders and Houghton, Columbia School, 1890 (destroyed)

Manuscripts, Special Collections, University Archives Division, University of Washington Libraries, photo by A. C. Warner, 27

All four buildings were two-story wood structures based on the same rectangular plan with a central hall and four classrooms on each floor. The exterior materials and detailing of each building were different as directed by the board. Columbia School, characterized as "Queen Anne," featured English Revival half-timbering at the second floor and probably closely matched Saunders's initial August 1889 proposal for the four schools (Fig. 6.13). Minor was a Colonial Revival design with a center gable on each side and a classical porch with a Palladian window above (Fig. 6.14). Mercer was a fairly simple block with relatively plain detailing that featured shingles at the gable and upper tower similar to the firm's Rainier Hotel and their Engine House Number 2. (Fig. 6.15) Rainier School was the most curious, with a mix of Renaissance and Romanesque features, even though executed in wood (Fig. 6.16). The use

6.14 Saunders and Houghton, T. T. Minor School, 1890 (destroyed)

Manuscripts, Special Collections, University Archives Division, University of Washington Libraries, photo by A. C. Warner, 36

6.15 Saunders and Houghton, Mercer School, 1890 (destroyed)

Manuscripts, Special Collections, University Archives Division, University of Washington Libraries, photo by A. C. Warner, UW6019

6.16 Saunders and Houghton, Rainier School, 1890–91 (destroyed), with addition by John Parkinson, 1891

Annual Report of the Board of Education of the City of Seattle for the School Year ending June 30, 1892; *Manuscripts, Special Collections, University Archives Division, University of Washington Libraries*

6.17 Denny School, with 1891 additions by John Parkinson (destroyed)

Manuscripts, Special Collections, University Archives Division, University of Washington Libraries, photo by Asahel Curtis, 4327

of Romanesque might be evidence of Richardson's influence, but, of course, Richardson would never have considered the Romanesque—essentially a lithic style—as an appropriate mode for wood construction.[35]

Even with the four new schools, crowding remained a major problem, but after the failure on 15 November of Baring Brothers and the subsequent Panic of 1890, new construction was limited to additions to existing buildings.[36] At their 22 April 1891 meeting, the board called for designs "in compatible styles" for additions to Rainier, Mercer, and Denny Schools (even though Rainier and Mercer Schools were less than six months old).[37] On 29 April, the board accepted designs by John Parkinson for two four-room additions to Denny School as well as four-room additions to Mercer and Rainier Schools (rejecting designs by Saunders and Houghton, even though two of the additions were to buildings that Saunders and Houghton had designed little more than a year before).[38] Bidding took place in May, and the additions were constructed under Parkinson's supervision over the next three months (Fig. 6.17). From this time, Parkinson had an informal relationship with the school board similar to the one that Saunders and Houghton had previously enjoyed.[39]

John Parkinson's full emergence as the leading school architect of Seattle in the early 1890s was marked by his winning the design competition for a new school just north of the Fremont neighborhood center in the area newly annexed to the city of Seattle. On 22 June 1891, Benjamin F. Day offered a site on the condition that the district "cause to be erected thereon a school building to cost not less than $25,000." The board formally accepted the land on 8 July, and soon authorized a design competition for a sixteen-room brick building, of which only an eight-room portion would be built initially.[40] By the end of the month, the board had received eleven submittals representing virtually all of the major architects practicing in Seattle. This response reflected the significance and visibility of this commission—a costly brick building that

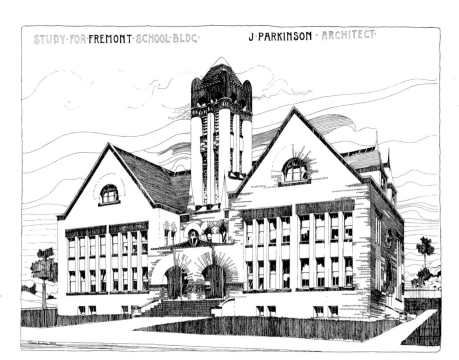

6.18 John Parkinson
(A. B. Chamberlin, del.),
B. F. Day School project,
1891–92

*American Architect and
Building News 30 (21 Nov.
1891), Library of Congress*

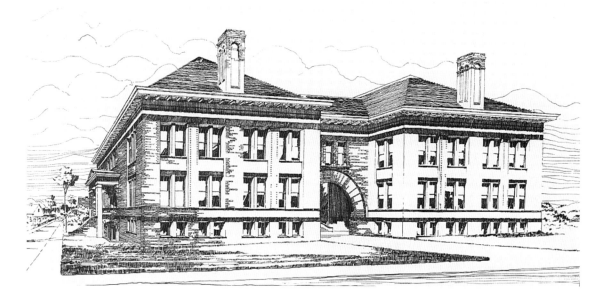

6.19 John Parkinson
(A. B. Chamberlin, del.),
B. F. Day School design,
1891–92

*American Architect and
Building News 31 (30 Jan.
1892), Library of Congress*

attracted more press attention than other school projects; it may also indicate the slowing of the post-fire commercial construction boom. The board selected Parkinson's design on 12 August.[41]

Parkinson later published two versions of his design. A drawing titled "Study for Fremont School Bldg.," apparently an early scheme, was published in *American Architect and Building News* on 2 November 1891. This showed a structure with two eight-room wings and an interconnecting entry lobby with a tall central tower. (Fig. 6.18) A drawing of the final design, titled "Day School Building, Seattle," also appeared in *American Architect* two months later. (Fig. 6.19) Although the general organization remained the same, Parkinson eliminated the more dramatic features, the tall tower and high gables, in favor of a

6.20 B. F. Day School
with 1900 addition
following Parkinson's
original design

*Manuscripts, Special
Collections, University
Archives Division, University
of Washington Libraries,
photo by Asahel Curtis, 4314*

lower hipped roof and a generally more horizontal treatment. In accordance
with the board's plan, only the south wing of Parkinson's design for the B. F.
Day School (1891–92, altered) was constructed initially: eight rooms in a four-
over-four configuration with a south-facing classical entrance portico. Bidding
took place in late September and construction began without delay. The day
after the dedication on 4 May 1892, the *Post-Intelligencer* described the new
Day School as "probably the best of its kind in the state."[42] Parkinson's
Romanesque-influenced, round-arched main entrance would not be constructed
until 1900, when the building was expanded in accordance with his design.[43]
(Fig. 6.20) With later additions, the B.F. Day School is still used today, the
oldest school in continuous operation in Seattle.

A successful bond referendum in March 1892 allowed the district to go forward with additional school construction.[44] To proceed with design, the board
decided to contract for the services of a single architect. Architectural services between January 1889 and March 1892 had cost $16,614—an average,
according to the board, of $437 per month. By employing one "Architect and
Superintendent of Construction," who would be paid a salary of $208.33 per
month, the board would save the district money.[45] On 20 April the board chose
John Parkinson (there were no other nominees recorded in the minutes) and
immediately authorized him to design a school in the Eastern Addition (a location roughly midway between Central, South, Minor, and Rainier Schools). For
the next two years Parkinson was responsible for the design of all new schools
in the city. Other architects complained about this arrangement and requested
design competitions for every building, but to no avail.[46]

The board accepted Parkinson's sixteen-room design for the new Pacific
School in early May 1892, but when bids exceeded the amount approved
by the voters, Parkinson reworked his proposal with only twelve rooms. His
revised design was approved on 11 June, a construction contract was signed

6.21 John Parkinson, Pacific School, 1892–93 (destroyed)

Manuscripts, Special Collections, University Archives Division, University of Washington Libraries, photo by Asahel Curtis, 4323

6.22 John Parkinson, Cascade School, 1893–94, with later additions by Saunders and Lawton and James Stephen following Parkinson's original design (destroyed)

Museum of History and Industry, PEMCO Webster & Stevens Collection, 83.10.7356

later that month, and the building was occupied in March 1893.[47] Pacific School (1892–93, destroyed) was a two-story brick structure with six rooms on each floor and two gymnasiums in the basement—the first true gymnasiums in the district. The building was strongly horizontal with a low hipped roof and windows simply arranged in groups reinforcing the horizontal character (Fig. 6.21). In his autobiography Parkinson recalled, "The Pacific School Building in Seattle, architecturally, has more interest, and the best design of the buildings I did in Seattle. All, however, were of sound practical construction."[48] In photographs, the building appears almost modern; by 1892 Richardson's influence was waning rapidly and the appearance of the Pacific School suggests that Parkinson's design was an economical response to functional requirements.

On 29 September 1892, the board asked Parkinson to prepare plans for a twelve-room school for a site south of Lake Union in an area that was becoming densely populated, but the project was shelved the following month.[49] The board did not consider this school again until March 1893 and then it asked

Parkinson to prepare plans for both a six-room and a twelve-room building. Parkinson developed a scheme for a larger twenty-room school that could be built in phases. The design for a two-story brick building had a central section and two wings in what Parkinson said was a "free treatment of the Elizabethan style."[50] Although the board approved Parkinson's scheme in April, it directed that only a six-room wing be built initially because of limited funds. Construction of the Cascade School (1893–94, destroyed) proceeded through the rest of the year, and the building was put in use when the school term began in January 1894.[51]

As initially constructed, Cascade School appeared curious because it was T-shaped with three projecting gabled bays and an almost windowless north elevation. However, this blank elevation was designed to form part of the wall of the central block when the school was enlarged. Four years later the district authorized construction of the main portion, enlarged from eight to twelve rooms; in 1904 the district would authorize the final six-room wing, thereby completing the balanced composition Parkinson had conceived.[52] (Fig 6.22)

Throughout the time Parkinson was under contract to the Seattle School District, he continued his independent practice. Although his office carried on a variety of residential and commercial work, he also successfully sought school commissions in districts outside the city, aided no doubt by his position as Seattle schools architect. In his autobiography, Parkinson claimed he had designed thirty-two schools during his years in the Northwest.[53] Because Seattle schools accounted for only a portion of them, many remain unidentified. Nonetheless, it seems clear that Parkinson was the most prolific designer of schools in Washington State in the 1890s. He traveled to lumber towns such as Snohomish, Sedro, and Hamilton, and recalled rowing four miles each way on Lake Washington to the School District of Ravenna Park, to carry out the design and construction of small buildings. He also published a design for a small elementary school in Whatcom (now part of Bellingham), in the November 1891 *Northwestern Architect*. (Fig. 6.23) Other projects were larger, such as the twelve-

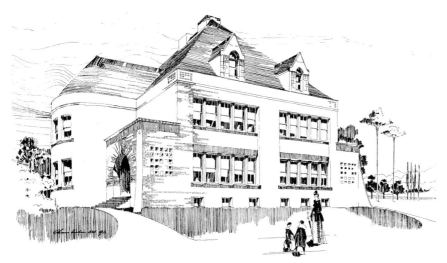

6.23 John Parkinson (A. B. Chamberlin, del.), Public School project, Whatcom, Washington, ca. 1891

Northwestern Architect 9/11 (Nov. 1891), Minnesota Historical Society

room Ballard Central School (1891, later Washington Irving School, destroyed) and the South Seattle School (1892, destroyed), an eight-room brick structure built in 1892. (Fig. 6.24)[54]

Parkinson also designed a variety of small projects for the Seattle School District, but he probably did not realize as much work from his position as Seattle schools architect as he had hoped. For example, he probably anticipated designing a high school costing $100,000 or more, but he never got the chance. High school bonds were defeated in March 1892 and in May 1893, and thereafter, the national economic collapse made any consideration of such a project impossible.[55]

Although Seattle continued to grow after 1891, prosperity never returned to the boom levels of the 1888–90 period. When the national depression began in May 1893, school construction, like other construction, gradually came to a halt, and thereafter the district faced increasing financial difficulties. At the board meeting on 14 February 1894, Parkinson, whose monthly salary had already been cut to $100, tendered his resignation, effective 1 April. He was then asked to advance the date to 1 March as there was "nothing for him to do."[56]

For the next year, the national economic collapse limited school construction in Seattle to only a few small projects.[57] But in 1895, when the state approved legislation to allow financially strapped school districts to restructure their indebtedness, the Seattle School District was able to proceed with a new school in the Queen Anne neighborhood.[58] However, the project was complicated by the new professional standards of the Washington State Chapter of the American Institute of Architects, formed in February and March 1894. The chapter wished to raise the professional standing of architects around the state. After the school board invited design submissions for the school, the chapter held a special meeting on 7 March 1895, determined that the instructions were "indefinite," and resolved that "all members of the Washington State Chapter A.I.A. decline to enter into the competition under the terms of the present notice."[59] Two leading members of the chapter, G. W. Bullard of Tacoma and Charles Bebb (who had moved to Seattle from Chicago), met with the board a week later. Because the board's invitation did not indicate the desired number or size of rooms or the relationships among them, specify who would make the final selection or what criteria would be used, or require anonymity of entries, the competition, they claimed, could not be fair.[60] The board, however, refused to change its procedures.

The AIA chapter could not prevent the competition, but, nonetheless, the chapter's boycott reduced the number of designs submitted to just five, a very low number considering the significance of this project in the otherwise extremely depressed market for architectural services.[61] On 22 June, the board accepted the proposal by Skillings and Corner—but not without controversy. Having displayed the competing entries before making a choice, the board allowed Skillings and Corner to modify the roof of their design as requested by some Queen Anne residents. Neither Warren P. Skillings nor James M. Corner was then a member of the AIA, but both AIA members who did submit

6.24 John Parkinson, South Seattle School, 1892 (destroyed)

Museum of History and Industry, PEMCO Webster & Stevens Collection, 83.10.6569

6.25 Skillings and Corner, Queen Anne School, 1895–96 (West Queen Anne Elementary School, altered)

Manuscripts, Special Collections, University Archives Division, University of Washington Libraries, UW13735

(William Willcox and A. B. Chamberlin) were subsequently expelled from the chapter.[62]

Skillings and Corner designed a two-story eight-room building, but even the lowest bid exceeded the funds available. As a result, the firm reworked the design, reducing it to six rooms, lowering the roof and substituting shingles for slate, and reducing the amount of stone. By late August the project was under way. Queen Anne School (1895–96, altered, later renamed West Queen Anne School) was completed in June and opened for classes in September 1896.[63] (Fig. 6.25) This was the last large school built in Seattle until the twentieth century.

The Seattle School District built six masonry structures between 1888 and 1896, but the Romanesque Revival had surprisingly little influence on school design in the city. This was partially because of timing; Central and South schools predated Boone's conversion to the Romanesque; Pacific, Cascade, and Queen Anne all were built after the Romanesque had been eclipsed. Richardson's influence in Seattle peaked between 1889 and 1891, and the schools of those years—Minor, Mercer, Columbia, and Rainier—were constructed of wood. Thus, among Seattle schools, only the arched entry to the B. F. Day School in Fremont, designed by John Parkinson in mid-1891, suggests the power of Richardson's example. Taken in sequence, these buildings are further evidence of the rapidity of both the rise and the fall of the Romanesque Revival.

Institutions of Higher Learning

The one part of Seattle's institutional framework that began to take physical form in the early 1890s that was not neighborhood-based was the city's network of colleges and universities. Seattle's state-supported university, the University of Washington, and two private universities, Seattle Pacific University and Seattle University, would all see major growth and development in the twentieth century, but the first building on each campus took place in the post-fire period.

The creation of these institutions was initiated in a national context that had seen the beginning of many new colleges and universities in the Midwest and West in the post–Civil War period. As noted by Paul Turner, the typical approach to college building before 1890 was to create a single, grand, all-purpose building that could house all collegiate functions initially and that would establish the identity and permanence of the new institution. If the institution prospered, more buildings would be added incrementally as required by the expanding educational program.[64] Even if a monumental building could not be afforded initially, the campus might still begin with a smaller multi-purpose structure, and this was the pattern followed for Seattle's early collegiate construction.

The University of Washington was the first of Seattle's three universities to proceed, although it proved to be the last to be completed. By 1890, the original ten-acre University of Washington campus was becoming inadequate and it would soon be enveloped by the city's growing downtown.[65] The state addressed the regents' call for a new campus on 7 March 1891 with legislation allocating a 160-acre site fronting on both Lake Washington and Lake Union (the section now called Portage Bay), and giving responsibility for its development to a newly created Board of University Land and Building Commissioners.[66] The legislature also set a deadline of 1 March 1893 for the university to move to its new location.[67]

The Board of University Land and Building Commissioners immediately began planning for the new campus. At their first meetings in Seattle in early April 1891, the board appointed William Boone as architect and superintendent of construction.[68] How he was selected was not revealed, but in a later

6.26 Willcox and Johnston, Shumway Hall, Shattuck School, Faribault, Minnesota, 1886–87

Minnesota Historical Society, St. Paul, MR7.9 FB5.25 p15

interview, Boone reported that he responded to an invitation and appeared before the board on 7 April. Asked if he would accept the position as architect and superintendent for the new university, he agreed to serve if there was no design competition, which he characterized as a "picture gallery."[69] With this understanding Boone accepted the appointment. (Given the 1893 deadline in the state legislation establishing the board, the commissioners felt they could not tolerate the delay that a competition would require.)

Although it was Boone who met with the board, he credited William Willcox, his partner since December 1890, for the design. Willcox had previously designed buildings on several campuses including the Shattuck School, Faribault, Minnesota, and Macalester College, St. Paul.[70] (Fig. 6.26) When the University of Washington designs were announced, the *Post-Intelligencer* cited Willcox's expertise, stating, "Mr. Wilcox [*sic*], the architect who designed the plans, has had experience in building other universities, and knows just what is needed."[71]

Boone later noted that once his firm was selected, they based their design on "as complete a study as practicable of the most noted and successful universities in other portions of the country."[72] Work on the campus plan proceeded rapidly: meeting in Olympia, the regents adopted the design on 21 August. It was made public in Seattle the next day.[73] On 25 August, the *Post-Intelligencer* reported that Professor Thomas Gatch, the president of the university, had "expressed great satisfaction with the plans."[74]

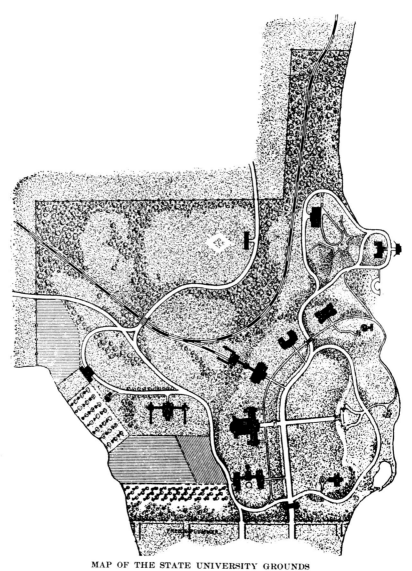

MAP OF THE STATE UNIVERSITY GROUNDS

SHOWING THE FINAL IMPROVEMENTS CONTEMPLATED FOR WHICH THE GRADING AND CLEARING WAS BEGUN.

6.27 Boone and Willcox, University of Washington campus plan proposal, 1891

Report of the University of Washington Land and Building Commissioners, 1892 *Manuscripts, Special Collections, University Archives Division, University of Washington Libraries, UW18233*

The Boone and Willcox plan proposed locations for sixteen buildings, placing all but one building south or east of the Seattle, Lake Shore and Eastern Railroad tracks that crossed the site (the alignment of the Burke-Gilman Trail today). (Fig. 6.27) They proposed that the main entrance to the campus, through an arch, would be from the south (across what today is the "Montlake Cut," which did not then exist). A secondary entrance was planned to the west (at a location between the present Pacific and Boat streets). The plan proposed five primary buildings facing east and southeast arrayed in a gentle arc overlooking Lake Washington (at the western edge of what is today the stadium and associated parking). From south to north these buildings were a dormitory and dining hall, the main administration building, a chemical and physical hall (connected to a power house, manual training facility, and school of mines), a Latin and legal hall (also described as serving law and medicine), and, across a ravine, a library and art hall. The other buildings were positioned in a picturesque arrangement in relationship to the shape of the land and the water. These included a botanical hall (also called biological hall) west of the administration building and north of proposed botanical gardens, a gymnasium located north of the art/library building, a club and boat house, an observatory, a chapel, a military training building, and stables. A running track and a baseball field were also planned.[75]

The picturesque character of the Boone and Willcox master plan reflected the typical approach to campus planning of the previous several decades. Notable examples of campus master plans by landscape architect Frederick Law Olmsted from the 1860s to the 1880s, such as his 1866 plan for the University of California at Berkeley, derived from his approach to park design, based on picturesque rather than formal composition, and emphasized the natural setting wherever possible.[76] However, the 1887 Stanford University master plan developed by Olmsted and Richardson's successors, Shepley, Rutan, and Coolidge, offered a marked departure as it featured a large formal quadrangle with buildings arranged symmetrically.[77] The construction of the central Stanford quadrangle was largely complete by 1891, but its formal organization (soon to become the norm in American campus planning) did not influence Boone and Willcox, who followed the earlier tradition.

The architects' report described the intentions of each of the buildings; for some they suggested the kinds of rooms on each floor.[78] The only building that was designed beyond a conceptual level was the Main Building (identified as the "Administration and Belles Lettres" building). Because this was to have been built first and would have housed the entire university initially, a complete set of construction documents and specifications was prepared. The building included two primary floors plus a finished basement and attic for a total of four floors of usable space. It was to include academic spaces (classrooms, lecture halls, professors' offices, library), administrative spaces (president's office, rooms for the regents and commissioners, and adjoining rooms), support spaces (cloak rooms, toilets, preparatory rooms), and a large double-height assembly hall at the rear. The building was to be constructed of fireproof materials throughout: exterior walls of rock-faced light-colored stone, interior of brick and hollow clay tile, and a floor system using steel beams and terra-cotta. Although both Willcox and Boone had had experience with the Romanesque, the style they chose for the building was characterized as "Scholastic Gothic."[79] The primary features of the exterior were the main entrance and bell tower with a large clock. No drawings are known for this building, so its design can only be surmised; it was very likely similar to the buildings of Shattuck School in Minnesota with which Willcox had previously been involved.

Unfortunately, although construction began about 1 October, it was halted after only ten days.[80] The state auditor in Olympia refused to issue warrants for payment, because of defects in the state enabling legislation.[81] Boone and Willcox initially hoped that a way might be found to allow construction to proceed, but it soon became clear that nothing would be done until the legisla-

ture met in its regular session in 1893.[82] The stoppage of the university project was a blow to their practice that could not be sustained. With very little work in hand, Boone and Willcox dissolved their partnership in June 1892.

While the University of Washington project was delayed, design and construction did go forward on the initial buildings of two newly formed private colleges. The first building of Seattle Pacific University was constructed as the "Seattle Seminary," a school created under the auspices of the Free Methodist Church. The denomination's Oregon and Washington Conference created an Education Committee in 1889 to investigate the establishment of a school where students could receive an education framed by religious principles. On 20 June 1891, at a meeting in Seattle, the committee recommended building a school as soon as funds could be raised. Members of the conference pledged varying amounts of support, and Nils B. Peterson, a Queen Anne resident, offered a five-acre site at the bottom of the north slope of Queen Anne Hill (in the community then known as Ross).[83] Ground was broken for the Seattle Seminary Building (1891–93) just four months later, on 29 October, and a drawing of the design by John Parkinson appeared the next month in *Northwestern Architect*.[84] (Fig. 6.28) The Board of Trustees probably selected Parkinson as the designer because of his school design experience. His four-story multipurpose structure provided space for all the needs of a boarding school, with a dining room, kitchen, lavatory, and associated spaces on the ground floor, a chapel and school rooms on the second floor, a library and additional school rooms on the third floor, and two dormitories and teachers residence rooms on the fourth floor. (Fig. 6.29) The building was a masonry block of dark brown

6.29 Seattle Seminary
Building (Alexander
Hall, Seattle Pacific
University)

*Museum of History and
Industry, Seattle Historical
Society Collection, 13249*

brick with stone trim and a hipped roof of slate. The *Post-Intelligencer* characterized the building as "substantial and commodious."[85] The four faceted corner towers gave the building a strong vertical emphasis and a medieval character, but the only Romanesque-inspired features were the round-arched main entrance at one end and the arched windows. Construction lagged because of financial difficulties, but the seminary was finished in early 1893 and the school term opened in April (with thirty-four students registering during the term). College-level instruction did not take place on the campus until 1910. When the Seattle Pacific University developed on this campus in the twentieth century, the Seminary Building was renamed Alexander Hall.

Parkinson was also the architect of the new Jesuit College and Church (1892–94, altered), the first building of a new Catholic college campus. The site at the corner of Madison and Broadway was acquired in November 1890, but the project proceeded slowly. Although Rev. Victor Garrand, S.J., arrived in Seattle in August 1891 with the goal of creating a Catholic college, his initial task was to take over Immaculate Conception (Parish) School. Planning for a new building did not begin until October 1892 and it was apparently at this time that Parkinson was hired.[86] When the *Post-Intelligencer* first reported the project in January 1893, the structure was described as "part of a comprehensive plan contemplating the ultimate erection of a splendid college."[87] Whether Parkinson had actually prepared a campus master plan is not known, but the structure that was built was apparently intended to be the first part of a larger "Main Building." Parkinson's design was a rectangular two-story brick block measuring 41 by 112 feet. The lower basement, accessible from

6.30 John Parkinson,
Jesuit College and
Church, 1892–94
(Garrand Building,
Seattle University, stair
and porch removed)

*Manuscripts, Special
Collections, University
Archives Division, University
of Washington Libraries,
photo by Asahel Curtis, 1249*

the outside, provided space for the refectory and two bedrooms (living quarters for the Jesuit community), the upper basement for two living rooms and four classrooms (initially for the older boys in the Immaculate Conception School); the two floors above, entered directly from Broadway across a bridge, contained the Immaculate Conception Church. By this time the Romanesque was clearly in decline and Parkinson turned in another direction. The design was described in newspaper reports as "Roman-Byzantine," but the building as erected was relatively plain, featuring only two-story brick pilasters with some minimal classical detail.[88] Construction above the foundation took place only after July 1894, when the building was carried forward without Parkinson's participation under the direction of Rev. Garrand.[89] (Fig. 6.30) It opened on 8 December. Parkinson's master plan for the college was apparently lost. The Seattle College, itself, was not incorporated until 1898, and the first college-level classes were offered two years later. Although a major expansion was proposed about 1908, substantial additional construction did not take place on the Seattle University campus until the 1940s. Parkinson's building is now known as the Garrand Building.[90]

The new campus for the University of Washington finally proceeded in 1893. New legislation provided for an enlarged site of 580 acres. It also dissolved the Board of University Land and Building Commissioners, returning authority over design and construction to the regents. $150,000 was provided for construction of the first building; the design was to be selected through a competition open to all architects in the state. The regents were directed to proceed at once.[91]

On 6 December 1893, based on a report by landscape architect and Seattle Parks Superintendent Edward O. Schwagerl, the regents selected a site on high

6.31 Unknown architect
(J. Anderson, del.),
University of Washington
competition project, 1893

*Manuscripts, Special
Collections, University
Archives Division, University
of Washington Libraries*

ground north of the center of the enlarged tract, with a view toward both Lake Union and Lake Washington. Schwagerl also argued that the ample grounds of the university campus would not require tall buildings and costs could be reduced by using "slow-burning construction" if no recitation rooms were allowed above the second floor of any building.[92]

Directions to architects were published in late December in papers around the state; these described the required rooms, specified the use of slow-burning construction, indicated a preference for a two-story building with a basement, noted that the heating plant would be located separately from the building, required both piping for gas and wiring for electric lighting, indicated a cost of $125,000, and stated that the winning design would become the property of the university.[93] By the due date, 17 February 1894, twenty-four submissions had been received. Little is known of these projects, although a watercolor perspective of one unidentified entry does survive. (Fig. 6.31) The winners were announced on 15 March: Charles Saunders's design for the building would be built; John Parkinson placed second; William Boone was third.[94] Saunders's building was constructed between May 1894 and August 1895. On 4 July 1894, a crowd of nearly 1000 attended the laying of the cornerstone. The building was named Denny Hall in September 1895 when it opened for classes.[95]

Denny Hall (1894–95, interior altered) was a two-story brick and stone block with a raised basement and a hipped roof. The building included six laboratories, ten recitation rooms, a museum, rooms for the president, regents, and faculty, a library, music room, lecture hall, and a 700-seat assembly room. The overall form of the symmetrical front of the building, with two projecting round bays, showed the direct influence of Richardson's Sever Hall at Harvard.

A City of Neighborhoods 237

However, the formal language at Denny Hall was not Richardson's, but derived instead from French chateau architecture; the new building was described as an "elegant" and "attractive" example of the "French Renaissance style."[96] (Fig. 6.32)

Places for Worship

Other than the first buildings at Seattle Pacific and Seattle universities, the only significant private institutions built during the period were churches. The fluid nature of downtown real estate after the fire may have contributed to a caution on the part of congregations toward rebuilding in the downtown core. Trinity Episcopal Congregation sold its burned-out property at Third and Jefferson for commercial use and moved to a site on First Hill. Members of the Methodist Episcopal Congregation briefly considered a church design (for their burned-out site at Second and Madison) that could be converted at a later time to office space should the real estate market make their land too valuable to retain for religious purposes.[97] As a result, new church buildings were constructed either just outside the developing commercial core or in the emerging residential neighborhoods.

The most progressive church design of the period, by Saunders and Houghton, was not built, and is known only from its publication in *Northwestern Architect* in February 1891. (Fig. 6.33) The volumetric clarity of the scheme was reinforced by the plain masonry surfaces rendered as a neutral field on which architectural elements of generally Romanesque character were exhibited. The congregation which commissioned this design remains unidentified.[98]

Post-fire construction typically continued the use of Gothic, not Romanesque, as the preferred mode for religious structures. And most churches were wood frame, as only three congregations were able to afford masonry. Boone and Willcox's brick Plymouth Congregational Church (1891–92, destroyed), located

6.33 Saunders and Houghton (A. B. Chamberlin, del.), unidentified church project, ca. 1890–91 (unbuilt)

Northwestern Architect 9/2 (Feb. 1891), Minnesota Historical Society

at Third and University, was the most substantial religious structure built in the period. (Fig. 6.34) Announced in March 1891, and completed the following year, its planning and design reflected Willcox's previous experience with church buildings in the Midwest.[99] The primary architectural character derived from the juxtaposition of clearly articulated volumes and fine brickwork. Detail was restrained and the simple mass composition strongly suggests the character of the Romanesque even though the vocabulary remained Gothic. Given Willcox's previous experience designing Romanesque churches, it may be that the congregation required a Gothic design. Boone and Willcox did design at least one Romanesque Revival church, an 1891 proposal for Trinity Methodist Church in West Seattle, but it was beyond the means of the congregation and was never built.[100]

Somewhat less ambitious was Trinity Episcopal Church (1890–92, altered), a stone building at Eighth and James by Henry F. Starbuck of Chicago. Construction of this prototypical English Gothic parish church was supervised by local architect Charles Alexander, who modified Starbuck's design to fit the sloping site.[101] The simple five-bay nave was lit with rows of lancet clerestory windows, and stained glass panels by Franz Mayer of Munich lit the main floor side aisles. One-story transept wings projected from the north and south nave walls. (Fig. 6.35) A proposed corner tower and porch were not added until a decade later following a fire that left the building an empty shell. Alexander, better known for his residential designs, was responsible for the shingled rectory to the north.

Montreal architects Maurice Perrault and Albert Mesnard furnished original designs for the third significant masonry church, the Church of the Sacred Heart

6.34 Boone and Willcox,
Plymouth Congregational
Church, 1891–92
(destroyed)

*Manuscripts, Special
Collections, University
Archives Division, University
of Washington Libraries,
photo by Asahel Curtis, 2619*

6.35 Henry F. Starbuck
(Charles A. Alexander,
superintending), Trinity
Episcopal Church,
1890–92 (altered)

The Commonwealth, *17 May
1902*

6.36 Herman Steinmann, Congregation Ohaveth Shalom Synagogue 1892, (destroyed)

Manuscripts, Special Collections, University Archives Division, University of Washington Libraries, UW18708

(1890–91, destroyed) at Sixth and Bell on Denny Hill. Local architect P. H. Donovan provided details and supervised the construction of this brick-veneer French Gothic structure, one of the more opulent of the post fire churches.[102] John Parkinson designed an accompanying wood frame rectory in a similar Gothic style in 1893.

Although other post-fire church construction was of wood, the detailing typically remained Gothic. For example, Elmer Fisher's First Methodist Protestant Church (1889–90, destroyed), at Third and Pine, was a wood frame structure with a cross-gable roof, two unequal towers at the front, flat siding and restrained Gothic detail.[103]

This period also saw the construction of Seattle's first substantial Jewish synagogue, by architect Herman Steinmann, for congregation Ohaveth Shalom (1892, destroyed), at Eighth and Seneca. Steinmann's wood frame design in a modified *rundbogenstil* mode differed little from that of Seattle's Christian houses of worship: a rectangular nave with round-arched windows, flanked in the front by two domed towers initially of equal height. In profile and plan it resembled synagogues in Portland and San Francisco, although it lacked the more elaborate decorative ornamentation of buildings in those cities.[104] (Fig. 6.36)

The Neighborhood Fabric

The leading architects of Seattle's post-fire period were primarily focused
on the rebuilding of the city's commercial core and on the creation of a network of public institutions, yet most of them were also occasionally engaged
in the design of residences. The explosive population growth of Seattle after
1885 had generated an unprecedented demand for new housing, only a frac-
tion of which could be addressed by professional architects.

While the streetcar and cable car network and land platting practices fostered a single-family residential fabric, some early rowhouse clusters were
constructed; Elmer Fisher's pre-fire Scurry Terrace at the northeast corner of
Third and James has already been noted. He had also designed similar terrace
housing in 1888 for Howard Lewis, on James between Third and Fourth, and for
Austin Bell, on Second at Bell, but after the fire, terrace house projects were
generally commissioned to "second rank" architects, as the leading firms were
too busy with commercial work. Notable wood rows were designed by J. A.
DeProsse at Eighth and Columbia and by Towle and Wilcox on Sixth Street and
on Yesler Avenue.[105] (Fig. 6.37) These rows typically were detailed with Queen
Anne bays, gables, brackets, and porch supports in their less complex forms.

The one exception was an unusual project by John Parkinson known as the
Stone Row (1892, destroyed). Parkinson was both developer and designer for
this project, a row of seven stone townhouses at the corner of Marion and Twelfth
(now Minor). When Parkinson announced the project in March 1892, he
claimed, "These dwellings will be the best west of the Rocky Mountains. I

shall rent them, and I am building them because I believe there is now a demand here for houses as fine as those of eastern cities."[106] But when the houses were finished in October, Parkinson sold them in a land swap to Charles Hopkins; it was in this way that Parkinson acquired the site on Front Street where he developed his Seattle Athletic Club building.[107] The Stone Row was constructed of Tenino "bluestone" finished smooth, with crisply incised openings for the doors and windows. Six three-story townhouses faced Marion and the seventh faced Twelfth; two-story wings projected back from the three-story block along the street. (Fig. 6.38) Each townhouse measured 20 by 70 feet and had twelve rooms. Parkinson stated that the smooth-faced stone followed the example of similar projects in Chicago and New York. The plumbing, heating, and interior finishes were described as all of the "best quality."[108] Parkinson's project offered a precedent for urbane residential construction on First Hill; indeed, it is possible to imagine First Hill becoming a dense urban residential district similar to Back Bay in Boston or the Upper West Side in New York, but the Panic of 1893 ended all such expensive residential development in Seattle and Parkinson's example was not followed when growth resumed after 1900. It remained the only example of late-nineteenth and early-twentieth-century masonry rowhouse construction in Seattle until its demolition after 1970.

In the 1890s and thereafter, Seattle's residential fabric was primarily composed of single-family houses on individual residential lots. This pattern was made feasible because the early implementation of cable car and streetcar lines relative to population growth made a large area of undeveloped land easily accessible. Except where topography interfered, land subdivision practices over most

6.38 John Parkinson, Stone Row, 1892 (Greystone Hotel, destroyed)

Puget Sound Regional Archives

of this area followed a relatively uniform north-south, east-west street grid with typical lots measuring approximately 50 by 100 feet. Higher-density areas were occasionally created by dividing several adjacent lots into narrower parcels or dividing corner lots in half so that four houses might be built where the initial plat had provided only three lots. In other locations, larger houses were built, usually on larger parcels created by combining lots.[109] (Fig. 6.39)

As in most cities, the residential fabric was primarily the product of contractor-builders, who were responsible for both design and construction of the residences they built. They, in turn, typically depended on the illustrated trade literature including plan and pattern books, although such sources were infrequently acknowledged.[110] However, the use of plan and pattern books and other published sources for residential designs in Seattle was not restricted to contractor-builders. In the mid-to-late 1880s, architects of the older generation, who spent a significant portion of their lives in the building trades, also occasionally turned to these sources for design ideas. For example, William Boone derived his design for the C. L. Denny House (1887, destroyed) from William Comstock's early 1880s pattern book, *Modern Architectural Designs and Details*, published in New York. Comstock illustrated a "Suburban House" by Howe and Dodd of Boston, providing plans, elevations, details, and a perspective. Boone's design, while not an exact copy, included many of the primary features in his Seattle project. (Figs. 6.40a, b) Elmer Fisher's Howard Lewis House (1889, destroyed) was copied from the *Scientific American Architects and Builders Edition* June 1887 "Residence Costing Five Thousand Dollars," based on the Mrs. W. B. Chapin House in Pomfret, Connecticut, by Howard Hoppin. Fisher not only copied the house design, he even duplicated the brick and rock wall surrounding the yard shown in the magazine illustration! (Figs. 6.41a, b)

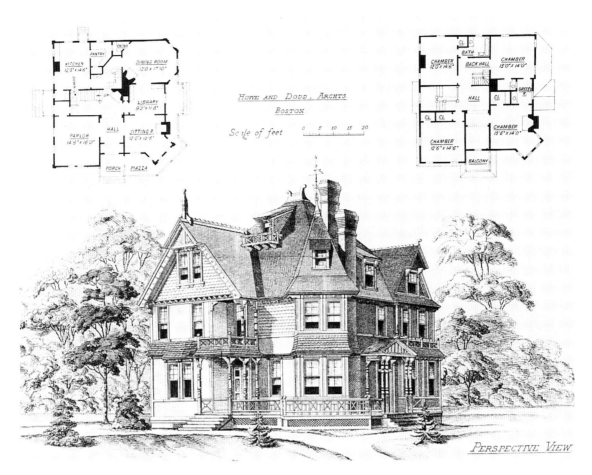

HOWE AND DODD, ARCHTS
BOSTON

Scale of feet   0   5   10   15   20

PERSPECTIVE VIEW

6.40a Howe and Dodd,
"Suburban House"
in William Comstock,
*Modern Architectural
Designs and Details*
(New York, c. 1881)

6.40b Boone and Meeker,
Charles L. Denny House,
1887 (destroyed)
Private collection

6.41a Howard Hoppin, "Residence Costing Five Thousand Dollars" (Mrs. W. B. Chapin House, Pomfret, Conn.), *Scientific American Architects and Builders Edition* (June 1887)

6.41b Elmer H. Fisher, Howard Lewis House, 1889 (destroyed)

Margaret P. Strachan, "Early Day Mansions, No. 12," Seattle Times (19 Nov. 1944); Manuscripts, Special Collections, University Archives Division, University of Washington Libraries, UW14814

In the post-fire period, however, architects generally turned away from pattern and plan books and trade publications, and responded instead to examples in the architectural press.

The residential designs of Seattle's leading architects varied widely in the early 1890s, reflecting the transitional state of American architecture more clearly than any other building type. Local newspaper reports on residential design reflect the absence of a clear direction. A *Times* article on 19 March 1890 suggested that the Queen Anne style was "going out of use" and referred to it as a fad; a year later the same paper commented on the unusual "Italian" of a new residence, and indicated that most new houses in the city reflected the "Queen Anne craze."[111] It is almost impossible to generalize about residential design in Seattle at the time. The range of production is perhaps best demonstrated in the work of Elmer Fisher and John Parkinson.

After the fire, Fisher seldom accepted residential projects, because he was so busy with commercial work. Nonetheless, he did produce some original residential designs. His John G. Scurry House (1889–91, destroyed) was apparently under way just before the fire; Fisher had probably accepted the commission because Scurry was already his client. A fifteen-room house, this two-story rectangular structure was built of stone to the second floor and wood above, and featured a variety of irregular dormers and gables.[112] The house freely mixed motifs including the Victorian square corner tower, the thin Eastlake porch supports, and the Queen Anne features of the gables. (Fig. 6.42) The primary rooms on the ground floor, entrance hall, parlor, living room, and dining room were finished in carved oak and mahogany. After the fire, one project Fisher could not refuse was a house for Otto Ranke, one of the leading contractors in Seattle, who was responsible for construction of Fisher's Pioneer, Starr-Boyd, Schwabacher, and State buildings. The Otto Ranke House (1890–91, destroyed), at the southeast corner of Madison and Tenth, was one of the few masonry residences in Seattle.[113] Built of brick with stone trim and a slate roof and surrounded by broad porches, this was marked by Queen Anne detail. (Fig. 6.43)

Parkinson's architecture suggests a personal search for an appropriate residential style and also shows his virtuosity in wood, likely as a result of his early experiences. In his residential projects, Parkinson seems to have deployed each of several design modes with some level of sensitivity as each design displays a degree of internal consistency. His Margaret J. Pontius House (1889, destroyed), near the streets now named Denny and Yale, a two-story wood-frame residence, included a large hall, front and back parlors, dining room, and kitchen on the ground floor, and five bedrooms on the second floor.[114] This house was generally rectangular, but featured a variety of towers, bays, gables, and dormers, and an extraordinary array of Queen Anne detail. (Fig. 6.44) Parkinson's skill at designing in wood was also evident in his Calkins Hotel (1889–90, destroyed), a richly detailed resort hotel on Mercer Island; the strong horizontals and simple roof form of this design lent overall coherence to the project.[115] (Fig. 6.45) By 1891, Parkinson's residential designs were considerably simplified, but they show continuing experimentation. The John A. Hatfield House (1891, destroyed), on Madison near Hyde, was composed of a few clearly expressed geometric forms and suggests the influence of published examples of "modern colonial" (shingle-style) architecture; a rendering appeared in *American Architect* in September 1892.[116] (Fig. 6.46) His Frank D. Black House (1891–92, destroyed), on Twelfth at Atlantic on Beacon Hill, was described in the *Post-Intelligencer* as in the "Swiss cottage style."[117] His unbuilt Guy Phinney House (1891–92), for a site near Woodland Park, showed a mix of Queen Anne and other influences; it was published in an extraordinary rendering in

6.42 Elmer H. Fisher,
John Scurry House,
1889–91 (destroyed)

*Manuscripts, Special
Collections, University
Archives Division, University
of Washington Libraries,
UW13785*

6.43 Elmer H. Fisher,
Otto Ranke House,
1890–91 (destroyed)

*Pacific Magazine 4/2
(Aug. 1891); University
of Washington Libraries,
Manuscripts, Special
Collections, University
Archives Division*

6.44 Parkinson and Evers, Margaret J. Pontius House, 1889 (destroyed)

Manuscripts, Special Collections, University Archives Division, University of Washington Libraries, photo by Asahel Curtis, 5330

6.45 Parkinson and Evers, Calkins Hotel, Mercer Island, 1889–90 (East Seattle Hotel, destroyed)

Manuscripts, Special Collections, University Archives Division, University of Washington Libraries, UW4815

6.46 John Parkinson (G. Lawton, del.), John Hatfield House, 1891 (destroyed)

American Architect and Building News *37 (17 Sept. 1892); Minnesota Historical Society*

6.47 John Parkinson (A. B. Chamberlin, del.), Guy Phinney House project, 1891–92 (unbuilt)

American Architect and Building News *31 (6 Feb. 1892), Library of Congress*

American Architect in February 1892.[118] (Fig. 6.47) And, his Joseph W. Wilkinson House (1892, destroyed), at the northwest corner of Broadway and Columbia, was a simple rectangle clad entirely in shingles, with a gambrel roof and an engaged round tower; a photograph was published in the Minnesota-based *Architect, Builder & Decorator* in September 1894.[119] (Fig. 6.48)

Overall, Richardson's example was of little use for residential construction in post-fire Seattle. In fact, no Romanesque Revival houses are known to have been built in the city in the 1890s. Further, residential design seems less a

6.48 John Parkinson, Joseph W. Wilkinson House, 1892 (destroyed)

Architect, Builder & Decorator 8/9 (Sept. 1894); Library of Congress

harbinger of the future of Seattle architecture than almost any other type of building in the period. The dominant single-family character of the city was established by the early 1890s, but it was not until the early twentieth century that the primary architectural directions of Seattle's wood frame residential fabric would emerge.[120]

The Limitations of Richardsonian Design

The difficulties faced by Seattle architects in making a convincing architecture outside the commercial core demonstrate the limitations of Richardson's influence and of the Romanesque Revival as a framework for architectural design. Seattle architects found the Romanesque to be a vehicle for the creation of a masonry commercial architecture of strength and solidity in the years after the 1889 fire. But for the city's neighborhoods, where wood construction was generally preferred and was often used for institutional as well as residential buildings, Richardson's example provided no useful model. Instead, an unstable mix of late-Victorian modes, such as the Queen Anne, contemporary approaches such as the "modern colonial" and emerging tendencies, prevailed.

In this regard Seattle contrasted strongly with both San Francisco and Portland. Academically trained architects such as A. Page Brown, Willis Polk, A. C. Sweinfurth, Ernest Coxehead, and Bernard Maybeck in San Francisco and William Whidden and Ion Lewis in Portland were emerging as leaders in the architecture of those cities in the 1890s, and their academic eclectic residential projects were already establishing design directions that would continue for several decades. In Seattle, architects with an equivalent level of academic training did not become influential until the twentieth century.[121]

VII

Creating a Civic Presence
Willis Ritchie and the Architecture of Public Buildings

Work has commenced on the Whatcom County Courthouse. When completed it will be the finest in the state.
— *Bellingham Bay Express* (Whatcom County), 15 April 1890

The new courthouse will be beyond question the handsomest in the State.
— *Morning Olympian* (Thurston County), 15 May 1891

When Seattle architects turned to the Romanesque in the reconstruction of downtown Seattle after the 1889 fire, they did so to create an architecture appropriate to the new urban core. The commercial buildings of H. H. Richardson, Burnham and Root, and others in Chicago, Minneapolis/St. Paul, and elsewhere provided numerous examples of a masonry architecture that could meet the requirements of the new building code while projecting an image of solidity and strength.

At the same time, the rapid urbanization of Washington also required new public architecture. In Seattle the commitment of the citizens to their emerging city was represented in the new networks of public institutions, primarily fire stations and schools. But new public buildings of all kinds were needed across the state, not just in Seattle. In a period of urban development, the new public architecture projected the aspirations of cities and towns to metropolitan status. Of these buildings, the new county courthouses were undoubtedly the most significant. Courthouses directly embodied the rule of law in the dramas played out in the courtrooms; and in the vital records kept by county officials, courthouses were the places where the legal system touched directly on every citizen. Of most importance, these buildings housed the records of land division, ownership, and transfer by which a community was established and secured. Thus, it is not surprising that the county courthouse took on a symbolic importance that required commensurate architectural treatment while simultaneously requiring the most completely fireproof construction possible. Richardson's work, particularly his Allegheny County Courthouse in Pittsburgh with its rock-faced walls, symbolic tower, and ranges of arched windows framed by colonettes with carved capitals, inspired a generation of American architects as they addressed the challenge of the new public architecture.

The most successful designer of public buildings in Washington in the period was Willis A. Ritchie (1863–1931). Among the youngest of the architects drawn to Seattle after the fire, and apparently without local connections before his

252

7.1 Elmer Fisher, Lottie
Roth Block, Whatcom
(now part of Bellingham),
Washington 1890–91

Whatcom Museum Archives,
1981.36.58

arrival in 1889, Ritchie nonetheless soon secured a series of design commissions for county courthouses, schools, fire stations, and similar structures across
western Washington. He was the first Northwest architect to achieve a statewide
reputation, practicing first in Seattle and subsequently in Spokane.[1] As a leading Romanesque Revival designer, the course of his career encapsulates the
vicissitudes of the Romanesque mode in the Northwest.[2]

Ritchie's success in winning commissions in Washington towns and cities
also reflects the ascendancy of Seattle as a regional economic center. Because
Seattle was the largest city on the sound, and because it had developed a network of economic links to the region, it had also become a center for the export
of architectural services. By 1890, Seattle city directories listed thirty architects and firms in practice locally, by far the largest number of architects in
practice in any city in the Northwest other than Portland, and Seattle practitioners had projects under way all across western Washington. This was facilitated because Seattle's business leaders were investing not only in Seattle,
but also elsewhere in the region. Through the patronage of William Bailey's
Washington Territory Investment Company (and its subsidiaries), Saunders
and Houghton were responsible for projects such as the shingled Hotel
Eisenbeis (1889–90, destroyed) in Port Townsend, a masonry hotel building
in Anacortes, and buildings in Sedro-Wooley.[3] Elmer Fisher's commercial practice focused primarily in Seattle, but he had continuing involvement in Port
Townsend, and was also responsible for business blocks such as the Lottie Roth
Block (1890–91) in Whatcom (now part of Bellingham), as well as others in
Ellensburg and possibly Yakima.[4] (Fig. 7.1) A house by Fisher has been identi-
fied as far away as Woodland, California.[5] John Parkinson's spreading practice

in school design included buildings in a variety of Puget Sound communities. Still, for all of these figures, Seattle remained the primary focus of their practices. For Ritchie, Seattle was just a beginning.

Background and Early Career

Willis Alexander Ritchie (né Richie) was born in Van Wert, a small town in northwest Ohio, on 14 July 1864. His family moved to Lima, Ohio, about 1868. Because he showed an aptitude for construction and design, Richie dropped out of high school just before he turned sixteen and was subsequently apprenticed to a carpenter and contractor. At the same time he apparently studied architecture through a correspondence course.[6] Soon thereafter, Richie may have been employed as a draftsman in architects' offices in Cincinnati or Toledo.[7] In 1883, although not yet nineteen, he opened his own office in Lima, where he practiced as an architect (or possibly as a contractor-builder) for the next two years.[8]

In July 1885, John Eaton, the vice president of the Farmers' Bank in Winfield, Kansas, invited Richie to visit and to design a new building for the bank. A small city forty miles south of Wichita, Winfield was enjoying a building boom brought on by the rapid settlement of southern and southwestern Kansas.[9] The town had drawn a substantial portion of its population from central Ohio, and about 1883 a group of Bucyrus, Ohio, capitalists, seeking to invest in Kansas, had chartered the Farmers' Bank. John Eaton, formerly the law partner of Walter Richie, Willis Richie's uncle, had moved from Bucyrus to Winfield to direct bank operations. By 16 July, Eaton was able to display Richie's plans for the bank building, and he subsequently commissioned Richie to design his own house. In August the Winfield school board consulted Richie about an addition to the Central School; by mid-September he was submitting proposals on other Winfield projects. Within a few months Richie was overwhelmed with commissions. He moved to Winfield permanently and, at this time, added a "t" to his last name.[10]

Ritchie's early Winfield buildings incorporated the typical compositional practices of the Victorian modes, but in a relatively simple and straightforward manner. Although economic factors may have limited embellishment, Kansans had a history of preferring design that was elemental rather than ornate, as noted by Richard Longstreth. Simple buildings were seen as practical and appropriate to the character of the state in contrast to the more highly agitated work thought to be typical in the East.[11] In addition, a fine local cream-colored limestone was the preferred building material in Winfield for commercial and public work, so the polychromatic variation often found in American Victorian architecture in the 1880s was generally absent in Winfield.[12]

Ritchie's first Winfield project, the Farmers' Bank Building (1885–86), was followed by his three-story First National Bank and Alexander Block (1885–86, altered), built for Winfield's largest bank.[13] (Fig. 7.2) He also won large institutional projects including the Southwestern Kansas Methodist Episcopal College

7.2 Willis A. Ritchie,
First National Bank
and Alexander Block,
Winfield, Kansas,
1885–86 (altered)

*Kansas State Historical
Society, Topeka, FK2.C10
W.5 9A.Mai5*1*

7.3 Willis A. Ritchie,
Winfield City Building,
Winfield, Kansas,
1885–86 (altered)

*Kansas State Historical
Society, Topeka, FK2.C10
W.1 F.*3*

(1885–86, destroyed) and the Winfield City Building (1885–86, altered).[14] (Fig. 7.3) By 1886, W. A. Ritchie and Co. was the most prominent architectural firm in Winfield, employing between five and ten draftsmen and building superintendents.[15] Ritchie's practice also expanded south and west and at one time he had branch offices in the nearby towns of Arkansas City and Wellington.[16] Ritchie's last major Winfield project was the Grand Opera House and Board of Trade Building (1886–88, destroyed). A two-story stone block, this displayed a regular bay system on both street elevations, with paired second-floor windows detailed with semi-circular arches, Ritchie's first use of a Richardsonian Romanesque motif; this feature may reflect the influence of new Romanesque work he had seen in Wichita.[17]

On 14 January 1886, Ritchie applied for the post of superintendent of construction for the new Federal Courthouse and Post Office at Wichita. In his let-

7.4 Mifflin E. Bell, Supervising Architect of the Treasury (Willis A. Ritchie, Superintendent), Federal Courthouse and Post Office, Wichita, Kansas, 1886–89 (destroyed)

*Kansas State Historical Society, Topeka, FK2.53 W.78 *3*

ter of application he wrote: "I was born at Van Wert, Ohio and am now 29 years of age. Have been engaged in Architecture eleven years and have had much experience in charge of the construction of many buildings in Ohio and in this state."[18] The outright lies are astonishing: at the time Ritchie was only twenty-one and at most could claim five years in practice. While his accomplishments were remarkable for one so young, they far exceeded his candor! At least eleven of Ritchie's clients and friends wrote letters of recommendation for the federal position, all emphasizing his experience—and also noting that he was a "loyal Democrat." He won the appointment in April 1886 and after February 1887 maintained an office in Wichita for this work. Initially estimated at $100,000, the final cost of the Wichita Federal Building was actually closer to $200,000. The building was internally complex as it housed not only the federal courts and post office, but also offices for a wide variety of federal departments. Then the tallest building in Wichita, it was also the first to include a passenger elevator. The design, by the Office of the Supervising Architect of the Treasury, was a generally symmetrical composition interrupted by the jarringly "picturesque" insertion of an offset tower in the front elevation. The walls were treated in smooth stone and punctuated by varied openings featuring classical detail.[19] (Fig. 7.4)

The Wichita Federal Building was extraordinarily important in Ritchie's career. Although Ritchie was not the designer, his supervisory role required that he become familiar with all aspects of the building, and the scale of the structure was clearly the largest in his limited experience. And, while the Federal Building was not stylistically notable, it did feature the most advanced fireproofing technology then available. Further, other construction under way in Wichita between 1887 and 1889, including Proudfoot and Bird's Romanesque Revival Garfield University, completed in 1888, and their Wichita City Hall, begun in 1889, incorporated a Richardsonian Romanesque vocabulary.[20] (See Figs. 4.26, 4.27) The design direction Ritchie took in his buildings in Washington State was clearly influenced by what he had observed in Wichita.

During his years as superintendent of the Federal Building, Ritchie maintained his Winfield architectural practice, though at a reduced scale, and Winfield continued as his primary residence.[21] In January 1887 he also began speculating in Winfield real estate. Although the Wichita Federal Building was not fully completed until 1890, Ritchie's supervisory role ended in May 1889. By that time the Kansas boom was collapsing and it was apparent that few large projects were being planned. Ritchie had incurred significant debts in his land development venture and to pay his creditors, he needed to find a more promising location in which to pursue architectural commissions.[22]

In July 1887, Ritchie had married Eliza Etta Reid. On 28 December 1888, the *Winfield Daily Courier* reported the sudden death of A. Lawson Reid, Ritchie's father-in-law, on a mining claim near Orting, Washington Territory.[23] Thus, Ritchie and his wife may have planned to come west in connection with mining property they inherited. Although he may also have considered moving to Salt Lake City, Ritchie no doubt was attracted to Seattle by the apparent architectural opportunities offered by the rebuilding after the 6 June fire. The *Post-Intelligencer*, on 4 July 1889, just one month after the fire, noted: "Mr. W. A. Ritchie of Wichita [*sic*], Kansas, is spending a few days in the city."[24]

Public Buildings in Western Washington, 1889–1890

By the time Ritchie arrived in Seattle, the rebuilding after the fire was already under way, and, without local connections, he was unable to secure local commercial projects. But his experience with the Wichita Federal Building gave him an expertise in fireproof construction that other Washington architects could not match. Further, 1889 was the worst year in Washington's history for fire losses: Seattle, Ellensburg, and Spokane each saw their business districts destroyed by fire that summer. In this context, knowledge of the latest fireproofing methods gave Ritchie an advantage in competing for new public projects not just in Seattle but across the Northwest, and from this his Washington career rapidly developed.

In contrast to the fire-resistive, heavy-timber frame commercial blocks built in Seattle's commercial core after the fire, Ritchie's masonry public buildings were more truly fireproof because he avoided the use of wood entirely except in the roof framing. Ritchie's designs were typically of load-bearing masonry construction throughout: the exterior walls were of stone and/or brick, and the

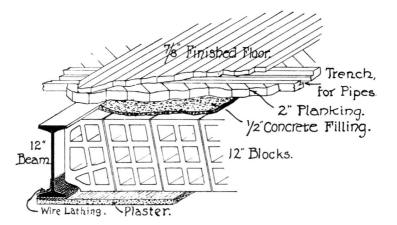

7.5 Illustration from John M. Carrère, "Interior Fireproof Construction," *Engineering Magazine* 4/1 (Oct. 1892): 103

interior walls were of brick or structural terra-cotta. Floors were constructed with parallel steel beams spanning between the load-bearing walls; these beams supported terra-cotta floor pieces to provide both fire protection (by encasing each beam) and the floor structure. (Fig. 7.5) The floors themselves were finished in tile. The only structural wood in these buildings was the framing of the sloped roof. Although this was sometimes left exposed in an attic (inaccessible except for maintenance), a plaster ceiling at the top floor in addition to the terra-cotta (attic) floor system provided the necessary separation to keep any fire from reaching this level. While this approach produced buildings that were almost completely fireproof, these buildings were also completely inflexible since most interior walls were load-bearing and, therefore, not movable. Nonetheless, at the time this was the best fireproof construction available in the Northwest and Ritchie clearly exploited his knowledge of this approach in seeking public building commissions.

The growth of Washington after 1885 was notable for the commitment made by cities and counties to new public construction as well as private development. As symbols of local attainment, public buildings usually drew high praise in the local press, reflecting the boosterish sentiment that their size and beauty demonstrated the stature of the community and indicated its prospects for the future. These public commissions were almost always awarded through a public process, usually an open competition. Typically local officials would advertise that a building of a certain type, size, and cost would be built and that architects might submit competitive designs. The architect of the selected project would then receive the commission to prepare the construction documents, and usually to advertise for bids and supervise construction. Competition among architects for these projects was intense, not only because of the attention the buildings would attract, but also because the relatively large scale of these public projects compared with commercial and residential construction meant large fees. These competitions were completely unregulated: There might or might not be guidelines for design, the submissions might or might not be anonymous, and the reviewing panel might or might not include individuals who had experience in design or construction. An advantage to competitions was that skilled but previously unrecognized designers had a chance at large projects.

7.6 Willis A. Ritchie,
King County Courthouse,
1889–91 (destroyed)

*Manuscripts, Special
Collections, University
Archives Division, University
of Washington Libraries,
photo by Asahel Curtis, 915*

However, vague selection criteria and opportunities for (or accusations of) inappropriate influence sometimes generated controversy.

On 4 July 1889, the King County Commissioners called for architects to submit designs by early September for a courthouse and jail not to exceed $185,000. Twelve sets of plans were received on 2 September (although only eight had the required accompanying contractors' bids), but on 13 September, all the designs were rejected as unsuitable. Instead, Ritchie was hired to prepare plans under the direction of the commissioners.[25] On 7 October, the *Post-Intelligencer* reported that Ritchie's plans were nearly complete, and added, "Ritchie's new plan is the same as that submitted by him in the competition . . . with the exception that a three story building is proposed instead of four and the interior arrangement is modified." This similarity led a group of the other competing architects to petition that since Ritchie had (in effect) won the first prize, the second and third prizes should also be awarded, including the monetary premiums advertised. The commissioners rejected this request, stating that the interior of Ritchie's final design was completely different from his competition submittal.[26]

Ritchie's King County Courthouse (1889–91, destroyed) occupied a prominent but inconvenient full-block site bounded by Seventh, Eighth, Terrace, and Alder at the crest of First Hill. (Fig. 7.6) The building was designed in a classical style, a surprising choice for Ritchie, who had little experience in classical design. The *Post-Intelligencer* on 3 November presented an illustration of the building and praised it, stating: "It will undoubtedly be the finest building of the kind on the coast."[27] The building was described as measuring 195 feet by 125 feet, with a raised basement at ground level, two floors above, and an observatory 80 feet above the street, beneath the crowning dome. The architect was also described: "Mr. Ritchie, although a young man has had a vast amount of experience in courthouse, city buildings, and government work, and he has made a general study of strict fireproof construction in buildings." In what would become his typical pattern, the first floor was the location of county offices and the second floor was used for court rooms, judges chambers, and related spaces; the raised basement was the location of the jail and a variety of support spaces. In November 1889 a San Francisco firm won the construction contract, but the project was slowed as the contractor unsuccessfully objected to Ritchie's role in construction supervision. The building was due in October 1890, but was not completed until 1891, because of delays resulting from materials shortages and a strike. The final cost exceeded $200,000. On 6 June 1891, King County officials celebrated the second anniversary of the 1889 fire by moving into the building.[28]

Ritchie's inexperience with classical design was particularly evident in the awkward dome, although the building was impressive in its monumentality. However, the county commissioners had probably been most impressed with Ritchie's experience with large institutional building construction, something no other local architect could equal. The courthouse, constructed of stone and brick with a steel beam and tile floor system, was nearly fully fireproof, but it also proved completely inflexible—a feature that was a frequent source of complaint until the building was demolished in 1931.

Ritchie's experience with city buildings in Kansas also aided him in winning the commissions for the two new Seattle fire stations at Battery and Fourth and Broadway at Terrace and Eleventh.[29] (See Figs. 6.7, 6.8) Ritchie's early success with these public projects might have elevated him to the top rank of Seattle's designers, but he had little success in winning other projects in the city. His only other identified Seattle work from this period is the Mrs. G. M. Bowman house (1890, destroyed), a shingled structure with Queen Anne detail, built near the center of Fremont.[30] (Fig. 7.7) Instead, Ritchie's work over the next eighteen months consisted primarily of large institutional structures located in smaller cities throughout western Washington. His knowledge of fireproof construction, plus his early success with the King County project, gave him credibility with officials in the smaller communities.

Ritchie's submission for the courthouse in Whatcom County (in what is now Bellingham) was selected on 27 January 1890, besting seventeen other proposals. When construction began in April, the *Bellingham Bay Express* described the new building as "the most complete, most admirably arranged, and most ornate structure of the kind yet undertaken in Washington, except for the larger and more expensive edifice under construction in Seattle, from

7.7 Willis A. Ritchie, Mary E. (Mrs. G. M.) Bowman house, 1890 (destroyed)

Pacific Magazine *4/2 (August 1891), University of Washington Libraries, Manuscripts, Special Collections, University Archives Division*

7.8 Willis A. Ritchie, Whatcom County Courthouse, Whatcom (Bellingham), Washington, 1889–91 (destroyed)

Whatcom Museum Archives, Galen Biery Collection

plans by the same architect."[31] The Whatcom County Courthouse (1889–91, destroyed) was a two-story stone structure, with a tower originally proposed at 100 feet tall. (Fig. 7.8) In contrast to the classical style he had used for King County, Ritchie here designed in the Richardsonian Romanesque mode that became his typical approach for large institutional buildings for the next three years. Although officials hoped that the building would be finished by October 1890, problems with the quality of the available stone and difficulties in obtain-

7.9 Willis A. Ritchie, DeMattos Block, Sehome (New Whatcom, Bellingham), Washington, 1890 (destroyed)

Whatcom Museum Archives, Galen Biery Collection

ing other materials contributed to delays. Construction, by contractor John Rigby, was not completed until February 1891 at a cost of $65,000.[32] The Whatcom Courthouse followed the King County model; it was a fireproof building with exterior stone walls, interior brick or tile partitions, and steel and tile floors; wood was used only for the roof structure. It was apparently the only project that Ritchie submitted for publication in a professional journal—it appeared in the Minneapolis-based *Northwestern Architect* in May 1891.[33] (See Fig. 4.45)

In contrast to Seattle, the cities on Bellingham Bay commissioned several commercial projects from Ritchie. Work on his DeMattos Block (1890, destroyed), a three-story stone building, began in May 1890 and was completed in September. The design resembled his Winfield commercial work, but featured semi-circular arches reflecting Ritchie's continuing use of Romanesque motifs. (Fig. 7.9) A second project, a four-story block for the Columbia National Bank, was commissioned in May 1890, but construction did not begin until the fall and apparently never proceeded beyond the foundation because of the Panic of 1890.[34]

By June 1890, Ritchie had also won commissions for three schools, one in Ellensburg and two in Olympia. The Ellensburg School Board had advertised in March for designs for a building to provide space for eight hundred students. A school bond vote was approved on 23 April, and on 8 May the *Ellensburg*

7.10 Willis A. Ritchie, Ellensburg School, Ellensburg, Washington, 1890–91 (destroyed)

Ellensburg Public Library, Local History Collection

Capital reported that the school board had selected Ritchie's design, stating "Mr. Ritchie designed the King County courthouse and the Whatcom County courthouse, the two finest buildings in the State, and he will no doubt erect a magnificent school building for the citizens of Ellensburg."[35] Officials hoped that the building would be ready by October. On 25 June, a contract for $38,650 was signed with the low bidder, John Scott of Ellensburg, whom the *Capital* described as a "pusher." Although the building was to open by 1 November 1890, problems with the school bonds delayed the project. When the building finally opened in September 1891, the *Capital* claimed it was the finest school building in Washington.[36] The Ellensburg School (1890–91, destroyed) was a symmetrical rectilinear composition in plan with six classrooms on each floor, but Ritchie's asymmetrical placement of Romanesque Revival elements resulted in a more picturesque appearance and the tower added a typical Victorian vertical emphasis. (Fig. 7.10)

In May 1890, the Olympia School District advertised in papers in Olympia, Tacoma, and Seattle for one design to be used for two eight-room schools, each costing not more than $25,000. Ten firms submitted designs by 20 May, and Ritchie's was selected. The construction contract was awarded in late June. The school names, Washington and Lincoln, were selected in September, but

the buildings were not completed until late March 1891.[37] The two buildings
were virtually identical—each was symmetrical, and nearly square in plan,
but, as at Ellensburg, the asymmetrical treatment of the roof and dormers produced a picturesque appearance; the vocabulary was Romanesque. (Fig. 7.11)

Spring 1890 was a busy season for Ritchie; he was also preparing a competitive design for the Jefferson County Courthouse in Port Townsend. Buoyed
by an anticipated railroad connection and the expected accompanying growth,
the Jefferson County Commissioners planned a $100,000 building. On 8 May
1890, they advertised for designs, and on 27 June, the local paper, *The Morning
Leader*, reported that eight sets of plans and specifications had been received,
indicating that "some of the best architects on the Sound" had submitted and
claiming "All of the plans submitted are beautiful and appropriate in design
so that the county is sure of a splendid building."[38] The next day, the *Leader*
identified the architects of each design, and noted that Comstock and Trotsche
of Seattle and San Diego, Whiteway and Schroeder of Port Townsend, and W. A.
Ritchie of Seattle were finalists. Finally, on 2 July, the *Leader* reported the
selection of Ritchie's scheme, which was described as the "only absolutely
fireproof" design among the eight proposals.[39] The *Leader* went on: "Taken as
the drawing of the building shows, it will certainly be one of the handsomest

buildings in this country, and, as the architect, Mr. Ritchie says, it is the very finest piece of architectural work he has ever designed or planned, which speaks volumes for our new Courthouse in style and beauty." The proposal by John Rigby (the contractor on Ritchie's Whatcom County Courthouse) to construct this building for $100,000 was also accepted.

The local architectural firm of Whiteway and Schroeder immediately complained. On 4 July, under the title "The Merry Sounds of Boodle," Whiteway was quoted as saying the building could not be built for that price, that it was not a fireproof design, and that Whiteway and Shroeder's second-place design was better planned. But, when questioned, County Commissioner Weymouth indicated that the Whiteway and Shroeder design had been placed second only to give the local firm publicity and their design was "at best really fourth or fifth." Ritchie was also quoted to the effect that John Rigby, because he owned a sash and door factory, could bid jobs closer than other contractors.[40] On 8 July, after a visit by Rigby to Port Townsend, the *Leader* confirmed that he would build the project for the $100,000 bid. In addition, Rigby planned to hire local workers.[41] Further, Ritchie stated that he had been unfairly accused of changing the Whatcom County Courthouse plans after he won the design competition because he made changes requested by the Whatcom County commissioners. He indicated that the plans submitted for the Jefferson County competition would remain in Port Townsend and two members of the Seattle office force would be brought to the city to make copies of the plans for use in Seattle. Although Whiteway had indicated he would campaign against the courthouse bonds, when the vote took place on 19 September, the project was approved overwhelmingly. Contracts were signed in early October, but the project went slowly.[42] The cornerstone ceremony took place on 2 July 1891, and construction proceeded through the next year. On 16 July 1892, the *Leader* finally announced that those conducting county business should now go to the new courthouse. The final project cost, including the heating plant and furnishings, was approximately $150,000.

The Jefferson County Courthouse (1890–92) is a large brick building with a partially raised stone basement, measuring 84 feet by 149 feet, with a 124-foot tower. (Figs. 7.12, 7.13, 7.14) As at his other courthouses, Ritchie used wood only for the roof structure. With details of stone and terra-cotta, the design was Ritchie's finest in the Richardsonian Romanesque mode, although his tendency to compose picturesquely is still evident. Features of the primary facade are similar to those of Garfield University in Wichita, a building Ritchie knew from his years in Kansas. (See Fig. 4.26) The dramatic scale of the building demonstrated the confidence that late-nineteenth-century Port Townsend civic leaders had in the future of their community. In their book on Victorian architecture in Port Townsend, Denison and Huntington offered this assessment of the courthouse:

> One might criticize Ritchie's work as being too facile, too undisciplined. But for all
> its faults the architecture of the Jefferson County Courthouse is rewarding for the

- JEFFERSON · COVNTY · COVRT · HOVSE. -

- SIDE · ELEVATION. -

- Scale 4"·1·0: -

- W. A. Ritchie, Arch.
- Seattle, Wash -

7.12 Willis A. Ritchie,
Jefferson County
Courthouse, Port Townsend,
Washington, 1890–92; side
elevation

Private collection

266   Creating a Civic Presence

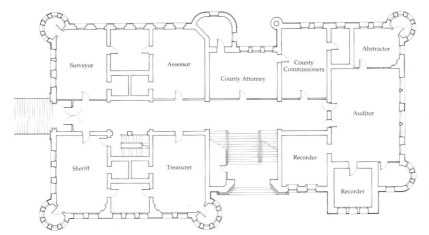

7.13 Willis A. Ritchie, Jefferson County Courthouse, first floor plan

Redrawn by Gretchen van Dusen and Youngmin Han from blueprint held by Jefferson County (courtesy Frank Gifford)

7.14 Willis A. Ritchie, Jefferson County Courthouse

Private collection

skilled manner in which the bulky massiveness of stone is juxtaposed against the smooth, flat areas of brick and rewarding as well for the high quality sculptured details in random and unpredictable locations.

Richardson himself had no rivals in his ability to handle the Romanesque forms that he popularized, but many architects handled the mode less skillfully than Ritchie and the great arched entry dominating the west façade is a powerful and impressive feature. Ironically, it is in the rear of the building where the more fashionable and sometimes too chaotic forms yield to the functional and unadorned parts of the build-

7.15 Willis A. Ritchie, Thurston County Courthouse, Olympia, 1890–92 (altered)

Manuscripts, Special Collections, University Archives Division, University of Washington Libraries, photo ca. 1900; UW4874

ing such as the smokestack, where Ritchie comes nearest to capturing the spirit of his famous predecessor.[43]

On 12 December 1890, the Thurston County Commissioners voted to employ Ritchie to design their new courthouse in Olympia. Whether he had already provided a preliminary scheme is unknown, but just a month later Ritchie submitted construction documents although the project did not go forward until the approval and sale of bonds in April 1891. On 15 May the *Morning Olympian* carried a lengthy description of the project, when ground was broken. Praised as "beyond question the handsomest in the State," the courthouse was described as "after the Romanesque in architecture, the style prevailing so extensively in new public buildings in recent years."[44] Again, the construction was characterized as "entirely fireproof." The building was completed in late summer 1892.[45]

The Thurston County Courthouse (1890–91, altered) was a symmetrical building constructed of Chuckanut stone barged to Olympia from the quarries in Whatcom County. The building measured 146 feet by 78 feet in plan and the central tower rose to a height of 150 feet. (Fig. 7.15) The design treatment was particularly disciplined, both in its symmetry and by the relative lack of ornament, allowing the rock-faced stone to read more strongly. As at the Jefferson County Courthouse, Ritchie appears to have drawn on his memories of buildings he knew in Kansas as some elements here recall those of the Wichita City Hall. (See Fig. 4.27) After preferring asymmetry for so long, why Ritchie turned to a symmetrical composition for Thurston County is unknown, but it might have been a design response to the anticipated construction of a new state capitol building in Olympia, which would traditionally have been a symmetrical building. Ernest Flagg's winning project in the 1893–94 State Capitol competition was, in fact, a symmetrical composition of classical design. However, that project never proceeded beyond the foundation. In 1901, the state legislature provided money to purchase Ritchie's building for use as the State Capitol. Ritchie was subsequently commissioned to design a new east wing to accommodate the legislature and additional state offices. The legislature moved into the building in 1905, and it served as the State Capitol until 1927.[46]

Not all of Ritchie's institutional commissions were as large as these courthouse and school projects. His Washington State Soldiers Home (1890–91, destroyed) in Orting was much more domestic in scale and design. The idea for a state soldiers' home developed in response to federal pensions for those who had served in the Civil War; in March 1890 the state legislature voted to provide appropriate accommodations for elderly and infirm veterans. Meetings of the commission responsible for the Soldiers Home were reported by newspapers across western Washington from August to October 1890. By late August the commission had determined on the "cottage plan" with a number of individual residences as well as a larger dining hall and dormitory building. In early November the commission decided to locate the facility at Orting and to retain Ritchie as architect. The Port Townsend *Morning Leader* stated, "Architect Ritchie has already done considerable work on the plans and will strive to make the several buildings for the home models for other States to follow. His plans have been warmly approved by the commission, members of which are highly pleased at securing the services of so excellent an architect."[47] Construction was completed by June 1891. In its report on the dedication, the *Post-Intelligencer* offered the following description: "The home is one of the most complete institutions in the state. It comprises a large main building with four handsome cottages located a short distance from the four corners. The main building is three stories in height. . . . The cottages are each one story high. There are accommodations for 150 persons in the buildings. They are fitted up in a tasteful and neat manner and are supplied with all necessary conveniences."[48] In fact, the buildings were wood structures painted white with colonial detail. (Fig. 7.16)

In the early 1890s, the New Year's day editions of the *Post-Intelligencer* usually included a lengthy review of the accomplishments of Seattle and Washington State in the preceding year. The issue for 1891 touted the rebuilding of Seattle in the eighteen months after the fire. It also included a stunning half-page advertisement titled "Work of September, 1889, to January, 1891," in which "W. A. Ritchie, Public Building Architect" described his four courthouses, three schools, the soldiers' home, two fire stations, and commercial buildings in

7.16 Willis A. Ritchie,
Washington State Soldiers'
Home (main building),
Orting, 1890–91
(destroyed)

West Shore 17 (7 Mar.
1891); Manuscripts, Special
Collections, University
Archives Division, University
of Washington Libraries

Sehome (Bellingham). Ritchie noted the cost of each building, and provided
large drawings of the Jefferson County and Thurston County courthouses. The
total cost listed for the work was $848,000, which clearly placed Ritchie among
the leading architects in Washington.[49] Why he chose to advertise in this manner, which was unprecedented for an architect in Seattle, is unknown. He may
have sensed a lessening of demand for architectural services and sought this
method to continue to draw commissions; his work was primarily located outside Seattle and he may have wanted to bring it to the attention of potential
Seattle clients. It may be that he was beginning to sense the impact on construction of the economic troubles that began in late 1890 and would continue
through 1891.

For all his success, it is important to recognize that Ritchie did not win every
competition he entered. Architects do not emphasize their unsuccessful
attempts to secure commissions, and the names of losing competitors were often
not recorded or published, so it is unknown how many such competitions Ritchie
lost. However, several have been identified. The first was a new school in Port
Townsend; on 16 July 1890, the *Morning Leader* named all eleven architects
who had presented school plans the day before, among them Ritchie; the commission was awarded to G. C. Clements, a Tacoma architect.[50] Ritchie also
submitted a design to the B. F. Day School competition in Seattle that was won
by John Parkinson in August 1891. And, for the State Normal School in
Ellensburg, the *Post-Intelligencer* listed Ritchie among the competitors on 27
April 1893, but an Ellensburg architect won that commission.[51]

Ritchie may also have wished to compete for the Pierce County Courthouse
in Tacoma in spring 1890, but he was prevented from doing so. The enmity
between Tacoma and Seattle as a result of their competition for ascendancy on
Puget Sound may have been one reason why the Pierce County commissioners, when calling for designs, insisted that "all plans should be drawn within

the County of Pierce." On 12 June 1890, after designs had been received, the *Tacoma Morning Globe* reported that selection would be delayed because a petition had been submitted claiming that the project by Charles H. Smith of Tacoma had actually been drawn by a Seattle architect. John C. Proctor of the Tacoma firm Proctor and Dennis protested that these plans were by "architect Riche [*sic*], of Seattle, who recently superintended erection of a schoolhouse at Olympia, there stated to a Tacoma architect that he would like to compete for the proposed courthouse."[52] Proctor claimed that Ritchie had paid Smith to submit the plans under his name—charges Smith denied. Within a few days Proctor's partner, Oliver P. Dennis, requested that the petition be dropped, and on 18 June the commissioners announced their selection of Proctor and Dennis's design for the Pierce County project; Charles Smith did not place. Whether Ritchie had actually designed Smith's project is not known.[53]

Ritchie's success engendered considerable jealousy within Seattle's architectural community. Some felt that his frequent selection was a result of his using unfair methods to compete. His first major commission in Washington, the King County Courthouse, had generated protests when the county commissioners terminated the competition. Rumors of changes in the plans and specifications had swirled around the Whatcom County Courthouse. Throughout his early career in Washington, Ritchie was frequently involved in controversy. Of course, public buildings were the focus of considerable attention, and the actions of architects and contractors received much scrutiny. Ritchie's youth or his manner (as revealed in the *Post-Intelligencer* advertisement) may have provoked other architects. Their irritation very likely increased when Ritchie was one of just two architects (Elmer Fisher was the other) profiled in the May 1891 issue of the Seattle-based *Northwestern Real Estate and Building Review*.[54] The writer asserted that Ritchie was "born an architect." He was credited with the complete design of the Wichita Federal Building. The writer glossed over the process of the King County Courthouse competition, only to say, "His triumph was complete." Following a list of his major projects, won "in the face of the keenest and most formidable competition," was the prediction "a great future lies before this talented and rising young architect." Given the lack of commissions in mid-1891 because of the recession, other Seattle architects could only have considered this excessive.

The distance between Ritchie and his fellow professionals is most clearly evident in John Parkinson's autobiography, published more than forty years later. Parkinson said little about other Seattle architects of the period, but specifically recalled Ritchie. His summary is also interesting as an indication of the conditions under which competitions were held at the time:

Generally competitions were carried out in a friendly and courteous way and the result accepted as satisfactory. There was one architect, Richie [*sic*], however, whom we all despised, but he managed to get the public buildings. In one Court House competition, as usual, he was awarded the job, whereas by his drawings he was entirely outclassed. After the award, the competing architects were standing in a group discussing the result, when Richie, who had a hard, slick looking face, joined the group. I accosted him, saying, 'You got this job by unfair means, in the next competition I will beat you.' He did not resent my accusation, but half grinned and turning, left us. A few months later, there was a competition for an eight room brick school building, south of Seattle. Both Seattle and Tacoma architects competed, including Richie. One member of the School Board had a feed store, sold grain, hay, etc. I used to call on him, and sitting on a bale of hay we would discuss the new school building and became very friendly. The architects were to submit their plans in the old school house, a wood building consisting of one room, located at the foot of a hill, where a few years before the timber had been cut leaving the old stumps projecting up through the ferns and underbrush. Each architect was to have twenty minutes to explain his plans. Some ten of us, including Richie were there. I knew his game which was to be the last man, and knew from my friend just how he stood with the Board, who were honest without exception. The room was about forty feet long by twenty-four feet wide; across the far corner a blanket hung and behind it each architect in turn explained the plans to the three members of the Board. I arranged with my friend to be first to have ten minutes, then excuse myself and have my final ten minutes after all the others were through. I took my ten minutes, was excused, left the school house and climbed the hill where, seated on a stump, I saw the various architects take trail for Seattle, leaving only Richie, then I entered the school. Richie was promptly told when his time was up that I was waiting for my remaining ten minutes. I grinned at him as he passed on his way out. After my remaining ten minutes, I came out from behind the curtain with the job and the building was erected.[55]

About the actual operation of Ritchie's office little is known. Because Ritchie had projects simultaneously under way in multiple cities in western Washington, he must have spent considerable time traveling and must, therefore, have depended significantly on his office staff. Among those who worked in his Seattle office were Theobald Buchinger, who later practiced independently and in partnership in Seattle, and Daniel J. Patterson, who later practiced in San Francisco. Both later claimed to have had major roles in the design of Ritchie's buildings. (Patterson drew the Whatcom Courthouse perspective that appeared in *Northwestern Architect*.) Others who worked in the office included Wert W. Reid, W. A. Villeneuve, Paul Bungart, and Ritchie's wife, Etta Reid Ritchie.[56]

Ritchie's Seattle Practice after 1890

Although Ritchie remained busy supervising his many buildings under construction in western Washington, he received fewer new projects in 1891. He did secure the Clark County Courthouse commission after the design by another architect could not be financed. On 25 February 1890, the old Clark County Courthouse burned, and following a successful bond election in April, Clark County advertised for designs for a brick courthouse and jail to cost $40,000. In early June the county received five submissions, including one by

7.17 Willis A. Ritchie,
Clark County Courthouse,
Vancouver, Washington,
1891–92 (destroyed)

*Washington State University
Libraries, Historical Photographs Collection, WSU
78–995*

Ritchie, but on 11 June, the *Vancouver Register* reported that the design by O. M. Hidden of Vancouver had been selected.[57] However, construction was delayed for a year due to difficulty in selling the bonds. In May 1891, Ritchie met with the commissioners to propose that his design be accepted; in return, the contractor he would bring to erect the building for $40,000 would accept the bonds in payment. This proposal was accepted and in June the contract was awarded to A. M. Evans of Seattle. The project went forward quickly thereafter, and was completed in early February 1892, when the *Register* reported, "Contractor A. M. Evans has given us a much better building in many respects than the specifications called for. The new building is substantial, well finished, an ornament to the city and a credit to the county."[58] Ritchie's design for the Clark County Courthouse (1890–92, destroyed) was actually a re-working of his Whatcom County design, executed in brick rather than stone. (Fig. 7.17) The general massing, placement of elements such as the tower, and pattern of fenestration all echoed the Whatcom building. However, in developing the Clark County building in brick, Ritchie turned away from a Romanesque Revival design. Rather, his scheme was surprisingly retrograde in the mix of window shapes and details that reflected earlier American Victorian convention.

In late 1891, Ritchie became embroiled in a controversy over the Washington State Building for the World's Columbian Exposition in Chicago. The state commission responsible for coordinating the Washington exhibits at the exposition had been formed in January 1891, and subsequently their executive committee held planning meetings in various cities. In early July the committee invited architects to submit designs for the state pavilion. Although the designs were

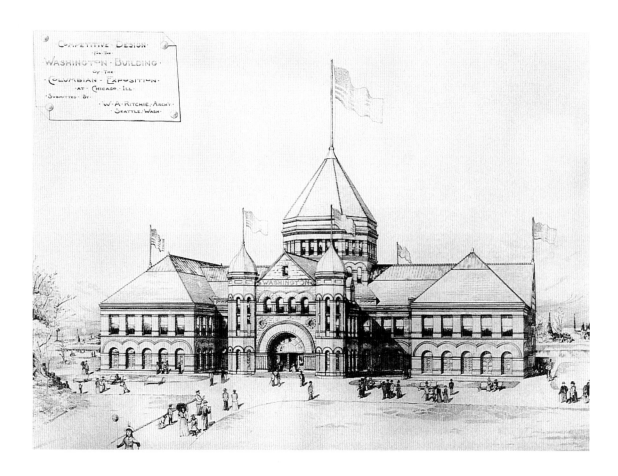

COMPETITIVE · DESIGN ·
for the
WASHINGTON · BUILDING ·
of the
COLUMBIAN · EXPOSITION ·
at · Chicago · Ill ·
Submitted · By ·
· W · A · Ritchie · Arch'y ·
· Seattle · Wash ·

7.18 Willis A. Ritchie, First Place Design for Washington State Building, World's Columbian Exposition, 1891–92 (unbuilt)

Manuscripts, Special Collections, University Archives Division, University of Washington Libraries

not due until November, architects began offering suggestions to the committee almost immediately. Spokane architect Herman Preusse's ideas were transmitted in a letter read at the committee's mid-July meeting in Port Townsend, and Ritchie addressed the same meeting.[59] The invitation for designs indicated that the building was to be built from materials found in the state and should be considered part of the exhibit. On 19 November, at their Seattle meeting, the executive committee selected the winning designs from the twenty-two entries they had received. According to newspaper reports, the first place scheme, by Ritchie, "won favor with the Committee chiefly on account of the excellence of the floor plan. There is no waste room, there are no niches, and no sharp angles"; the style was characterized as Romanesque.[60] (Fig. 7.18) Bullard and Haywood of Tacoma placed second, and Seattle architect Warren Skillings was third. However, when the state's selection was transmitted to Chicago for approval (which the commission assumed would be automatic), Daniel Burnham, the exposition's chief of construction, refused to accept Ritchie's design, which he described as "inferior in every way"[61] and "commonplace."[62] Instead, he chose Skillings's third-place scheme. Burnham's rejection of Ritchie's design produced considerable controversy in Washington, but he refused to alter his position. Although the state commission awarded Ritchie the $500 first-place prize and Skillings the $200 third-place prize in January 1892, two months later it capitulated to Burnham's decision and

approved Skillings's proposal, which was the design erected at the Chicago Fair.[63] (Fig. 7.19)

Ritchie had built his career in Washington through the series of public buildings he had designed in the Romanesque mode, and his proposed state pavilion reflected the same design approach. While the executive committee of the state commission had probably seen this as a positive feature, showing that the metropolitan development of Washington was comparable to that in the East, Burnham sought a design he considered more regionally expressive and therefore selected Skillings's rustic proposal. The issue was not that Ritchie's building was structurally or functionally inadequate, but rather it did not fit within the approach that Burnham envisioned for state buildings—an approach that reflected the unique character of each state as he saw it. Burnham's decision indicated his awareness of the latest national trends in design—the regionalist idea for the state pavilions was one direction within the new academic eclectic approach of the fair—while Ritchie's project reflected the Romanesque Revival design tendency that would soon be eclipsed.[64]

On 23 March 1892, the list of architects advertising their services in the *Spokane Review* expanded to include "W. A. Ritchie, Architect." Ritchie identified his expertise as "public buildings and fireproof work" and gave as his office address four rooms in Spokane's Auditorium Building.[65] Ritchie never stated publicly why he moved from Seattle to Spokane, but several factors

7.19 Warren P. Skillings, Third Place Design for Washington State Building, World's Columbian Exposition, accepted by D. H. Burnham and built in Chicago, 1891–93 (destroyed)

Manuscripts, Special Collections, University Archives Division, University of Washington Libraries

7.20 Willis A. Ritchie, Spokane City Building, Spokane, Washington, 1892–94 (destroyed)

Northwest Museum of Arts and Culture/Eastern Washington State Historical Society, Spokane

undoubtedly influenced his decision. The growth of Puget Sound cities was slowed by the recession of 1890–91, and the opportunities for additional major public building projects were becoming limited. Most counties that could afford to build new courthouses had already done so. And after John Parkinson won the commission for the B. F. Day School in Seattle in August 1891, he became the leading school designer in the city; when Parkinson was selected as the official architect of the Seattle School District in April 1892, that not only meant that there would be no Seattle schools for other architects but also that he would have an advantage in competing for schools outside Seattle.[66] In contrast, Spokane and the Inland Empire offered design opportunities that Seattle and Puget Sound could no longer match. By early 1892, there were discussions in Spokane of both a new city building and a new county courthouse. As Spokane had emerged as the center of the Inland Empire, it would be a location from which an architect could compete for projects in eastern Washington, Idaho, and western Montana. Finally, Spokane had comparatively fewer practicing architects than Seattle, and none of them could match Ritchie's public building experience.

Ritchie's move to Spokane almost immediately led to design commissions. On 11 April 1892, the Wallace, Idaho, School Board commissioned Ritchie to design a new school building, and soon after he also received school projects in Anaconda, Montana.[67] Subsequently he won the competition for the Spokane City Building (1892–94, destroyed) with a Richardsonian design.[68] (Fig. 7.20) His selection generated controversy, as some local architects protested award-

7.21 Willis A. Ritchie,
King County Hospital,
County Poor Farm, south
of Seattle, 1893–94
(destroyed)

Beginnings, Progress and
Achievement in the Medical
Work of King County,
Washington (Seattle: 1930?),
photo ca. 1902; University of
Washington Libraries, Special
Collections and Preservation
Division, UW15998

ing the commission to an architect who they claimed did not really intend to remain in Spokane.

In January 1893, Ritchie reopened his Seattle office, but he also maintained his practice in Spokane, and for the next six months he operated offices in both cities.[69] He returned to Seattle to design a single building, the King County Hospital (1893, destroyed). On 22 January, the *Post-Intelligencer* reported that the county commissioners had appointed Ritchie to plan a new joint county-city hospital to accommodate the indigent and sick on the Poor Farm grounds south of the city.[70] However, just two days later, the paper reported that the city would not participate and Ritchie had proposed a plan for a smaller building. Described as a plain, three-story building of brick with stone trim, this was fireproof throughout, with construction similar to Ritchie's courthouses. Separate wards were to be provided for each sex. The building was called "a model of convenience" and it was noted that the design had been examined and approved by physicians. The project was bid in March and April, and John Rigby was the low bidder at $79,400, but one of the wings, bid as an alternate, could not be afforded.[71] Thus, although the design was symmetrical, the constructed building was not; when the missing wing was added later, the design did not follow Ritchie's original scheme. Ritchie's design was a relatively utilitarian building of brick, with classical columns at the main entrance and second floor loggia. (Fig. 7.21)

When construction proceeded in June 1893, the *Post-Intelligencer* noted that Ritchie's selection without an open competition had been the subject of complaint, and that Rigby's price, which was several thousand dollars below the next bidder, had been questioned. Nonetheless, the project proceeded rapidly and by September the roof framing was under way. However, on 27 September the paper reported that the grand jury was investigating fraud in the design and construction of the hospital. For the next month, the paper frequently presented charges and counter-charges concerning the quality of the construction and alleged substitutions of less expensive materials. But on 8 November the grand jury report exonerated the county commissioners, the architect, and the contractor. They found that several changes had been ordered by the county commissioners and that the quality of the workmanship met construction industry norms. (Instead the grand jury attacked the quality of John Parkinson's Pacific School.) Just two days later several unhappy citizens filed a lawsuit to enjoin payment of Ritchie and Rigby and to stop construction, claiming the county lacked the authority to proceed. In mid-December, the courts upheld the right of the county to build the hospital; this would have seemed to bring the controversy to an end, but in January 1894 a citizens' committee, including John Parkinson and several business leaders, was formed to investigate Rigby's request for payment of extras in addition to his base bid. On 3 February this committee finally reported, approving Rigby's extras but deducting the savings he had achieved elsewhere in the project through substitutions of less expensive materials. This brought the controversy to an end.[72] Ritchie's work in Seattle also came to an end; he had already closed his Seattle office in mid-1893.

Even with the King County project, Ritchie's practice in spring and summer 1893 remained primarily in Spokane as he won two more public building commissions there.[73] The first was for the Union Park (later Edison) School (1893, destroyed). The second was the Spokane County Courthouse (1893–96), the largest commission of Ritchie's career, and his sixth courthouse. (Fig. 7.22) The overall form of this structure with a tall central tower was clearly derived from Richardson's Allegheny County Courthouse, and may have been influenced by Long and Kees's Hennepin County Courthouse in Minneapolis as well. (See Figs. 4.7, 4.41) But Ritchie did not adopt their Romanesque language. His building, executed in light buff brick with terra-cotta detail, is easily described as "chateauesque." Henry-Russell Hitchcock characterized the design as "altogether exceptional for the profusion and the accurate execution of its early French Renaissance detail."[74]

The course of Ritchie's career clearly shows the vicissitudes of Romanesque Revival design. Ritchie's early training, gained in construction and through a correspondence school, emphasized the practical aspects of architecture. His initial experience was gained in smaller towns and cities in the Midwest and his early work reflected American High Victorian design tendencies. Ritchie probably first saw Romanesque Revival design in Wichita, but he did not consistently adopt the Romanesque Revival until late 1889 or early 1890, and then his compositional approach remained picturesque even as his architectural vocabulary became Richardsonian. Ritchie's success in winning commissions was no doubt due in large part to his superior knowledge and experience in designing large fireproof institutional buildings. Although he had emerged as the leading architect in Washington by 1892, D. H. Burnham's rejection of his

design for the World's Columbian Exposition reflected the waning of the Roman-esque Revival. Ritchie's last major building in the mode was the Spokane City Hall. His career peaked with the Spokane County Courthouse, which showed a compositional strategy derived from Richardson's example, but a design vocabulary decidedly not Richardson's.

Ritchie was among the last of the leading architects of the post-fire period to arrive in Seattle; he was the first to depart. But, he was not long alone; by the mid-1890s many of Seattle's architects would choose to follow his example as the severity of the economic collapse on Puget Sound forced them to look elsewhere for opportunities to pursue their architectural careers.

7.22 Willis A. Ritchie, Spokane County Courthouse, Spokane, 1893–96

University of Washington Libraries, Special Collections and Preservation Division, UW13500

VIII

Toward the Turn of the Century
Seattle after 1895

Adverse conditions prevail in almost all branches of industry and business. The unexpected scarcity of money has resulted in the tying up of funds that would otherwise be invested and has frightened away more capital than any similar depression has done in recent memory.

—"Business Outlook," *Inland Architect* 22/2 (Sept. 1893): 24

By the summer of 1893, I had become quite a capitalist, and owed some one hundred fifty thousand dollars on the various properties. In the winter of 1893 and 1894, a serious business depression developed. There was neither business nor prospects. I was in a tight place.

—John Parkinson, *Incidents by the Way*, 165

Construction in Seattle never fully recovered after the Panic of 1890. Although building resumed by 1892, the level never approached that of the boom years of 1889 to 1890. But slow construction after 1890 became complete collapse in the aftermath of the Panic of 1893. The bank failures of May 1893 and the ensuing uncertainty in financial markets meant that credit virtually disappeared, interest rates rose to impossible levels, and money was no longer available for new investment. Tight money was felt throughout the economy. In early July 1893, Edwin Houghton optimistically looked forward to "many new buildings," but by late July the *Post-Intelligencer* was referring to "Hard Times."[1] Seattle architects finished work already under way, but few new commissions were forthcoming. (Fig. 8.1)

After August 1893 the city of Seattle began looking for ways to reduce expenses by cutting clerical staff, limiting the size of the police force, and reducing salaries. Some predicted that the economic troubles would be short-lived, but no improvement was apparent in Seattle for several years. The withdrawal of funds from the West by eastern investors had led to the collapse of construction. When confidence began to return, eastern capitalists initially supported new real estate projects in eastern and midwestern cities and were slower to make money available in cities in the West where their losses had been severe. As a result, the Panic of 1893 was much deeper and lasted much longer in most of the West than in the East.[2]

Seattle architects had hoped for better times. In December 1893, A. B. Chamberlin predicted that there would be more opportunities in 1894.[3] He suggested that projects such as the University of Washington and a new state

8.1 View north along
Commercial Street (now
First Avenue South), ca.
1904. Although photo-
graphed a decade later,
this view shows the post-
fire reconstruction that
was essentially complete
by 1894.

Paul Dorpat collection

capitol in Olympia would create demand for building and for architects' services. He also proposed that the completion of the Great Northern Railroad
would foster new development in Seattle. But few new buildings were actually
announced in 1894. Charles Saunders won the University of Washington competition, and that project did proceed into construction. New York architect
Ernest Flagg won the 1893–94 Washington State Capitol competition, but
his building proceeded only as far as the foundation due to the inability of the
state to pay for construction.[4] Other projects were announced, but never went
beyond planning. A notable example was the Yesler Avenue Hotel, a project
of Chicago real estate developer C. P. Dose. On 10 January 1894, the *Post-
Intelligencer* reported that Chicago architect "Frank L. Wright" had already
completed the plans for the six-story building at Yesler and Fifth. Wright's project
was mentioned again on 29 January and 26 March, but nothing came of these
reports.[5] The decline in construction proved severe and showed no evidence
of abating. Seattle building permits had exceeded $6 million in 1889, but fell
to only $240,000 in 1897, just 4 percent of the 1889 peak.[6]

One way architects responded to the crisis in building was by seeking to
enhance their professional standing. In 1889 and 1890, in the aftermath of the
fire, Seattle architects had been hard pressed to keep up with the demand for

their services. But, as demand began to slacken after 1890, concern arose about the professional status of architects, including the levels of their fees and the fairness of design competitions. Some complaints in this regard were soon voiced. In March 1893, a controversy arose over the architect selection process for the West Seattle School; apparently the choice had been influenced by differences in the fees requested by the competitors. Warren Skillings argued that architects in Seattle were not as valued as those in eastern cities, and proposed that fee schedules should be standardized so that competitions would truly be decided on the merits of the submitted designs.[7]

By 1894, the deepening recession was affecting all architects in Washington. On 13 March, architects from across the state met in Seattle to form the Washington State Chapter of the American Institute of Architects, the national professional organization. Seattle was the city most strongly represented and the officers selected included William Boone, William Willcox, and Charles Saunders. Other Seattle members included Emil DeNeuf, Arthur B. Chamberlin, Albert Wickersham, and Charles Bebb.[8] The Washington State chapter announced that it would seek to raise the standards for entry into the profession; the chapter passed a resolution stating, "only men of professional training shall be recognized as architects."[9] In January 1895, the AIA petitioned the University of Washington to create a professorship in architecture (the first step in what would be a nearly twenty-year process to create an architecture school at the university). And that March the chapter became involved in boycotting the Queen Anne School competition, which in turn led to the expulsion of two members (Willcox and Chamberlin).[10] Nonetheless, the AIA chapter could not overcome the faltering economy.

The Changing Face of the Profession

The impact of the continuing recession is nowhere more evident than in the Seattle city directories of the period in which the declining number of architects tells the story. In 1890, Seattle directories listed thirty firms offering architectural services; by 1897 the number was reduced to only eleven.[11] Indeed, by 1896, most of the leading architects of the post-fire period had left the city.

Elmer Fisher gave up the practice of architecture in 1891, and thereafter sought to live on income from the Abbott Hotel and from other investments.[12] Fisher had invested in several ventures including the city's first plant to provide steam for heat to downtown buildings. In March 1892 he tried local politics, running for alderman from the fifth ward on the Republican ticket. However, he lost as Democrats swept every city office.[13] Fisher's investments in real estate would have left him vulnerable at the onset of the Panic of 1893, but his difficulties were considerably compounded by a scandal that erupted early that year. On 15 February 1893, Fisher married a widow and daughter of a local clerk, Charlotte Mollie Willey. When the couple returned from their honeymoon in Portland, Fisher was named in a $10,000 lawsuit brought by

Mary H. Smith of Victoria, British Columbia, for breach of promise. Smith stated that she had met Fisher in Denver in 1884 and claimed they had made "a verbal agreement" to "live together . . . as husband and wife as long as they should live."[14] She had resided with Fisher in Colorado, Montana, and British Columbia, but she indicated that he had abandoned her in Victoria when he had come to Seattle. In the controversy that followed, Fisher admitted that Smith had been his mistress, and that he had introduced her as his wife in Victoria "to avoid public scandal," but he claimed that theirs was purely a business relationship. The case attracted headlines not only in Seattle but also in Tacoma. Finally settled in September 1893, when a jury found Fisher innocent of the breach of promise, the case nonetheless sullied Fisher's reputation.[15] The timing could not have been worse.

In May, Fisher had opened a new architectural practice in Seattle. Because he had transferred his earlier office to Emil DeNeuf, he was effectively starting over. His biggest clients previously had been Henry Yesler and Thomas Burke, but Yesler had died in December 1892 and Burke built no additional buildings after the collapse of the opera house project. Further, Fisher was identified with the architecture of 1889–91, and the direction of design was changing. Finally, it was the very same week that Fisher's new listing as an architect appeared in the *Post-Intelligencer* that reports began to appear of bank failures across the country.[16] Fisher's listing disappeared after only three months. No projects from this period of his career have been discovered. His name did not appear in Seattle directories in 1894. Fisher moved from Seattle to Los Angeles some time later and tried again to open an architectural practice. By June 1896, probably in lieu of unpaid rent, he turned over his office furnishings to T. D. Stimson for $1.[17] Thereafter, he may have worked as a carpenter and as a draftsman in John Parkinson's Los Angeles office. He may have died in Los Angeles about 1905, although his last years remain as obscure as his early life.[18]

John Parkinson was another of Seattle's post-fire architectural leaders who chose to pursue his career in Los Angeles. When Seattle voters failed to approve bonds to cover the existing school district debt in February 1894, any prospect for significant new school construction was eliminated. When Parkinson's resignation as schools architect took effect on 1 March, he no longer had a guaranteed income. Like Fisher, Parkinson had invested in Seattle real estate. He was the owner of the Seattle Athletic Club Building, but with the collapse of the Seattle economy, business blocks were not good investments and even the Athletic Club faced financial difficulties. Parkinson pursued every potential architectural opportunity, but he proved unlucky. For example, he developed a scheme for the Equitable Life Assurance Society's proposed Seattle headquarters, but nothing came of the project. (Fig. 8.2) In August 1893, he sued for unpaid fees of $5000, and alleged he had been induced to purchase $15,000 worth of life insurance as a condition of obtaining the project.[19] Parkinson also entered every open architectural competition in the region, but he was never

8.2 John Parkinson
(A. B. Chamberlin, del.),
Equitable Life Assurance
Building project, Seattle,
1890–91 (unbuilt)

*American Architect and
Building News 30 (12 Dec.
1891), Library of Congress*

·STVDY FOR THE·
·EQVITABLE·LIFE·ASSVRANCE·BVILDING·
·SEATTLE·

Jno·Parkinson·Architect·

8.3 John Parkinson
(A. B. Chamberlin, del.)
Washington State
Building competition
project, World's
Columbian Exposition,
Chicago, 1891 (unbuilt)

*American Architect and
Building News 33 (8 Oct.
1892), Library of Congress*

able to win a major building. His entry for the Washington World's Fair pavilion in 1892 was praised by the jury as "most artistic," but was rejected as too expensive; he did not place.[20] (Fig. 8.3) That year he also entered the British Columbia Parliament competition, but was not among the finalists. He entered the Spokane County Courthouse competition in July 1893, and was one of the six finalists after the first stage, but the three top finishers after the second stage were all residents of Spokane. In December 1893, he entered the Washington State Capitol competition that was won by Ernest Flagg the following April. And, in March 1894, his design came in second to that of Charles Saunders for the University of Washington building.

The announcement that Parkinson had placed second in the University of Washington competition came just two weeks after his schools position ended. With the limited opportunities available in Seattle, Parkinson had already begun looking to move. By the end of March, he was in Los Angeles, where, within a few years, he would become a leader in the city's architectural community, a position he would occupy until his death in 1935.[21] His best-known buildings are those he did in partnership with his son, Donald Parkinson, including the Los Angeles Coliseum, the Los Angeles City Hall, and Bullock's Wilshire (department store).

Other Seattle architects also sought better opportunities elsewhere. The architect who traveled farthest was Emil DeNeuf. His practice had never really expanded beyond those clients he had acquired from Elmer Fisher and by 1894, he was forced to close his office. From 1894 to 1900 he practiced architecture in Guatemala, but then returned to Seattle, where he formed a moderately successful partnership with Augustus Heide from 1901 to 1906.[22] He died in San Francisco in 1915.

William Willcox and Warren Skillings both tried California. Willcox had had little success in maintaining an independent practice in Seattle after his partnership with Boone was dissolved in 1892. In 1895, after he cut his ties with other members of the Seattle architecture profession by entering the Queen Anne School competition, he left the city and moved to Los Angeles. Willcox stayed there just three years, then moved again to San Francisco, where he practiced as an architect and then as a surveyor. He died in a veterans home at Yountville, in central California, in 1929, just before his ninety-seventh birthday.[23] His career had stretched across the continent, from New York in the East, to Chicago, Nebraska, and Minneapolis in the Midwest to Seattle and California in the West, reflecting the national growth of the architectural profession. After the completion of construction of the Queen Anne School in mid-1896, Warren Skillings also left Seattle, although the firm Skillings and Corner was listed in city directories though 1899. Skillings went briefly to Alaska, then moved to Eureka, California, where he practiced architecture until 1910. Skillings next moved to San Jose and continued in active practice until 1930. He died there in 1939.[24]

After his Collins Building was completed, Arthur B. Chamberlin won few other Seattle commissions, and like Willcox, he cut his ties with fellow professionals by entering the Queen Anne School competition. In 1896, he returned to Minneapolis, where he soon formed a partnership with George E. Bertrand. As was typical in the period, although Chamberlin had been a skilled delineator, once he became the owner of his own firm, he gave up the creation of architectural drawings. The only signed drawing by Chamberlin published after his return to Minneapolis was a small study of a Doric column that appeared in *Western Architect* in September 1902.[25] Bertrand and Chamberlin continued in practice until Bertrand's death in 1931 and Chamberlin's death in 1933. Although the firm's work varied, it was recognized as a local leader in the academic classical design of the period.[26]

Willis Ritchie had begun his architectural career in Ohio, had remained in Kansas only four years, and had been in Seattle little more than three when he moved to Spokane in 1892. Once Ritchie closed his Seattle office in mid-1893, the peripatetic part of his career came to an end. The focus of his practice during the depression years of the mid-1890s was the Spokane County Courthouse, and once settled in Spokane he did not move again, residing in the city for almost forty years until his death in 1931. Until 1905 he continued to win institutional projects, including two buildings at the University of Idaho, and the expansion of his Thurston County Courthouse to serve as the Washington State Capitol, but thereafter his work was primarily residential. The Spokane County Courthouse remained his most significant project.[27]

Only three of the prominent Seattle architects of the years from 1889 to 1895 had significant continuing practices in Seattle after 1898: William Boone, Charles Saunders, and Edwin Houghton. At an age when many architects might have been content to retire, William Boone continued in active practice. His career had begun in the building trades, but he was one of the leaders of the effort to establish architecture in Washington on a more professional basis in the 1890s. He was one of the instigators of the new AIA chapter and served as its first president. From 1900 to 1905 Boone joined with James Corner (who had earlier been in partnership with Warren Skillings), to form Boone and Corner. Their most important building was the first Seattle High School (1902–3, destroyed). (Fig. 8.4) After 1905 Boone reduced his practice activities and sometime after 1910 retired entirely from practice. Boone was feted by the AIA in 1920 on his nintieth birthday. He died in Seattle the next year, in October 1921.[28]

Neither Charles Saunders nor Edwin Houghton appears to have had much work in the lean years of the mid-1890s, but subsequently both had moderately successful Seattle practices. In 1898 Saunders and his draftsman, George Lawton, formed the partnership Saunders and Lawton, which endured until 1915. Their practice included a variety of building types, but few commissions that approached the scale or significance of the work Saunders had undertaken for William Bailey. After 1915 Saunders practiced at a reduced level, and from 1923 to 1932 served in the state legislature, where he was a leader in early conservation legislation. He died in 1935.[29] Edwin Houghton's practice after 1898 involved a variety of building types, but he became especially identified with the design of theaters, not only in Seattle, but also in cities across the Northwest. He continued in active practice until his death in 1927.[30]

In general, the careers of Seattle's leading architects after the fire peaked in the years between 1889 and 1893. Only Boone had had a significant pre-

fire career and only Parkinson would have a truly prominent post-1900 career (and that was in Los Angeles, not Seattle).

Charles Bebb was the one exception to this pattern, as he came permanently from Chicago to Seattle in 1893 and his career flowered in the twentieth century. Bebb had first come to Seattle to supervise the Adler and Sullivan opera house project, and when that project was terminated by the Panic of 1890, he returned to Chicago. But Bebb had formed a strong attachment to Seattle and, with the assistance of Thomas Burke, invested in several lots in the city. Bebb's efforts to move to Seattle took several forms, including trying construction; in September 1891, Bebb was the low bidder on the construction of Boone and Willcox's proposed University of Washington building, but all the bids were rejected.[31] In March 1892, while Bebb was still in Chicago, he and Burke corresponded on financial matters as Bebb was having trouble keeping up payments on his Seattle lots. He still expressed the hope that the opera house project would go forward. Six months later Bebb wrote, "I sincerely hope I shall get back to Seattle inside of two years to remain for good. I have not the slightest doubt of Seattle's future, in fact am considered by my friends a crank upon the subject."[32] But following the string of bank failures that initiated the Panic in May 1893, Bebb asked Burke to sell his lots. Bebb recognized he would get little for the land but his financial plight was becoming severe.[33] On 14 June he repeated his request and described his situation as "no work and no money saved." His description of Adler and Sullivan in the deepening national reces-

8.4 Boone and Corner, Seattle High School, (Washington High School; Broadway High School) 1902–03 (destroyed)

University of Washington Libraries, Manuscripts, Special Collections, University Archives Division, UW5040

sion was particularly revealing: "The condition of all lines of business in Chicago is deplorable. Adler and Sullivan are doing nothing and Mr. Adler told me he could not even make collections of moneys due him, and consequently has had to reduce the office force to three men, and these three have nothing to do. I have found that all architects and contractors are in the same or even worse shape."[34] In late June, Bebb asked Burke if there was any chance of any employment in Seattle and suggested that he and his wife would "come at once" with the "slightest inducement."[35] On 19 July 1893, Bebb asked if Burke would advance him $200 against the future sale of the lots so he could meet pressing obligations. Of Adler and Sullivan he wrote, "Adler having reduced the office to 3 men, as a matter of fact, is borrowing from friends each week to pay his pay-roll."[36]

Charles Bebb left Adler and Sullivan and moved to Seattle in fall 1893. He took a position as architectural engineer with the Denny Clay Company, local manufacturer of pipe and other utilitarian clay products. Under his direction they became a leading regional manufacturer of architectural terra-cotta.[37] But Bebb always saw himself as an architect, and he was an early and active member in the new Washington State AIA Chapter. Bebb was also to have been the local architect for Frank Lloyd Wright's 1894 Seattle hotel project, but that did not go forward.[38] Bebb remained with the Denny Clay Company five years, then opened his office in Seattle in 1898. In 1901 he formed a partnership with Louis L. Mendel, and their firm, Bebb and Mendel, was one of the most prominent architectural practices in Seattle until 1914.[39] Their early work frequently featured Sullivanesque terra-cotta ornament. (Fig. 8.5) In 1914, Bebb formed a new partnership, Bebb and Gould, with Carl F. Gould, and this firm, too, was a leader in the city until Gould's death in 1939. Bebb died just three years later in June 1942.[40] Begun in 1890, Bebb's career in Seattle architecture lasted half a century, linking the emerging city of the 1890s to the modern Seattle of the mid-twentieth century.

Seattle after 1896

The 17 July 1897 arrival of the steamer *Portland* from Alaska, reportedly with a "ton of gold" on board, initiated the Klondike gold rush. This event finally broke the economic depression that had gripped Seattle for four long years. The city capitalized on its geographic location and became the primary point of embarkation, where prospectors were outfitted before departing for the Yukon. The gold fields were in Canada and the Canadian government required that prospectors have supplies to last one year in order to enter the country. Seattle dry goods merchants, such as the Schwabacher Company, became leading suppliers for those rushing to the Klondike. In turn, Seattle renewed its position as one of the primary centers of trade on the Pacific Coast.

With the rebound of the economy, the city's population continued to swell, reaching 80,861 in 1900, and 237,194 in 1910. Growth eventually renewed the demand for architectural services, although prosperity for architects did

8.5 Bebb and Mendel, Schwabacher Hardware Company Warehouse (now part of Merrill Place), 1903–5, entrance
Photo by John Stamets, 2001

not fully return until 1900. In downtown, it was several years before the backlog of space in the city's business blocks was absorbed. New institutional construction also awaited growing confidence and improved public revenues before projects could be undertaken. Thus, construction did not really pick up after the Panic of 1893 until the turn of the century. It was not until 1902 that the value of building permits in the city finally exceeded the level of 1889.[41]

The patterns of Seattle's urban development after 1900 were generally those initiated in the years from 1889 to 1893. The city's system of small neighborhood institutions expanded rapidly to keep pace with the explosive growth of the first decade of the twentieth century, and the previous pattern of small, neighborhood-based fire stations and schools continued. Following the example of building several buildings from a single prototype plan—the example set by Boone and Meeker and Saunders and Houghton—the school district identified a "model school" prototype based on the Green Lake School designed in 1901 by James Stephen, who subsequently served as school district architect. Multiple neighborhood-based elementary school buildings over the next decade were designed from his model school plan. Many of the schools Stephen designed or influenced survive today; the pattern of their locations reflects the expansion of city neighborhoods that developed over the years between 1903 and 1909 when Stephen held the schools architect position.[42] The pattern of multiple similar neighborhood-based public buildings was further reinforced between 1908 and 1915 when the city constructed its first group of neighborhood (Carnegie) branch libraries.[43] Almost none of Seattle's pre-1900 public buildings survive, but their legacy in terms of urban pattern remains.[44] The pre-1900 period was of critical importance in establishing the shape of Seattle's neighborhoods and the character of its public institutions.

While the single-family pattern of Seattle neighborhoods was largely established in the 1890s, the later development of the city's residential architecture was not predictable from pre-1900 construction. Although a wide variety of houses were built in the city after the turn of the century, the influence of Arts and Crafts ideas and the example of California meant that the house type that emerged as dominant was the bungalow, a form unknown in the early 1890s. The houses of the 1890s had shown a mix of late Victorian, Queen Anne, "modern colonial" (shingle-style), and classical influences, and some preference for Queen Anne in its half-timbered and Tudoresque modes can be discerned. The shingled "modern colonial" was less influential in Seattle than in the East; the last significant example was Edwin Houghton's Charles A. Riddle House (1899, altered) on Queen Anne Hill. After 1900, Seattle houses seemed to reflect two primary tendencies, a loose interpretation of classical motifs, particularly as applied in the two-story, four-square house locally identified as the "Seattle box" or the "classic box," and several freely composed Arts and Crafts–influenced types, including half-timbered and Tudoresque designs as well as a variety of interpretations of the one- to one-and-one-half-story bungalow. Between 1900 and 1920, when the city's population grew from just over 80,000 to nearly 330,000, an abundance of pattern books, plan books, and popular periodicals promoting modes related to both "classical" and Arts and Crafts shaped the character of Seattle's residential buildings.[45] Their influence is seen today throughout the residential fabric of the city's extant older neighborhoods.

The downtown construction of the post-fire era had established a metropolitan character and scale for Seattle's commercial core. But the rebuilding of downtown Seattle after the 1889 fire took place just prior to the technological revolution that soon overtook American architecture. When construction resumed after 1900, the new Seattle downtown office buildings were technologically modern, in that they were supported by steel frames with exterior cladding, rather than by load-bearing walls. The first steel-framed downtown high-rise was the fourteen-story Alaska Building (1903–4), at Second and Cherry, by Eames and Young of St. Louis, with Saunders and Lawton serving as supervising architects in Seattle. This was soon followed by the American Savings Bank/Empire Building (1904–6, destroyed), on Second at Madison,

by A. Warren Gould. These buildings and others brought a new scale to the city along with the new approach to construction. However, slow-burning heavy timber construction continued to be used for new warehouses, such as Bebb and Mendel's Schwabacher Company warehouse (1903–5), at First South and Jackson. (See Fig. 8.5)

The commercial core of downtown gradually followed the new office blocks north from the old center. As in the early years of settlement, the intersection of Front and Commercial at Yesler Avenue was the center of the city after the 1889 fire and this remained the center until 1900. But by 1910, most of the new high-rise construction had clustered along Second, and the center of downtown commercial activity had permanently moved north of Yesler. (Fig. 8.6) In the following decade, the commercial core rapidly spread northward, and new office blocks had been erected north of Pike Street by 1914. Those who had invested in property at the south end of downtown resisted the shift, fearing reduced property values, and the construction at Second and Yesler of the thirty-six-story Smith Tower (1910–14, altered), designed by Gaggin and Gaggin

8.7 Looking east on Yesler Way after the 13 April 1949 earthquake, which caused significant damage in Pioneer Square. The debris is from the Occidental Hotel (Seattle Hotel); the Seattle National Bank Building (Interurban Building) is in the background.

Museum of History and Industry, PEMCO Webster and Stevens Collection, 83.10.16963

of Syracuse, New York, was an attempt to anchor the downtown on Yesler for the future; instead, this building thereafter marked the south end of the city's twentieth-century business core.

The shift of downtown development to north of Yesler had two effects. First, it led to the destruction of Seattle's residential district of early day mansions as these were replaced by new commercial construction. Second, it left behind the old commercial core created in the 1889 to 1893 period; this area declined and became known as "skid row."[46] Most of the buildings erected after the 1889 fire remained intact, although many gradually deteriorated between the 1920s and the 1950s. (Fig. 8.7) Over time, several structures were demolished for parking lots, and partial redevelopment through urban renewal was proposed for the area in the 1950s and early 1960s. But, the buildings of the post-fire commercial center were rediscovered in the 1960s by architects and developers who recognized both the historical significance and reuse potential of the district.[47] Their efforts (and the demolition of the Occidental Hotel for a parking garage in 1963) attracted the attention of the community and the city. Faculty and students from the University of Washington inventoried buildings in the area in 1968 and 1969 in order to prepare a nomination for the National Register of Historic Places. In 1970, the area, now called Pioneer Square, became the city's first locally designated historic district.

Today the Pioneer Square Historic District is a vital mixed-use community as well as one of the best preserved collections of late-nineteenth-century commercial architecture in the United States. Woodbridge and Montgomery wrote: "Today we need not regret that the commercial center moved on, leaving the area to stagnate. This lack of interest and investment insured that a remarkable stand of urbanistically compatible buildings from the end of the nineteenth century would remain. Streetscapes like that from Pioneer Square south along First Avenue are rare in a modern metropolis forced to reuse the same downtown area over and over."[48] Although cars now fill the streets, and restaurants, bars, and stores fill the ground floors of the buildings (and professional offices and condominiums are found above), it is still possible to walk through the area and have some sense of what this place was like a century ago, and what these buildings meant to people struggling to make their city into a modern metropolitan center.[49] (Fig. 8.8)

Seattle and H. H. Richardson

Montgomery Schuyler's 1891 essays in *Architectural Record* and *Harper's Magazine* celebrated the Romanesque Revival and spoke of its further development. Henry Van Brunt's January 1891 obituary for John Root had also addressed the "Americo-Romanesque experiment" and elsewhere he wrote of this direction as the basis for an appropriate American architecture. Yet, by 1891, the Richardson-influenced Romanesque Revival had already passed its apogee, although its downward trajectory was just beginning to be apparent. In 1891, D. H. Burnham rejected Willis Ritchie's Romanesque designs proposed for the 1893 World's Columbian Exposition in Chicago, calling them "commonplace."[50] By 1893, the decline of the Romanesque Revival would become apparent to all.

The Romanesque Revival can be characterized as a relatively successful national mode of design. But its period of ascendancy was brief—in Seattle it was the dominant mode of design for just four years, 1889 to 1893—and even in that period, it was strongest only from 1889 to 1891. As the buildings in Seattle demonstrate, the Romanesque Revival mode has often appeared to later observers much more coherent than it actually was in its time. Richardson's example, which served as the broad inspiration for American architects as understood through publications, never appeared to offer a single direction for development. In addition to the "proto-modern" architect that modern historians found by focusing on some of Richardson's works at the expense of others, there was also a "Victorian" Richardson and a "picturesque" Richardson, as well as the familiar "Romanesque Revival" Richardson.[51]

As understood by Seattle architects, Richardson's example presented a new architectural vocabulary which could be absorbed within the framework of the freely inventive design approach that had coalesced in America after the Civil War. How Seattle's architects used the Romanesque Revival vocabulary varied depending upon their backgrounds and their abilities to intuit at least some of the lessons of Richardson's example, either from Richardson's own work in publication, or from the many published examples of works which attempted further development of the Romanesque "experiment." Seattle architects faced a situation of rapid change with new building types and new fire-resistive technologies and in their own emerging professionalism. The

Romanesque Revival offered a language of design that allowed them to meet these challenges. Their work often still betrays a preference for the ornamented rather than the unadorned surface, for the emphatically vertical rather than the quietly horizontal, and for agitation rather than repose, yet in these works there is a sense that these architects were always striving, and at least sometimes succeeding, in making an architecture appropriate to an emerging metropolitan community.

The fate of the Romanesque Revival mode, already on the wane, was sealed by the Panic of 1893, the most severe depression the nation had experienced to that time. This ended the land and building boom that had begun in the late 1870s. After May 1893 construction in most parts of the United States slowed rapidly, and by 1894 it came to a halt.

When construction resumed nationally by the late 1890s, Romanesque design was an outmoded form. It survived only in smaller cities and towns, generally in the central and western states, reflecting their cultural conservatism and the cultural lag between younger architects who were quick to adopt academic eclecticism and the older architects and contractor-builders who continued to build in the Romanesque mode, at least for a time. Where Romanesque design had proved appropriate to indigenous building traditions and materials, especially where rustication was the easiest method for treating native stone, it survived into the twentieth century. But even in out-of-the-way locations, the Romanesque Revival had disappeared by 1910.[52]

The final legacy of the Richardsonian era was the buildings it left behind. These form the record of the last period of widespread city-making in the United States. By the late 1890s, the network of American cities was almost completely established. The many towns and cities which had tried to outdo each other in the boom years from the 1870s to the 1890s drove themselves to build imposing civic, institutional, and commercial buildings. Often these were scaled to the hope of future growth rather than the reality of immediate needs. The Panic of 1893 ended many of these hopes. Still, their aspirations survive, crystallized in the many variations of Romanesque Revival design across the United States.

What is evident is that the force of Henry Hobson Richardson's architecture altered the design development of every architect of his time. The pull of his example was so powerful as to "impose itself" (as Montgomery Schuyler later wrote) on the architecture of a generation.[53]

8.8 First Avenue South,
looking north from South
Main Street, Pioneer
Square Historic District,
January 2001

Photo by John Stamets

Appendix

Known Buildings of Seattle's
Major Post-Fire Architects, 1880–1895

Known buildings, projects and competition entries for Seattle's major post-fire architects are listed in order by date as compiled from available evidence. Most of the buildings listed have been identified from newspaper reports; other surviving evidence (such as school board records) has also been used to supplement the newspaper accounts. Building names are as indicated in contemporary accounts with later names added (in parentheses) for clarification. Addresses are based on historical locations and street names (with current locations in parentheses). Dating is based on contemporary accounts; dates are indicated from the earliest report of the commission to the completion of construction. Approximated dates, where exact evidence is not available, are indicated by the use of "ca." Occasional notes and clarifications are provided as appropriate throughout these lists.

Architects are listed roughly in the order of their arrival in Seattle. Emil DeNeuf is an exception—he follows immediately after Elmer Fisher, whose practice he took over. In some cases architects entered into or dissolved partnerships at some point during a building's design and construction—partnership information is listed immediately after the dates for each building.

Lists of buildings by Fisher in British Columbia and by Ritchie in Kansas are known to be incomplete; and, because all lists were compiled primarily from newspapers, there are likely omissions for other architects as well. Some buildings may never have been mentioned in publication and others may simply have been missed.

William E. Boone

City Building, 1882
e. side S. Third (Second S.), between Main and Washington
Seattle
destroyed (fire 1889)

Marshall Building, 1882
Commercial (First S.)
Seattle
destroyed (fire 1889)

Boyd & Poncin Store, 1882
Front (First)
Seattle
destroyed (fire 1889)

McNaught, Walker & Renton Building, 1882–1883
Commercial (First S.)
Seattle
destroyed (fire 1889)

Yesler-Leary Building, 1882–1883 (Boone and Meeker)
n.w. corner Front (First) at Mill (Yesler)
Seattle
destroyed (fire 1889)

Yesler-Leary Building Addition project, 1883 (Boone and Meeker)
Mill (Yesler)
Seattle
unbuilt

C. P. Stone Building, 1883–1885 (Boone and Meeker)
625 Front (First)
Seattle
destroyed (fire 1889)

Schwabacher Building, 1883 (Boone and Meeker)
Mill (Yesler) opposite Post
Seattle
destroyed (fire 1889)

Henry Yesler House, 1883–1884 (Boone and Meeker)
Third, between Jefferson and James
Seattle
destroyed (fire 1901)

Denny School (North School) competition project, 1883 (Boone and Meeker)
Seattle
unbuilt

Wah Chong Building, 1883 (Boone and Meeker)
S. Third (Second S.)
Seattle
destroyed (fire 1889)

Watson Squire Building, 1883 (Boone and Meeker)
S. Second (Occidental S.)
Seattle
destroyed (fire 1889)

Eben A. Osborne House, 1884 (Boone and Meeker)
1123 Fourth
Seattle
destroyed

Bishop Paddock House, 1884 (Boone and Meeker)
corner Division and Tacoma
Tacoma
destroyed

Samuel Wilkeson House, 1884 (Boone and Meeker)
n.w. corner C Street at S. Seventh
Tacoma
probably destroyed

H. A. Atkins House, 1884 (Boone and Meeker)
location unidentified
Tacoma
probably destroyed

Wilkeson Block (Wilkeson & Kandle Building), 1884 (Boone and Meeker)
Pacific, near 11th
Tacoma
destroyed

Seattle Safe Deposit Building/Merchants National Bank, 1884–1885 (Boone
and Meeker)
Front (First), near Cherry
Seattle
destroyed (fire 1889)

Gordon Hardware Company Building, 1884–1885 (Boone and Meeker)
927 Front (First), near Cherry
Seattle
destroyed (fire 1889)

Annie Wright Seminary, 1884 (Boone and Meeker)
Tacoma, between N. First and Division
Tacoma
destroyed

E. C. Smith House, 1885 (Boone and Meeker)
C, between 4th and 5th
Tacoma
destroyed

Washington Academy, 1885 (Boone and Meeker)
S. Tacoma, between S. 7th and S. 8th
Tacoma
destroyed

Washington Territorial Insane Asylum, 1886–1887 (Boone and Meeker)
Steilacoom
destroyed

Charles L. Denny House, 1887 (Boone and Meeker)
s.w. corner Third at Union
Seattle
destroyed

Sol Simpson House, 1887 (Boone and Meeker)
near Sixth
Seattle
destroyed

Houses for King County Investment Company, 1887 (Boone and Meeker)
s.w. corner 12th at Madison
Seattle
destroyed

Fred Sander House, 1887–1888 (Boone and Meeker)
1525 Eighth
Seattle
destroyed

Toklas & Singerman Building, 1887–1888 (Boone and Meeker)
s.w. corner Front (First) at Columbia
Seattle
destroyed (fire 1889)

Boston Block, 1887–1888 (Boone, local superintending architect)
s.e. corner Second at Columbia
Seattle
destroyed
(architect: Bradley, Winslow & Witherall of Boston, MA)

Yesler-Leary Building Addition (Yesler Block), 1887–1888 (Boone and Meeker)
Mill (Yesler), between Yesler-Leary and Post buildings
Seattle
destroyed (fire 1889)

Chapin Block (Colonial Block), 1888 (Boone and Meeker)
n.e. corner Second at Columbia
Seattle
destroyed

Central School, 1888–1889 (Boone and Meeker)
Sixth at Madison
Seattle
destroyed

South School, 1888–1889 (Boone and Meeker)
e. side 11th, between Lane and Weller
Seattle
destroyed

Abraham W. Engle House, 1888 (Boone and Meeker)
414 Tenth
Seattle
destroyed

Oren O. Denny House, 1889 (Boone and Meeker)
1108 Seneca
Seattle
destroyed

I.O.O.F. Building (Barnes Building), 1889 (Boone and Meeker)
Front (First) near Bell
Seattle

Phinney Building (Carleton Block, Ramona Hotel), 1889
Front (First) at Seneca
Seattle
destroyed

Wah Chong Building (Phoenix Hotel), 1889
n.e. corner S. Third (Second S.) at Washington
Seattle
destroyed

McNaught Building, 1889
s.e corner S. Sixth (Fifth S.) at Jackson
Seattle
destroyed

Squire Block, 1889
Second, between Yesler and Jefferson
Seattle
destroyed

Starr Block, 1889
1115–1117 Front (First)
Seattle
destroyed

Dexter Horton Building (Occidental Block), 1889
n.w. corner Third at Cherry
Seattle
destroyed

Sanderson Block (Merchants Cafe), 1889
Yesler Way, between S. Second (Occidental S.) and Commercial (First S.)
Seattle

Y.M.C.A., 1889–1890
1417 Front (First), near Union
Seattle
destroyed

New York Building, 1889–1892 (Boone; Boone and Willcox)
n.e. corner Second at Cherry
Seattle
destroyed

Seattle School District Offices, 1889–1890
Sixth at Madison (Central School grounds)
Seattle
destroyed

Sanderson Block, 1890
s.e. corner S. Third (Second S.) at Washington
Seattle
destroyed

Post-Edwards Block, 1890
w. side Front (First), between University and Union
Seattle
partially destroyed

Masonic Temple project, 1890
n.e. corner Second at Pike
Seattle
unbuilt

Marshall-Walker Building (Globe Hotel; Globe Building), 1890–1891
(Boone; Boone and Willcox)
s.e. corner Commercial (First S.) at Main
Seattle

McKenney Block, 1890–1891 (Boone; Boone and Willcox)
Fourth and Main
Olympia

Trinity Methodist Church project, 1891 (Boone and Willcox)
Mercer and Kentucky
Seattle
unbuilt

Plymouth Congregational Church, 1891–1892 (Boone and Willcox)
n.e. corner Third at University
Seattle
destroyed

Yesler/Baxter Opera House project, 1891 (Boone and Willcox)
s.e. corner Yesler at S. Fourth (Third S.)
Seattle
unbuilt

Store for F. Sander, 1891 (Boone and Willcox)
1012–1016 Front (First)
Seattle
destroyed

Ten Houses, 1891 (Boone and Willcox)
Fourth and Columbia
Seattle
destroyed

John M. Frink House, 1891 (Boone and Willcox)
s.e. corner Rainier at Weller
Seattle
destroyed

Judge Julius Stratton House (Thomas Burke House), 1891
(Boone and Willcox)
n.e. corner 14th at Madison
Seattle
destroyed

William R. Bentley House, 1891 (Boone and Willcox)
s.w. corner Allee at Light
Seattle
destroyed

Rectory for St. Mark's Episcopal Church, 1891 (Boone and Willcox)
Fifth near Stewart
Seattle
destroyed

John H. Sanderson House, 1891 (Boone and Willcox)
n.e. corner 12th at Columbia
Seattle
destroyed

Armstrong House, 1891 (Boone and Willcox)
location unidentified
Seattle
unknown

Alfred Hohman House, 1891 (Boone and Willcox)
n.e. corner 13th at Columbia
Seattle
destroyed

Oliver C. Shorey House, 1891 (Boone and Willcox)
n.e. corner 13th at Seneca
Seattle
destroyed

H. Fuhrman House, 1891 (Boone and Willcox)
east side of Lake Union
Seattle
destroyed

H. Pumphrey House, 1891 (Boone and Willcox)
1530 Eighth
Seattle
destroyed

Rees Daniels House project, 1891 (Boone and Willcox)
Seattle
unbuilt

Cyrus Walker Building, 1891–1892 (Boone and Willcox; Boone)
S. Second (Occidental S.), between Yesler and Washington
Seattle
(only one floor constructed)

B.F. Day School competition project, 1891 (Boone and Willcox)
Fremont and N. 39th
Seattle
unbuilt

University of Washington Campus Plan and Administration Building project, 1891
(Boone and Willcox)
University of Washington campus
Seattle
unbuilt

J. M. Frink Building (Washington Iron Works Building; Washington Shoe Building),
1891–1892 (Boone and Willcox; Boone)
s.e. corner S. Second (Occidental S.) at Jackson
Seattle
altered (two floors added 1912)

Leary-Walker Building, 1893
Second Street, between Madison and Spring
Seattle
destroyed

Main Building (Denny Hall) competition project, 1893–1894
University of Washington campus
Seattle
unbuilt (awarded third place)

Elmer H. Fisher

Spencer's Arcade, 1886
Government/Broad
Victoria, British Columbia
destroyed

Denny Building (business building for William Denny), 1886
Broad adjacent to Spencer's Arcade
Victoria, British Columbia
destroyed

Reid House, 1886
Esquimault Road
Victoria, British Columbia
unidentified

Business Buildings, 1886
Carroll and Water Streets
Vancouver, British Columbia
unidentified

Willes Bakery, 1887
537 Johnston
Victoria, British Columbia

Goldstream Hotel (Phair's Hotel), 1887
Goldstream, British Columbia
destroyed

McCurdy Block, 1887–1888
n.e. corner Water at Taylor
Port Townsend

Byrnes Block (business block for George Byrnes), 1887
2 Water
Vancouver, British Columbia

Bank of British Columbia, 1887
New Westminster, British Columbia
destroyed

Courthouse, 1887
Nanaimo, British Columbia
destroyed

McLennen and McFeely Building, 1887
Vancouver, British Columbia
unidentified

Pimbury Building, 1887
Nanaimo, British Columbia
unidentified

Colman Building project, 1887 (Fisher and Clark)
w. side Front (First), between Columbia and Marion
Seattle
unbuilt

Korn Building, 1887–1889 (Fisher and Clark)
Mill and S. Second (117–119 Yesler Avenue at Occidental S.)
Seattle
destroyed (fire 1889)

White House (Fisher and Wilson)
Government
Victoria, British Columbia

Croft & Norris Stores (Fisher and Wilson)
1319–1329 Douglas
Victoria, British Columbia

W. G. Cameron Building, 1888 (Fisher and Wilson)
579–581 Johnson
Victoria, British Columbia

Armory (First Regiment Armory B), 1888 (Fisher and Clark)
s. side Union, between Third and Fourth
Seattle
destroyed

Lewis Terrace, 1888 (Fisher and Clark)
James, between Third and Fourth
Seattle
destroyed

Austin A. Bell Row Houses, 1888 (Fisher and Clark)
Second at Bell
Seattle
destroyed

Elmer H. Fisher House, 1888 (Fisher and Clark)
North Seattle (now lower Queen Anne)
Seattle
destroyed

South School competition project, 1888 (Fisher and Clark)
Seattle
unbuilt

Gilmore & Kirkman Building (Bay Building, Arlington Hotel), 1888–1890 (Fisher and Clark; Fisher)
s.w. corner Front at University (1215 First Avenue)
Seattle
destroyed (1974)

James & Hastings Building, 1888–1889 (Fisher and Clark)
n.e. corner Water at Tyler
Port Townsend

Naher Terrace, 1889
Yesler near Seventh
Seattle
destroyed

Denny Hotel competition project, 1889
Denny Hill
Seattle
unbuilt

Scurry Terrace, 1889
600–610 Third
Seattle
destroyed

N. D. Hill Building, 1889
s.e. corner Water at Quincy
Port Townsend

Hastings Building, 1889–1890
s.e. corner Water at Taylor
Port Townsend

Howard Lewis House, 1889
n.e. corner Terry at Jefferson (506 Tenth)
Seattle
destroyed

Burke's New York Block, 1889
1401–1415 Third
Seattle
destroyed

Austin A. Bell Building (Belle Apartments), 1889–1890
Front near Bell (2324 First Avenue)
Seattle
destroyed (facade survives)

Alonzo Hull Building, 1889–1890
n.w. corner Front at Battery (2401 First Avenue)
Seattle

Kittinger Block (project?), ca. 1889
S. Second (Occidental S.) near Washington
Seattle
probably unbuilt

Dr. John J. Scurry House (Scurry-Lippy House), 1889–1891
s.w. corner 11th (Boren) at James
Seattle
destroyed

Pioneer Building, 1889–1891
602–610 Front (First)
Seattle
altered (tower removed, 1949)

Burke Building, 1889–1891
901–909 Second
Seattle
destroyed (fragments incorporated in Federal Building plaza)

Times Building, 1889
s. side Columbia, between Front (First) and Second
Seattle
destroyed

Haller Building, 1889–1890
801–805 Second at Columbia
Seattle
destroyed

Sullivan Building, 1889–1891
706–716 Front (First)
Seattle
destroyed

Korn Building, 1889
117–119 Yesler at S. Second (Occidental S.)
Seattle
altered (cornice removed, masonry painted)

Starr-Boyd Building, 1889–1890
615–623 Front (First)
Seattle
destroyed (1949, 1956)

Lebanon Building (J.W. George & Kinnear Building, Jesse George Building, Touraine Hotel), 1889–1891
212 S. Second (Occidental S.)
Seattle
destroyed

Schwabacher Building (Gatzert Building), 1889–1890
103–107 Commercial (First S.) and 105–107 Yesler
Seattle
altered (Commercial Street facade reconstruction by Emil deNeuf following 1892 fire)

Rengstorff Building (Downs Block), 1889–1890
707–711 Second
Seattle
destroyed

New England Hotel (Harmon Building), 1889–1890
n.w. corner Commercial at Main (217–219 First S.)
Seattle
altered (cornice removed)

Y.M.C.A. project, 1889
Front (First)
Seattle
unbuilt

Abbott Hotel (Fisher Building), 1889–1890
301–311 Pike
Seattle
destroyed

Washington Building (Poncin Block), 1889–1890
703–707 Front (First)
Seattle
destroyed

Homer Hill Building (Press Building) (project?), 1889–1891
s. side Yesler, between S. Third and S. Fourth (Second S. and Third S.)
Seattle
likely unbuilt beyond foundation

First Methodist Protestant Church, 1889–1890
s.e. corner Third at Pine
Seattle
destroyed

Kline & Rosenberg Building (Kline Building), 1889
s.w. corner Second at University
Seattle
destroyed (only two floors built)

Gatzert & McDonald Building project, 1889
corner Front (First) at Madison
Seattle
unbuilt (did not proceed beyond foundation)

Trinity Episcopal Church (project?), ca. 1889
Seattle
likely unbuilt

Pease Building, 1889
2113–2117 Front (First), near Lenora
Seattle
destroyed

Terrence O'Brien House, 1889–1890
n.w. corner S. Ninth (Eighth) at King
Seattle
destroyed

Bow Building project, ca. 1889
near Commercial (First S.) and Main
Seattle
unbuilt

McDonald Building (Douthitt Building, Haller Building Annex), 1890
807–811 Second
Seattle
destroyed

Mrs. Edmund R. Lowe House, 1890
458 First
Woodland, California

Fisher Building, 1890
S. Second (Occidental S.), between Washington and Main
Seattle
destroyed (only one floor may have been built)

H. K. Owens Building project, 1890–1891
w. side S. Third (s.w. corner Second S. and Yesler)
Seattle
unbuilt (site later developed by Yesler, 1892–1893;
see: Emil DeNeuf list)

Eagle Cafe (Padden Block), 1890–1890
111 Yesler
Seattle

Yesler Building (Bank of Commerce), 1890–1891
95 Yesler/101 Commercial (First S.)
Seattle
altered (third floor by Albert Wickersham after 1900)

Yesler Building (Mutual Life Building), 1890–1891
n.w. corner Front (First S.) at Yesler
Seattle
altered (only first floor was built; for upper floors,
see: Emil DeNeuf list)

State Building (Schwabacher Building), 1890–1891
300–310 Second S. (Occidental S.)
Seattle

Lottie Roth Block, 1890–1891
Bellingham (Whatcom)

Otto Ranke House, 1890–1891
1104 Tenth (s.e. cor. Terry at Madison)
Seattle
destroyed

Fischer & McDonald Building (Feuer Building, Post Hotel), 1889, 1892
88–90 Yesler
Seattle
(constructed under supervision of Emil DeNeuf, 1892–1893)

Elmer Fisher House, 1892
s.e. corner Lane at Wilfred
Seattle
destroyed

Emil DeNeuf

Fischer & McDonald Building (Feurer Building, Post Hotel), 1889, 1892 (DeNeuf,
supervising architect)
88–90 Yesler
Seattle
(design architect: Elmer Fisher)

Metropole Building (H. K. Owens Building), 1892–1893
w. side S. Third (s.w. corner Second S. at Yesler)
Seattle
altered
(design architect possibly Elmer Fisher)

Yesler Building upper floors (Mutual Life Building), 1892–1893
n.w. corner Front (First S.) at Yesler
Seattle
altered (addition to west; cornice altered)

Lowman & Hanford Building, 1892
Front Street (First), between present Lowman Building and Tremont Building
Seattle
altered (three floors added)

William P. Boyd House, 1892
corner Tenth and Spring
Seattle
destroyed

W.D. Carkeek House, 1892
Everett and Depot
Seattle
destroyed

Schwabacher Building (reconstruction), 1893
103–107 Commercial (First S.)
Seattle

John Parkinson

Bank of Napa, 1888
Napa, California
destroyed

High School project, 1888
Napa, California
unbuilt

Courthouse project, 1888
Redding, California
unbuilt

William R. Ballard Flats, 1889
Seattle
unidentified

Odd Fellows Lodge Hall project, 1889
Seattle
unbuilt

First National Bank, 1889 (Parkinson and Evers)
415–417 Main
Olympia
destroyed

Olympia Hotel (Hotel Olympia), 1889–1890 (Parkinson and Evers)
Main at Eighth
Olympia
destroyed

Butler Block (Butler Hotel; Butler Garage), 1889–1890 (Parkinson and Evers)
n.w. corner Second at James
Seattle
destroyed except for first floor facade (upper stories replaced by parking garage)

Martin Ballard House, 1889–1890 (Parkinson and Evers)
225 Lenora
Seattle
destroyed

Margaret Pontius House, 1889 (Parkinson and Evers)
Depot, between Lincoln and Howard (2000 Denny Way)
Seattle
destroyed

Wallingford Block, 1889 (Parkinson and Evers)
e. side Second, between Union and Pike
Seattle
destroyed

McGuire Building, 1889 (Parkinson and Evers)
e. side S. Third (Second S.), between Jackson and King
Seattle
destroyed

Epler Block, 1889–1890 (Parkinson and Evers)
811–815 Second, between Columbia and Marion
Seattle
destroyed

Calkins Hotel (Mercer Island Hotel, Seattle Hygienic Sanitarium, East Seattle Hotel),
1889–1890 (Parkinson and Evers)
Mercer Island
destroyed (fire 1908)

Presbyterian Church project, 1890 (Parkinson and Evers)
Mercer Island
unbuilt

Whatcom County Courthouse competition project, 1890 (Parkinson and Evers)
Bellingham
unbuilt

Seattle National Bank (Smith Tower Annex, Interurban Building), 1890–1891
(Parkinson and Evers; Parkinson)
S. Second (Occidental S.) at Yesler
Seattle

G. H. Hilton Double House, 1890 (Parkinson and Evers; Parkinson)
Fourth at Lenora
Seattle
destroyed

Portland City Hall competition project, 1890
Portland, Oregon
unbuilt

Chamber of Commerce Building competition project, 1890 (Parkinson co-designer
with J.B. Hamme)
Portland, Oregon
unbuilt

John Parkinson House, 1890
Joy at Madison (16th at Madison)
Seattle
destroyed

Denny School Addition, 1891
Sixth at Wall
Seattle
destroyed

Rainier School Addition, 1891
between King and Lane Streets, 23rd and 24th
Seattle
destroyed

Mercer School Addition, 1891
s.e. slope Queen Anne Hill (Valley and Aloha, Fourth N., and Nob Hill N.)
Seattle
destroyed

John A. Hatfield House, 1891
Hyde at Madison Streets (18th at Madison)
Seattle
destroyed

George W. Watson House, 1891
1208 Seventh Avenue
Seattle
destroyed

Ballard Central School (Washington Irving School), 1891–1892
Tallman Avenue near Broadway (near present Ballard Hospital)
Ballard (now Seattle)
destroyed

School, ca. 1891
Snohomish
unidentified

School, ca. 1891
Hamilton (near Sedro-Wooley)
unidentified

School, ca. 1891
Sedro-Wooley
unidentified

Green Lake School, 1891
e. side Green Lake (Sunnyside N. and 65th)
Seattle
destroyed

B.F. Day School, 1891–1892
Fremont and N. 39th
Seattle
altered

Seattle Seminary (Alexander Hall/Seattle Pacific University), 1891–1893
n. slope Queen Anne Hill (W. Dravus and Third W.)
Seattle

Whatcom School (project?), 1891
Bellingham
unidentified

Equitable Life Assurance Society Building project, 1891
Seattle
unbuilt

Washington State Building competition project, 1891
World's Columbian Exposition
Chicago, Illinois
unbuilt

Guy Phinney House project, ca. 1891–1892
Woodland Park
Seattle
unbuilt

Stone Row, 1892
Marion at 12th (Minor)
Seattle
destroyed

Pacific School, 1892–1893
between James and Jefferson, 11th and 12th
Seattle
destroyed

J. H. Ohman House (project?), 1892
Market and Weller
Seattle
unidentified

Joseph W. Wilkinson House, 1892
n.w. corner Broadway at Columbia
Seattle
destroyed

Rees Daniels House, 1892
n.e. corner Pennsylvania and Stacy (8th W. and Lee)
Seattle
destroyed

Duwamish School, 1892
Duwamish (now Seattle)
destroyed

Frank D. Black House, 1891–1892
12th at Atlantic
Seattle
destroyed

J. G. Kenyon Block, 1892–1893
n.w. corner Front at Madison
Seattle
destroyed

Queen Anne School project, 1892, 1893
Seattle
unbuilt

Lake Union School project, 1892
Seattle
unbuilt

J. G. Kenyon Block, 1892–1893
e. side Front at Seneca
Seattle
destroyed

South Seattle School, 1892
Oregon at Sansome
South Seattle (now Seattle)
destroyed

Jesuit College and Church (Garrand Building/Seattle University), 1892–1894
Broadway at Madison
Seattle
altered

Daniel Jones House (project?), ca. 1892
location unidentified
Seattle
probably unbuilt

School, ca. 1892
Ravenna Park (Seattle)
destroyed

Seattle Athletic Club, 1892–1893
n. w. corner Front at Seneca
Seattle
destroyed

Provincial Parliament Building competition project, 1892–1893
Victoria, British Columbia
unbuilt

T. W. Prosch Building, 1892–1893
Ninth at Cherry
Seattle

Seattle School District Offices Addition, 1893
Sixth at Madison (Central School grounds)
Seattle
destroyed

Dobson and Denton Building, 1892–1893
Front (First), between Seneca and Spring
Seattle
destroyed

School/Rectory for Redemptorist Fathers/Sacred Heart Church, 1893
near Sixth and Bell
Seattle
destroyed (Denny Regrade)

Homer F. Norton House, 1893
1233 Chestnut (17th S.)
Seattle
destroyed

Cascade School, 1893–1894
between Harrison and Thomas, Pontius and Howard
Seattle
destroyed

Spokane County Courthouse competition project, 1893
Spokane
unbuilt (one of the six finalists)

Washington State Capitol competition project, 1893
Olympia
unbuilt

Main Building (Denny Hall) competition project, 1893–1894
University of Washington campus
Seattle
unbuilt (placed second)

Charles Saunders and Edwin Houghton

Dr. William F. Channing House, ca. 1884 (Charles Saunders and Mary Saunders)
Orange Grove Boulevard and Walnut Avenue
Pasadena, California
destroyed (burned 1900)

Charles and Mary Saunders House, ca. 1887 (Charles Saunders and Mary Saunders)
Walnut Avenue
Pasadena, California

Washington Territory Investment Company Building, 1889–1890 (Saunders;
Saunders and Houghton)
n.w. corner Second at Cherry
Seattle
destroyed

*Bailey Building (Harrisburg Block, Broderick Building, Railway Exchange
Building)* 1889–1892 (Saunders; Saunders and Houghton; Houghton)
619 Second (s.w. corner Second at Cherry)
Seattle

Rainier Hotel (Hotel Rainier), 1889 (Saunders; Saunders and Houghton)
between Fifth and Sixth, Marion and Columbia
Seattle
destroyed (1910)

Maud Building (Hotel for William Maud), 1889–1890 (Saunders; Saunders and
Houghton)
w. side Commercial (First S.), between Washington and Jackson
Seattle

T. T. Minor School, 1889– 1890 (Charles Saunders, Saunders and Houghton)
between Pike and Union, 17th and 18th
Seattle
destroyed

Mercer School, 1889–1890 (Saunders; Saunders and Houghton)
between Valley and Aloha, Fourth N. and Nob Hill
Seattle
destroyed

Columbia School, 1889–1890 (Saunders; Saunders and Houghton)
between 11th and Federal, Mercer and Roy
Seattle
destroyed

Rainier School, 1889–1891 (Saunders; Saunders and Houghton)
between King and Lane, 23rd and 24th
Seattle
destroyed

Manhattan Building project, 1889–1890 (Saunders and Houghton)
s.e. corner Second at Union
Seattle
unbuilt

Olympic Building (Starr-Colman Block; Cascade Hotel), 1889–1890 (Saunders and
Houghton)
105–107 Yesler (s.e. corner Yesler at Commercial [First S.])
Seattle
destroyed

Terry-Denny Building (Northern Hotel), 1889–1891 (Saunders and Houghton)
109–115 Commercial (First S.)
Seattle

Seattle Fire Department Headquarters Building, 1889–1890 (Saunders and Houghton)
615 Columbia (s.w. corner Seventh at Columbia)
Seattle
destroyed

Seattle Fire Department Engine House Number 2, 1889–1890 (Saunders and Houghton)
302 Pine (n.w. corner Third at Pine)
Seattle
destroyed

Hotel Eisenbeis, 1889–1890 (Saunders and Houghton)
Port Townsend
destroyed

Store Building for Sedro Land & Improvement Co., ca. 1890 (Saunders and Houghton)
Sedro-Wooley
unidentified

Anacortes Hotel, ca. 1890 (Saunders and Houghton)
Anacortes
destroyed

M. F. Backus Double House, 1890 (Saunders and Houghton)
s.e. corner 11th at Columbia
Seattle
destroyed

Denny School Addition competition project, 1891 (Saunders and Houghton)
Seattle
unbuilt

Rainier School Addition competition project, 1891 (Saunders and Houghton)
Seattle
unbuilt

Mercer School Addition competition project, 1891 (Saunders and Houghton)
Seattle
unbuilt

Edward Graves House, ca. 1891 (Saunders and Houghton)
1120 Jefferson (near 12th)
Seattle
destroyed

Rainier Avenue Electrical Station, 1891 (Saunders and Houghton)
Rainier Avenue
Seattle
destroyed

Field and Club House, ca. 1891 (Saunders and Houghton)
Rainier Avenue
Seattle
destroyed

B. F. Day School competition project, 1891 (Saunders and Houghton)
Fremont at N. 39th
Seattle
unbuilt

QUEEN ANNE AVENUE BOOKS
1629 QUEEN ANNE AVE N. SEATTLE WA 98109
(206)283-5624
OPEN 7 DAYS A WEEK!

A   7288 05/28/04 11:03

23276 1 DISTANT CORNER   60.00   60.00
   12 1 GREETING CARD   2.25   2.25

       2   Subtotal: 62.25
             Tax: 5.48
SALE   Total due: 67.73
             Check   67.73
5

Returns may be made for in-store credit.
Sorry, we are not able to do refunds.
*****
Thank you for supporting your local
independent bookstore!

Charles W. Saunders

Seattle Theater and Rainier Club, 1892
n.e. corner Third at Cherry
Seattle
destroyed

Seattle Fire Department Engine House Number 6, 1893–1894
Yesler Way at Taylor (101 23rd S.)
Seattle
destroyed

Seattle Fire Department Engine House Number 7, 1893–1895
Harrison at N. 15th (402 15th E.)
Seattle
destroyed

Main Building (Denny Hall), 1893–94
University of Washington campus
Seattle

Cudahy Packing Plant, 1895–1896 (Saunders, local supervising architect)
Dearborn at S. Eighth
Seattle
unidentified
(architect: Cudahy Company designers based in Omaha)

Observatory, 1895
University of Washington campus
Seattle

Gymnasium, 1895
University of Washington campus
Seattle
destroyed

Power House, 1895
University of Washington campus
Seattle
destroyed

Edwin W. Houghton

C. A. Walsh House, 1892
Anna at Swim Streets (n.w. corner Fourth W. at W. Comstock)
Seattle
destroyed

Beacon Light Company Power House, 1892
near Lake Washington
Seattle
destroyed

R. A. Brown House, 1893
Rose, north of Madison
Seattle
unidentified

D. Emmons House, 1893–1894
428 Dyer
Seattle
destroyed

Willis Alexander Ritchie

(Unable to verify projects in Lima, Ohio, and surrounding areas, 1880–1885)

Farmers' Bank Building (Cowley County Bank), 1885–1886
Winfield, Kansas

Central School Addition, 1885–1886
Winfield, Kansas
destroyed

John A. Eaton House, 1885
Winfield, Kansas

Southwestern Kansas Methodist Episcopal College Main Building (North Hall),
1885–1887
Southwestern Kansas Methodist Episcopal College campus
Winfield, Kansas
destroyed (1949)

City Building, 1885–1886
Winfield, Kansas
altered (third floor, tower removed 1931; other severe changes)

First National Bank and Alexander Block, 1885–1886
Winfield, Kansas
altered (floor added 1904)

St. James Hotel, 1885–1886
Winfield, Kansas
altered (first floor completely changed)

State National Bank Building, 1886–1887
Wellington, Kansas
destroyed (burned 1981)

Second Ward School, 1886
Arkansas City, Kansas
destroyed (1931)

City Building, 1886–1888
Arkansas City, Kansas
destroyed

Savings Bank, Winfield, 1886
Winfield, Kansas
unidentified

Gladstone Hotel, 1886–1887
Arkansas City, Kansas
destroyed (burned 1980, demolished 1985)

Judge I.H. Bonsall's Building (three-story business building), 1886
Arkansas City, Kansas
unidentified

Frank Hess Building, 1886
Arkansas City, Kansas
unidentified

John L. Howard's Building, 1886
Arkansas City, Kansas
unidentified

Business block, 1886
Arkansas City, Kansas
unidentified

Cracker Factory, 1886
Arkansas City, Kansas
destroyed

Winfield Opera House and Board of Trade Building, 1886–1888
Winfield, Kansas
destroyed

U.S. Court House, Post Office, Land Office, 1886–1889 (Ritchie local
superintending architect)
Wichita, Kansas
destroyed (1932)
(design architect: Office of the Supervising Architect of the U.S. Treasury)

Barbour (now Barber) County Courthouse, 1886–1887
Medicine Lodge, Kansas
destroyed (1956)

First National Bank (Farmers and Stockgrowers Bank), 1887–1888 (W.A. Ritchie
& Co., contractor)
Ashland, Kansas
(architect: F.A. Weston of Colorado)

Block 32 (four buildings including city hall and opera house), 1887–1888
Ashland, Kansas
partially destroyed

D. Rodocker Building, 1887
Ashland, Kansas
unidentified

School Building, 1887–1888
Ashland, Kansas
destroyed

Meade City Hall/County Courthouse, 1888
Meade, Kansas
destroyed (1928)

King County Courthouse, 1889–1890
Terrace at Alder
Seattle
destroyed (1931)

Seattle Fire Department Engine House Number 4, 1889–1890
n.e. corner Fourth at Battery (402 Battery)
Seattle
destroyed

Seattle Fire Department Chemical Engine House Number 2, 1889–1890
Broadway, Terrace, and 11th
Seattle
destroyed

Whatcom County Courthouse, 1890–1891
Ellsworth
Bellingham
destroyed (1953)

Ellensburg School, 1890–1891
Ellensburg
destroyed

DeMattos Building (Sunset Block), 1890–1891
corner Elk and Holly
Bellingham
destroyed

Columbia National Bank project, 1890
Bellingham
unbuilt

Dibble Building (project?), 1890
Bellingham
unidentified

Washington School, 1890–1891
between Fifth and Sixth, Quince and East
Olympia
destroyed (1925?)

Lincoln School, 1890– 1891
between Fremont and Swan, Cherry and Chestnut
Olympia
destroyed (1922)

Jefferson County Courthouse, 1890–1892
between Franklin and Jefferson, Walker and Cass
Port Townsend

Pierce County Courthouse competition project, 1890
Tacoma
unbuilt (project submitted by Charles Smith attributed to Ritchie)

Port Townsend School competition project, 1890
Port Townsend
unbuilt

Mrs. G. M. (Mary) Bowman House, 1890
Woodland Park N. near N. 36th
Seattle (Fremont)
destroyed

Thurston County Courthouse, 1890–1892 (served as Washington State Capitol
1905–1927; now Superintendent of Public Instruction)
Olympia
altered (tower removed, entrance altered; addition by Ritchie for State Capitol)

Washington State Soldiers' Home, 1890–1891
Orting
destroyed

Clark County Courthouse, 1890–1892
Vancouver
destroyed (1941)

T. M. Reed Building (project?), 1891
Olympia
unidentified

Washington State Building competition project, 1891
World's Columbian Exposition
Chicago, Illinois
unbuilt

B.F. Day School competition project, 1891
Fremont at N. 39th
Seattle
unbuilt

South Seattle School competition project, 1892
Oregon at Sansome
South Seattle (now Seattle)
unbuilt

Wallace School, 1892
Wallace, Idaho
destroyed

Spokane City Hall, 1892–1894
n.e. corner Trent at Howard
Spokane
destroyed (1913)

Prescott School, 1892–1893
W. Park
Anaconda, Montana
destroyed

Lincoln School, 1892, 1894
Chestnut
Anaconda, Montana
destroyed (fire 1897)

King County Hospital, 1893–1894
King County Poor Farm
south of Seattle
destroyed

Union Park School (Edison School), 1893
Spokane
destroyed

State Normal School competition project, 1893
Ellensburg
unbuilt

Spokane County Courthouse, 1893–1895
n. side Broadway, Jefferson to Madison
Spokane

Warren Porter Skillings

John F. Conant House, 1889
1109 Cherry
Seattle
destroyed

California Block (San Francisco Store; MacDougall-Southwick Store), 1889–1890
(Skillings, local superintending architect)
s.w. corner Front (First) at Columbia
Seattle
destroyed
(architect: Copeland & Pierce of San Francisco, California)

Four Frame and Brick Cottages, 1890
Kirkland
unidentified

Congregational Church, 1890–1891
Snohomish
unidentified

Washington State Building, 1891–1893
World's Columbian Exposition
Chicago, Illinois
destroyed

B.F. Day School competition project, 1891
Fremont at N. 39th
Seattle
unbuilt

Dearborn Building, 1891–1892
311 S. Third (Second S.)
Seattle
destroyed (1927)

Harrington & Smith Building, 1892
n.e. corner Washington at Railroad (Alaskan Way)
Seattle

Four Houses for Gilbert Meem, 1892
corner 13th at Seneca
Seattle
destroyed

Alexander E. MacClusky House, 1892
1310 12th (corner 12th and University)
Seattle
destroyed

T. M. Daulton House, 1892
Joy, near Madison (n.e. corner 16th at Madison)
Seattle
destroyed

Two Cottages for Von Rosen, 1892 (Skillings and Corner)
Rose (15th), near Madison
Seattle
unidentified

Provincial Parliament Building competition project, 1892–1893 (Skillings and Corner)
Victoria, British Columbia
unbuilt (one of five finalists)

Watson Squire Building, 1893 (Skillings and Corner)
n.w. corner S. Second (Occidental S.) at Main
Seattle
destroyed

Amos Brown House, 1893 (Skillings and Corner)
California
Seattle (West Seattle)
(partially built in 1893; not completed until 1902 by Edwin Houghton; destroyed)

Coal, Lumber and Mineral Palace (Exhibit Hall), 1892–1893 (Skillings and Corner)
Pioneer Place Park
Seattle
destroyed

Union Trust Block, 1893 (Skillings and Corner)
115–117 S. Main (s.w. corner Occidental S. at Main)
Seattle

The Rialto (Frederick & Nelson Building), 1893–1894 (Skillings and Corner)
w. side Second, between Madison and Spring
Seattle
destroyed

Washington State Capitol competition project, 1893 (Skillings and Corner)
Olympia
unbuilt

Queen Anne School (West Queen Anne School), 1895–1896 (Skillings and Corner)
between 5th and 6th, Lee and Galer
Seattle
altered (twice enlarged; converted to condominiums)

State Normal School, 1895–1896 (Skillings and Corner)
(now Western Washington University campus)
Bellingham

Arthur Bishop Chamberlin

Collins Block, 1893–1894
s.e. corner Second at James
Seattle

Judge Richard Osborn House, 1894 (Chamberlin and Siebrand)
Ninth near Jefferson
Seattle
destroyed

Ellen McElroy Building, 1894 (Chamberlin and Siebrand)
s. side Columbia, between Second and Third
Seattle
destroyed

T. T. Minor School Addition, 1894 (Chamberlin and Siebrand)
between Pike and Union, 17th and 18th
Seattle
destroyed

Denny-Fuhrman School, 1894–1895 (Chamberlin and Siebrand)
Louisa and Lynn, Franklin and Boylston
Seattle
altered (enlarged by James Stephen after 1900; now part of Seward School)

Navy Yard Buildings, 1895–1897 (Chamberlin and Siebrand; Siebrand)
Port Orchard
some structures survive
(Siebrand retained commission when Chamberlin and Siebrand dissolved)

Queen Anne School competition project, 1895
Seattle
unbuilt

Notes

Frequently cited periodicals are abbreviated as follows:

AABN   *American Architect and Building News*
IA   *Inland Architect*
JSAH   *Journal of the Society of Architectural Historians*
NREBR *Northwestern Real Estate and Building Review*
P.I.   *Seattle Post-Intelligencer*
PNQ   *Pacific Northwest Quarterly*
Times   *Seattle Times* (including *Seattle Press-Times*)

I. Introduction:
Seattle and Nineteenth-Century American Architecture

1. *P.I.*, 22 Nov. 1889, 3.

2. Only three deaths are thought to have occurred as an immediate result of the fire. With the collapse, on 27 June 1889, of a brick wall still standing among the ruins, one additional death can also be attributed to the fire.

The fire is addressed in many of the general histories of Seattle. One recent book on the fire and its aftermath is: James R. Warren, *The Day Seattle Burned: June 6, 1889* (Seattle: n.p., 1989).

3. *P.I.*, 1 Jan. 1890, 13.

4. The advertising sections of Seattle city directories from this period give a clear indication of the rise of the architecture profession after the fire. In 1888, six firms are listed; in 1889 there are sixteen firms; in 1890 the number rises to thirty.

5. For example, the proposed Seattle Opera House was initially announced in these terms: "The building when completed will be one of the finest in the West." *Northwestern Architect* 7 (Dec. 1889): Advertisers Trade Supplement, n.p. Similar language continued to appear in later descriptions: "It [the opera house] will be one of the most important structures in the West." *P.I.*, 5 Aug. 1890, 3.

6. The challenge of placing the buildings of late-nineteenth-century Seattle in the architectural and urban context of their time is complicated by two issues. First, documentary sources for the period are limited and research depends significantly on newspaper accounts in order to generate accurate information regarding dating and attribution of projects as well as an understanding of how these buildings were seen by contemporaries. Second, retroactive interpretations that have been applied to all architecture of the period must be regarded as problematic unless they can be shown to be rooted in ideas and attitudes that architects, builders, or clients would have had at the time these buildings were actually created.

7. *P.I.*, 19 Oct. 1889, 5. Although the architect who cites Richardson is unnamed, the buildings he cites as "Romanesque" following Richardson's example are all by Elmer Fisher; thus, it appears that Fisher is the architect quoted. Note: The full quotation appears at the beginning of chapter 4.

8. Addressing Richardsonian architecture in Kansas, Richard Longstreth wrote: "it is tempting for one not familiar with Richardsonian work there [in a remote location] to postulate that it would be little more than an echo, one seldom expressed in a very

sophisticated manner, and occurring, more likely than not, later than in places well-recognized for their architectural achievements. What is fundamentally wrong with this approach is not only that it places too much value on stereotypical assumptions, but that it posits Richardson's oeuvre as the one valid basis for architectural assessment rather than examining the diffusion of the mode on its own terms. . . . [p]eople in a remote region can absorb a tendency while it is still new, and they can use it for their own reasons." See: Richard Longstreth, "Richardsonian Architecture in Kansas," in *The Spirit of H. H. Richardson on the Midland Prairies: Regional Transformations of an Architectural Style,* edited by Paul C. Larson with Susan M. Brown (Minneapolis: University Art Museum, and Ames: Iowa State University Press, 1988), 67. A similar argument is made by Henry Glassie: "there is no area in the Anglo-American world where the architecture is either wholly fashionable or wholly traditional. Saying that a building is an expression of some fashion may indicate a relationship between the design of localities, but it explains nothing. What needs explanation is why that particular fashion was accepted." Although Glassie is primarily discussing vernacular architecture, his argument can apply equally well to any similar question of influence in architectural history. See: Henry Glassie, *Folk Housing in Middle Virginia: A Structural Analysis of Historic Artifacts* (Knoxville: University of Tennessee Press, 1975), 188.

9. The firm, McKim, Mead and White, is the subject of several books. Both Charles McKim and Stanford White began their professional careers in Richardson's office, but their firm is recognized primarily for their work in academic eclecticism rather than the Richardsonian Romanesque. The careers of Richardson apprentices Alexander Longfellow and Frank Alden were addressed in Margaret Henderson Floyd, *Architecture after Richardson: Regionalism before Modernism—Longfellow, Alden, and Harlow in Boston and Pittsburgh* (Pittsburgh: Pittsburgh History and Landmarks Foundation, and Chicago and London: University of Chicago Press, 1994). There is no recent monograph on Richardson's direct heirs, Shepley, Rutan and Coolidge; a contemporary publication was: Russell Sturgis, *A Critique of the Work of Shepley, Rutan & Coolidge and Peabody & Stearns: Great American Architects Series* 3 (New York: Architectural Record Co., July 1896; reprint edition: New York: DaCapo Press, 1977), 1–52; a brief analysis of Richardson's successors is: J. D. Forbes, "Shepley, Bulfinch, Richardson & Abbott, Architects: An Introduction," *JSAH* 17/3 (Fall 1958): 19–31. Material prepared for the 1972 tour of the Society of Architectural Historians was compiled in a special issue of *JSAH* on Richardson and his contemporaries: *JSAH* 32/2 (May 1973), with articles on Peabody and Stearns, Hartwell and Richardson, and William Appleton Potter. Richardsonian architecture in the central states was the subject of an exhibit at the University of Minnesota in 1988; the collection of essays published to accompany the exhibit is: Larson and Brown, eds., *The Spirit of H. H. Richardson on the Midland Prairies.* An unpublished thesis broadly addressing the Richardsonian Romanesque is: Leland B. Grant, "Richardsonian Architecture in America: 1886–1893" (M.A. thesis, New York University, June 1974).

10. Lewis Mumford, *Brown Decades: A Study of the Arts in America, 1865–1895* (New York: Harcourt Brace, 1931), 114–132; see also: Lewis Mumford, *Sticks and Stones: A Study of American Architecture and Civilization* (New York: Boni & Liveright, 1924), 44–48.

11. Henry-Russell Hitchcock, *The Architecture of H. H. Richardson and His Times* (New York: Museum of Modern Art, 1936).

12. Henry-Russell Hitchcock, *The Architecture of H. H. Richardson and His Times,* 2nd ed. (Hampden, Conn.: Archon Books, 1961); rev. paperback (Cambridge, Mass., and London: MIT Press, 1966).

13. James F. O'Gorman, *H. H. Richardson: Architectural Forms for an American Society* (Chicago and London: University of Chicago Press, 1987).

14. James F. O'Gorman, *Henry Hobson Richardson and His Office: Selected Drawings*

(Boston: David R. Godine, 1974; paperback edition, Cambridge, Mass., and London: MIT Press, 1982), 31, n.3.

15.   For a discussion of how Hitchcock built his case, see: Jeffrey Karl Ochsner, "Seeing Richardson in His Time: The Problem of the Romanesque Revival," in *H. H. Richardson: The Architect, His Peers, and Their Era*, edited by Maureen Meister (Cambridge, Mass., and London: MIT Press, 1999), 102–145.

16.   Hitchcock, *Richardson and His Times* (1966), 290. In later writings Hitchcock reassessed Richardson's contributions and eliminated some of the most evident biases of his early work. His published lecture, *Richardson as a Victorian Architect*, placed the first part of Richardson's career more directly within its Victorian context, and saw his evolution as a creative synthesis of contemporary French and English tendencies. See: Henry-Russell Hitchcock, *Richardson as a Victorian Architect* (Baltimore: Smith College at Barton-Gillette Co., 1966).

17.   James F. O'Gorman, *Three American Architects: Richardson, Sullivan, and Wright, 1865–1915* (Chicago and London: University of Chicago Press, 1991).

18.   Floyd, *Architecture after Richardson*, 8–9. O'Gorman wrote: "It takes nothing away from Richardson's stature as an architect to envision him as part of a group of interacting individuals who together contributed to the work we for convenience call *his*." See: O'Gorman, *Selected Drawings*, 29–30.

19.   Floyd argued that Hitchcock was able to present Richardson as a lone proto-modern genius because he routinely credited the non-modern features of Richardson's buildings to the office staff. Floyd, *Architecture after Richardson*, 5–7. Hitchcock did call early staff members such as Stanford White "one-eyed," and the later staff were described as entirely "blind." Hitchcock, *Richardson and His Times* (1966), 128, 163–164, 241.

20.   On Hitchcock's interpretation of Richardson and some of his errors, see: Ochsner, "Seeing Richardson in His Time," 102–145.

21.   Floyd, *Architecture after Richardson*, 10.

22.   Modern historians like Mumford and Hitchcock explored the evidence of Richardson's works, but largely ignored the pattern of contemporary publication of his buildings. As a result, their approach was one which depended on induction of an interpretive framework based on Richardson's own works, but it cannot be considered as reflective of how Richardson's works came to be known and understood by his contemporaries.

23.   A few have been more positive about the Richardsonian Romanesque; Breisch called it "one of the most successful styles of building in the United States during the last two decades of the nineteenth century." See: Kenneth A. Breisch, review of *H. H. Richardson: Architectural Forms for an American Society* by James F. O'Gorman, *Winterthur Portfolio* 23/1 (Spring 1988): 94–95.

24.   The book *The Spirit of H. H. Richardson on the Midland Prairies* was prepared as a catalogue to accompany an exhibition of the same title held at the University Art Museum of the University of Minnesota from March to May 1988 (which subsequently toured to other sites from August 1988 to November 1990). Prepared on a very tight schedule and drawing on the work of multiple contributors, the book was a pioneering effort, but suffers from some unevenness among the essays and occasional inaccuracies in dating and attribution. (See note 8 for complete bibliographic citation.)

25.   One of the few scholarly articles that outlines the development of American Victorian architecture is: Stephen Fox, "High Victorian Architecture in Texas," *Texas Architect* 36/3 (May/June 1986): 88–95.

26.   Colin Rowe and John Hejduk, "Lockhart, Texas," *Architectural Record*, 121/3 (March 1957): 201–206

27.   A complete history of the preservation and rehabilitation of Pioneer Square has not been written. Some parts of the story are addressed in Lawrence Kreisman, *Made to Last: Historic Preservation in Seattle and King County* (Seattle: Historic Seattle

Preservation Foundation; Seattle and London: University of Washington Press, 1999), especially pages 83–95. A brief discussion of the preservation of the Pioneer Square District is found in: Randolph Delahanty, *Preserving the West: California, Arizona, Nevada, Utah, Idaho, Oregon, Washington* (New York: Pantheon Books, 1985), 157–164.

II. Pre-Fire Seattle:
Architects and Architecture

1. Cited in David Buerge, *Seattle in the 1880s* (Seattle: Historical Society of Seattle and King County, 1986), 12.

2. "There are abundant grounds for the prediction that Tacoma . . . will rapidly become one of the greatest industrial centers of the world." Louis W. Pratt, *Tacoma: Electric City of the Pacific Coast* (Tacoma: Tacoma Chamber of Commerce, [1903]), 5–6. "This means . . . at Tacoma another New York with at least five million people in the next fifty years." "Tacoma: The Second Greater New York," *The Forum* [Tacoma] 8/12 (21 Dec. 1907): 3. A photo caption in this article reads: "Pacific Avenue, The Future Broadway of the West." As late as 1913 a local writer published a booklet at his own expense to try to prove the future greatness of Tacoma: Randolph F. Radebaugh, *The Pacific Metropolis: Where and Why* (Tacoma: R. F. Radebaugh, 1913).

3. Henry Leiter Yesler (1810–1892) was among the most important of Seattle's earliest settlers. Yesler's steam sawmill was almost the only industry in Seattle in the city's first decade. Yesler built the city's first grist mill and its first crude water system. He served as the first clerk of King County and at various times was a King County commissioner and Seattle mayor. He invested in banks, railroads, and real estate. Yesler is a key figure in almost every history of Seattle. For a biographical summary, see: Clarence Bagley, *History of Seattle from the Earliest Settlement to the Present Time* (Chicago: S. J. Clarke, 1916), 2: 708–710.

4. For the history of railroads and nineteenth-century Seattle, see: Kurt E. Armbruster, *Orphan Road: The Railroad Comes to Seattle, 1853–1911* (Pullman: Washington State University Press, 1999). The history of the Northern Pacific Railroad is particularly complex as it suffered through mismanagement, failures, reorganizations, and mergers. As a result there is no complete history of the railroad and those histories that do exist occasionally disagree with regard to basic facts. The first history of the railroad, commissioned by Henry Villard during his presidency, Eugene V. Smalley, *History of the Northern Pacific Railroad* (New York, 1883), remains the best history to 1883. The railroad's own *Annual Reports* (various locations, 1877–1905) supplement the Smalley history as does James B. Hedges, *Henry Villard and the Railways of the Northwest* (New Haven: 1930). Recent accounts include Louis T. Renz, *The History of the Northern Pacific Railroad* (Fairfield, Wash.: Ye Galleon Press, 1980), and Charles Wood, *The Northern Pacific: Main Street of the Northwest* (Seattle: Superior, 1968). An excellent short summary of Northern Pacific Railroad history is found in Edward W. Nolan, *Northern Pacific Views: The Railroad Photography of F. Jay Haynes, 1876–1905* (Helena: Montana Historical Society Press, 1983). A history of Pacific Northwest railroads in terms of their impact on regional development is: Carlos A. Schwantes, *Railroad Signatures across the Pacific Northwest* (Seattle and London: University of Washington Press, 1993). Brief accounts include Randall V. Mills, "A History of Transportation in the Pacific Northwest," *Oregon Historical Quarterly* 47 (Sept. 1946): 281–312; Hanford W. Fairweather, "The Northern Pacific Railroad and Some of Its History," *Washington Historical Quarterly* 10 (April 1919): 95–100; and David Lavender, *Land of Giants: The Drive to the Pacific Northwest, 1750–1950* (Garden City, N.Y.: Doubleday, 1958), 375–400. For a recent discussion of the coming of the Great Northern Railroad to Seattle, see: Frank Leonard, "'Wise, Swift, and Sure'? The Great Northern Entry into Seattle, 1889–1894," *PNQ* 92/2 (Spring 2001): 81–90.

5. "Message of Governor Marshall Moore, December 7, 1867," in *Messages of the Governors of the Territory of Washington to the Legislative Assembly, 1854–1889*, edited by Charles M. Gates (Seattle: University of Washington Press, 1940), 142.

6. G. Thomas Edwards, "'Terminus Disease': The Clark P. Crandall Description of Puget Sound in 1871," *PNQ* 70/4 (October 1979): 163–177. Crandall, an editor of the Portland *Oregonian*, made a three-week tour of Puget Sound towns in 1871. His report appeared in the *Oregonian* Sept. 4, 6, and 7, 1871.

7. *Washington Standard*, 15 Apr. 1871, 2; cited in Edwards, "'Terminus Disease,'" 165.

8. In response to the Northern Pacific selection of Tacoma as terminus, Seattle business and civic leaders organized to build the Seattle and Walla Walla Railroad across the Cascades. A survey of the route was completed in 1874, but no financing could be obtained due to the depressed national economy. On 14 May 1874, citizens started to try to build the railroad themselves. By October enthusiasm lagged—only thirteen miles had been graded and no track laid. Seattle entrepreneur J. M. Colman acquired the line in 1876 and completed it as far as Renton, where he tapped newly discovered coal fields. Thereafter, Seattle became an exporter of coal to other West Coast cities. Although Seattle was not selected as the Northern Pacific terminus, the city became the center of a local transportation network and developed a more diverse economy than other Puget Sound towns. See: Armbruster, *Orphan Road*, 48–59; Sol H. Lewis, "A History of the Railroads in Washington," *Washington Historical Quarterly* 3 (July 1912): 186–197; and Roger Sale, *Seattle Past to Present* (Seattle and London: University of Washington Press, 1976), 33–34.

9. Buerge, *Seattle in the 1880s*, 36, 42.

10. Ibid., 46.

11. Rudyard Kipling, *American Notes* (New York: Manhattan Press, n.d. [1910?]); reprint edition: *American Notes: Rudyard Kipling's West*, edited and with an introduction by Arrell M. Gibson (Norman: University of Oklahoma Press, 1981), 68. Kipling's quote was specifically about Tacoma, but could almost equally well have applied to Seattle.

12. Quoted in Murray Morgan, *Puget's Sound: A Narrative of Early Tacoma and the Southern Sound* (Seattle and London: University of Washington Press, 1979), 273.

Elsewhere similar contests were played out at various scales. In eastern Washington, intense competition developed among cities such as Ellensburg, Yakima, Walla Walla, Sprague, and Spokane. A typical example is the article enumerating the advantages of Ellensburg and denigrating rival Yakima that appeared in the local paper: "Plain Truths," *Ellensburg Capitol*, 26 Sept. 1889, 1.

13. Buerge, *Seattle in the 1880s*, 46–47.

14. For example, the *Post-Intelligencer* described the anticipated opening of the Frye Opera House in 1884: "Another long step will be taken in the city's progress toward metropolitan estate." The paper stated that the building was "an index to our city's future." *P.I.*, 30 Nov. 1884, 3.

15. *Weekly Pacific Tribune*, 16 Oct. 1869, 3. Two months later the paper reported Abbott's design for a bank building as "the first brick building in Olympia"; *Weekly Pacific Tribune*, 25 Dec. 1869, 3.

16. The Washington Territorial University building, erected in 1861, was the work of John Pike (1814–1903), a local builder. Pike came west with the Denny party, but settled initially in Corvallis, Oregon. He moved to Seattle in 1858. He left Seattle in 1873, and died on Orcas Island on 6 November 1903. See: undated obituary in the pamphlet file at Manuscripts, Special Collections, University Archives Division, University of Washington Libraries.

17. The term "freely eclectic" is used here to distinguish the Victorian approach from the term "academic eclectic." Both involve choice (the Greek root of "eclectic" means "to choose" or "to pick out"), but academic eclecticism demanded scholarly

knowledge of past architectural styles so that educated choices could be made and historically inappropriate combinations could be avoided. American Victorian eclecticism was not bound by such limits.

18. Uvalde Price, *An Essay on the Picturesque, as compared with the Sublime and the Beautiful* (London: 1796), I.61; for a summary of Price's text, see: "Price on Picturesque Planning," *Architectural Review* 95 (Feb. 1944), 47–50. For further discussion of the picturesque see: Thomas D. Lauder, *Sir Uvalde Price on the Picturesque* (Edinburgh and London: 1842); Christopher Hussey, *The Picturesque* (London and New York: G. P. Putnam's Sons, 1927); and Nikolaus Pevsner, "The Genesis of the Picturesque," *Architectural Review* 96 (Nov. 1944): 139–143.

19. Andrew Jackson Downing, *The Architecture of Country Houses* (New York: 1850; reprint edition with new introduction by George Tatum, New York: Da Capo, 1968), 204.

20. An example of an influential immigrant Victorian architect is Frederick Withers. See: Francis R. Kowsky, *The Architecture of Frederick Clarke Withers and the Progress of the Gothic Revival in America after 1850* (Middletown, Conn.: Weslayan University Press, 1980).

21. Henry Van Brunt's statement is quoted in Roger Stein, *John Ruskin and Aesthetic Thought in America, 1840–1900* (Cambridge, Mass.: Harvard University Press, 1967), 201–202.

22. For a discussion of Alfred B. Mullett, see: Lawrence Wodehouse, "Alfred B. Mullett and His French Style Government Buildings," *JSAH* 21/1 (March 1972): 22–37.

23. For example, the first building in Texas to appear in *AABN*, the Galveston Cotton Exchange completed in 1878, has been described by Stephen Fox as "a virtual case study of American High Victorian techniques of composition. The two street elevations were organized in a compositional grid with belt courses and pilasters defining a rhythmic pattern of compartments into which openings were inserted. Within the depth of the masonry bearing walls, shallow planar layers were defined to create a sense of plasticity. In contrast to the regularity implied by this architectural frame, individual components were highly differentiated through variations in shape, material, surface texture, and color. Architectural ornament was divided into a hierarchy of types, as icons of the building's civic standing, its typological antecedents, and for its tectonic, spatial and material composition." Fox, "High Victorian Architecture in Texas," 90.

24. The initiation of the first national professional architectural journal, *American Architect and Building News,* based in Boston, served both as a vehicle for the dissemination of new directions in American architecture and as a record of the design work during its years of publication. For information on this and other early professional architectural journals, see: Mary Norman Woods, "The *American Architect and Building News, 1876–1907*" (Ph.D. diss., Columbia University, 1983). A summary of some of this material is: Mary Norman Woods, "The First American Architectural Journals: The Profession's Voice," *JSAH* 48/2 (June 1989): 117–138.

25. The history presented here generally follows that outlined by Stephen Fox, who uses the term "constructive ornament" to describe the ornament of mid- to late-nineteenth-century buildings that appears related to a real or an implied structural rationale. The frequent use of flat pilasters and belt courses on load-bearing masonry walls in American Victorian architecture implied a kind of structural grid; other ornamental embellishments appear at window and door heads, roof-wall connections, or points where interior framing intersects the exterior load-bearing walls. The detail did not literally reveal the actual connection but frequently tended to emphasize points of connection or load transfer. See: Stephen Fox, *Houston Architectural Guide* (Houston, Tex.: AIA/Houston Chapter and Herring Press, 1990), 52–57; see also: Fox, "High Victorian Architecture in Texas," 88–92.

26. On Street's introduction of classicizing tendencies into the Victorian Gothic, see: David B. Brownlee, *The Law Courts: The Architecture of George Edmund Street* (New York: Architectural History Foundation, and Cambridge, Mass., and London: MIT Press, 1984).

27. A very brief introduction to pattern books and their influence is David Gebhard, "Pattern Books," in *Master Builders: A Guide to Famous American Architects*, edited by Diane Maddex (Washington, D.C.: Preservation Press, 1985), 68–73, 197; for the use of pattern books relative to nineteenth-century residential building, see: Dell Upton, "Pattern Books and Professionalism: Aspects of the Transformation of Domestic Architecture in America, 1800–1860," *Winterthur Portfolio* 19/2–3 (Summer–Autumn 1984): 107–150. Also see: Daniel D. Reiff, *Houses from Books: Treatises, Pattern Books and Catalogs in American Architecture, 1738–1950: A History and Guide* (University Park, Penn.: Pennsylvania State University Press, 2000).

28. Arthur Doyle (1819–1899) was born in Ireland, but came to Lexington, Mississippi, at an early age. He served as mayor of Lexington, and later served as a colonel in the Confederate Army. After the Civil War, he lived in Mobile, Alabama, and Denver, Colorado, before arriving in Seattle in 1871. He retired from active practice in 1884.

29. For Squire's Opera House, see: *P.I.*, 31 Aug. 1879, 3. For the Stacy House, see: *P.I.*, 4 Nov. 1883, 2; also see: Margaret P. Strachan, "Early Day Mansions #17: Martin Van Buren Stacy," *Times*, 24 Dec. 1944, magazine section, 2.

30. For the First Presbyterian Church, see: *P.I.*, 19 July 1876, 3; 17 Aug. 1876, 3. For the nineteenth-century history of the First Presbyterian Church, see: Ida Grace Corkey, *Seattle Churches as Known through Seattle Newspapers* (Seattle?: 1939?), 23–25; unfortunately this includes nothing about the church building.

31. For the comparison of Seattle to a New England coastal town, see: Buerge, *Seattle in the 1880s*, 90.

32. *P.I.*, 9 Apr. 1882, 4; 13 Apr. 1882, 4.

33. *P.I.*, 19 May 1882, 4.

34. The cast-iron front of Arthur Doyle's Frauenthal Building was imported from San Francisco; see: *Weekly Pacific Tribune*, 19 May 1876, 2.

35. Cheryl Sjoblom, "Mother Joseph of the Sacred Heart (Esther Pariseault)," in *Shaping Seattle Architecture: A Historical Guide to the Architects*, edited by Jeffrey Karl Ochsner (Seattle and London: University of Washington Press, with AIA Seattle, 1994, 6–9, 301–302, 326, is an accurate short account. There is extensive literature on Mother Joseph; however, some published essays appear to have been based on limited original research and may contain inaccuracies or exaggerations regarding her role as architect and builder.

36. David A. Rash discovered that there were two Donald MacKays subsequent to the publication of David A. Rash, "Donald MacKay," in *Shaping Seattle Architecture*, 10–15, 300–301, 326. Rash notes that the history prior to 1882 presented in that essay applies to Mackay the Portland, Oregon, contractor. After the arrival in Seattle of the other MacKay, the contractor-builder who had been in Walla Walla from 1880 to 1882, the essay is substantially correct. (Personal communication from David Rash, 8 June 1999.)

37. *P.I.*, 29 Oct. 1882, 4. For the construction history of Providence Hospital, see: *P.I.*, 20 Apr. 1882, 4; 23 April 1882, 4; 26 Apr. 1882, 4; 29 Apr. 1882, 4; 8 Sept. 1882, 4; 19 Jan. 1883, 4.

38. On Our Lady of Good Hope Church, see: *P.I.*, 21 Apr. 1882, 4; 6 May 1882, 4; 9 May 1882, 4; 14 May 1882, 4; 13 Oct. 1882, 4.

39. John Collins (1835–1903) was born in Ireland in 1835 and came to New York City at age ten. In 1851, he went to Machias, Maine, to work in the lumber business. He moved to Puget Sound to work for the Puget Mill Company in Port Gamble in the mid-1850s and arrived in Seattle a decade later. After 1869, Collins served on the city

council, as mayor, and in the territorial legislature. He joined other Seattle business leaders in investing in the Seattle and Walla Walla Railroad, in mining properties, and in Seattle real estate.

40. For Occidental Hotel construction history, see: *P.I.*, 6 May 1882, 4; 10 June 1882, 4; 17 June 1882, 4; 21 Sept. 1882, 4; 25 Feb. 1883, 2; 14 Mar. 1883, 2; 1 June 1883, 2; 19 Aug. 1883, 2; 28 June 1884, 2. An addition to the Occidental Hotel was made in 1888, to fill the complete triangular block. This was designed by architect Otto Kleemann of Portland, Oregon. See: *P.I.*, 7 Aug. 1887, 3; 4 Oct. 1887, 3. (The paper misspelled his name "Kleemer.") Otto Kleemann was a long-time Portland architect who designed many Catholic churches in the Portland area. For a brief biography, see: Joseph Gaston, *Portland, Oregon: Its History and Builders*, 2 (Chicago: S. J. Clark, 1911), 91.

41. For a selection of Boone's Yesler-Leary design, see: *P.I.*, 23 July 1882, 4; 25 July 1882, 4; 10 Aug. 1882, 4 (design selected and described).

42. For the Academy of Holy Names, see: *P.I.*, 1 May 1883, 2; 9 Oct. 1883, 2. MacKay's other designs in 1883 included the Seattle Engine House No. 1 (1883–84, destroyed) and a commercial block for Amos Brown (1883, destroyed).

David Rash has discovered that MacKay remained in Portland only a few years; he had moved to Vancouver, British Columbia, by 1887. However, Margaret MacKay is listed as his widow in the Portland city directory in 1888. (Personal communication from David Rash, 8 June 1999.)

43. William Boone's career was remarkable in its longevity and unusual for an architect who began in the building trades. His career in the 1880s and 1890s is described in detail in this book. A short overview of his career is: Jeffrey Karl Ochsner, "William E. Boone," in *Shaping Seattle Architecture*, 16–21, 295, 319.

44. Boone's practice is first mentioned in the *P.I.*, 28 Apr. 1882, 4; he is first included in the newspaper professional listings on 30 Apr. 1882. Boone may also have lived and practiced briefly in Puyallup.

45. For the Boone and Meeker partnership, see: *P.I.*, 3 July 1882, 2 (although the partnership had already submitted plans for the North School, *P.I.*, 29 June 1883, 2). Meeker is described as "an experienced architect." Information on Boone's partner, George C. Meeker, is scarce, as he never maintained a permanent residence in Seattle. From 1878 to 1883–84, and from 1888 to 1892–93, he is listed in Oakland city directories, and from 1892–1902, he is listed in San Jose city directories; thereafter he resided in Oakland until his death in 1919 at age sixty-nine. Meeker may have lived in Puyallup after 1884, but in March 1886 he returned permanently to California to become "assistant architect" on a state insane asylum in San Jose; see *P.I.*, 2 Mar. 1886, 1. The firm still advertised as Boone and Meeker in early 1888, but by February 1889, Boone was listed alone. The firm name "Boone and Meeker" never appeared in city directories in California.

46. For Boone's early projects, see: City Building: *P.I.*, 29 Apr. 1882, 4; 27 May 1882, 4; 13 July 1882, 4; 26 Oct. 1882, 4; 27 Oct. 1882, 4; 9 Dec. 1882, 4; Marshall Building: *P.I.*, 19 May 1882, 4; McNaught, Walker and Renton Building: *P.I.*, 18 June 1882, 4; Boyd and Poncin Store: *P.I.*, 16 June 1882, 4; 19 June 1882, 4.

47. "When completed the Leary Block, will be the finest structure in appearance, for its size, north of San Francisco." *P.I.*, 10 Aug. 1882, 4. For Yesler-Leary Building history, see: *P.I.*, 12 May 1882, 4; 23 July 1882, 4; 25 July 1882, 4; 13 Aug. 1882, 4; 23 Sep. 1882, 4; 13 Mar. 1883, 2; 12 May 1883, 2; 23 June 1883, 2; 28 June 1883, 2.

48. John Leary (1837–1905) was a Canadian lumber merchant who came to Seattle in 1869.

49. For the decision to build the Methodist Protestant Church in wood, due to unavailability of brick, see: *P.I.*, 19 Aug. 1882, 4. For construction delays due to lack of brick and stone, see: *P.I.*, 24 Aug. 1882, 4. Unavailability of brick continued to be a problem in 1883; see: *P.I.*, 26 June 1883, 2.

50. For Boone's 1883 commercial blocks, see: Yesler-Leary addition (unbuilt): *P.I.*, 21 Mar. 1883, 2; 15 Apr. 1883, 2; 28 June 1883, 2; C. P. Stone Block: *P.I.*, 17 Mar. 1883, 2; 1 Apr. 1883, 2; 7 Apr. 1883, 2; 15 Apr. 1883, 2; 23 June 1883, 2; 26 Oct. 1883, 2; 5 June 1884, 2; 18 June 1884, 2; 18 Jan. 1885, 4; Schwabacher Building: *P.I.*, 15 Apr. 1883, 2; 23 June 1883, 2; 8 July 1883, 2; 13 July 1883, 2; 24 Nov. 1883, 2; Wah Chong Building: *P.I.*, 29 June 1883, 2; 13 July 1883, 2; 21 July 1883, 2; 27 Sep. 1883, 2; Squire Building: *P.I.*, 12 Aug. 1883, 3; 27 Sept. 1883, 2 (substitution of wood for brick); 11 Nov. 1883, 4; 9 Dec. 1883, 4.

51. For Yesler house, see: *P.I.*, 15 Apr. 1883, 2 ("Eastlake style"); 15 July 1883, 2; 21 July 1883, 2; 1 Jan. 1885, 5.

52. For Boone and Meeker's commercial projects in 1884, see: Gordon Hardware Company Building: *P.I.*, 31 July 1884, 2; 1 Jan. 1885, 5; 18 Jan. 1885, 4; Seattle Safe Deposit Building: *P.I.*, 9 May 1884, 2; 10 May 1884, 2; 23 May 1884, 2; 19 July 1884, 2; 1 Jan. 1885, 5; 18 Jan. 1885, 4.

53. The Tacoma paper described the Annie Wright Seminary: "It has been termed composite, and if to this we add the word American, a better idea would scarcely be given of the style of the building than by the use of any other. In fact, there is scarcely a school of architecture, save the Egyptian, that its architect has not borrowed from." *Tacoma News*, 21 Aug. 1884, 1.

Other works by Boone and Meeker in Tacoma included: Wilkeson & Kandle Building (1884), Bishop Paddock house (1884), Samuel Wilkeson house (1884), and E. S. Smith house (1885); the Smith house was inherited from Donald MacKay.

54. Of John Nestor's early life and previous practice of architecture in Indiana (where he designed several theaters) and San Francisco, little is known. His works in Portland included the Ladd and Tilton Bank Building (1868, destroyed); fragments of this were saved and integrated into a bank of Nestor's design in Salem. See: William J. Hawkins, *The Grand Era of Cast Iron Architecture in Portland* (Portland, Oreg.: Binford & Mort, 1976), 16, 32.

55. For a description of the Frye Opera House, see: *P.I.*, 30 Nov. 1884, 3 (qtn.); for its history, see: 12 Oct. 1883, 2; 13 Oct. 1883, 2; 1 Nov. 1883, 2; 9 Nov. 1883, 2; 14 Dec. 1883, 2; 13 May 1884, 2; 23 Aug. 1884, 2; 30 Nov. 1884, 3; 2 Dec. 1884, 3; 1 Jan. 1885, 5; 18 Jan. 1885, 4.

56. For selection of the architects and their roles, see: "Minutes of Proceedings of the Board of Trustees of the First Methodist Episcopal Church of Seattle," Volume A: 4 June 1887: plans by William Stokes adopted with changes; 13 June 1887: plans by Stokes approved; 21 June 1887: agreement to employ John Nestor as superintendent; June–July 1887: changes to plans delay bidding; 10 Aug. 1887: J.E. Bennett of Portland low bidder at $24,500; 15 Aug. 1887: Bennett raises bid to $28,500; decision to terminate Stokes and employ Nestor to make changes and continue as architect as well as superintendent; 23 Aug. 1887: construction contract delayed pending settlement with Stokes; 30 Aug. 1887: Nestor requested to complete drawings; 20 Sept. 1887: bid of $14,400 by Moses McKeezer of Seattle accepted. Construction proceeded thereafter and was nearly complete by July 1888; however, interior finishes were bid separately and the church was not finished until May 1889.

57. Seattle's earlier schools were one- or two-room schools later described as "shack schools." They were built by local builders and very likely did not involve architectural input. For a discussion of the early history of the Seattle School District and its buildings, see chapter 6.

58. *P.I.*, 28 Oct. 1872, 3. Isaac A. Palmer (born ca. 1835 in Pennsylvania) was active in Seattle in the early and mid-1870s. He designed and built a number of commercial buildings and residences in 1872, notably the L.V. Wyckoff residence at the southeast corner of Second and Cherry, and the First Baptist Church on Fourth Avenue. His design for a pretentious stone courthouse for King County, described with much enthusiasm in Seattle newspapers late in 1876, was never built. He moved to Dayton,

Washington Territory, sometime in late 1877 or early 1878, then returned to Seattle in late summer of 1881. He advertised as an architect in Seattle, Dayton, and Walla Walla newspapers and operated in several partnerships, including Palmer Brothers, Palmer Brothers and Ball, and Odell and Palmer. (Thanks to David Rash for this biographical information.)

59. For a description of Central School, see: *P.I.*, 28 Apr. 1883, 2; for its history: *P.I.*, 21 Apr. 1882, 4; 21 May 1882, 4; 28 May 1882, 4; 8 June 1882, 4; 13 June 1882, 4; 30 June 1882, 4; 6 July 1882, 4; 14 July 1882, 4; 23 July 1882, 4; 25 July 1882, 4; 8 Aug. 1882, 4; 24 Sept. 1882, 4; 5 Nov. 1882, 4; 19 Dec. 1882, 4.

60. For the Denny School design competition, see: *P.I.*, 15 June 1883, 2; 29 June 1883, 2 (submissions), 30 June 1883, 2 (selection). For the history of construction, see: *P.I.*, 8 July 1883, 2; 11 July 1883, 2; 24 July 1883, 2; 26 July 1883, 2; 1 Aug. 1883, 2; 9 Aug. 1883, 2; 10 Aug. 1883, 2; 4 Sep. 1883, 2; 23 Oct. 1883, 2; 9 Nov. 1883, 2; 27 Jan. 1884, 2; 4 June 1884, 2; 22 July 1884, 2; 31 Aug. 1884, 2; 1 Jan. 1885, 5.

61. The partnership between James P. Donovan and Stephen Meany lasted only a few months. Its dissolution was noted in *P.I.*, 9 Oct. 1883, 2. Following complaints about Donovan's inadequate supervision of construction at North School, Meany was hired as superintendent for the project; *P.I.*, 23 Oct. 1883, 2; 9 Nov. 1883, 2. Donovan left the city and subsequently practiced in Victoria, British Columbia.

62. *P.I.*, 30 June 1883, 2.

63. Of Stephen Meany's early life in San Jose, California, little is known. In 1879 the Seattle city directory listed his profession as "mariner"; by 1882 he was identified as a draftsman. His early architectural career mixed independent practice and working as a draftsman for others; see: *P.I.*, 1 Mar. 1884, 2. For his commercial buildings in 1884, see: Poncin Block: *P.I.*, 24 June 1884, 2; 1 Jan. 1885, 5; 18 Jan. 1885, 4; Kenney Block: *P.I.*, 1 Oct. 1884, 2; 7 Oct. 1884, 3; 1 Jan. 1885, 5; 18 Jan. 1885, 4.

64. On the McNaught House, see: *P.I.*, 3 Oct. 1883, 2; 1 Jan. 1885, 5; also see: Margaret P. Strachan, "Early Day Mansions #5: James McNaught," *Times*, 1 Oct. 1944, magazine section, 3.

65. Palliser and Palliser had advertised their pattern and plan book series in the Seattle newspapers from the mid-1880s. The Carkeek House appears to have been an independent commission from Palliser and Palliser as a matching design in their published pattern books has not been discovered. A front elevation drawing is on display in the Swedish Hospital annex; this was created by Olson/Sundberg Architects from historic photographs (including photographs of the floor plans) at University of Washington Libraries, Manuscripts, Special Collections, University Archives Division.

66. On the Kinnear House, see: *P.I.*, 3 July 1887, 7; 1 Jan. 1889, 7, 11. Plans and a perspective of the design appeared in *The Architectural Era* 2/2 (Feb. 1888): 26–27. (Thanks to David Rash for pointing out these citations.) Also see: Margaret P. Strachan, "Early Day Mansions #24: George Kinnear," *Times*, 11 Feb. 1945, magazine section, 3.

67. For the Washington Teritorial Insane Asylum, see: newspaper clipping files, Washington State Historical Society, Tacoma (undated clippings from the *Tacoma Daily Ledger*, April–Oct. 1886). Also see: *Washington Magazine* 1 (Nov. 1889): 31. As a result of problems with the quality of construction, John C. Proctor, of the Tacoma firm Daniels and Proctor, replaced Boone as superintendent in September 1886.

68. For the Toklas and Singerman Building, see: *P.I.*, 12 Mar. 1887, 3; 3 Apr. 1887, 3; 11 Mar. 1888, 3.

69. For the Boston Block, see: *P.I.*, 7 Sept. 1887, 3; 13 Jan. 1888; 21 Jan. 1888; 18 Apr. 1888, 3; 22 Apr. 1888, 3; 23 May 1888, 3. Also see: *IA* 12 (Dec. 1888): 16.

70. For the Yesler Block, see: *P.I.*, 29 Sept. 1887, 3; 7 Dec. 1887, 3; 18 Apr. 1888, 3; 29 Apr. 1888, 5. For the earlier Yesler Block proposal, see: note 50.

71. For Boone and Meeker's projects see: I.O.O.F. Building: *P.I.*, 28 Feb. 1889, 2; Phinney Building: *P.I.*, 26 Mar. 1889, 3; 1 Dec. 1889, 5. Boone and Meeker were also

responsible for the Chapin Building, a three-story wood commercial block adjacent to the Boston Block; see: *P.I.*, 8 Mar. 1888, 4; 10 Apr. 1888, 3; 23 May 1888, 3.

72. For Central School fire, see: *P.I.*, 11 Apr. 1888, 3; for the new Central and South Schools, see: *P.I.*, 11 Apr. 1888, 3; 12 Apr. 1888, 2, 3; 13 Apr. 1888, 2, 3; 22 Apr. 1888, 5; 5 May 1888, 3; 6 May 1888, 4; 7 June 1888, 4; 10 Nov. 1888, 3; 2 Feb. 1889, 3; 15 Oct. 1889, 5. Also see: School Board "Minutes," April 2, 1888.

73. Fisher's date of birth and year of immigration are approximations based on calculations from later accounts. No primary sources documenting his early life have been discovered.

74. Fisher's immigration to the United States from Edinburgh at age 17, and his working for five years for "Boyd & Sons," an "eminent" architectural office in Worcester, Massachusetts, where he gained "his first knowledge of his profession," are all described in *NREBR* 1/3 (May 1891): 8. However, no record of Fisher's presence in Worcester has been discovered in city directories or other records between 1850 and 1860, leading to some doubts regarding this account. There was no firm in Worcester by the name of Boyd and Sons; the leading architect in Worcester in this period was Elbridge Boyden (1810–1898), and it must be to Boyden that the Seattle account refers. Boyden has been recognized for his early use of cast-iron fronts in commercial buildings; see: Henry-Russell Hitchcock, *Architecture: Nineteenth and Twentieth Centuries* (Baltimore: Penguin Books, 1958), 192.

When Fisher ran for City Council in 1892, a brief published biographical summary indicated that Fisher had served in the Civil War in the 25th Massachusetts Volunteers, had transferred to "the sharpshooters" in 1864, and then was wounded in the siege of Richmond. See *Times*, 7 Mar. 1892, 1. However, military records of the period include no mention of Elmer H. Fisher or even E. H. Fisher. Nor are there any records for other spellings such as "Fischer." One explanation might be that Fisher changed his name between 1865 and 1880.

75. Denver city directories indicate Fisher's presence in Denver and his participation in Corrin and Fisher. Because Corrin and Fisher was very likely constructing projects of its own design, Fisher may have designed some Denver buildings, but none of the firm's Denver projects have been identified.

76. Victoria, founded as a Hudson's Bay Company outpost, became the seat of British Columbia's provincial government in 1856. Transformed into a bustling city following the Fraser River gold rush in 1858, Victoria was the leading city on the West Coast of Canada until completion of the Canadian Pacific Railroad to Vancouver in 1887. Vancouver's population equaled Victoria's by 1891 and surpassed it thereafter.

77. Fisher first advertised in the *Victoria Colonist*, 6 Feb. 1886, 2. For Spencer's Arcade, see: *Victoria Colonist*, 30 Mar. 1886, 3; 16 May 1886, 7; 2 Oct. 1886, 3.

78. For the death of James P. Donovan, see: *Victoria Colonist*, 21 May 1886, 3. Donovan had previously practiced in Seattle, but had moved to Victoria in late 1883; see: note 61.

With the description of Spencer's Arcade, the *Colonist* noted, "Mr. Fisher is entitled to great credit for the designing and constructing of the whole building, the whole having been under his personal supervision from the first, and while he is a comparative stranger to most of us, yet his manner of designing and constructing this building alone is sufficient to ensure his success in this city." *Victoria Colonist*, 2 Oct. 1886, 3.

79. *Victoria Colonist*, 3 Oct. 1886, 3.

80. For Fisher's British Columbia buildings, see: Hotel at Goldstream: *Victoria Colonist*, 3 Feb. 1887, 3; Vancouver commercial buildings: *Victoria Colonist*, 27 Apr. 1887, 3; 7 Aug. 1887, 1; Bank of British Columbia at New Westminster: *Victoria Colonist*, 9 June 1887, 1; Courthouse at Nanaimo: *Victoria Colonist*, 21 July 1887, 4; 11 Aug. 1887, 1; Nanaimo commercial buildings: *Victoria Colonist*, 7 Oct. 1887, 1; various residences: *Victoria Colonist*, 1 Mar. 1887, 3; 3 June 1887, 1; 30 July 1887, 1.

81. Anthony A. Barrett and Rhodri Windsor Liscombe, *Francis Rattenbury and*

British Columbia: Architecture and Challenge in the Imperial Age (Vancouver: University of British Columbia Press, 1983), 54.

82. For the McCurdy Block, see: *Victoria Colonist,* 8 Feb. 1887, 1.

83. Port Townsend, on the Olympic Peninsula, enjoyed a rail-related boom in 1888–90, when the Union Pacific subsidary, the Oregon Improvement Company, acquired the interests of the Port Townsend Railroad and announced plans to extend its line to the city. In the financial stringency of late 1890 the boom collapsed and the project was abandoned. Today most of the buildings on Water Street, the main street in downtown Port Townsend, date from the 1888–90 period. For the history and architecture of Port Townsend, see: Allen T. Denison and Wallace K. Huntington, *Victorian Architecture of Port Townsend Washington* (Saanichton, B.C., and Seattle: Hancock House Publishers, 1978); Peter Simpson and James Hermanson, *Port Townsend, Years That Are Gone: An Illustrated History* (Port Townsend: Quimper Press, 1979).

84. For Fisher's Port Townsend buildings, see: Denison and Huntington, *Victorian Architecture,* 56–70; and Simpson and Hermanson, *Port Townsend,* 117, 127, 134. For James and Hastings Building, see: *P.I.,* 13 Oct. 1888, 2 (bid notice); for Hastings Building, see: *P.I.,* 30 Mar. 1889, 2.

85. Fisher maintained his Victoria practice by entering into a partnership with William Ridgway Wilson in late 1887; this partnership endured until April 1889, and was responsible for several commercial and residential structures in Victoria and nearby communities. (Thanks to Don Luxton for this information.)

86. *P.I.,* 17 Nov. 1887, 3; Goddard remains unknown, although a Samuel Goddard is listed as a draftsman working for William Boone in the 1890 Polk directory for Seattle.

87. *P.I.,* 7 Dec. 1887, 3. For Colman Building, see: *Victoria Colonist,* 20 Dec. 1887, 3.

88. For Meany's design for the Colman Building, see: *P.I.,* 17 Apr. 1889, 5; 25 May 1889, 3; 7 Nov. 1889, 8; 6 June 1889, 8.

89. *Victoria Colonist,* 20 Dec. 1887, 3. For the (first) Korn Building, see: *P.I.,* 20 Jan. 1888, 3; 27 May 1888, 3; 19 June 1888, 3; 1 Jan. 1889, 15; 3 Feb. 1889, 5.

90. For Scurry Terrace, see: *P.I.,* 17 Feb. 1889, 5; 24 Apr. 1889, 5; 1 Jan. 1890, 13.

91. For Gilmore and Kirkman Building, see: *P.I.,* 19 May 1888, 3; 24 May 1888, 3; 30 Oct. 1888, 3; 11 Jan. 1889, 5; 24 Jan. 1889, 3; 28 Feb. 1889, 3; 17 Oct. 1889, 8; 19 Oct. 1889, 8; 1 Jan. 1890, 13; 6 June 1890, 8; *Times,* 10, Aug. 1889, 1, 8.

92. For Bell Building, see: *P.I.,* 15 Mar. 1889, 3; 21 Mar. 1889, 2; 3 Aug. 1889, 3; 18 Oct. 1889, 5; 1 Jan. 1890, 13; *Times,* 10 Aug. 1889, 1. The facade of the Bell Building was designed to coordinate with the adjacent I.O.O.F. Building by William Boone; see: note 71.

93. The Denny Hotel, the project of Arthur A. Denny, was built near the top of Denny Hill, north of downtown Seattle. As a result of financial problems the building had a long and complex history; it finally opened in 1903 as the Washington Hotel. For its early history see: *P.I.,* 16 Sept. 1888, 2; 16 Nov. 1888, 3; 18 Jan. 1889, 5; 13 Feb. 1889, 5; 20 Feb. 1889, 4; 2 Apr. 1889, 5.

94. *P.I.,* 16 Feb. 1889, 5.

95. Thomas Burke (1849–1925) was the most significant of Seattle's late-nineteenth-century civic leaders. The son of Irish immigrants, Burke was born in Clinton County, New York. He received his schooling in Ypsilanti, Michigan, then attended the University of Michigan. Burke read law with an attorney in Marshall, Michigan, then came to Seattle in 1875. He was probate judge for King County from 1876 to 1880, and served a temporary term as chief justice of the Washington Territory Supreme Court from 1888 to 1889. Burke invested in real estate, newspapers, streetcar lines, and railroads. After the 1889 fire, he was responsible for several major business blocks in the city. Burke was chief counsel for the western division of the Great Northern Railroad from 1893 to 1904. For a full discussion of Burke's impact on Seattle see: Robert C.

Nesbit, *He Built Seattle: A Biography of Judge Thomas Burke* (Seattle: University of Washington Press, 1961).

96. For Burke's New York Block, see: *P.I.*, 11 Jan. 1889, 5; 12 Mar. 1889, 5; 1 Jan. 1890, 13. Initially this was called Burke's Block, but the name was later changed to New York Block. This three-story structure should not be confused with the much larger Burke Building, designed by Fisher and erected after the June 1889 fire. Burke's New York Block also should not be confused with the later New York Building designed by William Boone for Dexter Horton.

97. For the Yesler Building and the Burke Building, see: chapter 5.

98. The most important source for Parkinson's early life is his own autobiography: John Parkinson, *Incidents by the Way* (Los Angeles: George Rice and Sons, 1935), 1–169. See also: Robert H. Tracy, "John Parkinson and the Beaux-Arts City Beautiful Movement in Downtown Los Angeles, 1894–1935" (Ph.D. diss., University of California, Los Angeles, 1982); however, Tracy drew primarily on *Incidents by the Way* for his coverage of Parkinson before his move to Los Angeles in the mid-1890s.

99. For background on Bolton's Mechanic's Institute, see: Tracy, "John Parkinson," 62–107.

100. Parkinson, *Incidents*, 45.

101. Ibid., 108–109.

102. For Bank of Napa, see: *Register* (Napa), 23 Mar. 1888, 1.

103. Parkinson, *Incidents*, 125–128.

104. For Parkinson's first Seattle advertisement, see: *P.I.*, 22 Feb. 1889.

105. Parkinson, *Incidents*, 133.

106. William Rankin Ballard (1847–1929) was born in Ohio but moved with his family to Oregon in 1858. Beginning in 1866 he held positions first as a teacher, then as a government surveyor, and finally as captain on a coastal steamer.

107. For First National Bank, Olympia, see: Parkinson, *Incidents*, 134–135.

108. The First National Bank in Olympia marked Parkinson's first use of terra-cotta ornament, which was furnished by Gladding, McBean and Company of California. Parkinson's building was only the eighth project for which Gladding, McBean supplied terra-cotta, but the relationship Parkinson established with the firm was to last through his entire career. Records of Gladding, McBean are at the California Room of the California State Library, Sacramento. (Librarian Gary Kurutz kindly allowed the authors access to the unprocessed collection and furnished copies of the Washington state job inventories of Gladding, McBean. The authors also thank Bill Wyatt, plant historian at Gladding, McBean, for allowing access to these materials while they were still in the possession of the Gladding, McBean Company.) For an overview of the company and its projects in California see: Gary F. Kurutz, *Architectural Terra Cotta of Gladding, McBean* (Sausalito: Windgate Press, 1989); however, the company's projects outside California are not addressed by Kurutz.

109. Parkinson, *Incidents*, 136–142.

110. William Farrand Prosser, *History of Puget Sound Country* (New York and Chicago: Lewis Publishing, 1903) 1, 466. This description is included in a biography of E. N. Tunin, the Olympia Hotel manager. The design was described in: *Washington Standard*, 26 Apr. 1889, 1. A drawing appeared in *West Shore* 15/4 (Apr. 1889): 169. Also see: Parkinson, *Incidents*, 138.

111. Other architects active in Seattle before the 1889 fire would also contribute to the rebuilding of the commercial core. Of these, the most important figure not previously mentioned was Hermann Steinmann (1860–1905), who had practiced architecture in St. Louis from 1883 to 1887 before coming to Seattle. Steinmann had an active practice in 1888 and 1889 designing smaller commercial blocks, institutional buildings, terrace houses, and single-family residences. His most important pre-fire commercial structure was the Squire Building (1888), which was destroyed in the June 1889 fire.

III. The Fire and Its Aftermath:
Technology, Construction, and Design

1. For a history of the 1889 Seattle fire and its immediate aftermath, see: Warren, *Day Seattle Burned.* Brief accounts of the fire and its effects on the city are found in virtually every history of Seattle; see, for example: Bagley, *History of Seattle,* 1, 419–428; also see Buerge, *Seattle in the 1880s,* 108–115. The earliest history of the fire, apparently published in July 1889, was the pamphlet by C. W. Austin and H. S. Scott, *The Great Seattle Fire of June 6, 1889: Containing a Succinct and Complete Account of the Greatest Conflagration on the Pacific Coast* (Tacoma, Wash.: Puget Sound Printing Co., 1889).

2. Tacoma papers reported that that the remains of three bodies were found after the fire; see *Tacoma Daily Ledger,* 12 June 1889, 4. Subsequently an unstable wall left standing after the fire collapsed causing an additional death; see *Times,* 28 June 1889, 1; cited in Warren, *Day Seattle Burned,* 28–29.

3. "The people of Seattle have decided to rebuild the city in brick and stone. The decision was reached quickly and almost unanimously." *P.I.,* 8 June 1889, 1.

4. *P.I.,* 8 June 1889, 1; cited in Warren, *Day Seattle Burned,* 46.

5. The need to implement a building permit system and to limit the construction of frame buildings in downtown Seattle was noted in *P.I.,* 14 Feb. 1888, 3; the danger of wood buildings in the downtown was noted in *P.I.,* 24 May 1888, 3. Questions concerning the continued adequacy of the volunteer fire department were raised in *P.I.,* 11 Apr. 1888, 2; a professional paid department was advocated in *P.I.,* 13 Apr. 1888, 3. The widening of streets was discussed in *P.I.,* 6 Sept. 1888, 3 (Front Street); 7 Sept. 1888, 5 (Commercial Street). The need to improve sewage and drainage was noted in *P.I.,* 20 Jan. 1889, 4.

6. For the replat, see: *P.I.,* 22 June 1889, 4; 23 June 1889, 4; 29 June 1889, 4; 30 June 1889, 1; 1 July 1889, 1.

7. Tacoma citizens sent $7,000 to aid those who had suffered in the fire. At the same time Tacoma newspapers headlined the deaths that resulted from the fire and also reported on difficulties some building owners were having in receiving payments from their insurance companies.

8. On insurance companies paying claims after the fire, see: "The Great Seattle Conflagration," *West Shore* 15/6 (June 1889): 284; Warren, *Day Seattle Burned,* 49. For examples of notices by companies inviting policy holders to make claims, see: *Times,* 15 June 1889, 2; 17 June 1889, 2. However, there apparently were problems with the insurance for the Toklas and Singerman Building; see *Tacoma Daily Ledger,* 19 June 1889, 5.

9. *P.I.,* 9 June 1889, 1.

10. The perception of fire as a regenerative force in city development is not unique to Seattle, but has been played out in many cities; see, for example: Ross Miller, *American Apocalypse: The Great Fire and the Myth of Chicago* (Chicago and London: University of Chicago Press, 1990); Christine Meisner Rosen, *The Limits of Power: Great Fires and the Process of City Growth in America* (Cambridge: Cambridge University Press, 1986).

11. *P.I.,* 26 June 1889, Supplement, 1. See also: Warren, *Day Seattle Burned,* 67–69; Buerge, *Seattle in the 1880s,* 108–115; Sale, *Seattle Past to Present,* 50–53.

12. For a broad discussion of the role of fire in American culture, see: Margaret Hindle Hazen and Robert M. Hazen, *Keepers of the Flame: The Role of Fire in American Culture, 1775–1925* (Princeton: Princeton University Press, 1992). For a brief overview of fires in the West, see: Ralph W. Andrews, *Historic Fires of the West* (Seattle: Superior Publishing Co., 1966).

13. *P.I.,* 20 July 1883, 2.

14. Frank Kidder, *Architects and Builders Pocketbook* (New York: John Wiley and Sons, 1885), 383–391.

15. The county courthouses designed by Willis Ritchie all employed this fireproof building technology; see: chapter 7.

16. Sara E. Wermiel, *The Fireproof Building: Technology and Public Safety in the Nineteenth-Century American City* (Baltimore and London: Johns Hopkins University Press, 2000), 104–137. Wermiel notes that the terms "mill construction" and "slow-burning" are synonymous; "semi-fireproof" and "fire-resistant" are less precise and have broader reference. A brief discussion of some aspects of fire-resistant construction and its application to nineteenth-century warehouse construction is found in Leonard Eaton, *Gateway Cities and Other Essays* (Ames, Iowa: Iowa State University Press, 1989), 3–17.

17. Wermiel cites numerous publications by Atkinson and others, including articles and letters in *AABN* beginning in 1879. Atkinson described the approach in the popular press in Edward Atkinson, "Slow-Burning Construction," *Century Magazine* 37/4 (Feb. 1889): 566–579.

18. Kidder, *Architects and Builders Pocketbook*, 375; International Correspondence Schools, *A Treatise on Architecture and Building Construction* (Scranton, Pa.: Colliery Engineer Co., 1899) 2, 132–143.

19. Kidder, *Architects and Builders Pocketbook*, 375; quoted in: Eaton, *Gateway Cities*, 10.

20. Wermiel, *Fireproof Building*, 116–128.

21. Atkinson advocated horizontally spreading mill buildings of no more than two stories, in contrast to the earlier, taller mills found in New England. But urban buildings on constricted sites needed to be taller, so presented challenges quite different from mills. Similarly, mills had largely open interiors, but urban office blocks and hotels were divided by multiple interior partitions, another critical difference.

22. Personal communication from Sara Wermiel, 10 Jan. 2002.

23. "These anchors and caps are protected by United States patents, but may be cast in any foundry on payment of one-eighth of a cent per pound to the Goetz-Mitchell Company of New Albany, Indiana." International Correspondence Schools, *Treatise on Architecture*, 2: 140. (The anchors and caps are illustrated and discussed on pages 138–140.)

24. Atkinson, "Slow-Burning Construction," However, Wermiel questions whether the Field Store was truly slow-burning as surviving plans suggest it lacked stair and elevator enclosures or fire suppression equipment. Personal communication from Sara Wermiel, 20 Dec. 2001. For the Field Store, see: James F. O'Gorman, "The Marshall Field Wholesale Store: Materials Toward a Monograph," *JSAH* 37/3 (Oct. 1978): 175–194.

25. International Correspondence Schools, *Treatise on Architecture*, 2: 131.

26. *P.I.*, 20 June 1889, 3 ("Reducing the Fire Hazard: How Seattle's Buildings Should Be Constructed").

27. *P.I.*, 28 June 1889, 4; 2 July 1889, 4.

28. For full text of the new building ordinance, Ordinance 1147, see: *P.I.*, 5 July 1889, 6. This was actually Seattle's third building ordinance addressing fire protection. Ordinance 20, approved 19 Aug. 1870, required that every business building have at least one 40-gallon cask of water for fighting fires. Ordinance 185, approved 8 Aug. 1879, established the city's first "fire limits" and required the use of plaster on the interior of new wood-frame buildings in this area. It did not, however, require masonry construction. Copies of all three ordinances are available at the City of Seattle Archives. (Thanks to Scott Cline for information regarding the early fire ordinances.)

29. Kidder, *Architects and Builders Pocketbook*, 378; International Correspondence Schools, *Treatise on Architecture*, 2: 134–135. Of course, these sizes were based on northwestern hardwoods, not Puget Sound softwoods.

30. The most prominent bay window constructed on a downtown building after the fire, the corner bay on the Winehill Block (1889–90) at Commercial and Main

by Bucheler and Hummel, was subsequently the target of a lawsuit; see *P.I.*, 3 Apr. 1890, 8.

31. *P.I.*, 4 July 1889, 4.

32. "Report of Fire Commissioners," in *Seattle Municipal Reports for the Fiscal Year Ending December 31, 1891* (Seattle: 1892), 187. Cited in Daniel E. Turbeville III, "Cities of Kindling: Geographical Implications of the Urban Fire Hazard on the Pacific Northwest Coast Frontier, 1851–1920" (Ph.D. diss., Simon Fraser University, 1985), 109–111. (Copies of both these publications are available at University of Washington Libraries, Manuscripts, Special Collections, University Archives Division.)

33. *P.I.*, 28 June 1892, 8.

34. In June 1893, the city adopted a revised building code (Ordinance 2833) that made some changes to the 1889 ordinance, but the general approach of the 1889 ordinance was maintained. However, since this was adopted one month after the bank failures that initiated the Panic of 1893, which brought a halt to construction, Ordinance 2833 had little effect on building. See: *Revised Ordinances of the City of Seattle* (Seattle: Sunset Publishing Co., 1893). In 1901 the city adopted a stronger building ordinance that addressed many of the failings of the 1889 and 1893 laws, and subsequent revisions to the city's building ordinances have further strengthened fire prevention measures. See: Turbeville, "Cities of Kindling," 218–221.

35. Sarah Bradford Landau and Carl W. Condit, *Rise of the New York Skyscraper, 1865–1913* (New Haven and London: Yale University Press, 1996), 8–9.

36. *P.I.*, 5 July 1889, 6.

37. Russell Sturgis, "The Warehouse and the Factory in Architecture," *Architectural Record* 15/1 (Jan. 1904): 1–2; cited in Eaton, *Gateway Cities*, 9.

38. Dankmar Adler, "Light in Tall Office Buildings," *Engineering Magazine* 4/2 (Nov. 1892): 171–186; also see: Adler, "The Tall Office Building—Past and Future," *Engineering Magazine*, 3/12 (Sept. 1892): 766–767. Both of these essays are cited by Joseph Siry, "Adler & Sullivan's Guaranty Building in Buffalo," *JSAH* 55/1 (March 1996): 10–13. Also see: George Hill, "Some Practical Limiting Conditions in the Design of the Modern Office Building," *Architectural Record* 2/2 (Apr.–June 1893): 445–468.

39. *P.I.*, 1 Nov. 1889, 5.

40. In some places where the city was slow in raising the grades of the streets, what would become the basement floors of the new buildings was initially used as the ground floor. Today these can be seen on the tour of "Underground Seattle" which begins at the Pioneer Building. However, it should be recognized that some of the stories told on that tour may include occasional exaggerations.

41. Eaton indicates that the term "gateway city" actually derives from novels by Carl Jonas about the city of Omaha, which he called "Gateway City." See: Eaton, *Gateway Cities*, 7–9.

42. The rail-related warehouse district in Tacoma developed along Pacific Avenue, especially from South 17th Street to South 23rd Street; today this is recognized as the Union Station/Warehouse Historic District. For a discussion of the cultural resources in this district and their significance, see: National Park Service, *Tacoma: The Union Depot District* (Tacoma: National Park Service, 1981). Wholesale warehouse buildings in this area designed by Tacoma architects Proctor and Dennis were published in *Northwestern Architect* 9/4 (April 1891—Business Block for Garretson, Woodruff, Pratt, Co., Tacoma, Wash.) and 9/7 (July 1891–Business Block [West Coast Grocery Company], Tacoma, Wash.).

43. On the Schwabacher Buildings, see: chapter 5. For the mention of the 500-pounds-per-square-foot load capacity of the State Building, see: *NREBR* 1/3 (May 1891): 9.

44. Eaton, *Gateway Cities*, 13–15. Also see: Sturgis, "Warehouse and Factory," 1–2.

45. Landau and Condit, *Rise of the New York Skyscraper*, 15–18.

46. Paul Groth, *Living Downtown: The History of Residential Hotels in the United*

States (Berkeley, Los Angeles, and London: University of California Press, 1994), 188; also see chapters 3–5 (pages 56–167).

47. Leland M. Roth, *McKim, Mead & White* (New York: Harper & Row, 1983), 90–94. Also see: Leland M. Roth, "The Architectural Patronage of Henry Villard, 1879–1895," unpublished typescript, 1987.

48. The only presently surviving pre-fire wood structure in downtown Seattle is the now partially derelict Drexel Hotel, at the southwest corner of Third Avenue and James Street. For its history, see: Masayuki Sono, "The Second Transformation: Intervention to the Drexel Hotel—The Last Pre-Fire Building in Downtown Seattle" (unpublished M.Arch. thesis, University of Washington, 1996), 13–41.

49. For the Rainier Hotel, see chapter 5.

50. For Occidential Hotel design by architect Stephen Meany, see: *P.I.*, 18 June 1889, 4; 26 June 1889, 4; 16 July 1889, 4; 7 Nov. 1889, 8; 1 Jan. 1890, 13; 6 June 1890, 8; 1 Jan. 1891, 5.

51. For the Denny Hotel, see: chapter 2, note 93.

52. When the conversion of the Butler Block was announced in early May, it was reported that it would open as soon as possible after 1 June. Although it did open some time thereafter, renovation actually continued until October. *P.I.*, 8 May 1894, 8; 28 Oct. 1894, 8.

53. After 1910, many of the residential hotels in Pioneer Square were managed by Japanese Americans. A good description of what these hotels were like is Monica Sone, *Nisei Daughter* (Boston: Little, Brown and Company, 1953; reprint, Seattle and London: University of Washington Press, 1979), 3–19.

54. *Times*, 10 Aug. 1889, 1.

55. Graduate students in an architectural design studio at the University of Washington in Spring Quarter 1996 documented the Austin Bell Building interior. Initially it was surmised that the Bell Building had been designed as an office building because the interior seemed similar in character to Fisher's earlier business blocks in Port Townsend and his later Pioneer Building in Seattle. However, contemporary newspaper accounts clearly indicate the Bell Building was a residential apartment block.

56. Landau and Condit, *Rise of the New York Skyscraper*, 39.

57. David A. Knoblach, "Washington's Stone Industry—A History," *Washington Geology* 21/4 (Dec. 1993): 3–17.

58. For background on the Gladding, McBean Company, see: chapter 2, note 108. Architectural terra-cotta manufacturing in the Seattle area began about 1898. See: Mark Smith, "The History of American Terra Cotta and Its Local Manufacture," in *Impressions of Imagination: Terra Cotta Seattle* (Seattle: Allied Arts of Seattle, 1986), 1–6.

59. *P.I.*, 20 June 1889, 3; also see: Warren, *Day Seattle Burned*, 49–51.

60. *P.I.*, 5 July 1889, 4.

61. *P.I.*, 18 Aug. 1889, 8; 24 Aug. 1889, 4.

62. *P.I.*, 7 Nov. 1889, 5.

63. *P.I.*, 1 Oct. 1889, 8.

64. *P.I.*, 15 Oct. 1889, 8; 2 Nov. 1889, 5.

65. See chapter 5.

66. *P.I.*, 6 July 1889, 4 ("They Are Brick Buildings—Why Carpenters from Abroad are Disappointed"); also see: Warren, *Day Seattle Burned*, 53–54.

67. Parkinson, *Incidents*, 139–140.

68. *P.I.*, 23 June 1889, 4.

69. The *P.I.* published a copy of Fisher's letter to the Hall Standard Safe Company in which he reported the survival of his drawings and papers in one of their safes. *P.I.*, 23 June 1889, 4.

70. For post-fire buildings by Boone and Fisher, see: chapter 5.

71. *P.I.*, 18 June 1889, 4; 16 July 1889, 4.

72. Parkinson, *Incidents*, 140.

73. Over 100 drawings of the Pioneer Building from Elmer Fisher's office survive in the University of Washington Libraries, Manuscripts, Special Collections, University Archives Division (collection 73). These include floor plans, elevations, sections, interior and detail drawings on linen, some matching floor plans, sections, as well as larger scale partial plans, partial sections, and structural drawings on construction paper. Some of these detail drawings may have been sent to fabricators or, more likely, hand-drawn copies were sent to fabricators. The collection does not include any shop drawings. Presumably detailed shop drawings were prepared by cast-iron and terra-cotta manufacturers, sent to the architect's office for review, and then returned to the manufacturers who would have retained them.

Shop drawings for terra-cotta for the Pioneer Building and for other Seattle buildings were prepared by and returned to Gladding, McBean in California. Tens of thousands of uncatalogued Gladding, McBean shop drawings are now at the California State Library in Sacramento, so it is impossible to determine if they might include any shop drawings for the Pioneer Building or other Seattle buildings of the period. For Gladding, McBean, see: chapter 2, note 108.

74. Blueprinting for accurate reproduction of architectural drawings began in the 1870s, based on a process first developed in 1840 in England. City directories in Seattle do not list blueprinting as an available service. However, David Rash discovered a full-page advertisement in an 1890 directory in which Richardson Nevins, Jr., civil engineer and surveyor, lists "photo blue prints" as an available service; see: *Corbett & Co.'s First Annual Seattle City Directory . . . 1890* (Seattle: Corbett and Company, 1890), 888. For the early history of blueprinting, see: J. Norman Jensen, "The Early History of Blueprinting," *Architectural Record* 71/5 (May 1932): 335; also see: "The 'Blue' Copying Process," *AABN* 4 (3 Aug. 1878): 44.

75. Draftsmen could also get additional training through architectural sketch clubs. Although they generally disappeared after 1914, from the 1880s to 1910 architectural sketch clubs could be found in most larger cities; they filled an educational vacuum not addressed by other institutions, particularly as professional education in the new architectural schools was available only to a few. Architectural sketch clubs (sometimes called "draftsmen's clubs") originated as both educational and social organizations. The first such American club is thought to have been the Portfolio Club of Boston, founded about 1879. The model for most clubs in the Midwest and West was the Chicago Architectural Sketch Club, founded in 1885. This sketch club was fostered by *Inland Architect*, which occasionally reported on its activities. In a similar fashion, the Minnesota Architectural Sketch Club was formed in Minneapolis in late 1888 at the instigation of *Northwestern Architect;* an associated St. Paul group was formed in early 1889.

The character of architectural sketch clubs varied from place to place, but most sponsored drawing classes, competitions, exhibitions, lectures, and social gatherings. Some clubs met in their own quarters in rented space, where they assembled collections of books, photographs, and multiple architectural journals. The club rooms were also used for lectures and drawing classes. Lectures might address architectural history or recent work, but most often emphasized practical aspects of materials and construction. Drawing classes were central to the club's activities and were usually conducted by the leading delineators in the local area. Various media were introduced, including pencil, pen and ink, watercolor, and charcoal. Competitions, usually monthly, were generally for simple structures so that the emphasis might be on the quality of presentation. While practicing professional architects and senior employees did play a role in the sketch clubs, even to the point of being welcomed as honorary members, these clubs were draftsmen's organizations. When draftsmen began to practice independently (or, in later years, assumed a partnership or senior position in a large firm), they, in a sense, "graduated" from the sketch clubs; as practicing architects, they generally joined the professional associations. For a contemporary discussion of architectural draftsmen's clubs, see: William Bryce Mundie, "Architectural Sketch Clubs," *IA* 13/4 (Apr. 1889): 55–56. For a summary of the development of such clubs, see: Eileen Manning Michels, "A Developmental Study of the Drawings published in *American Architect* and *Inland Architect* through 1895" (Ph.D. diss., University of Minnesota, 1971), 138–142.

The formation of an architectural sketch club in Seattle in February 1890 may reflect the early maturation of the local profession. By April the *Post-Intelligencer* reported that this club had thirty members and was setting up club rooms. Their first competition was held in May. See: *P.I.*, 13 Feb. 1890, 3; 10 Apr. 1890, 8; 12 May 1890, 5; 15 May 1890, 8.

76. For the chronologies of the Burke Building and the Bailey Building, see chapter 5.

77. *P.I.*, 7 Nov. 1889, 8; 7 Dec. 1889, 8; 3 Apr. 1890, 8. Kline and Rosenberg built several buildings after the fire. This structure by Towle and Wilcox was among the earliest. Located on the south side of Washington between Commercial and South Second (now Occidental), it was at a location where the sawdust may have extended to twenty-five feet below grade. Apparently the piles under the building were not deep enough and gave way beneath the weight of one of the walls.

78. *P.I.*, 23 Mar. 1890, 8; 21 May 1890, 5. The 21 May article in the *Post-Intelligencer* directly questioned Meany's competence: "The collapse . . . ought to show . . . the necessity of employing a first class architect, who would not allow himself to be persuaded by the impecunious views of owners or prospective builders."

79. On the visual impact of the electric lighting in the Seattle Theater, see: *P.I.*, 6 Dec. 1892, 8.

80. On the electrification of the Pioneer Building, see: *Times*, 10 Aug. 1889, 1. For the Seattle Seminary building, see: *P.I.*, 19 Sept. 1892, 5. The request for designs for the first building on the University of Washington campus specified both gas and electricity in the building. *P.I.*, 24 Dec. 1893, 5.

81. *P.I.*, 6 June 90, 4.

82. On the subject of the complexity of technology addressed in late-nineteenth-century architectural practices, see: Jeffrey Karl Ochsner, "The First Modern Practice? H. H. Richardson and His Office," *Proceedings of the 81st Annual Meeting of the ACSA, Charleston South Carolina, March 13–16, 1993* (Washington, D.C.: ACSA Press, 1993), 232–235.

IV. The Architectural Context:
The Influence of Richardson and the Romanesque Revival

1. Montgomery Schuyler, "The Romanesque Revival in America," *Architectural Record* 1/2 (Oct.–Dec. 1891): 194; reprinted in Montgomery Schuyler, *American Architecture and Other Writings*, William H. Jordy and Ralph Coe, eds. (Cambridge: Belknap Press of Harvard University Press, 1961), 222. (Thanks to Jay Henry for bringing this quotation to our attention.)

2. *IA* 9/3 (Mar. 1887), 23.

3. Henry Glassie has argued: "The architectural historian who operates without a totalizing definition of architecture may focus on isolated detail—an object too small. As a consequence he often finds himself having to explain architectural change as a series of unconnected revolutions instead of the gradual development that he would find to be the case if he examined architectural wholes." The varied production that gradual change implies suggests that at any point a range of work will be produced, some forward-looking, some backward-looking, but all reflecting the state of the architectural culture at that particular time. See: Glassie, *Folk Housing in Middle Virginia*, 8–9.

4. All research on Richardson begins with the biography published just two years

after his death: Marianna Griswold Van Rensselaer, *Henry Hobson Richardson and His Works* (Boston: Houghton-Mifflin, 1888; facsimile edition with introduction by James D. Van Trump, Park Forest, Ill.: Prairie School Press, 1967; paperback facsimile edition with introduction by William Morgan, New York: Dover, 1969); see also: note 28 (below). The complete catalogue of Richardson's buildings is: Jeffrey Karl Ochsner, *H. H. Richardson: Complete Architectural Works* (Cambridge, Mass., and London: MIT Press, 1982, revised paperback edition 1984); this should be consulted for complete histories and references for individual buildings as well as images of buildings not presented here. Two significant interpretive studies of Richardson's work have been discussed in the introduction: Hitchcock, *The Architecture of H. H. Richardson and His Times*, and O'Gorman, *H. H. Richardson: Architectural Forms for an American Society*. Other important works on Richardson previously noted are: Hitchcock, *Richardson as a Victorian Architect*, and O'Gorman, *Henry Hobson Richardson and His Office: Selected Drawings*. Recent works include: Margaret Henderson Floyd, *Henry Hobson Richardson: A Genius for Architecture* (New York: Monacelli Press, 1997), a well-illustrated interpretive study; James F. O'Gorman, *Living Architecture: A Biography of H. H. Richardson* (New York: Simon & Schuster Editions, 1997), an illustrated biography; and Maureen Meister, ed., *H. H. Richardson: The Architect, His Peers, and Their Era* (Cambridge, Mass., and London: MIT Press, 1999), a collection of scholarly essays.

5. See: chapter 2, note 24.

6. Richardson's description of the building appears in: *Consecration Services of Trinity Church, Boston, February 9, 1877; with the consecration sermon by Rev. A. H. Vinton, D.D., an historical sermon by Rev. Phillips Brooks, and a description of the church edifice by H. H. Richardson, architect* (Boston: Trinity Church, 1877). A reprint of Richardson's description appeared in *AABN* 2 (11 Aug. 1877): 254, 258–259.

Recent scholarly articles on Trinity Church include: Ann Jensen Adams, "Birth of a Style: Henry Hobson Richardson and the Competition Drawings for Trinity Church, Boston," *Art Bulletin* 62 (Sept. 1980): 409–433; Kathleen Curran, "The Romanesque Revival, Mural Painting, and Protestant Patronage in America," *Art Bulletin* 81 (Dec. 1999): 693–722; Theodore E. Stebbins, Jr., "Richardson and Trinity Church: The Evolution of a Building," *JSAH* 27 (Dec. 1968): 281–298; and Helene Barbara Weinberg, "John La Farge and the Decoration of Trinity Church, Boston," *JSAH* 33 (Dec. 1974): 323–353.

7. For example, Trinity Church received five pages of discussion in an article on churches in the popular *Century Magazine* in 1885; see: Marianna Griswold Van Rensselaer, "Recent Architecture in America, IV—Churches," *Century Magazine* 29/3 (Jan. 1885): 328–333.

Images of Trinity Church were widely published in architectural periodicals at the time of its design and construction: *Architectural Sketch Book* 1 (Aug. 1873): 5; *New York Sketch Book of Architecture* 1 (Aug. 1874): pl. 32; *AABN* 2 (3 Feb. 1877): 22 (31 Dec. 1887); proposed alterations appeared in *AABN* 45 (11 Aug. 1894). Trinity Church was also the subject of one of *AABN* monographs; see: note 33.

8. "The Ten Best Buildings in the United States," *AABN* 17 (13 June 1885): 282. The continuing high regard for Trinity Church is reflected in the fact that it was also included in similar lists in the mid-twentieth century; see: "One Hundred Years of Significant Building," *Architectural Record* 120 (Oct. 1956): 193; and "Highlights of American Architecture," *AIA Journal* 65 (July 1976): 106–107.

9. For a detailed analysis of Richardson's series of small public libraries, see: Kenneth A. Breisch, *Henry Hobson Richardson and the Small Public Library in America: A Study in Typology* (Cambridge, Mass., and London: MIT Press, 1997).

10. Van Rensselaer, *Richardson and His Works*, 70.

11. For a discussion of Ames Hall in Ruskinian terms, see: Thomas C. Hubka, "The Picturesque in the Design Method of H. H. Richardson: Memorial Hall, North Easton," in Meister, ed., *H. H. Richardson*, 2–32.

12. Austin Hall appeared in *AABN* 17 (28 Mar. 1885); it was also the subject of an *AABN* monograph; see: note 33. A drawing of the Billings Library appeared in *AABN* 29 (29 Dec. 1888); the building was the subject of a monograph by the publisher; see: note 33. Six detailed presentation drawings of the unbuilt All Saints Cathedral project appeared in *AABN* 14 (1 Sept. 1883).

Richardson also generated designs that showed a greater independence from historical sources, such as the series of railroad stations that he designed between 1881 and 1886 which were relatively simple structures providing shelter at trackside, almost without historical reference. However, unlike Richardson's larger institutional buildings, photographs of the stations rarely appeared in contemporary architectural journals. The only railroad station to be published by *AABN* in a photograph was the Boston and Albany Station at Chestnut Hill; see: *AABN* 16 (13 Dec. 1884). *AABN* did include a series of small line drawings of Richardson's stations after his death; see: *AABN* 21 (2 Feb. 1887): 103. The stations at Palmer and North Easton were also illustrated in line drawings in Van Rensselaer, "Recent Architecture in America, II—Public Buildings," *Century Magazine* 28/3 (July 1884): 333. For an analysis of Richardson's railroad stations, see: Jeffrey Karl Ochsner, "Architecture for the Boston & Albany Railroad, 1881–1894," *JSAH* 47/2 (June 1988): 109–131. A suggestion of a link between the stations and Japanese architecture is offered by Floyd; see: Floyd, *Genius for Architecture*, 192–201.

The shingled houses that Richardson designed after 1880 were similarly without specific historical reference, but few of these were illustrated in contemporary publications. The M. F. Stoughton House, Cambridge, Mass. (1882–1883), appeared in George W. Sheldon, *Artistic Country Seats: Types of Recent American Villa and Cottage Architecture with Instances of Country Club-Houses* (New York: D. Appleton, 1886–1887; facsimile edition, New York: Da Capo, 1979) I: 157; and in Russell Sturgis et al., *Homes in City and Country* (New York: C. Scribner's Sons, 1893), 84–85. The study of shingled residential architecture which places Richardson's houses in context is: Vincent J. Scully, Jr., *The Shingle Style and the Stick Style*, rev. ed. (New Haven, Conn.: Yale University Press, 1973).

13. H. H. Richardson, *Description of Drawings for the New County Buildings for Allegheny County, Penn.* (Boston: 1884).

14. Quoted in Van Rensselaer, *Richardson and His Works*, 23. Van Rensselaer also quoted Richardson, then in failing health, as saying "Let me have time to finish Pittsburgh . . . and I should be content without another day"; then she added her own evaluation: "Taken as a whole the design of this vast and complex structure, both inside and out, is a marvel of good sense as well as architectural beauty."

15. Images of the Allegheny County Buildings were published in *AABN* 28 (24 May 1890); 38 (12 Nov. 1892; 19 Nov. 1892); 41 (5 Aug. 1893); ten images were published in *IA* 13/5 (May 1889), 13/7 (June 1889); and images also appeared in *Architectural Record* 1/2 (Oct.–Dec. 1891): 154–157, 160, 196.

16. Montgomery Schuyler, "The Buildings of Pittsburgh, Part II: The Business Quarter and the Commercial Buildings," *Architectural Record* 30/3 (Sept. 1911): 226–227.

17. Richardson's initial Romanesque-inspired solution to the commercial block was the Cheney Building, Hartford (1875–76, altered), which introduced Richardson's pattern of layered arcades with fenestration sequentially reduced in scale at the upper floors. A similar pattern was subsequently applied on an irregular site for the Ames Store, Bedford Street, Boston (1882–83, destroyed). However, for the Marshall Field Store, this approach was reduced to its essentials, then expanded to the scale of a seven-story structure filling an entire Chicago city block.

18. Van Rensselaer, *Richardson and His Works*, 97

19. A photograph of the Field Store appeared in *IA* 12/3 (Oct. 1888).

20. Six photographs of the Chamber of Commerce were published in *IA* 12/9 (Jan. 1889); two photographs appeared in *AABN* 27 (1 Mar. 1890), and 29 (12 July 1890); a drawing was published in *Architectural Record* 1/2 (Oct.–Dec. 1891): 158.

21. Although of conventional load-bearing construction, the exterior wall of the Ames Building on Harrison Avenue, Boston, can be read as suggesting the possibility of skeletal construction; see: Hitchcock, *Richardson and His Times* (1966), 283. This was published in *AABN* 21 (14 May 1887).

22. During his 1885 visit to Chicago, Richardson called on Burnham and Root, the city's leading commercial architects, to discuss the foundations of the Field Store. Richardson almost certainly also saw design work that Burnham and Root then had under way. Their Chicago work, discussed below, seems to be echoed in his Ames Building on Harrison Avenue. See: Donald Hoffman, *The Architecture of John Wellborn Root* (Baltimore and London: Johns Hopkins University Press, 1973), 45–47.

23. The messages conveyed by these Richardson buildings are diverse: Trinity Church could be seen as an example of historical eclecticism; Ames Hall as a model of picturesque Queen Anne/Arts and Crafts design; Sever as a building distinguished by simplification, symmetrical balance, and restrained detail; and Albany City Hall as similar to Ames Hall but simplified with a picturesquely positioned tower. Because the New York State Capitol project involved multiple architects working over a period of more than thirty years (and it was incomplete in 1885), the meaning of its inclusion on the list of the "ten best" is unclear. See Ochsner, *Richardson: Complete Works*, 157–167.

24. Van Rensselaer, "Recent Architecture in America, I—Public Buildings," *Century Magazine* 28/1 (May 1884): 53–64 (includes Crane Library, Sever Hall Ames Hall, Austin Hall, New York State Capitol Senate Chamber, Albany City Hall); "Recent Architecture in America, II—Public Buildings," *Century Magazine* 28/3 (July 1884): 333 (railroad stations at Palmer, North Easton); "Recent Architecture in America, III—Commercial Buildings," *Century Magazine* 28/4 (Aug. 1884): 512–515 (Ames Building on Bedford Street, Boston); "Recent Architecture in America, IV—Churches," *Century Magazine* 29/3 (Jan. 1885): 328–333 (Trinity Church, Brattle Square Church, North Congregational Church, Springfield). Richardson's masonry houses are criticized in "Recent Architecture in America, IV—City Dwellings," *Century Magazine* 31/5 (Mar. 1886): 681.

25. *AABN* 19 (1 May 1886): 205–206.

26. *IA* 7/7 (May 1886): 57.

27. For a list of obituaries, see: O'Gorman: *Richardson: Architectural Forms*, 145–146.

28. *Henry Hobson Richardson and His Works* was commissioned by Richardson's neighbors and friends, Charles Sprague Sargent and Frederick Law Olmsted. Mariana Griswold Van Rensselaer, a contemporary critic, provided an account of Richardson's life and work, with background on his education, approach to design, and office operations. The coverage of Richardson's built work is relatively complete, but the only unbuilt project discussed is the Albany Cathedral (although a few others are illustrated in sketches). Printed in large format with 36 full-page plates, as well as many sketches and drawings in the text, the book offered a perceptive analysis of his practice and many of his buildings. However, this book was a biography and although it did present a clear chronology of Richardson's works, an overarching interpretive framework focusing on a single evolutionary tendency in Richardson's career was not offered. For specific publication history, see: note 4 (above). Although only 500 copies were printed in 1888, some did find their way as far west as Chicago and Minneapolis.

For background on Van Rensselaer, see: Cynthia D. Kinnard, "The Life and Works of Mariana Griswold Van Rensselaer, American Art Critic" (Ph.D. diss., Johns Hopkins University, 1977), especially pages 135–174.

29. *AABN* editors were aware of their role in promoting Richardson as they later stated: "Mr. Richardson soon became one of our kindest friends, and if reputation and employment are things to be desired by an architect, we may say with all due modesty—that what he did for us was repaid to him a hundred fold, for great as was

his talent, it must without the publicity given to his work through means like ours, have had for years only a local influence." "Our International Edition," *AABN* 27 (11 Jan. 1890): 17–18.

30. *AABN* carried seventeen images of Richardson's works between January 1876 and April 1886, the month of his death. In September 1883 *AABN* also published Richardson's competition drawings for the Albany Cathedral. Between May 1886 and October 1895, an additional 26 images of Richardson buildings were published. In addition, Richardson's major buildings were documented in a series of small sketches in September 1886, and additional sketches of railroad stations were published in February 1887. Two photographs of the New York State Capitol appeared in 1898, but these were not identified with Richardson.

31. For details of the publication sequence of Richardson's buildings and the impression this gave of his work, see: Ochsner, "Seeing Richardson in His Time," 102–145.

32. The *American Architect* publication of the YMA Library project after Richardson's death was the first publication of an unbuilt project by Richardson since the James Cheney House in May 1878, with the exception of the publication of the competition drawings for the Albany Cathedral which appeared in 1883. With the publication of the YMA Library, the editors felt compelled to explain that Richardson had not wanted drawings of his unfinished work published because he believed he could improve his buildings during construction. In fact, Richardson paid a fee to the magazine so that his work would be published only in photographs. See: "Design Submitted for Young Men's Christian [*sic*] Association Building, Buffalo, N.Y.," *AABN* 21 (23 Apr. 1887): 199.

33. "Our International Edition," *AABN* 27 (11 Jan. 1890): 17–18. The popularity of the illustrations in *American Architect* led the publisher to issue a series of folios of plates titled *Monographs of American Architecture*. Richardson's works were the subjects of three of the first five volumes. These folios also tended to present Richardson as an eclectic designer working primarily from Romanesque sources. The folio series included: H. H. Richardson, *Austin Hall, Harvard Law School, Cambridge, Mass.*, Monographs of American Architecture 1 (Boston: Ticknor and Company, 1885 [and 1886]); H. H. Richardson, *The Ames Memorial Buildings, North Easton, Mass.*, Monographs of American Architecture 3 (Boston: Ticknor and Company, 1886); H. H. Richardson, *Trinity Church, Boston*, Monographs of American Architecture 5 (Boston: Ticknor and Company, 1888). A similar folio published separately was: H. H. Richardson, *The Billings Library: The Gift to the University of Vermont of Frederick Billings* (Boston: Ticknor and Company, ca. 1888).

34. *Inland Architect* published a "Photogravure Edition" beginning in 1887, allowing subscribers who paid more to receive photographic plates in addition to the less expensive line drawings. Photographic images of Richardson's building were published as follows: Adams house: *IA* 9/8 (June 1887); MacVeagh house (two images): *IA* 10/6 (Nov. 1887), 11/6 (May 1888); Glessner house: *IA* 11/1 (Feb. 1888); Warder house (two images): *IA* 11/3 (March 1888); J. R. Lionberger house: *IA* 11/7 (June 1888); Marshall Field Store: *IA* 12/3 (Oct. 1888); Cincinnati Chamber of Commerce (four images): *IA* 12/9 (Jan. 1889); Allegheny County Courthouse (ten images): *IA* 13/3 (May 1889), 13/5 (June 1889); Gratwick house: *IA* 14/7 (Dec. 1889). In addition, *Inland Architect* carried a series titled "Boston Sketches" in 1888–89, including drawings of Richardson's Brattle Square and Trinity churches (Dec. 1888), and the Harrison Avenue Ames Building or J. H. Pray Store (Jan. 1889).

35. *American Architect* appeared weekly, with 52 issues per year. The number of plates (drawings and photographs) per issue was usually more than four, although the number was smaller in the early years and increased thereafter. In 1885 and 1886, *American Architect* launched the Imperial and the Gelatine editions; for an increased price, a subscriber would receive additional photographic plates. This further increased the num-

ber of published images, although not all subscribers received all images thereafter. With fewer than 45 plates in the period, Richardson's percentage of the total number of published images may have been even less than the 1.2 percent stated in the text.

36. O'Gorman's chapter titles in *H. H. Richardson: Architectural Forms for an American Society* included "Urbanism," "Ruralism," and "Commuterism," indicating an implicit recognition of Richardson's contributions to the different building types found in different contexts. In this sense—that is that Richardson was among the first architects to face this wide array of building types—Mumford was correct, Richardson was "the first architect of distinction ready to face the totality of modern life." See: Mumford, *Brown Decades*, 53.

37. To cite just one example, the article included a drawing of the Syracuse City Hall (1889–92), a Romanesque Revival building by local architect Charles E. Colton. See: Barr Ferree, "The City Hall in America," *Engineering Magazine* 4/2 (Nov. 1892): 201–220.

38. See: Breisch, *Richardson and the Small Public Library*, 256–269.

39. A relatively early Richardson building, Brattle Square Church, Boston (1869–73), appeared in *AABN* 3 (29 June 1878) and *AABN* 43 (24 Mar. 1894). Its tower was sometimes copied by architects working in the Romanesque Revival.

40. A few Romanesque Revival houses could be found, for example, on private streets in St. Louis and on Summit Avenue in St. Paul, Minnesota. See: Charles C. Savage, *Architecture of the Private Streets of St. Louis: The Architects and the Houses They Designed* (Columbia: University of Missouri Press, 1987); Julius K. Hunter, *Westmoreland and Portland Places: the History and Architecture of America's Premier Private Streets, 1888–1988* (Columbia: University of Missouri Press, 1988); and Ernest R. Sandeen, *St. Paul's Historic Summit Avenue* (St. Paul: Macalester College Museum, 1978).

41. Richardson did prepare descriptive materials for some competition entries including the Connecticut State Capitol, Hartford; Allegheny County Buildings, Pittsburgh; Chamber of Commerce, Cincinnati; and Hoyt Public Library, East Saginaw, Michigan. He also contributed a description for the dedication of Trinity Church. For a complete chronological bibliography, see: O'Gorman, *Richardson: Architectural Forms*, 143–159.

42. The use of the term "project" here is derived from its use in psychology and psychoanalysis; to project is "to externalize (a thought or feeling) unconsciously so that it appears to have objective reality." Because it is a thought or feeling that is (unconsciously) projected, there must be something (an object or a person) which appears to embody the projection. Through the process of projection, it was possible for a contemporary of Richardson's to see a Richardson building in a particular way, not because that specific way of seeing the building was inherent in the design, but because the architect "projected" a particular framework on the building through which it was then seen. The projection is unconscious—that is, the architect does not consciously intend to see the work in this way. Richardson's work may be considered receptive not only to the (unconscious) projections of his contemporaries, but also to projections of architectural historians. Since Richardson did not provide a framework through which we may see the work, some of what we see in it we provide ourselves.

43. "St. Paul Correspondence," signed "Doric," in *Building Budget* 6 (May 1890): 60; quoted in Paul C. Larson, "H. H. Richardson Goes West: The Rise and Fall of an Eastern Star," in Larson and Brown, *Spirit of Richardson*, 23, 138.

44. Although the Masonic Temple reflected Victorian compositional practices with a Romanesque vocabulary, Long and Kees did design a series of very creditable Richardsonian buildings in Minneapolis, and they did publish their work in *American Architect* and in *Northwestern Architect;* see: note 97 (below)

45. Hitchcock mistakenly identified Newton Center Baptist Church as a Richardson building in the first edition of *Richardson and His Times*. In the 1966 edition, Hitch-

cock added lengthy endnotes to bring the book up-to-date and corrected his error. See: Hitchcock, *Richardson and His Times* (1966), 262–263, 327 (n. XIII–24).

46. For Newton Center Baptist Church, see: *IA* 13/4 (Apr. 1889).

47. O'Gorman, *Richardson: Architectural Forms*, 67–68.

48. For Boston Water Works, Chestnut Hill, see: *Northwestern Architect* 7/2 (Feb. 1889).

49. See: Floyd, *Architecture after Richardson*, 21–64.

50. The Cambridge City Hall design was published in a drawing in *AABN* 24 (28 July 1888).

51. Hunt's atelier, modeled on his experience at the Ecole des Beaux-Arts, offered the best trainng then available in the United States. For a description see: Paul R. Baker, *Richard Morris Hunt* (Cambridge, Mass., and London: MIT Press, 1980), 98–105. For background on Henry Van Brunt, see: William J. Hennessey, "The Architectural Works of Henry Van Brunt" (Ph.D. diss., Columbia University, 1979). A good summary is the introduction to William A. Coles, ed., *Architecture and Society: Selected Essays of Henry Van Brunt* (Cambridge, Mass.: Belknap Press of Harvard University Press, 1969).

52. The Richardsonian features of Van Brunt's library proved controversial in Topeka, where the other Victorian modes still held sway. See: Hennessey, "Works of Van Brunt," 143–144; the local impact of the building is also noted in Longstreth, "Richardsonian Architecture in Kansas," 67–68. Van Brunt and Howe opened an office in Kansas City in 1885, placing them among the earliest Richardsonian practitioners in the West; see: Hennessey, "Works of Van Brunt," 199–206.

53. Van Brunt and Howe's Rindge Public Library, Cambridge, Mass. (1887–89), was widely published: *IA* 16 (Jan. 1890); *AABN* 36 (11 June 1892). The firm's Richardsonian railroad stations for the Union and Central Pacific Railroads appeared as follows: Ogden, Utah, in *AABN* 20 (6 Nov. 1886), and Cheyenne, Wyoming, in *AABN* 21 (8 Jan. 1887).

54. Henry Van Brunt, "On the Present Condition of Architecture," *Atlantic Monthly* 57 (March 1886): 382; reprinted in Coles, *Architecture and Society*, 166–167.

55. Henry Van Brunt, "Henry Hobson Richardson, Architect," *Atlantic Monthly* 58 (Nov. 1886): 685–693; reprinted in Coles, *Architecture and Society*, 170–179.

56. Henry Van Brunt, "Architecture in the West," *Atlantic Monthly* 62 (Dec. 1889): 772–784; reprinted in Coles, *Architecture and Society*, 180–194.

57. Montgomery Schuyler offered the theory of the incomplete development of the historical Romanesque multiple times. See, for example, Montgomery Schuyler, "The Romanesque Revival in New York," *Architectural Record* 1/1 (July–Sept. 1891): 38 (this section omitted in Schuyler, *American Architecture*); and Montgomery Schuyler, *A Critique of the Works of Adler & Sullivan, D. H. Burnham & Co., Henry Ives Cobb—Great American Architects Series* 2 (New York: Architectural Record Co., July 1896; reprint edition: New York: DaCapo Press, 1977), 81.

Given this understanding of the Romanesque as a style capable of further development, the decision by *Inland Architect* to run a series of articles beginning in March 1889 on the history of the Romanesque in medieval Europe can be seen not as the basis for creating a revival, but rather as an attempt to show contemporary architects places to begin its further development.

58. Wheaton A. Holden, "The Peabody Touch: Peabody & Stearns of Boston, 1870–1917," *JSAH* 32 (May 1973): 114–131. Another exemplary Peabody and Stearns project in the Richardsonian Romanesque mode was their Memorial Hall at the Lawrenceville School, Lawrenceville, New Jersey (1884–85), published in *Architectural Record* 1/2 (Oct.–Dec. 1891), 162. Although Peabody and Stearns did buildings of a variety of types in a Richardsonian mode, they also worked in other styles over the same period; see: Sturgis, *A Critique of the Work of Shepley, Rutan & Coolidge and Peabody & Stearns*, 53–97.

59. George Foster Shepley (1858–1903) and Charles Allerton Coolidge (1858–1936) had both studied architecture at MIT and worked at Ware and Van Brunt before join-

ing Richardson in the early 1880s. Charles Hercules Rutan (1851–1914) had been at Richardson's office since 1869, but his expertise was primarily in management and technical aspects of projects. For sources for Shepley, Rutan, and Coolidge, see: Chapter 1, note 9.

60. The seamless transition from Richardson to Shepley, Rutan, and Coolidge was reflected in railroad station commissions received from the Boston and Albany Railroad. The successor firm's stations were virtually indistinguishable from Richardson's, with their simple stone construction, horizontal character, broad overhanging roofs, and absence of historical detail. Shepley, Rutan, and Coolidge also had the opportunity to design much larger stations such as the Boston and Albany station at Springfield, Massachusetts; the design for this appeared in *AABN* 23 (31 Mar. 1888); images of the constructed building were published in *Architectural Record* 1/2 (Oct.–Dec. 1891): 189, 191. For a full discusion of the Shepley, Rutan, and Coolidge stations, see: Ochsner, "Architecture for the Boston & Albany," 109–131.

The successors' debt to Richardson is reflected in other work such as the Shadyside Presbyterian Church, Pittsburgh (1888–90); its overall form recalled Richardson's Trinity Church, but Shadyside was much lower and more simply resolved. See: James D. Van Trump, "The Mountain and the City: A History of Shadyside Presbyterian Church, Pittsburgh, as Seen through Its Architecture," *Western Pennsylvania Magazine* 64 (Mar. 1961): 21–34.

61. At Stanford, individual campus buildings were based on specific precedents in Richardson's work, but in the overall design, buildings connected by arcades formed a series of enclosed courtyards that recalled the Spanish missions. The allusion to Spanish architecture was enhanced by a palette of red tile roofs and yellow, rock-faced limestone walls. The Stanford project was significant as the first that demonstrated how a variation on the Richardson Romanesque mode might be developed as a regionally responsive architecture. Contemporary publication of the Stanford campus included an image in *IA* 17/3 (Apr. 1891). For a recent discussion of the original architecture of Stanford University, see: Paul V. Turner, "The Collaborative Design of Stanford University," in *The Founders and the Architects: The Design of Stanford University*, edited by Paul V. Turner, Marcia E. Vetrocq, and Karen Weitzel (Stanford: Stanford University Department of Art, 1976), 28–47; see also: Paul V. Turner, *Campus: An American Planning Tradition* (New York: Architectural History Foundation, and Cambridge, Mass., and London: MIT Press, 1984), 169–177.

62. According to Woods, 58 designs by Shepley, Rutan, and Coolidge were published in *American Architect* between 1887 and 1907. This made them the fifth most well-published firm. See Woods, "The *American Architect*," 252, n. 1.

63. Schuyler, "Romanesque Revival in America," 151–198. Five years later the firm was profiled in the "Great American Architects" series in *Architectural Record*, but this was after the decline of the Romanesque Revival and so had little effect on its spread; see: note 4.

64. The three partners in Longfellow, Alden, and Harlow met at MIT. Frank Ellis Alden (1859–1908) entered Richardson's office in 1880 and in 1884 moved to Pittsburgh to supervise Richardson's work in the city; he resigned his position shortly after Richardson's death. Alexander Wadsworth Longfellow, Jr. (1854–1934), had studied at the Ecole des Beaux-Arts and joined Richardson in 1881, remaining until March 1886. Alfred Branch Harlow (1857–1927) had worked for McKim, Mead, and White from 1881 to 1886 before joining Longfellow and Alden. As Floyd describes in detail, this firm, with offices in both Boston and Pittsburgh, was able to secure major commissions in both New England and Pennsylvania. Their most prominent early New England building was the Cambridge City Hall. Their Pittsburgh office emerged as the preeminent firm in that city and similarly followed Richardsonian Romanesque precedent in projects such as the Duquesne Club (1887–89), Vandergrift Building (1889–92), and in their early Pennsylvania churches and residences. Longfellow, Alden, and Harlow

were not as well published as some other Richardsonian Romanesque practitioners, but their presence in Pittsburgh as well as Boston clearly contributed to the spread of Romanesque Revival design. See: Floyd, *Architecture after Richardson*, 21–59. Also see: James D. Van Trump, "Romanesque Revival in Pittsburgh," *JSAH* 16 (Oct. 1957): 22–29.

65. A drawing of the *New York Times* Building, New York, appeared in *Architectural Record* 1/1 (July–Sept. 1891): 33. A drawing of the Union Trust Company Building appeared in *Architectural Record* 1/1 (July–Sept. 1891): 35; and in *AABN* 42 (21 Oct. 1893). On Post's Romanesque Revival commercial buildings, see: Sarah Bradford Landau, *George B. Post, Architect: Picturesque Designer and Determined Realist* (New York: Monacelli Press, 1998), and Winston Weisman, "The Commercial Architecture of George B. Post," *JSAH* 31/3 (Oct. 1972): 176–203. For an overview of Post's work, see: Russell Sturgis, *A Review of the Work of George B. Post—Great American Architects, Series* 4 (New York: Architectural Record Co., June 1898; reprint edition: New York: DaCapo Press, 1977).

66. On the Office of the Supervising Architect, see: Antoinette J. Lee, *Architects to the Nation: The Rise and Decline of the Supervising Architect's Office* (New York and London: Oxford University Press, 2000). Also see: Lois A. Craig and the Staff of the Federal Architecture Project, *The Federal Presence: Architecture, Politics, and National Design* (Cambridge, Mass., and London: MIT Press, 1984), 162–169; and Bates Lowry, *Building a National Image: Architectural Drawings for the American Democracy, 1879–1912* (Washington, D.C.: National Building Museum, 1985), 58–88. Montgomery Schuyler thought that the Office of the Supervising Architect reached its nadir under Mifflin Bell. See: Montgomery Schuyler, "Federal Buildings," *Art and Progress* 1 (Mar. 1910), 115–162; (Apr. 1910): 159–162; cited in Schuyler, *American Architecture*, 294.

67. Kenneth Breisch, "The Richardsonian Interlude in Texas: A Quest for Meaning and Order at the End of the Nineteenth Century," in Larson and Brown, *Spirit of Richardson*, 90–91; and Jay C. Henry, "The Richardsonian Romanesque in Texas: An Interpretation," *Texas Architect* 31/2 (Mar.–Apr. 1981): 52–53.

68. Bell's successors at the Treasury who continued to produce Richardsonian designs were William A. Freret (1887–88), James H. Windrim (1888–90), W. J. Edbrooke (1891–92), Jeremiah O'Rourke (1893–94), and William M. Aitken (1895–96). (Richardson once employed Aitken.) See: Lee, *Architects to the Nation*, 124–162.

The Port Townsend Custom House and Post Office had a particularly complex history. Congress first appropriated funds for the building in March 1885; after several changes of plans and additional appropriations, the first contract was awarded in 1887, but by 1889 only the foundation was complete. To save money, only three stories of the planned six-story tower were built. As finally realized, the building is Romanesque, but seems less directly related to Richardson's work than to German medieval precedent. See: Denison and Huntington, *Victorian Architecture*, 86–89.

69. *American Architect* and *Inland Architect* have each been the subject of scholarly analyses. For *AABN* see: Woods, "The *American Architect*"; also see: Woods, "The First American Architectural Journals," 117–138. For *IA*, see: Robert Prestiano, *The Inland Architect: Chicago's Major Architectural Journal, 1883–1908* (Ann Arbor, Mich.: UMI Research Press, 1985). The Minneapolis-based *Northwestern Architect* has not received similar study and is now difficult to use as a complete run does not survive; see: note 110 (below).

Competing journals in New York and Chicago included *Building* (later *Architecture and Building*) (New York, 1882), and *Building Budget* (Chicago, 1885). Other regional architectural journals in other cities in the period included *Western Architect and Builder* (St. Louis, 1879), *California Architect and Building News* (San Francisco, 1879), *Western Architect and Builder* (Cincinnati, 1881), *Southern Architect* (Atlanta, 1885), *Western Architect and Building News* (Denver, 1889), and *Architect and Builder* (Milwaukee, 1893).

70. The San Francisco–based *California Architect and Building News* might have

emerged as the most important periodical in the Pacific Northwest, but it had a tightly constrained geographical focus and only illustrated work in California, primarily in the Bay Area. It never published any illustrations of works in Seattle, Tacoma, or Spokane. Further, because California architecture was dominated by the High Victorian modes in the mid-1880s, the journal illustrated Richardsonian buildings infrequently. Two California Richardsonian works were published: the Los Angeles County Courthouse in *California Architect* 9 (Aug. 1888) and the California State Bank in Sacramento in *California Architect* 11 (Aug. 1890).

The San Francisco–based builders' journal *Daily Pacific Builder*, which began in 1892, may have covered Washington building construction in the period and might be a useful source. However, the entire run of *Pacific Builder* prior to 1908 has been lost; no issues from the 1890s survive.

Architectural Record began publication in New York in 1891 and initially appeared quarterly. As indicated by its title, it served primarily as a record of built work. It was not influential in Seattle until the twentieth century.

71. Eileen Manning Michels, "A Developmental Study of the Drawings published in *American Architect* and *Inland Architect* through 1895" (Ph.D. diss., University of Minnesota, 1971). This is summarized in Eileen Manning Michels, "Late-Nineteenth-Century Published American Perspective Drawing," *JSAH* 31 (Oct. 1972): 291–308.

72. A good example is the leading Richardsonian architect in Texas, James Riely Gordon (1863–1937), who designed a series of highly compact, generally symmetrical courthouses that displayed a sophisticated use of the Richardsonian Romanesque vocabulary, yet they are all emphatically vertical compositions featuring tall central towers. For background on Gordon, see: Breisch, "Richardsonian Interlude in Texas," 89–101; and Henry, "Richardsonian Romanesque in Texas," 53–55. See also: Paul Goeldner, "Central Symbols: Historic Texas Courthouses, *Texas Architect* 36/3 (May/June 1986): 78–85. Examples of Richardsonian courthouses by Gordon and others are illustrated and discussed in Henry-Russell Hitchcock, "Notes on the Architecture," in *Courthouse: A Photographic Document*, edited by Richard Pare (New York: Horizon Press, 1978), 208–224. Contemporary publication of these projects was apparently limited to drawings of two courthouses by James Riely Gordon and D. E. Laub: Victoria County Courthouse, Victoria (1891–92), in *AABN* 54 (17 Oct. 1896); Bexar County Courthouse, San Antonio (1892–95), in *AABN* 46 (20 Oct. 1894).

73. Longstreth, "Richardsonian Architecture in Kansas," 77.

74. The watercolor of the Pierce County Courthouse, Tacoma (1890–92), design appeared in *Northwestern Architect* 8/8 (Oct. 1890).

75. The Los Angeles County Courthouse, Los Angeles (1886–91), appeared in *Architectural Record* 1/1 (July–Sept. 1891): 56.

76. R. H. Robertson's unbuilt project for the *New York World* appeared in *AABN* 24 (9 Feb. 1889). Its picturesque profile was adapted for Chauncey Seaton's Review Publishing Company Building, Spokane (1890–91).

77. Schuyler, "Romanesque Revival in America," 192; this section was omitted in Schuyler, *American Architecture* (Jordy and Cole, eds.).

78. Ibid., 193–194; reprinted in Jordy and Coe, *American Architecture*, 222.

79. See: chapter 5.

80. The definitive study of John Wellborn Root (1850–91) is Hoffman, *The Architecture of John Wellborn Root* (see: note 22 for complete citation), which provides analyses and illustrations of all of the important works of Burnham and Root. A similar study of Root's partner, Daniel Hudson Burnham (1846–1912), is Thomas S. Hines, *Burnham of Chicago: Architect and Planner* (New York and London: Oxford University Press, 1974); because Burnham was less directly involved in design, this does not provide the same level of design analysis for the partnership's works. An early biography of Root is: Harriet Monroe, *John Wellborn Root: A Study of His Life and Work* (Boston: Houghton-Mifflin, 1896; facsimile edition with introduction by Reyner Banham, Park

Forest, Ill.: Prairie School Press, 1966); however, as this was written by Root's sister-in-law, it is often considered overly adulatory. A contemporary overview of the firm is included in Schuyler, *A Critique of the Works of Adler and Sullivan, D. H. Burnham and Co., Henry Ives Cobb,* 49–71. The architectural context for Burnham and Root's work in Chicago is presented in Carl W. Condit, *The Chicago School of Architecture: A History of Commercial and Public Building in the Chicago Area, 1875–1925* (Chicago and London: University of Chicago Press, 1964). Condit's interpretive framework has been challenged in Daniel Bluestone, *Constructing Chicago* (New Haven: Yale University Press, 1991).

81. Henry Van Brunt, "John Wellborn Root," *IA* 16/8 (Jan. 1891): 85–88; reprinted in Coles, 219.

82. Hoffman notes that the entrance to the Counselman Building, Chicago (1883–84, destroyed), a ten-story brick office block, was marked by a Richardsonian arch, but was otherwise without Richardsonian influence. Similarly his Rialto Building, Chicago (1883–86, destroyed), featured massive piers supporting heavy balconies at the ninth floor, a feature that Hoffman suggests may have been derived from a less conspicuous detail on Richardson's Cheney Block. Hoffman, *Architecture of Root,* 42–43. For the Atchinson, Topeka, and Santa Fe Railroad Building, Topeka, see: Ibid., 36, 38–39; also see: Longstreth, "Richardsonian Architecture in Kansas," 67–68.

83. Hoffman has suggested that the fine quality of the brickwork of the Insurance Exchange was comparable to that at Richardson's Sever Hall. Hoffman, *Architecture of Root,* 43–45; a photograph of the Insurance Exchange appeared in *IA* 5/6 (July 1885): Supplement.

84. Hoffman, *Architecture of Root,* 45, 47.

85. Root sometimes retained the Victorian eclectic tendency to combine details drawn from a variety of sources, especially in his non-commercial buildings. Burnham and Root's E. E. Ayer House, Chicago (1885–86), displayed a clear debt to Richardson, both in its overall massing and in individual details such as the entry arch which recalled similar arches by Richardson, but the house also had Moorish detail, including an onion dome at one corner creating a picturesque effect; see: ibid., 49, 56–57.

Burnham and Root's success with commercial construction brought them a wide variety of work in the later 1880s, and in some of these projects Root applied elements derived from Richardson's designs. The broad unornamented granite walls of his V. C. Turner House, Chicago (1886–87), show the influence of Richardson's MacVeagh House, which was built at the same time in Chicago. Root's Church of the Covenant, Chicago (1886–87), displayed a Richardsonian exterior of brick marked by two levels of arcaded fenestration that provided light to the central auditorium. Burnham and Root also continued to incorporate other influences. Hoffman has suggested that after the publication of McKim, Mead, and White's Boston Public Library, Root used a Renaissance proportional system in his competition entry for the otherwise Richardsonian Boatman Savings Bank Building, St. Louis (1888). See: Hoffman, *Architecture of Root,* 107, 114, 116–121, 138–139.

86. Montgomery Schuyler, "Glimpses of Western Architecture: Chicago I," *Harper's Monthly* 83 (Aug. 1891): 400; reprinted in Schuyler, *American Architecture,* 256–257.

87. W. H. Howard, "The New Chicago," *Harper's Weekly* 32 (June 1888): 451 (cited in Hoffman, *Architecture of Root,* 68).

88. The Rookery appeared in six views in *IA* 11/8 (July 1888).

89. John W. Root, "Style" *IA* 8/10 (Jan. 1887): 99–101; partially reprinted in Monroe, *John Wellborn Root,* 76–94.

90. John W. Root, "A Great Architectural Problem," *IA* 15/5 (June 1890): 67–71; quoted in Monroe, *John Wellborn Root,* 107.

91. Hoffman, *Architecture of Root,* 127–129 (Chronicle Building), 146, 148 (Tacoma buildings). The Chronicle Building appeared in *IA* 11/1 (Feb. 1888). Hoffman points out the similarity of the Fidelity Trust Company building in Tacoma to Adler

and Sullivan's warehouse for Martin Ryerson published in *IA* 13/4 (Apr. 1889), later called the Walker Warehouse. This building, in turn, had been directly influenced by Richardson's Marshall Field Wholesale Store (see: notes 93, 94).

92. The official relationship between *Inland Architect* and the Western Association of Architects ended in 1888, the year before the Western Association and the American Institute of Architects merged.

93. On Sullivan's fascination with the Field Store, see: William H. Jordy, "The Tall Buildings," in *Louis Sullivan: The Function of Ornament*, edited by Wim de Wit (New York and London: W. W. Norton, 1986): 67–73; and William H. Jordy, *American Buildings and Their Architects 3: Progressive and Academic Ideals at the Turn of the Twentieth Century* (Garden City, N.Y.: Doubleday, 1972), 28–38, 100–120. Schuyler also comments on the relationship of Adler and Sullivan to Richardson: Schuyler, *A Critique of the Works of Adler & Sullivan, D. H. Burnham & Co., Henry Ives Cobb*, 1–48.

94. The auditorium design appeared in *IA* 9/6 (May 1887); a section of the auditorium appeared in *IA* 11/8 (July 1888). The "Wholesale Store for M. A. Ryerson" design (later known as Walker Warehouse) appeared in *IA* 13/4 (Apr. 1889).

95. Montgomery Schuyler, "Glimpses of Western Architecture: Minneapolis and St. Paul," *Harper's Monthly* 83 (October 1891): 736–755; reprinted in Schuyler, *American Architecture*, 292–328.

96. A brief overview of the economic development of Minneapolis and St. Paul is: Mildred L. Hartsough, *The Twin Cities as a Metropolitan Market* (Minneapolis: University of Minnesota, 1925), 20–37, 51–71. A summary of Minneapolis and St. Paul architectural history is given in the introduction in: David Gebhard and Tom Martinson, *A Guide to Architecture in Minnesota* (Minneapolis: University of Minnesota Press, 1977), 3–20. A broader introduction to the architecture of these cities in the context of the state is: Donald R. Torbert, *A Century of Architecture in Minnesota* (Minneapolis: University of Minnesota Press, 1958). The best treatment of the Minneapolis architects of the 1880s and 1890s remains: Donald R. Torbert, "Minneapolis Architecture and Architects, 1848–1908: A Study of Style Trends in Architecture in a Midwestern City Together with a Catalogue of Representative Buildings" (Ph.D. diss., University of Minnesota, 1953). A partial summary is: Donald R. Torbert, "The Advent of Modern Architecture in Minnesota," *JSAH* 13 (March 1954): 18–23 (although this focuses largely on buildings which were seen as precursors to Modernism).

97. Franklin Bidwell Long (1842–1912) and Frederick G. Kees (1852–1927) maintained their partnership from 1884 to 1897. Biographical summaries for Long and Kees are presented in Torbert, "Minneapolis Architecture," 419–421, 440–441; for their Richardsonian buildings, see pages 269–272, 275–278, 280–285. Some of their Richardsonian work is discussed in Larson, "Richardson Goes West," in Larson and Brown, *Spirit of Richardson*, 19–43. The firm also published a volume on its own work, *The Architecture of Long and Kees* (Minneapolis: ca. 1891).

98. The contrast between the roughness and massiveness of the stone typically used in Minneapolis and the need for large window openings to maximize natural light due to the northern latitude and long winters proved difficult to resolve for many architects. Long's earlier Kasota Block, Minneapolis (1884), of rock-faced masonry, included tourelles and a broad entry arch, but these were not well resolved and the large number and size of the openings seemed to contradict the heavy surface treatment. The design of the Kasota Block also suffered from a decision to add floors, in response to the city's booming growth, after construction had begun.

99. The commercial work of Long and Kees was not always so successful; they were also responsible for the *retardataire* Masonic Temple, Minneapolis (1885–89); see: note 43 (above).

100. E. Townsend Mix (1831–1890) had previously practiced in Chicago and Milwaukee. For a partial biographical summary, see: Torbert, "Minneapolis Archi-

tecture," 452–453; for his buildings, see pages 278–279, 285–289. Mix's Guaranty Loan Building is more often cited for its innovative metal-framed and skylit twelve-story interior course; see, for example, Marcus Whiffen and Frederick Koeper, *American Architecture, 1607–1976* (Cambridge, Mass.: MIT Press, 1981), 252–253.

101. Harry Wild Jones (1859–1935), originally from Minnesota, was a student in the architecture program at MIT in 1880–82 and is reported to have worked in Richardson's office in 1883. For a partial biographical summary, see: Torbert, "Minneapolis Architecture," 448–449; for National Bank of Commerce, see 279–280. A drawing of the National Bank of Commerce appeared in the supplement to *Northwest Builder, Decorator and Furnisher* 1 (Nov. 1887). The completed building was described and illustrated in *Northwestern Architect* 7/5 (May 1889).

102. The Minneapolis Public Library was published in *Northwestern Architect* 8/8 (Aug. 1890). Six of the perspective drawings submitted to the competition for the city hall and courthouse appeared in an illustrated supplement to *Northwestern Architect* 6/4 (Apr. 1888); unfortunately no copies of this are known to survive in accessible collections. The competitive design by Long and Kees appeared in *AABN* 23 (7 Apr. 1888); their revised design appeared in *Northwestern Architect* 6/8 (Aug. 1888). The competition is also discussed in Torbert, "Minneapolis Architecture," 280–285.

103. For St. Paul urban and architectural history, see: Leonard Eaton, *Gateway Cities and Other Essays* (Ames: Iowa State University Press, 1989), 39–59. Also see: H. F. Koeper, *Historic St. Paul Buildings: A Report of the Historic Sites Committee, a Special Citizens Group: Named by the St. Paul City Planning Board* (St. Paul: City Planning Board, 1964); also see: Gebhard and Martinson, *Guide to Architecture in Minnesota*, 81–107.

104. J. Walter Stevens (1857–1937), a transplanted New Englander, practiced in St. Paul after 1880. The views of the West Publishing Company appeared in *AABN* 20 (19 Feb. 1887).

105. On the Noyes-Cutler Warehouse, see: Eaton, *Gateway Cities*, 46–49. However, Eaton's dating is incorrect; the building was permitted in 1886, before, not after, the publication of Adler and Sullivan's Ryerson Building/Walker Warehouse design.

106. An image of Laurel Terrace by Willcox and Johnston appeared in *Northwestern Architect* 6/6 (June 1888).

107. On Summit Avenue, see: Sandeen, *St. Paul's Historic Summit Avenue*.

108. There is currently no published biography of Ellis. The best source of information regarding Ellis remains Eileen Manning, "The Architectural Designs of Harvey Ellis" (M.A. thesis, University of Minnesota, 1953). Ellis's career is summarized in the collection of essays, Jean R. France, ed., *A Rediscovery—Harvey Ellis: Artist, Architect* (Rochester, N.Y.: Memorial Art Gallery, University of Rochester, 1972). A more recent study, Ellen Threinen, "Harvey Ellis as Architect and Draftsman: A Clarification and Re-evaluation" (M.A. thesis, University of New Mexico, 1976), clarifies some points about Ellis's life, but is incomplete because the author apparently failed to examine any of Ellis's drawings published in *Northwestern Architect*. As a result, it presents highly questionable judgments about Ellis's contribution to architecture. M. E. Lipscomb, "The Architecture of Harvey Ellis in Rochester, N.Y." (M.A. thesis, University of Rochester, 1969), is limited to Ellis's Rochester practice. Two articles by Roger Kennedy, "The Long Shadow of Harvey Ellis," *Minnesota History* 40 (fall 1966): 97–108, and "Long Dark Corridors: Harvey Ellis," *Prairie School Review* 5 (First–Second Quarter 1968): 5–18, offer a summary of Ellis's life and contributions, but both contain some errors and unsupported conjectures and must be used with caution. Kennedy also discusses Ellis in "Guest Speaker: Roger G. Kennedy: Harvey Ellis— Reconsidering an Elusive American Genius," *Architectural Digest* 47 (Oct. 1990): 32–33, 36, 40, 44. A summary of Ellis's background and a discussion of his contribution to St. Louis architecture appears in Savage, *Architecture of the Private Streets of St. Louis*, 207–218. Other biographical articles about Ellis include C. Bragdon, "Harvey Ellis: A Portrait Sketch," *Architectural Review* 15 (Dec. 1908): 173–183;

H. Garden, "Harvey Ellis, Designer and Draftsman," *Architectural Review* 15 (Dec. 1908): 184–188; and F. Swales, "Master Draftsmen III: Harvey Ellis," *Pencil Points* 5 (July 1924): 49–55, 79.

The impact of Ellis on other delineators at this time is documented in Michels, "A Developmental Study," 116–142, and Michels, "Late-Nineteenth-Century Published American Perspective Drawing," 303–306, and is mentioned in Larson, "Richardson Goes West" in *Spirit of H. H. Richardson*.

109. LeRoy Sunderland Buffington (1847–1931), who had emerged as the city's leading designer in the 1870s, was among the best-known Minnesota architects in the 1880s and 1890s. Through the early 1880s his work reflected the Victorian modes, and he was eclipsed by his younger colleagues in the late 1880s. Still he produced a number of notable Romanesque Revival designs when Harvey Ellis was in his office; in particular, Pillsbury Hall (1887–89) at the University of Minnesota, presents an extraordinary combination of Richardsonian Romanesque massing, polychromatic stone, and a variety of detail drawn from Richardson's Austin Hall.

Buffington's career is summarized in Muriel B. Christison, "LeRoy S. Buffington and the Minneapolis Boom of the 1880s," *Minnesota History* 23 (September 1942): 219–232. A brief biography appears in Torbert, "Minneapolis Architecture," 421–424. However, Buffington is now best known for his claim to have invented the skeleton frame system that made skyscraper construction possible. These claims were discussed in Everard M. Upjohn, "Buffington and the Skyscraper," *Art Bulletin* 17 (Mar. 1935): 48–70; Hugh Morrison, "Buffington and the Invention of the Skyscraper," *Art Bulletin* 26 (Mar. 1944): 1–2; Dmitri Tselos, "The Enigma of Buffington's Skyscraper," *Art Bulletin* 26 (Mar. 1944): 3–4; and Muriel B. Christison, "How Buffington Staked His Claim," *Art Bulletin* 26 (Mar. 1944): 13–24. Although these articles generally concluded that Buffington's claims were unfounded, recent research has reopened this question; see: Gerald R. Larson, "The Iron Skeleton Frame: Interactions between Europe and the United States," in *Chicago Architecture, 1872–1922: Birth of a Metropolis*, edited by John Zukowsky (Chicago: Art Institute of Chicago, and Munich: Prestel-Verlag, 1987), 50–52.

110. A summary chronology of *Northwestern Architect:*

Northwestern Architect and Improvement Record, 10 Nov. 1882 through Dec. 1890; absorbed *Building Budget,* Jan. 1891

Northwestern Architect and Building Budget, Jan. 1891 through May 1893; merged with *Builder and Decorator,* Aug. 1893

Architect, Builder and Decorator, Aug. 1893 through May 1895; absorbed by *Improvement Bulletin,* 31 May 1895

(Note: *Builder and Decorator* was titled *Northwest Builder, Decorator and Furnisher,* Jan.–Oct. 1889, then *Northwest Builder and Decorator,* Nov. 1889–Jan. 1892; then *Builder and Decorator,* Jan.–July 1893.)

Northwestern Architect is very difficult to use. Nothing survives of its earliest years, and only selected plates survive for the period before 1888. Partial runs survive in libraries in Minneapolis, Chicago, St. Louis, and Washington, D.C., but these do not add up to a complete run of the publication.

111. The first building in Washington to appear in an architectural journal was: "Hotel and Office Building, Spokane Falls, W. Ty.," Joy and Fitzpatrick, Architects, Minneapolis, *Northwestern Architect* 5/5 (May 1887).

112. On the concept of "gateway city," see: Eaton, *Gateway Cities,* especially 3–17.

113. The relationship between Minneapolis and St. Paul and the Pacific Northwest was due in part to the promotion of settlement in Oregon and Washington by the Northern Pacific and Great Northern railroads, and in part to the fact that settlers in Washington (which grew from a population of 75,116 in 1880 to 349,390 in 1890) came primarily from states in the upper and central Midwest, including Ilinois, Iowa, Ohio, Wisconsin, and Minnesota, plus New York and Pennsylvania. See: James B. Hedges, "Promotion

of Immigration to the Pacific Northwest by the Railroads," *Mississippi Valley Historical Review* 15 (Sept. 1928): 183–203; and Lancaster Pollard, "The Pacific Northwest," in Merrill Jensen, ed., *Regionalism in America* (Madison: University of Wisconsin Press, 1951), 187–212.

114. Other Washington architects of this period who had come through Minneapolis or St. Paul included Tacoma's William Farrell and Oliver P. Dennis and Spokane's Chauncey B. Seaton.

115. Parkinson, *Incidents by the Way*, 145–146.

116. Wallace K. Huntington, "Victorian Architecture," in *Space Style and Structure: Building in Northwest America*, edited by Thomas Vaughan and Virginia G. Ferriday (Portland: Oregon Historical Society, 1974), 285.

117. This understanding of the traditional design method seen in contrast to a progressive, modern, or scientific design method derives from the discussion of vernacular design offered in Thomas Hubka, "Just Folks Designing: Vernacular Designers and the Generation of Form," *JAE: Journal of Architectural Education* 32 (1979): 27–29; reprinted in Dell Upton and John Michael Vlach, eds., *Common Places: Readings in American Vernacular Architecture* (Athens, Ga., and London: University of Georgia Press, 1986): 426–432.

Hubka's argument draws upon the work of Levi-Strauss, who contrasts the mental process of the "scientist" (which involves the use of concepts) with that of the "bricoleur" (which involves the use of "signs"). Signs, in this sense, are seen as being halfway between images or percepts (which are completely concrete) and concepts (which are completely abstract). Signs are said to resemble images in that they are concrete entities, but they simultaneously resemble concepts in their powers of reference. Both signs and concepts are said to have powers of reference beyond themselves, but signs are constrained by their concrete aspects whereas concepts have a theoretically unlimited capacity in this respect. Images coexist with ideas in signs—it is the concreteness of the image that limits the number of relationships into which the sign can enter. Concepts, lacking this concreteness, can have theoretically unlimited relationships with other entities. Claude Levi-Strauss, *The Savage Mind* (Paris: Librairie Plon, 1962; English translation: Chicago: University of Chicago Press, 1966), 1–18.

118. Architectural design theory was seldom discussed in the nineteenth-century architectural press. For the most part, articles focused on professional concerns, practical design issues, and occasionally architectural history. Richardson never wrote about his designs or his design method. Richardson's application of architectural compositional principles that he learned at the Ecole des Beaux-Arts would have been most clearly evident in the plans of his designs, but the contemporary architectural press rarely carried plans of his buildings. Although Louis Sullivan was later highly critical of the education given at the Ecole, his lifelong search for generalized abstract principles of design is evident in his familiar statement: "Form follows function."

119. This phrase is taken from its original context in which it was intended to describe the methods of folk designers within traditional cultures and the author may not agree with my use of this phrase in the context of this book. See: Henry Glassie, "Folk Art," in *Folklore and Folklife: An Introduction*, edited by Richard M. Dorson (Chicago and London: University of Chicago Press, 1972), 253–280.

120. Even in Seattle, because evidence of the design methods of the post-fire architects is limited to surviving buildings and, in a few cases, surviving drawings, this theory of their design method remains conjectural.

V. The New Commercial Core:
Architecture for a Metropolitan Center, 1889–1895

1. This chapter focuses on the most significant contributors in the post-fire period, Elmer Fisher, William Boone, John Parkinson, and the firm Saunders and Houghton.

However, others also played important roles. For example, Stephen Meany designed the new Occidental Hotel (1889–90 [later Seattle Hotel], destroyed), and the Colman Building (1889–90, altered). Others who participated in the design of the new city included Comstock and Troetsche, whose most important post-fire works were: Marshall Block, now J & M Cardroom and Bar (1889), Squire-Latimer Block, now Grand Central Hotel (1889–90); Towle and Wilcox, whose important post-fire works were: Cort's Theatre, later Smith's Standard Theatre (1889, destroyed), Gottstein Block (1889–90, destroyed), Kline and Rosenberg Building (1889–90, altered); and Hermann Steinmann, whose important post-fire works included: Harms and Dickman Building (1889, destroyed), Golden Rule Bazaar Building (1889, destroyed), Phinney Block (1889, destroyed), Campbell Building (1889–90, destroyed), Terry-Kittinger Building (Delmar Building) (1889–90, altered).

2. For examples of local accounts that characterize these buildings as Romanesque Revival, see: Caroline Tobin, *Downtown Seattle Walking Tours* (Seattle: City of Seattle, 1985), 8; J. Kingston Pierce, *Seattle Access* (New York: Harper Collins, 1993), 13.

3. For Fisher's emergence as Seattle's leading architect, see: chapter 2.

4. *P.I.*, 15 June 1889, 4.

5. For Korn Building, see: *P.I.*, 18 June 1889, 4; 1 Aug. 1889, 4; 17 Oct. 1889, 8; 1 Nov. 1889, 5; 7 Dec. 1889, 8; 1 Jan. 1890, 13; 6 June 1890, 8.

6. For Sullivan Building, see: *P.I.*, 17 Apr. 1889, 5; 15 June 1889, 4; 31 July 1889, 4; 17 Oct. 1889, 8; 19 Oct. 1889, 5; 1 Jan. 1890, 13; 6 June 1890, 8; 28 July 1890, 5; 11 Aug. 1890, 5; 1 Jan. 1891, 5; 6 June 1891, 12.

7. *Northwestern Architect* 8/9 (Sept. 1890).

8. *P.I.*, 19 Oct. 1889, 5.

9. *Times*, 10 Aug. 1889, 8. For construction history of the Starr-Boyd Building: *P.I.*, 18 June 1889, 4; 11 July 1889, 4; 8 Oct. 1889, 4; 17 Oct. 1889, 8; 19 Oct. 1889, 5; 17 Nov. 1889, 3; 1 Jan. 1890, 13; 6 June 1890, 8.

10. For Haller Building, see: *P.I.*, 15 June 1889, 4; 11 July 1889, 4; 1 Aug. 1889, 4; 18 Aug. 1889, 5; 17 Oct. 1889, 8; 19 Oct. 1889, 5; 1 Nov. 1889, 5; 1 Jan. 1890, 13; 6 June 1890, 8; 11 Sept. 1890, 5; *Times*, 10 Aug. 1889, 8.

11. For Lebanon Building, see: *P.I.*, 3 July 1889, 4; 17 Oct. 1889, 8; 1 Jan. 1890, 13; 6 June 1890, 8; *NREBR* 1/2 (Mar.–Apr. 1891): 16.

12. For New England Hotel, see: *P.I.*, 21 June 1889, 4 (Meany); 24 July 1889, 5 (Comstock and Troetsche); 31 July 1889, 4; 17 Oct. 1889, 8; 1 Jan. 1890, 13; 6 June 1890, 8.

13. For Schwabacher Building, see: *P.I.*, 11 July 1889, 4; 17 Oct. 1889, 8; 19 Oct. 1889, 5; 1 Jan. 1890, 13; 6 June 1890, 8; 1 Jan. 1891, 5; *Times*, 10 Aug. 1889, 8.

14. The Commercial Street (First South) portion of the building was destroyed by fire in 1892 and the reconstructed facade was an original design not conforming to Fisher's original, as discussed later in this chapter.

15. Some works by Fisher seem much more related to his pre-fire designs. For example, his Rengstorff Building (1889–90, destroyed), later called the Downs Block, on Second between Cherry and Columbia, featured a central entrance bay topped by a high pediment and included a mix of detailing with round arches only at the fourth floor. For the Rengstorff Block, see: *P.I.*, 4 July 1889, 4; 14 July 1889, 8; 1 Jan. 1890, 13; 6 June 1890, 8; *NREBR* 1/2 (Mar.–Apr. 1891), 16. For demolition see: *Times*, 20 July 1937, 19.

16. *P.I.*, 1 Jan. 1890, 22.

17. City directories list at least some of Fisher's draftsmen: the 1890 Polk Directory lists Emil DeNeuf, George Elsey, and John C. N. Keith; the 1890 Corbett Directory also includes Joseph Middlebrook ("Superintendent"), William Kaufman, and Julius Krause; the 1891 Polk Directory lists Emil DeNeuf, Joseph Middlebrook ("Superintendent"), and Frank A. I. Hall. DeNeuf would eventually take over Fisher's practice as described later in this chapter.

18. *P.I.*, 20 Sept. 1888, 3; 11 Jan. 1889, 5.

19. *P.I.*, 8 Feb. 1889, 5; 17 Feb. 1889, 5; 7 Apr. 1889, 5.

20. Quoted in *P.I.*, 18 Oct. 1889, 8.

21. For Pioneer Building, see: *Times*, 10 Aug. 1889, 1; *P.I.*, 31 Aug. 1889, 4; 8 Oct. 1889, 4; 19 Oct. 1889, 5; 1 Jan. 1890, 13, 22; 28 July 1890, 5; 11 Aug. 1890, 5; 5 Sept. 1890, 12; 16 Oct. 1890, 12; 1 Jan. 1891, 5; *NREBR* 1/2 (Mar.–Apr. 1891), 16.

22. The intended two-phase construction was noted in *P.I.*, 11 Jan. 1889, 5. The more than 100 sheets of drawings for the Pioneer Building produced by Elmer Fisher's office, found at the University of Washington Libraries, Manuscripts, Special Collections, Archives Division, are numbered to reflect the two-phase sequence. Sheets 1–59 are identified as drawings for the "Pioneer Building"; sheets 60–75 are identified as "Pioneer Building Extension"; sheets 76–88 are undifferentiated as they are details of grilles, stairs, windows, and similar features which may apply to either or both portions of the building. A few of the numbered sheets between 1 and 88 appear to be missing. There are also approximately twenty unnumbered sheets that are either early studies or hand-drawn copies of numbered drawings. Also see: chapter 3, note 63.

23. Newspaper reports comments on these columns: "The two striking stone columns which run up the building are 113 feet high from the street. . . ." *P.I.*, 16 Oct. 1890, 12. The source for the design of these columns is unknown although there may have been a relationship between the rusticity of these columns and raw logs and an association to Henry Yesler's having made his fortune in the lumber business. Today these are often colloquially characterized as "tootsie roll" columns.

24. *Washington Magazine* 1/1 (Sept. 1889): 42–43.

25. *NREBR* 1/1 (Feb. 1891): 10.

26. For Burke's New York Block, see: chapter 3. (Note: Burke's New York Block should not be confused with Dexter Horton's New York Building designed by William Boone, discussed later in this chapter.)

27. *P.I.*, 12 Mar. 1889, 5.

28. When Burke wrote to Fisher about the terra-cotta supplier, he used Chicago as a standard of reference: "Unless it is certain that Gladding, McBean can furnish first-class terra cotta equal to Chicago, I will not accept their bid." Burke to Fisher, 4 Dec. 1889, Box 20, letterpress book 3, 477, Thomas Burke Papers, Manuscripts, Special Collections, University Archives Division, University of Washington Libraries. For the reference to the Rookery, see: *P.I.*, 12 Mar. 1889, 5.

29. For Burke Building, see: *Times*, 10 Aug. 1889, 1; *P.I.*, 17 Oct. 1889, 8; 1 Nov. 1889, 5; 1 Jan. 1890, 13, 22; 6 June 1890, 8; 28 June 1890, 12; 28 July 1890, 5; 11 Aug. 1890, 5; 1 Jan. 1891, 5; *NREBR* 1/2 (Mar.–Apr. 1891): 16.

30. This plate is similar in style to those published in *West Shore*. However, it appeared only in a small undated booklet of similar images of Seattle buildings. (The date is surmised from the inclusion of images of multiple buildings that were only finished a month or two before the June 1889 fire.) *Seattle: Queen City of the Pacific* (Seattle: Charles Kittinger, n.d.), n.p. (copy at University of Washington Libraries, Manuscripts Special Collections, University Archives Division).

31. *Times*, 10 Aug. 1889, 1; *Northwestern Architect* 8/6 (June 1890).

32. Burke's concern about terra-cotta was first evident in his three letters to Fisher about contracting with Gladding, McBean; Burke to Fisher, 4 Dec. 1889, 6 Dec. 1889, 8 Dec. 1889, Box 20, letterpress book 3, 477, 479, 480, Burke Papers. Once Gladding, McBean received the contract, Burke was even more adamant in correspondence with them that the color of the terra-cotta exactly match the pressed brick to be used on the Burke Building. He stated that he thought Fisher's desire for color contrast was "wrong," writing that shadows on the facade would offer enough contrast. Burke also rejected glazed terra-cotta, which he called "shiny," and would only accept "slightly semi-glazed" terra-cotta, which he thought would be closer in character to the brick. Burke to Gladding, McBean, 4 Jan. 1890, 6 Jan. 1890, 8 Jan. 1890, 16 Jan. 1890, 30 Jan. 1890,

10 Feb. 1890, 13 Feb. 1890, Box 20, letterpress book 1, 63, 64–65, 85–86, 122–123, 196, 281, 326, Burke Papers.

33. *Times*, 10 Aug. 1889, 1.

34. *NREBR* 1/2 (Mar.–Apr. 1891): 16.

35. *P.I.*, 18 June 1889, 1; 19 June 1889, 4; 17 Oct. 1889, 8; 7 Dec. 1889, 8; 1 Jan. 1890, 13.

36. Boone's other early post-fire work included several smaller buildings: McNaught Building, at Sixth (now Fifth) and Jackson; Sanderson Block, on Yesler; Squire Block on Second north of Yesler; and the Starr Block, on Front.

37. For Dexter Horton Building, see: *P.I.*, 2 July 1889, 4; 21 July 1889, 8; 23 Oct. 1889, 5; 1 Nov. 1889, 5; 1 Jan. 1890, 13.

38. Dexter Horton was born in New York State, but little is known of his early life until he joined Thomas Mercer's party in Illinois to come to Seattle, arriving in 1853. He worked initially at Yesler's Mill, later opened a store and began to lend money. After living in San Francisco from 1866 to 1870, he returned to Seattle to found the city's first bank. Thereafter he became an important business leader, investing in real estate and in Seattle's first gas and electric companies.

39. Dexter Horton's buildings at Second and Cherry and Third and Cherry were together called the "Seattle Block" in *P.I.*, 9 Oct. 1889, 3. However, this name was sometimes used only for Horton's building at Third and Cherry, although this was also called "Dexter Horton Building" (and later was called the "Occidental Block"). In 1890 and 1891, the building at Second and Cherry was usually identified by the owner's name, "Dexter Horton's building," as in *NREBR* 1/2 (Mar.–Apr. 1891): 16. The name by which the second of Dexter Horton's buildings was subsequently known, "New York Building," appeared in *P.I.*, 2 Apr. 1892, 5.

40. *P.I.*, 9 Oct. 1889, 3.

41. *NREBR* 1/2 (Mar.–Apr. 1891): 16.

42. According to the accompanying text, the drawing of the New York Building was based on a photograph. However, as the building was only a few floors above the street, the remainder had to have been based on information provided by the architects. *NREBR* 1/2 (Mar.–Apr. 1891): 14 (identified as "The Horton Block").

43. For New York Building, see: *P.I.*, 28 July 1890, 5; 11 Aug. 1890, 5; 1 Jan. 1891, 5; 6 June 1891, 12; 8 Sept. 1891, 8; 2 Apr. 1892, 5; also see: *Times*, 26 June 1891, 6; *Northwest Magazine* 9/2 (Feb. 1891), 25.

44. William Willcox's background is discussed later in this chapter; see: note 141.

45. It may be that Boone was aided in the fireproofing design by Willcox. Willcox, who had had experience with large masonry buildings, had included a discussion of fireproofing approaches in his book: William H. Willcox, *Hints to Those Who Propose to Build—Also a Description of Improved Plan and Construction of Churches* (St. Paul, Minn.: Pioneer Press, 1884). Willcox also brought first-hand familiarity with the new tall buildings in Minneapolis and St. Paul—buildings that sometimes incorporated similar fireproofing techniques.

46. *NREBR* 1/2 (Mar.–Apr.1891): 16.

47. The New York Building and the (first) Dexter Horton Building were demolished in 1922 so that the (second) Dexter Horton Building, designed by John Graham, could be built. See: Grant Hildebrand, "John Graham, Sr.," in *Shaping Seattle Architecture*, 91, 93.

48. William Elder Bailey (1860–1925) was the son of Charles L. Bailey, a prominent iron and steel manufacturer in Harrisburg, Pennsylvania. He joined his father's company after graduating from Yale in 1882. Bailey first visited Seattle on an extended vacation in 1888–89, and invested in Seattle property before leaving for California. He returned to the city immediately after the Seattle fire in June 1889. Bailey was proposed for the state senate in September 1889 but withdrew from consideration; he also served as a member of the Seattle Parks Board.

49. *P.I.*, 28 June 1889, 2.

50. Charles Willard Saunders came from a large family in Cambridge, Massachusetts, who were all descended from Martin Saunders, who arrived in Boston in 1635. A copy of the privately printed family genealogy is available at the Cambridge Public Library.

51. Charles Saunders was listed in Cambridge city directories as a clerk in Boston from 1879 to 1881, and then in the lumber business from 1882 to 1885; in 1886 his listing indicated that he had moved to California. Saunders was twenty-one years of age in 1879, so he may have attended college for several years, but no record of his education has been discovered.

52. The joint architectural practice of Mary Saunders and Charles Saunders is indicated in the Pasadena business directories. The house designed for Charles Saunders's father-in-law, was a symmetrical shingle-style building that volumetrically echoed Richardson's Sever Hall, which Saunders would have known from his years in Cambridge. Destroyed by fire about 1900, it is illustrated in David Gebhard and Harriette Von Breton, *Architecture in California, 1868–1968*, exh. cat. (Santa Barbara: University of California, Santa Barbara, 1968), n.p. The house that Charles and Mary Saunders designed for themselves is now one of the few shingle-style houses still standing in the city.

53. Limited information is available on Edwin Walker Houghton's background and education. The career of his uncle, Thomas M. Houghton, was briefly profiled in *The Builder*, 11 Feb. 1916. (Andrew Saint provided this information.) On his death certificate, Thomas M. Houghton's occupation was listed as quantity surveyor. When Edwin Houghton married in 1884, at age 29, he identified his occupation as "farmer."

54. Edwin Houghton's personal history was largely compiled from original sources and family records by his grandson, John Houghton, who graciously shared this information. A brief profile of Edwin Houghton's early life is also found in *Illustrated History of Los Angeles County* (Chicago: Lewis Publishing Co., 1889), 778.

55. *P.I.*, 18 Sept. 1889, 2. During the partnership, projects were credited to Saunders and Houghton jointly. After the partnership dissolved, Houghton took over supervision and completion of the firm's work. Thus, he is sometimes credited with work that may actually have been designed by Saunders.

56. Seattle Chamber of Commerce, *Seattle Illustrated: Containing a Careful Compilation and Review of the Resources, Terminal Advantages, Climate, and General Industries of the "Queen City" and the Country Tributary to It* (Chicago: Baldwin, Calcutt and Blakely, 1890), 59.

57. For Washington Territory Investment Company building construction, see: *P.I.*, 7 Aug. 1889, 4; 29 Aug. 1889, 4; 17 Oct. 1889, 8; 7 Dec. 1889, 8; 1 Jan. 1890, 13; 6 June 1890, 8; 28 July 1890, 5; 1 Jan. 1891, 5.

58. *P.I.*, 24 Jan. 1889, 3.

59. *P.I.*, 4 July 1889, 4.

60. *P.I.*, 14 July 1889, 8.

61. For Harrisburg Block/Bailey Building, see: *P.I.*, 5 Oct. 1889, 5; 17 Oct. 1889, 8; 1 Nov. 1889, 5; 2 Nov. 1889, 5; 7 Dec. 1889, 8; 1 Jan. 1890, 13; 26 Apr. 1890, 8; 6 June 1890, 8; 28 July 1890, 5; 11 Aug. 1890, 5; 16 Oct. 1890, 12; 1 Jan. 1891, 5; 6 June 1891, 12; 8 Sept. 1891, 8; 21 Oct. 1891, 8; *Times*, 26 Mar. 1892, 2. Also see: note 67 (below).

62. *The Graphic* (Oct. 1891) "Washington Supplement."

63. *NREBR* 1/2 (Mar.–Apr. 1891): 16.

64. The *P.I.* identified this as the "Harrisburg Building" or "Harrisburg Block" beginning in November 1889, and this continued through 1891. However, a rendering published in October 1891 identified the building as the "Bailey Building" and this name was used by the *Press-Times* when the building was finished in 1892. In its later history, this was also known as the Broderick Building and as the Railway Exchange Building.

65. *NREBR* 1/2 (Mar.–Apr. 1891): 16; *Times*, 26 Mar. 1892, 2.

66. *Times*, 26 Mar. 1892, 2. It may also be that the building was delayed by William Bailey's continuing financial difficulties.

67. The advanced character of the Bailey Building design has occasionally led to questions about its authorship. Charles H. Bebb, who had been sent to Seattle in October 1890 by Adler and Sullivan in connection with the Seattle Opera House project, may have become involved in consulting on some aspects of the Bailey Building construction. What Bebb contributed is unknown, but given the timing, it is unlikely that his contribution included significant elements of the exterior design.

68. *P.I.*, 21 July 1889, 8.

69. Thomas Ewing (1837–?), like Burke and Bailey, was an investor in real estate and other ventures. Ewing was born in Ohio and went to California as a grocery clerk in 1857. He engaged in dry goods business at various times in Idaho, Nevada, and Arizona, while also investing in mining securities. In 1888 he came to Seattle and immediately began to promote the development of West Seattle. At one time he was owner and president of companies that supplied water, electricity, ferry, and streetcar service to West Seattle and also president of a West Seattle real estate company.

70. For Rainier Hotel, see: *P.I.*, 27 July 1889, 4; 28 July 1889, 8; 9 Oct. 1889, 3; 18 Oct. 1889, 5; 25 Oct. 1889, 8; 29 Oct. 1889, 8; 2 Nov. 1889, 5; 13 Nov. 1889, 8; 17 Nov. 1889, 5.

71. For easily accessible contemporary illustrations of similar shingled buildings, see: Vincent J. Scully, Jr., *The Architecture of the American Summer: The Flowering of the Shingle Style* (New York: Rizzoli, 1989), especially plates 33, 39, 66, 68, 85, 94, 105, 127.

72. Saunders and Houghton were also responsible for the design of the Hotel Eisenbeis, a shingled hotel in Port Townsend modeled after the Rainier Hotel. See: Denison and Huntington, *Victorian Architecture of Port Townsend*, 19–20.

73. For Manhattan Building history, see: *P.I.*, 24 Sept. 1889, 5; 17 Oct. 1889, 8; 1 Nov. 1889, 5; 2 Nov. 1889, 5; 7 Dec. 1889, 8; 1 Jan. 1890, 13; 6 June 1890, 8; 6 June 1891, 12. Drawings of the Manhattan Block appeared in *Northwestern Architect* 8/11 (Nov. 1890); and in *Seattle Illustrated*, 40.

74. For Olympic Building, see: *P.I.*, 5 Oct. 1889, 5; 1 Jan. 1890, 13; 6 June 1890, 8; 28 July 1890, 5; 1 Jan. 1891, 5; 6 June 1891, 12.

75. For Terry-Denny Building, see: *P.I.*, 17 Oct. 1889, 8; 7 Dec. 1889, 8; 6 June 1890, 8; 28 July 1890, 5; 16 Oct. 1890, 12; 1 Jan. 1891, 5; 6 June 1891, 12; *NREBR* 1/2 (Mar.–Apr. 1891): 16.

76. The background and history of this building is little known. The architect Albert Wickersham may have been involved in superintending the project at one point as his correspondence regarding terra-cotta for the structure survives at Gladding, McBean.

77. Other works by Saunders and Houghton are equally puzzling. For example, the small Maud Building (1889–90), on the west side of Commercial between Washington and Jackson, presents a very flat facade of red-orange brick, with lighter colored brick trimming the windows. See: *P.I.*, 29 Aug. 1889, 4; 5 Oct. 1889, 5; 7 Dec. 1889, 8; 6 June 1890, 8.

78. Parkinson, *Incidents*, 139–140.

79. *P.I.*, 3 July 1889, 4.

80. Guy C. Phinney (1852–1893) was born and raised in Nova Scotia. He attended Phillips Exeter Academy, Bishops College (Lenoxville, Quebec), and studied law for one year at McGill College in Montreal, leaving to join a gold rush in British Columbia. After several years in mining, and a short stay in San Francisco, Phinney came to Seattle in 1881. He worked briefly as a clerk, then opened his partnership offering services in law, collections, and insurance. He invested his profits in Seattle real estate and by 1890 had focused his efforts in banking and real estate development. At the time of

his death, he was transforming his residential property into Woodland Park (which today is part of the park system of Seattle).

81. In January 1891, Guy Phinney purchased Daniel Jones's 40% interest in the project; *P.I.*, 29 Jan. 1891, 5. He later sold the building to Boston investors; *P.I.*, 13 Sept. 1893, 8. Also see: chapter 3 for discussion of the conversion of the building to a hotel in 1894.

82. Parkinson, *Incidents*, 140.

83. For Butler Block, see: *P.I.*, 21 July 1889, 8; 2 Aug. 1889, 3; 30 Sept. 1889, 3; 17 Oct. 1889, 8; 1 Jan. 1890, 13; 11 Aug. 1890, 5; 1 Jan. 1891, 5; 29 Jan. 1891, 5; 6 June 1891, 12. The Butler Block was also for a time the location of the Seattle City Hall; see: *P.I.*, 21 Oct. 1890, 7.

Parkinson and Evers "signed" the building to indicate their authorship. Their names can be found carved into the stone at the northeast corner of the surviving first floor facade (the north corner on Second Avenue).

84. *Washington Magazine* 1/4 (Dec. 1889): 26.

85. Even with this early success, Parkinson and Evers received few other commercial commissions. Their Epler Block (1889–90, destroyed), located on the west side of Second between Columbia and Marion, was announced in October. This four-story brick and stone office block filled a single 60-foot-wide mid-block lot. See: *P.I.*, 12 Oct. 1889, 5. Their other works in 1889 were primarily suburban commercial and residential projects; for these, see: chapter 6.

86. *P.I.*, 2 Apr. 1890, 8; 3 Apr. 1890, 7.

87. For example, Ballard commissioned at least one building to Fisher; see: *P.I.*, 23 Feb. 1890, 8.

88. For Seattle National Bank, see: *P.I.*, 23 Apr. 1890, 6; 30 Apr. 1890, 8; 28 July 1890, 5; 11 Aug. 1890, 5; 15 Aug, 1890, 8; 5 Sept. 1890, 12; 16 Oct. 1890, 12; 1 Jan. 1891, 5; 6 June 1891, 12; 8 Sept. 1891, 8.

89. *P.I.*, 30 Apr. 1890, 8.

90. For publication of the Seattle National Bank, in architectural journals, see *AABN* 29 (5 July 1890) and *IA* 23/2 (Mar. 1894). The perspective that appeared in *AABN* was also published, along with a description of the building, in *NREBR* 1/1 (Feb. 1891): 7–8.

Parkinson also "signed" this building; his name is inscribed in the red sandstone at the northeast corner of the building (facing the alley).

91. Saunders and Houghton received new commissions elsewhere, but their downtown Seattle commercial work in 1890 was limited to projects already under way.

92. For Marshall-Walker Building, see: *P.I.*, 16 May 1890, 12; 28 July 1890, 5; 11 Aug. 1890, 5; 16 Oct. 1890, 12; 1 Jan. 1891, 5; 6 June 1891, 12.

The primary investor in the Marshall-Walker Building was Cyrus Walker (1827–1913), a leading Puget Sound lumberman. As head of the Puget Mill Company, Walker preferred to live in Port Ludlow, but he profited handsomely from his Seattle real estate investments.

93. In April 1890 Boone also received the commission for the Post-Edwards Block, on Front Street, between University and Union. See: *P.I.*, 3 Apr. 1890, 5.

94. *P.I.*, 30 May 1890, 12; 28 June 1890, 12.

95. For Bank of Commerce construction history, see: *P.I.*, 28 July 1890, 5; 11 Aug. 1890, 5; 13 Sept. 1890, 5; 1 Jan. 1891, 5; 6 June 1891, 12. *NREBR* 1/2 (Mar.–Apr. 1891): 16.

96. *NREBR* 1/2 (Mar.–Apr. 1891): 16. The stone was identified as "Colorado red sandstone" in *P.I.*, 11 Aug. 1890, 5; it was changed to "Salt Lake red sandstone" in *P.I.*, 13 Sept. 1890, 5.

97. *Pacific Mason* 2/6 (June 1896), facing page 164. In addition, the Minnesota-based *Northwest Magazine*'s February 1891 issue on Seattle included a drawing of the city's central square in which the partially visible Yesler Building is shown completed

in accordance with Fisher's design. Other than the rustic stone first floor, the most notable features of the design are two rusticated stone columns which mirror those on the Pioneer Building across the park. See: *Northwest Magazine* 9/2 (Feb. 1891): 17. When the construction above the first floor resumed in 1892, it did not match Fisher's projected design (as discussed later in this chapter).

98. For the early history of the Yesler building, see: *P.I.*, 11 Aug. 1890, 5; 13 Sept. 1890, 5; 1 Jan. 1891, 5; 6 June 1891, 12; 24 Apr. 1892, 7; *NREBR* 1/1 (Feb. 1891): 11; 1/2 (Mar.–Apr. 1891): 16.

99. For State Building, see: *P.I.*, 28 June 1890, 12; 11 Aug. 1890, 5; 13 Sept. 1890, 5; 1 Jan. 1891, 5; 6 June 1891, 12; *NREBR* 1/2 (Mar.–Apr. 1891): 16; *Trade Register* 1/3 (15 Feb. 1893): 1.

100. *IA* 13/4 (April 1889).

101. *NREBR* 1/3 (May 1891): 8.

102. *P.I.*, 9 Oct. 1889, 8, 10 Oct. 1889, 4.

103. *P.I.*, 5 Dec. 1889, 8. The Seattle Operahouse Company was the first of three corporations that were created in sequence to try to build the Opera House. It was followed by the Seattle Building Company, incorporated 2 June 1890, and the Seattle Finance and Building Company, incorporated 3 November 1891, each for the specific purpose of building the Opera House. Therefore, Adler and Sullivan's client was actually the Seattle Building Company.

A pledge list for the initial corporation found in the Burke Papers includes pledges of $80,000, but a note on the binder indicates that the stock was never issued. Articles of incorporation for the two successor corporations are also found in the Burke Papers. Box 48–7, Burke Papers.

104. Burke, Bailey, Leary, and Ewing have been identified previously. Amos Brown (1833–1899) was born in New Hampshire and worked in lumber camps from age ten. He first came to Seattle in 1863, returned in 1867, and engaged in the lumber business alone or in various partnerships until his retirement in the mid-1890s. When the second corporation, the Seattle Building Company, was formed in June 1890, Ewing dropped out and was replaced as trustee by William Ballard.

105. *P.I.*, 25 May 1890, 5. This report may have been prompted by the actions of a rival group, headed by L. H. Griffith Realty and Banking Company, who had begun promoting their own opera house project and who proposed as designer Chicago architect J. M. Wood, who had designed theaters in cities across the West, including Denver, San Francisco, Portland, and Tacoma. *P.I.*, 24 May 1890, 5; 28 May 1890, 12.

106. *P.I.*, 19 June 1890, 2. Financial statements in the Burke Papers indicate that the cost of civil engineering and grading totaled $2322.70. Burke to Brown, 1 Aug. 1890, Box 48–7, Burke Papers.

107. "Seattle is to have a new Opera House, the cost of which including the site for same will be not quite $300,000. Competition will be advertised for, so that all architects of the country will have a chance. The promoters of this enterprise are Thomas Ewing, John Leary and others." *California Architect and Building News* 15 (15 Nov. 1889): 146. *Northwestern Architect* also carried a notice regarding the project: "The Seattle opera house company has filled [*sic*] articles of incorporation. The opera house is to be constructed at the corner of 3rd [in fact 2nd] and University streets, work will soon be commenced and pushed rapidly forward. The building when completed will be one of the finest in the West." *Northwestern Architect* 7/12 (Dec. 1889), Advertisers Trade Supplement.

108. The opening of the Chicago Auditorium was extensively reported in Seattle the next day. *P.I.*, 10 Dec. 1889, 2.

109. For the Pueblo Opera House, see: Lloyd C. Engelbrecht, "Adler & Sullivan's Pueblo Opera House: City Status for a New Town in the Rockies," *Art Bulletin* 67 (June 1985): 277–295; for Adler and Sullivan's work in the West, see: Robert Twombly, "Beyond Chicago: Louis Sullivan in the American West," *Pacific Historical Review* 54 (Nov.

1985): 405–438. The Pueblo Opera House commission was specifically cited as the connection for the Seattle project in Hugh Morrison, *Louis Sullivan: Prophet of Modern Architecture* (New York: Museum of Modern Art and W. W. Norton and Co., 1935).

110. *Spokesman-Review*, 3 Aug. 1890, 5; Sullivan to Burke, 3 Aug. 1890, Box 15–84, Burke Papers.

111. *P.I.*, 5 Aug. 1890, 3; 6 Aug. 1890, 8; 7 Aug. 1890, 8; 8 Aug. 1890, 8.

112. *P.I.*, 9 Aug. 1890, 5.

113. *Telegraph*, 16 Aug. 1890, 5. The actual site was the northeast corner of the intersection of Second and University, not the southeast corner.

114. Sullivan to Burke, 28 Aug. 1890, Box 15–84. Apparently the Seattle Building Company had considered acquiring the entire half-block facing Second Street. However, Burke's letter indicated that the decision had been made to acquire only three lots. Burke to Adler and Sullivan, 1 Sept. 1890, Box 20, letterpress book 3, 97, Burke Papers. A receipt signed by Bailey indicates that Burke contributed $6,120 on 3 Sept. 1890 as his share of the amount due on one of the parcels the Seattle Building Company was acquiring. Seattle Building Co. to Burke, 3 Sept. 1890, Box 48–7, Burke Papers.

115. Adler and Sullivan, letter to Burke, quoted in: *Telegraph*, 14 Sept. 1890, 6.

116. The Northwest Architectural Archives, University of Minnesota Libraries, collection includes five ink on linen drawings which are bound in one set. The cover sheet reads:

SEATTLE OPERA HOUSE BUILDING, SEATTLE, WN. ADLER AND SULLIVAN ARCHITECTS CHICAGO. PLANS MADE IN 1890. NEVER BUILT BECAUSE OF FINANCIAL DIFFICULTIES. SET OF FIVE LINEN TRACINGS. THESE TRACINGS FROM THE RECORDS OF PURCELL AND ELMSLIE, ARCHITECTS IN MINNEAPOLIS AND CHICAGO, 1910–1922 ARE DEDICATED TO THE ART DEPARTMENT OF THE UNIVERSITY OF MINNESOTA AS A CONTRIBUTION TO THEIR 'LOUIS HENRI SULLIVAN' DOCUMENTS. BY: WILLIAM GRAY PURCELL, A.I.A. PASADENA, CALIFORNIA APRIL 1953.

The first four sheets are plans scaled at 1/16" to 1'-0" for the first, second, fourth, and sixth floors. They measure approximately 13" by 18". The final sheet is a longitudinal section drawn at the same scale and measuring approximately 15" by 18".

117. Charles H. Bebb was born in Surrey, 10 Apr. 1858. He was educated at King's College, London, and at preparatory schools in Switzerland, before attending the University of Lausanne. He furthered his education at the School of Mines in London, then spent five years in South Africa with the engineering department of the Cape government railroad. He returned to England in the mid-1880s and then went to Chicago, intending to work for the Illinois Central Railroad. Instead, he remained in Chicago and joined the Illinois Terra Cotta Lumber Company as a construction engineer involved in the development of fireproofing systems for buildings. In 1888, this company received the fireproofing contract for Adler and Sullivan's Chicago Auditorium. Near the end of construction, he was hired by Adler and Sullivan as a superintending architect for their office. A brief notice of Bebb's joining Adler and Sullivan as a superintendent appeared in *IA* 16 (July 1890): 91. Bebb's article, "Fire Losses in Fire-Proof Buildings," appeared in *Engineering Magazine* 4 (Feb. 1893): 731–743.

118. *Telegraph*, 12 Oct. 1890, 3

119. The failure of Baring Brothers and Company, the great British financial house, precipitated the Panic of 1890, a brief recession, which has been largely overshadowed by the much more severe Panic of 1893. Owing to a crisis in Argentine finance that limited the salability of South American securities, British financiers began selling off American railroad stocks and bonds and other negotiable securities to raise funds, resulting in a general outflow of gold from the United States and a decline in the value of American securities. Combined with the continuing demand for money in the growing central and western states, where substantial new construction had been

under way, this outflow eventually caused a severe tightening of the American money market. By fall 1890, interest rates had risen to extraordinary levels (at times credit was virtually suspended) and the announcement of the Baring failure in November shattered confidence and led to a further decline in stock prices. Many businesses were driven into bankruptcy.

Construction of the Seattle Opera House foundation was started without full project financing in place. In a memorandum copied in his letterpress book (undated, but immediately preceding the 4 Nov. letter to Adler and Sullivan), Burke valued the land and the building together at $450,000 and indicated the need to seek a loan for $250,000. Burke memorandum, n.d., Box 20, letterpress book 3, 116, Burke Papers. The loss of confidence after the failure of Baring Brothers, combined with the economic stringency that had already been developing, must have made it impossible to obtain financing. A subsequent Burke letter indicates he was was still seeking financing in spring 1891. Burke to A.L. Parker, 4 Apr. 1891, Box 20 letterpress book 3, 244–245, Burke Papers. By 1891, Seattle's boom had leveled off. Seattle had less share in the improved economy of late 1891 than cities farther east since it did not benefit directly from the improved harvest or from the movement of grain exports to Europe. That the failure of Baring Brothers caused the demise of the Seattle Opera House project is also noted in Bebb's short biography in Clarence Bagley, *History of Seattle*, 3: 117.

120. In mid-December, Burke wrote a letter of introduction to the mayor of Fairhaven (now part of Bellingham) for Charles Bebb. Fairhaven was evidently considering building an opera house, and Bebb was traveling there to make inquiries. Burke to E.A. Turner, 13 Dec. 1890, Box 20, letterpress book 3, 150, Burke Papers.

121. According to Eileen Michels, the typical lag between submittal of drawings and publication in the architectural press at this time was from two to six months. Michels, "Late-Nineteenth-Century Perspective Drawing," 293. Thus, Adler and Sullivan most likely submitted the drawings for publication in October as soon as the design was complete and construction appeared imminent.

In addition to the perspective view of the project, *Inland Architect* published presentation plans for the second, fourth, and sixth floors. These plans are nearly identical to those found in the Northwest Archives (see: note 116); the only difference is that the published plans were more neatly drafted and the dimension strings omitted. No other drawings for the project have been discovered. A drawing tentatively identified by Paul Sprague as a study for the Seattle Opera House has since been identified as the proscenium with drop curtain of the Pueblo Opera House. See Paul E. Sprague, *The Drawings of Louis Henry Sullivan: A Catalogue of the Frank Lloyd Wright Collection at the Avery Architectural Library* (Princeton: Princeton University Press, 1979), 9, 38; and Lloyd Englebrecht, "Adler and Sullivan's Pueblo Opera House," 287, 290.

122. Burke to Adler and Sullivan, 4 Nov. 1890, 16 Apr. 1891, 27 Apr. 1891, 8 May 1891, Box 20, letterpress book 3, 117, 256, 271, 276, Burke Papers. See also: "Seattle Building Company in Account with Thomas Burke," 7 Nov. 1891, Box 20, letterpress book 3, 489, Burke Papers.

123. Charles Bebb to Burke, 30 Mar. 1892, Box 2–1, Burke Papers. Unfortunately, by late August 1892, all hope of building the Opera House was abandoned. The site was sold and the project came to an end. Indentures of Sale by Seattle Finance and Building Company, 26 Aug. 1892, Box 48–7, Burke Papers. However, Charles Bebb did eventually return to Seattle (as discussed in chapter 8).

124. Morrison, *Louis Sullivan*, 118, Frank Lloyd Wright used the phrase "office tragedies" in his autobiography in reference to Adler and Sullivan's Ontario Hotel project in Salt Lake City; Morrison used the phrase in reference to the Seattle Opera House.

125. *P.I.*, 2 Apr. 1891, 5.

126. *P.I.*, 20 Mar. 1892, 8.

127. *P.I.*, 9 Jan. 1893, 8. The values of construction annually were listed as follows: 1889: $5,789,000; 1890: $4,311,000; 1891: $1,815,000; 1892: $1,373,000.

128. *NREBR* 1/3 (May 1891): 8.

129. For Fisher's investment in the steam plant see: *P.I.*, 24 Nov. 1889, 8; for the Abbott Hotel (also called the Fisher Block), see: *P.I.*, 11 Aug. 1889, 8; 1 Jan. 1890, 13; 6 June 1890, 8; *NREBR* 1/2 (Mar.–Apr. 1891): 16; for the Fisher Building, see: *P.I.*, 1 Apr. 1890, 5; 6 June 1890, 8. Fisher did subsequently design a residence for himself; see: *P.I.*, 12 Dec. 1892, 8.

130. DeNeuf's first project for Yesler was construction of the four-story Fischer and McDonald Wholesale Store (1892), at the corner of Yesler and Post Avenue. Elmer Fisher had done a design for the Feurer Building for this site in 1889, but it had not gone forward. Whether DeNeuf redesigned the structure is unknown. Construction of the simply detailed narrow block of red brick with stone trim began in March and was completed by the end of June 1892, at a cost of $23,000. See: *P.I.*, 7 Nov. 1889, 8; 1 Jan. 1890, 19; 6 June 1890, 8; 4 Mar. 1892, 5; 2 May 1892, 5; 22 May 1892, 5; 12 June 1892, 7; 27 June 1892, 8; *Trade Register* 1/8 (1 May 1893), 1.

131. For Yesler Building, see: *P.I.*, 24 Apr. 1892, 7; 9 May 1892, 8; 30 May 1892, 5; 12 June 1892, 7; 1 Aug. 1892, 5; 29 Aug. 1892, 8; 5 Sept. 1892, 5; 27 Feb. 1893, 5; 31 July 1893, 6; 11 Sept.1893, 8; for purchase by Mutual Life Insurance Company, see: *P.I.*, 1 May 1895, 8.

132. After 1900, the Mutual Life Building was enlarged by an addition on its west side facing Yesler. Architects Robertson and Blackwell, who were responsible for the addition, also redesigned the cornice of the older building, creating its present horizontal appearance.

133. DeNeuf may also have been responsible for a three-story commercial block for Yesler on the nearly triangular site at the southwest corner of Yesler and South Third (now South Second). Although this site once belonged to H. K. Owens, he later traded it to Yesler for the trapezoidal parcel immediately to the south. Yesler's building, now called the Metropole Building, was constructed on the triangular site in 1892–93, and was often included in the *P.I.* reports that described the buildings by DeNeuf for Yesler; see: *P.I.*, 2 May 1892, 5; 9 May 1892, 8; 12 June 1892, 7; 4 July 1892, 5; 25 July 1892, 5; 1 Aug. 1892, 5; 29 Aug. 1892, 8; 17 Dec. 1892, 8.

134. For Lowman and Hanford Building, see: *P.I.*, 9 May 1892, 8; 12 June 1892, 7; 4 July 1892, 5; 25 July 1892, 5; 29 Aug. 1892, 8.

135. For the Schwabacher fire, see: *P.I.*, 28 June 1892, 8; for the reconstruction see: *P.I.*, 24 Feb. 1893, 5; 27 Feb. 1893, 5; 13 Mar. 1893, 5; 27 Mar. 1893, 5; 3 Apr. 1893, 7; 17 July 1893, 6.

136. For the "notice of dissolution" of the partnership (dated 12 Sept. 1891), see: *P.I.*, 17 Sept. 1891, 6. This notice ran in the paper for five days. Thereafter, "Saunders and Houghton" continued to be listed in the paper until 30 Dec. 1891; Houghton's first individual listing appeared 7 Jan. 1892.

137. *P.I.*, 30 June 1892, 5. According to the article, Houghton sued for unpaid fees of $5,558. From 1 May 1889 to 1 June 1891 the value of services was indicated as $16,588.33 of which only $9,030.33 had been paid. (There is a $1,000 error in the reported figures.)

138. By January 1891, evidence suggests that there was much less confidence in the ability of Burke's group, the Seattle Building Company, to proceed with the Seattle Operahouse project by Adler and Sullivan. On 10 Jan. 1891, the *P.I.* reported that the rival opera house group (led by L.H. Griffith Realty and Banking Company, see: note 105), that had apparently been dormant since May 1890, had formed a stock company, by the name of the Seattle Grand Operahouse Company, with a capital stock of $200,000. This group claimed that it had options on four potential sites and was prepared to start

construction within a few weeks with completion due in six months. The group actually leased a site in April 1891 at Third Street and Cherry Street. The Seattle Theater by Charles Saunders was built on this site. *P.I.*, 10 Jan. 1891, 5; 18 Jan. 1891, 10; 30 Jan. 1891, 5; 11 Apr. 1891, 5.

139. For Seattle Theater and Rainier Club, see: *P.I.*, 12 Apr. 1892, 8; 22 May 1892, 5; 6 June 1892, 8; 4 July 1892, 5; 11 July 1892, 8; 25 July 1892, 5; 29 Aug. 1892, 8; 19 Sept. 1892, 8; 24 Oct. 1892, 5; 18 Nov. 1892, 5; 5 Dec. 1892, 8; 6 Dec. 1892, 8. It should be noted that this building was exclusively the work of Charles Saunders not the Saunders and Houghton partnership that had dissolved. Subsequently Houghton would become one of the leading theater designers in the Northwest, but available evidence indicates that he had no role in the Seattle Theater and Rainier Club.

140. *P.I.*, 17 Dec. 1890, 6.

141. Background information on William H. Willcox is scattered. Primary sources are city directories in the various cities in which he worked. The 58-page booklet Willcox published in 1884, *Hints to Those Who Propose to Build—Also a Description of Improved Plans for the Construction of Churches* (St. Paul: Pioneer Press, 1884), included a list of his most important projects to that date. A copy is available at the Minnesota Historical Society in St. Paul. Clarence Johnston (1859–1936), with whom Willcox formed a partnership in 1886, later became a leading architect in Minneapolis/St. Paul. While Willcox and Johnston apparently never received commercial commissions, they did design a series of picturesque Romanesque Revival row houses and residences in St. Paul's Summit Avenue neighborhood, including the brick and stone Laurel Terrace row houses (illustrated in chapter 4).

142. *Northwest Magazine* 9/2 (Feb. 1891): 25.

143. For Plymouth Congregational Church, see: chapter 6.

144. For the Yesler/Baxter opera house project, see: *P.I.*, 28 May 1891, 8; 29 May 1891, 8; 16 July 1891, 5; 31 July 1891, 5; 8 Sept. 1891, 8; Baxter/Sanders: 28 Aug. 1892, 8; 11 Sept. 1892, 5; *Times*, 26 June 1891, 6.

145. For Walker Building, see: *P.I.*, 16 July 1891, 8; 8 Sept. 1891, 8; 2 Apr. 1892, 5. Although the April 1892 newspaper article described the building as four stories, only the basement and first story were actually constructed. (Thanks to Tim O'Brien for assistance in verifying that this was never built above the first story.)

146. For Frink Building, see: *P.I.*, 8 Sept. 1891, 8; 2 Apr. 1892, 5; 24 Apr. 1892, 5; 2 May 1892, 5; 24 Mar. 1895, 5. Two additional stories, designed by Blackwell and Baker, were added in 1912; the art deco stonework at the ground floor was added in the 1920s.

147. For J. G. Kenyon's block on the west side of Front at Madison, see: *P.I.*, 6 June 1892, 8; 25 July 1892, 5; 29 Aug. 1892, 8; 10 Oct. 1892, 8; 23 Dec. 1892, 8. For Kenyon's block on the east side of Front at Seneca, see: *P.I.*, 18 July 1892, 8; 29 Aug. 1892, 8; 10 Oct. 1892, 8; 31 Oct. 1892, 3; 23 Dec. 1892, 8; 3 Apr. 1893, 7; 31 July 1893, 6.

J. Gardner Kenyon (1834–1892), Parkinson's client, came to the Pacific Coast between 1852 and 1856, and after a short stint in mining, made his living for ten years performing as a ventriloquist. In the late 1860s, he used his savings to acquire timber land in Humboldt County, California, and after 1870 he lived in western Washington, investing in property in Port Townsend and Seattle in addition to his California holdings.

148. *P.I.*, 3 Nov. 1892, 5; 4 Nov. 1892, 8.

149. For the founding of the Seattle Athletic Club, see: *P.I.*, 18 Apr. 1890, 5. For construction of the Seattle Athletic Club building, see: *P.I.*, 4 Nov. 1892, 8; 19 Dec. 1892, 8; 2 Jan. 1893, 5; 12 June 1893, 5; 17 July 1893, 5; 31 July 1893, 3; 4 Aug. 1893, 9. For a description of their facilities, see: *P.I.*, 4 Nov. 1892, 8; 4 Aug. 1893, 9.

150. For Dobson and Denton Building, see: *P.I.*, 24 Feb. 1893, 5; 27 Feb. 1893, 5;

6 Mar. 1893, 5; 20 Mar. 1893, 8; 12 June 1893, 5; 2 Oct. 1893, 8. For the Gilmore and Kirkman Building/Arlington Hotel by Elmer Fisher, see chapter 2.

151. Little is known about Albert Wickersham's background. He arrived in Seattle from Portland, Oregon, in 1889, to serve as superintending architect for the Denny Hotel designed by A. B. Jennings. When that project was delayed, he may have provided services to other architects; for example, his name is found on correspondence in connection with terra-cotta for the Terry-Denny Building by Saunders and Houghton (see: note 76). At some point in 1892, with the Denny Hotel indefinitely delayed, Wickersham began seeking projects under his own name.

152. *P.I.*, 2 May 1892, 19 Sept. 1892, 8. About 1906, the Dexter Horton Bank was renamed the Maynard Building, the name by which it is known today.

153. Sally B. Woodbridge and Roger Montgomery, *A Guide to Architecture in Washington State* (Seattle and London: University of Washington Press, 1980), 113.

154. For background on Arthur B. Chamberlin, see: Jeffrey Karl Ochsner, "A. B. Chamberlin: The Illustration of Seattle Architecture, 1890–1896," *PNQ* 81/4 (Oct. 1990), 130–144.

155. For Collins Building, see: *P.I.*, 8 May 1893, 5; 12 June 1893, 5; 2 Oct. 1893, 8; 23 Oct. 1893, 8; 7 May 1894, 8. For the decision by the library to lease space in the Collins Building, see: *P.I.*, 8 May 1893, 5; 16 Dec. 1893, 5; 31 Dec. 1893, 5; 7 May 1894, 8.

156. For background on Skillings, see: *P.I.*, 17 Apr. 1892, 8. For the California Block (1889–90, destroyed), by San Francisco architects Copeland and Pierce, see: *P.I.*, 25 Oct. 1889, 8. Prior to 1892, Skillings's projects had also included a few smaller business blocks (McDougal & Southwick Building, Harrington & Smith Building), plus several single family residences.

157. For the Dearborn Building at 311 South Third Street, see: *P.I.*, 25 Sept. 1891, 4; 20 Dec. 1891, 8. Thanks to Paul Dorpat for this information.

158. For Skillings's Washington State Building, see: chapter 7. Also see: Jeffrey Karl Ochsner, "In Search of Regional Expression: The Washington State Building at the World's Columbian Exposition, Chicago, 1893," *PNQ* 86/4 (Fall 1995): 165–177.

159 James N. Corner was born and raised in Boston. He was the co-author, with E. E. Soderholtz, of *Examples of Domestic Colonial Architecture in New England* (1891) and *Examples of Colonial Architecture in Maryland and Virginia* (1892) (both later reissued without Corner's name).

160. *P.I.*, 16 Jan. 1893, 8. A total of 65 design submittals were received in the British Columbia Parliament competition. Skillings and Corner were among the five finalists.

161. *P.I.*, 16 Jan. 1893, 8.

162. For the Coal, Lumber and Mineral Palace, see: *P.I.*, 27 Feb. 1893, 5; 9 Apr. 1893, 8; 13 June 1893, 8; 28 June 1893, 8; 4 July 1893, 8.

163. For Union Trust Block, see: *P.I.*, 13 Mar. 1893, 5; 17 Apr. 1893, 5; 8 May 1893, 5; 12 June 1893, 5; 17 July 1893, 6; 28 Aug. 1893, 8; 11 Sept. 1893, 8; 2 Oct. 1893, 8.

164. For Rialto, see: *P.I.*, 7 June 1893, 5; 12 June 1893, 5; 17 June 1893, 6; 28 Aug. 1893, 8; 11 Sept. 1893, 8; 25 Sept. 1893, 5; 2 Oct. 1893, 8; 16 Oct. 1893, 8; 19 Nov. 1893, 8; 6 Mar. 1894, 3. In the early twentieth century, the Rialto would become the site of the Frederick and Nelson Department Store and was often called the Frederick and Nelson Building.

165. For Leary-Walker store building, see: *P.I.*, 9 Apr., 1893, 7; 8 May 1893, 5; 15 May 1893, 5; 12 June 1893, 5; 17 July 1893, 6; 28 Aug. 1893, 8; 11 Sept. 1893, 8.

166. *P.I.*, 26 July 1889, 4.

167. *P.I.*, 19 Mar. 1893, 5.

168. *P.I.*, 17 Apr. 1893, 5.

169. *P.I.,* 9 Apr. 1893, 8.

170. *P.I.,* 10 May 1893, 2; 12 May 1893, 3; 13 May 1893, 3; 14 May 1893, 7; 16 May 1893, 2; 17 May 1893, 2.

171. *P.I.,* 18 June 1893, 3; 29 July 1893, 8.

172. *P.I.,* 17 July 1893, 6.

VI. A City of Neighborhoods:
The Network of Public Institutions, 1889–1895

1. Population figures for the early 1890s are from *P.I.,* 22 Sept. 1892, 8.

2. For background information on proposals for a park and parkways system by Seattle Parks Superintendent E. O. Schwagerl, see: David A. Rash, "Edward Otto Schwagerl," *Shaping Seattle Architecture,* 52–57, 307; also see: William H. Wilson, *The City Beautiful Movement* (Baltimore and London: Johns Hopkins University Press, 1989), 147–150. (This book erroneously identifies Schwagerl's first name as "Eugene" and includes a few other minor errors of fact.)

3. Marianna Griswold Van Rensselaer, "Recent Architecture in America, IV— City Dwellings II," *Century Magazine* 31/5 (Mar. 1886): 681.

4. For the general history of fire departments, see: Rebecca Zurier, *The American Firehouse: An Architectural and Social History* (New York: Abbeville, 1982).

5. For the early history of the Seattle fire department, see: *Twentieth Century Souvenir of the Fire Department of Seattle* (Seattle: Seattle Fire Department Relief Association, 1901). Also see: Warren, *Day Seattle Burned,* 4–12, 58–66. For an overview of the department's history, including its buildings, see: *Seattle Fire Department Centennial Commemorative, 1889–1989* (Seattle: Taylor Publishing, 1989).

6. *P.I.,* 12 Oct. 1889, 5.

7. *P.I.,* 29 Oct. 1889, 8.

8. For a brief history of fire stations, see: Rebecca Zurier, "Firehouses," in *Built in the U.S.A.: American Buildings from Airports to Zoos,* edited by Diane Maddex (Washington, D.C.: Preservation Press, 1985), 78–81; and Zurier, *American Firehouse.*

9. *P.I.,* 29 Oct. 1889, 8; 31 Oct. 1889, 5.

10. *P.I.,* 21 Nov. 1889, 6.

11. For the construction history of the Headquarters Building, see: *P.I.,* 26 Nov. 1889, 8; 4 Dec. 1889, 5; 25 Feb. 1890, 5; 19 Apr. 1890, 8; 24 Aug. 1890, 8; 16 Oct. 1890, 12; for a complete description of the design see: *P.I.,* 5 Dec. 1889, 5. Also see: *Seattle Fire Department Centennial Commemorative,* 70.

12. For the construction history of Engine House Number 2, see: *P.I.,* 26 Nov. 1889, 8; 4 Dec. 1889, 5; 5 Dec. 1889, 5, 25 Feb. 1890, 5; 19 Apr. 1890, 8; 13 July 1890, 5; 20 July 1890, 16; 9 Aug. 1890, 8. Also see: *Seattle Fire Department Centennial Commemorative,* 71.

13. For the construction history of Engine House Number 4, see: *P.I.,* 26 Nov. 1889, 8; 4 Dec. 1889, 5; 5 Dec. 1889, 5; 25 Feb. 1890, 5; 19 Apr. 1890, 8; 9 July 1890, 6. Also see: *Seattle Fire Department Centennial Commemorative,* 72–73.

14. For the construction history of Chemical Engine House Number 2, see: *P.I.,* 26 Nov. 1889, 8; 4 Dec. 1889, 5; 5 Dec. 1889, 5; 25 Feb. 1890, 5; 19 Apr. 1890, 8; 14 Aug. 1890, 12; 30 Sept. 1890, 3; 11 Oct. 1890, 12. Also see: *Seattle Fire Department Centennial Commemorative,* 79.

15. Charles A. Alexander was an architect who had come from Minneapolis, arriving in Seattle in 1889. He served as supervising architect for Trinity Episcopal Church (discussed later in this chapter) and designed several residences, but had only limited success in Seattle and left the city before 1898. For the construction history of Engine House Number 3, see: *P.I.,* 26 Nov. 1889, 8; 4 Dec. 1889, 5; 5 Dec. 1889, 5; 25 Feb. 1890, 5; 20 Mar. 1890, 5, 21; 14 Aug. 1890, 12; 23 Aug. 1890, 8. Also see: *Seattle Fire Department Centennial Commemorative,* 72.

16. *P.I.*, 10 Jan. 1891, 12; 3 Jan. 1894, 8; 21 June 1894, 8. Also see: *Seattle Fire Department Centennial Commemorative*, 74, 75.

17. It was the interior of Engine House Number 6 that served as the setting in 1916 for "live action" photos of fire company activity. See: Figs. 6.3, 6.4.

18. To extend protection to Queen Anne, a small chemical engine company was housed in Chemical Engine House Number 3 at Lee Street and First West. See: *Seattle Fire Department Centennial Commemorative*, 75; also see: *Twentieth Century Souvenir*, 175.

19. Fred E. H. Schroeder, "Schoolhouses," in *Built in the U.S.A.*, 150–153; Sherry B. Ahrentzen, "Elementary Education Facilities," in *Encyclopedia of Architecture, Design, Engineering & Construction* (New York: John Wiley & Sons, 1988), II: 331–337; and Andrew Gulliford, *America's Country Schools* (Washington, D.C.: Preservation Press, 1984).

20. Design problems associated with school buildings were occasionally addressed in the professional architectural press after this period. See, for example: William Paul Gerhard, "Essentials of School Sanitation," *AABN* 87 (3 June 1905), 177–179; (10 June 1905), 183–185; Frank Irving Cooper, "The Planning of School Houses," *American Architect* 96 (17 Nov. 1909), 189–195; Rawson W. Haddon, "Modern American Schoolhouses: Some Recent Examples of Specialized Buildings, Guibert & Betelle, Architects," *Architectural Record* 36 (Sept. 1914), 244–263; Rawson W. Haddon, "Recent Schoolhouses Planned with Reference to the New Educational Facilities," *Architectural Record* 36 (Dec. 1914), 511–523.

21. For the relationship between Seattle's schools and neighborhoods, see: Bryce E. Nelson, *Good Schools: The Seattle Public School System, 1901–1930* (Seattle and London: University of Washington Press, 1988), 3–4, 16–22. However, Nelson argues that the school/neighborhood pattern dates from the years after 1900, a viewpoint that this chapter disputes.

22. There has been only limited research and writing on the history of the Seattle School District and even less on the history of the school buildings. For the early history of the district, see: Frederick Merick Lash, "An Historical and Functional Study of Public Education in Seattle, Washington" (Ph.D. diss., University of Washington, 1934); and Otto Wayne Bardarson, "A History of Elementary and Secondary Education in Seattle" (Ph.D. diss., University of Washington, 1928).

In the 1980s the Seattle School District commissioned the Historic Seattle Preservation and Development Authority to develop a detailed historical survey of its existing schools. This appeared as *Seattle Public Schools: Historic Building Survey* (Seattle: Historic Seattle Preservation and Development Authority, 1990). This important document provides a detailed building-by-building survey of the buildings erected before 1940 still remaining in the ownership of the district and serves as a critical document to support the preservation of these buildings. The report also contains an overview history covering the pre-1900 period from which few buildings survive. Unfortunately, it appears that this report relied on a previous school summary from the 1950s in reference to the pre-1900 period, so that errors in the earlier document are sometimes repeated.

23. For the early buildings of the Seattle school system dating from the early 1880s, see chapter 2. For a more detailed history of school development and construction in this period with a greater emphasis on policy and funding issues, see: Jeffrey Karl Ochsner and Dennis Alan Andersen, "Architecture for Seattle Schools, 1880–1900," *PNQ* 83/4 (Oct. 1992): 128–143.

24. For a description of the Central School fire, see: *P.I.* 11 Apr. 1888, 3. The "Minutes" list six firms submitting designs for South School, T.G. Bird, J. Cash, Hermann Steinmann, P. H. Donovan, Fisher and Clark, and Boone and Meeker; however, Bird and Cash must have been in partnership because only six sets of plans were received and Boone and Meeker submitted two designs. See: Seattle School Board Minutes, 1, 274 (2 Apr. 1888); *P.I.* 11 Apr. 1888, 2; 12 Apr. 1888, 3.

25. The bond issue of up to $120,000 and the question of materials were reported in *P.I.*, 13 Apr. 1888, 2, 3; 4 May 1888, 2, 3; 5 May 1888, 3; 10 Nov. 1888, 3; 11 Nov. 1888, 3. The bid authorization was noted in School Board Minutes, 1, 281 (7 May 1888); *P.I.*, 13 May 1888, 3.

26. While South School was apparently ready in February, it was later reported that the building did not open until September. See: *P.I.*, 2 Feb. 1889, 3; 18 Dec. 1889, 8. For the description of Central School see: *P.I.*, 15 Oct. 1889, 5.

27. *P.I.*, 20 Aug. 1889, 4. The day after the fall 1889 term commenced, two 60-seat classrooms for the lower grades at Denny and Central had 125 and 135 pupils. In fall 1888 the district had counted approximately 1700 students; on the first day of class in 1889 the number approached 2600, with several hundred more expected within a few weeks. *P.I.*, 4 Sept. 1889, 4. Temporary two-room buildings were also occasionally built as an expedient solution to overcrowding at existing schools. A list of all school facilities in use by the district appeared in *P.I.*, 18 Dec. 1889, 8.

28. *P.I.*, 10 Aug. 1889, 3; 17 Aug. 1889, 4. This report listed competitive design submittals from Hermann Steinmann, William Boone, Larkin and Smith, and Buchele and Hummel, yet in late August the design by Charles Saunders was accepted; see: School Board Minutes, 1, 411 (30 Aug. 1889).

29. For Saunders's designs, see *P.I.*, 14 Sept. 1889, 4.

30. *P.I.*, 19 Oct. 1889, 8. Contractors may have been too busy or materials too scarce in late 1889. In addition, contractors may have been concerned about receiving payment in school scrip.

31. Temporary two-room buildings were constructed at the Denny and South Schools and at the new sites in Queen Anne and on Madison in the Renton Addition. These cost about $500 each, see: *P.I.*, 26 Oct. 1889, 8; 9 Nov. 1889, 8; 16 Nov. 1889, 5; 22 Nov. 1889, 3; 11 Dec. 1889, 5; 7 Jan. 1890, 5; 28 Jan. 1890, 5.

32. School Board Minutes 2, 13 (25 Nov. 1889), 15 (2 Dec. 1889), 27 (30 Dec. 1889); *P.I.*, 11 Nov. 1889, 8; 28 Jan. 1890, 5.

33. *P.I.*, 2 Feb. 1890, 5; 11 Feb. 1890, 5; 18 Feb. 1890, 8; 25 Feb. 1890, 8; 4 Mar. 1890, 8; 18 Mar. 1890, 5; and School Board Minutes 2, 77 (28 Apr. 1890).

34. For school bond votes, see: *P.I.*, 28 Jan. 1890, 5; 4 Mar. 1890, 5; 22 Apr. 1890, 4; 3 June 1890, 6. For school construction, see: *P.I.*, 24 June 1890, 8; 11 July 1890, 5; 18 Aug. 1890, 8; 6 Sept. 1890, 5; 9 Sept. 1890, 12; 22 Jan. 1891, 5; also see: School Board Minutes 2, 100 (23 June 1890), 200 (21 Jan. 1891).

35. For Richardson the Romanesque mode was appropriate only to design in brick or stone. When Saunders applied the Romanesque to the wood frame Rainier School, the arched windows could only have been seen as appropriate if the Romanesque were understood as imagery applied to the surface and not integral to the material. However, this was not just a "provincial" response. Even Montgomery Schuyler once suggested that the Romanesque Revival might be applicable to all buildings, writing: "Romanesque architecture, in the Norman, German, and Provencal phases of it, constitutes an architectural language that is applicable to all our needs." Montgomery Schuyler, "Romanesque Revival in New York," 38. Just three months later he completely revised his opinion: "Romanesque is indeed not applicable to all our needs. . . . It is essentially and almost exclusively an architecture of stone-work. It furnishes no precedents for timber construction and very few for brick work." Schuyler, "Romanesque Revival in America," 197.

36. For school crowding, see: *P.I.*, 16 Sept. 1890, 5; 7 Oct. 1890, 5; 18 Oct. 1890, 8. For the financial problems of the School District see: *P.I.*, 22 Jan. 1891, 5.

37. *P.I.*, 16 Apr. 1891, 5; 23 Apr. 1891, 8; School Board Minutes 2, 217 (22 Apr. 1891).

38. School Board Minutes 2, 219, 220 (29 Apr. 1891); *P.I.*, 30 Apr. 1891, 8. For construction of these additions, see: *P.I.*, 5 May 1891, 5; 5 June 1891, 8.

39. Although Saunders and Houghton had received multiple school commissions

in 1889 and 1890, the partnership was never designated the exclusive schools architect, and the board occasionally gave work to other firms as well. See: Ochsner and Andersen, "Architecture for Seattle Schools," 136–137.

40. *P.I.*, 23 June 1891, 8; 9 July 1891, 5; 21 July 1891, 8; School Board Minutes 2, 262 (20 July 1891).

41. Plans were submitted for the Day School by Hermann Steinmann, Gleichman and Lane, T.G. Bird, J. B. Tarleton, C. H. Smith, Willis A. Ritchie, N. K. Aldrich, Boone and Willcox, Saunders and Houghton, Warren P. Skillings, and John Parkinson. See School Board Minutes 2, 264 (29 July 1891), 269 (12 Aug. 1891); also see: *P.I.*, 24 Sept. 1891, 8.

42. For Day School, see: *P.I.*, 24 Sept. 1891, 8; 9 Apr. 1892, 8; 5 May 1892, 5; 9 June 1892, 8.

43. In 1900, the district proceeded with the north wing of Day School. James Stephen, the architect of record, followed Parkinson's original design. When the enlargement took place it included Parkinson's central lobby space and east-facing arched entry.

44. For the bond issue, see *P.I.*, 28 Jan. 1892, 5; 11 Feb. 1892, 8; 6 Mar. 1892, 8; 7 Mar. 1892, 8. For sites acquisition, see: *P.I.*, 5 Apr. 1892, 8.

45. The monthly payment of 208.33\frac{1}{3}$ to the Seattle schools architect was calculated as follows: architect, $125.00; assistant, $50.00; rent and incidentals, $33.33–1/3; see: *P.I.*, 21 Apr. 1892, 5; see also: School Board Minutes 2, 340 (20 Apr. 1892), 343 (22 Apr. 1892), 345 (5 May 1892).

46. *P.I.*, 23 Apr. 1892, 5; 4 May 1892, 8.

47. *P.I.*, 23 Apr. 1892, 5; 6 May 1892, 5; 9 June 1892, 8; 12 June 1892, 5; see also: School Board Minutes 2, 343 (22 Apr. 1892), 345 (5 May 1892), 360 (11 June 1892). For Pacific School construction, see: *P.I.*, 1 Aug. 1892, 5; 23 Aug. 1892, 5; 15 Dec. 1892, 8; 18 Feb. 1893, 8; 4 Mar. 1893, 5; 6 Mar. 1893, 5; 9 Mar. 1893, 8; 19 Mar. 1893, 7.

48. Parkinson, *Incidents by the Way*, 145.

49. School Board Minutes 2, 403 (Sept. 29, 1892); *P.I.*, 30 Sept. 1892, 5; 13 Oct. 1892, 5. Crowding remained a problem: When the 1892 fall term began, enrollment was about 4350 pupils, but by January 1893 it was approaching 4700. See: *P.I.*, 13 Oct. 1892, 5; 11 Jan. 1893, 5.

50. School Board Minutes 2, 444 (31 Mar. 1893), 454 (20 Apr. 1893), 457 (12 May 1893), 458 (24 May 1893); *P.I.*, 1 Apr. 1893, 5; 21 Apr. 1893, 3.

51. *P.I.*, 13 May 1893, 5; 2 June 1893, 5; 15 June 1893. For Cascade School, see: *P.I.*, 2 Oct. 1893, 8; 16 Oct. 1893, 8; 23 Nov. 1893, 6; 2 Dec. 1893, 8; 6 Jan. 1894, 5; 11 Jan. 1894, 8.

52. Saunders and Lawton, the architects for the 1898 enlargement of Cascade School, generally followed Parkinson's original design when they added the central hipped-roof twelve-room portion. In 1904 the final six-room north wing, mirroring Parkinson's initial portion, created a symmetrical 24-room building fairly closely following the design originally conceived by Parkinson. As a result, although Saunders and Lawton are often cited as the architects of record, Parkinson should be credited as the designer of the Cascade School building. Not until all three portions were completed was a balanced composition produced.

53. Parkinson, *Incidents by the Way*, 146–152, 158.

54. Parkinson's Ballard Central School was later renamed Washington Irving School; see: *Times*, 26 June 1891, 6.

The South Seattle School was located at a site at Oregon and Sansome. Some students living in the southern portions of the Seattle School District also attended this school; see: *P.I.*, 10 Oct. 1892, 8; 1 Jan. 1893, 8.

Parkinson was also responsible for a school in the Duwamish School District, south of the South Seattle District, completed in October 1892; see: *P.I.*, 4 July 1892, 5; 10 Oct. 1892, 8.

55. Parkinson also made proposals for schools in the Queen Anne and Lake Union neighborhoods, but these were not carried out; see: School Board Minutes 2, 369 (22 June 1892); *P.I.*, 14 July 1892, 3; 10 Aug. 1893, 5; 14 Dec. 1893, 8. Parkinson designed an expansion to the school district office building at Central School and this was built; see: *P.I.* 12 Jan. 1893, 5; 27 July 1893, 8.

56. On 10 February 1894, voters rejected a new bond issue, leaving the district in a difficult financial position. See: *P.I.*, 11 Feb. 1894, 7; 12 Feb. 1894, 8; 15 Feb. 1894, 8. For Parkinson's resignation, see: School Board Minutes 3, 88 (14 Feb. 1894); *P.I.*, 15 Feb. 1894, 8.

57. In 1894, the board commissioned the firm Chamberlin and Siebrand to design an addition to the Minor School; see: School Board Minutes 3, 116 (20 July 1894), 120 (9 Aug. 1894); *P.I.*, 28 July 1894, 8; 9 Aug. 1894, 5; 26 Oct. 1894, 8; 13 Dec. 1894, 5. Chamberlin and Siebrand were commissioned to design the "temporary" two-room wood Denny-Fuhrman School (1894–95, altered) in the developing Eastlake neighborhood just east of Lake Union. Designed and bid in September and October, this was completed by early February 1895. See: *P.I.*, 13 Sept. 1894, 8; 11 Oct. 1894, 5; 8 Feb. 1895, 6; School Board Minutes 3, 174 (14 Feb. 1895). Amazingly, this survives in expanded form today as part of the Seward School, the oldest wood building still in use by the district.

58. For board discussions of cuts in teacher salaries and other retrenchments, see: *P.I.*, 12 Feb. 1894, 3; 1 Mar. 1894, 8; 12 Apr. 1894, 5; 10 May 1894, 8; 13 May 1894, 8; 21 Mar. 1896, 8; 8 May 1896, 8. On school district financial problems, see: *P.I.*, 16 Mar. 1895, 5; 23 Mar. 1895, 8; 24 Mar. 1895, 8; 2 Apr. 1895, 5; 10 Apr. 1895, 2; 21 Apr. 1895, 6; 25 Apr. 1895, 5; 26 Apr. 1895, 5; 27 Apr. 1895, 8; 28 Apr. 1895, 8; 2 May 1895, 5; 9 May 1895, 6.

59. Minutes of the Washington State Chapter of the American Institute of Architects, 7 Mar. 1895, 11 Apr. 1895, 9 May 1895, 14 May 1895, 17 May 1895. For early history of the chapter, see: *P.I.*, 16 Mar. 1894, 5; 13 May 1894, 8; 11 Jan. 1895, 8. (Thanks to Thomas Veith for this information.)

60. On Bebb and Bullard's meeting with the board, see: *P.I.* 13 Mar. 1895, 14.

61. The five firms submitting on the Queen Anne School were Skillings and Corner, Willcox and McQuaid, T. G. Bird, Charles A. Alexander, and A. B. Chamberlin. See: School Board Minutes 3, 240 (22 June 1895), 241 (24 June 1895).

62. Willcox and Chamberlin were expelled from the AIA chapter. Willcox claimed he had resigned from the AIA before he submitted his design. See: AIA Minutes, 13 June 1895, 3 July 1895; also see: *P.I.*, 1 July 1895, 8; 3 July 1895, 5.

63. On Queen Anne School construction, see: *P.I.*, 6 Aug. 1895, 5; 20 Aug. 1895, 8; 9 June 1896, 5.

64. Paul Venable Turner, *Campus: An American Planning Tradition* (New York: Architectural History Foundation; Cambridge, Mass. and London: MIT Press, 1984), 150.

65. For the early history of the University of Washington, see: Charles M. Gates, *The First Century at the University of Washington, 1861–1961* (Seattle: University of Washington, 1961), 3–45. For the original campus, see also Neal O. Hines, *Denny's Knoll: A History of the Metropolitan Tract of the University of Washington* (Seattle and London: University of Washington Press, 1980), 3–17; and Norman J. Johnston, *The Fountain and the Mountain: The University of Washington Campus, 1895–1995* (Woodinville, Wash.: Documentary Book Publishers; Seattle: University of Washington, 1995), 15–17.

For details of the period 1889–95, with a focus on the new campus, including policy and site selection issues not addressed here, see: Jeffrey Karl Ochsner, "The University that Never Was: The 1891 Boone and Willcox Plan for the University of Washington," *PNQ* 90/2 (Spring 1999): 59–67. Important sources for the history of the campus in this period are the *Annual Reports* of the Board of the University and reports and other documents in the Edmond S. Meany Papers at the University of

Washington, especially Edmond S. Meany, "A History of the University of Washington," n.d., typescript at University of Washington Libraries, Manuscripts, Special Collections, University Archives Division.

66. During a visit to Seattle in early February 1891 a legislative committee led by Edmond Meany selected the site fronting on Lake Washington and on Lake Union. Meany wished a larger site, but the legislature approved only 160 acres. *P.I.*, 6 Feb. 1891, 8; 7 Feb. 1891, 8; 8 Feb. 1891, 8; Edmond S. Meany, "History of the University," 79–80; Victor J. Farrar, "History of the University," *Washington Alumnus* 8/6 (March 1922): 11.

67. According to Meany, the creation of the Board of University Land and Building Commissioners was directly at the behest of the regents. He wrote, "The regents did not relish the responsibility and labor associated with the University lands and buildings and the proposed relocation of the institution. Their request for relief caused to be enacted the law approved on March 7, 1891." Meany, "History of the University," 79. For details of the Board of University Land and Building Commissioners, see Ochsner, "The University That Never Was," 66, n. 9. Also see: *Report of the University Land and Building Commissioners, 1892* (Olympia, Wash.: State of Washington, 1892), 3–8.

68. The Board of University Land and Building Commissioners also selected Fred Gordon Plummer (1864–1913) as the engineer and surveyor for the new campus. See Ochsner, "The University That Never Was," 67–68.

69. Edmond Meany prepared a set of typed notes recording the visit of the joint legislative committee to Seattle in February 1893. During this visit Boone gave this account of his hiring: "'All I can say is: I did not seek the work. The first I knew about it was the 7th of April 1891. I was notified to appear before the Board of University Land and Building Commissioners and asked if I would accept the position of architect for the Board. I asked if they were a lawful commission and whether there was any possibility of it becoming a political matter. They replied that, so far as they were concerned, the law was mandatory, and they were appointed for four years. . . . I said I would accept.'" The next part was later crossed out by Meany, but is still readable; thus, the original continued: "'if they did not advertise for plans. This position no architect could refuse. It would become a picture gallery if other architects were to compete.'" Untitled, undated typescript, 3–4, Edmond S. Meany Papers, Acc. No. 106–70–12, Box 101–20, Manuscripts and Archives Division, University of Washington Libraries.

70. For Willcox's background see: chapter 5. The previous educational building and campus planning experience of William Willcox is indicated by the building list in his own booklet, Willcox, *Hints to Those Who Propose to Build*, 28 (churches), 57 (other buildings); and also by the building list included in notice of the formation of Willcox and Johnston in the St. Paul *Pioneer Press*, 1 March 1886.

71. *P.I.*, 25 Aug. 1891, 8.

72. William E. Boone, "The Architect's Report," 19 Aug. 1891, 1; included as part of the "Report of the Board," Ferry papers. The complete text of this report was published in *P.I.*, 23 Aug. 1891, 8; and in *Report of the University Land and Building Commissioners, 1892*, 10–16. Boone argued that most Eastern schools had developed without planning for growth with unfortunate results, but the University of Washington could insure against such an outcome. Boone and Willcox wrote to American and European universities seeking information on designs for different building types; correspondence was apparently received from as far away as Berlin. See: Untitled, undated typescript, 3–4, Meany Papers, Acc. No. 106–70–12.

73. *Times*, 22 Aug. 1891, 5; *P.I.*, 23 Aug. 1891, 8; *Telegraph*, 23 Aug. 1891, 5.

74. *P.I.*, 25 Aug. 1891, 8.

75. Boone and Willcox's design for the campus is known primarily from the map that was published in *Report of the University Land and Building Commissioners, 1892*, 38; this was reprinted in John Paul Jones, *The History of the Development of the Present*

Campus Plan for the University of Washington (Seattle: University of Washington, 1940), n.p.; and again in Johnston, *The Fountain and the Mountain*, 20. Boone's description of the buildings skips around the site and is hard to follow; the report by Fred Plummer, the university's engineer, identifies each building by location. See: "Report of the Board," 59–60. A perspective of the Boone and Willcox scheme is thought to have been produced, but has not been discovered.

76. Turner, *Campus: An American Planning Tradition*, 140–150.

77. Turner, Vetrocq, and Weitze, *The Founders and the Architects*, 22–39, 93.

78. Boone, "Architect's Report," 2–14; included in "Report of the Board," Ferry Papers; also published in *P.I.*, 23 Aug. 1891, 8; and in *Report of the University Land and Building Commissioners, 1892*, 10–16.

79. Boone's term, "Scholastic Gothic," appears to be a variant of the much more commonly used term, "Collegiate Gothic." According to Turner, the first American architect to use the term "Collegiate Gothic" was probably Alexander Jackson Davis, who was a leading American college architect from 1830 to 1860. Turner suggests that Davis used "Collegiate Gothic" to mean "the late medieval styles found at the English universities," but adds that Davis "used the term loosely to include various styles and building types." Turner, *Campus: An American Planning Tradition*, 124. Boone's usage of "Scholastic Gothic" is similarly imprecise. The selection of gothic not only reflects its connection to English universities, but also Willcox's experience with gothic in his earlier career.

80. *P.I.*, 10 Oct. 1891, 3; 11 Oct. 1891, 7; 13 Oct. 1891, 8.

81. The auditor's action was a total surprise; just a month earlier the auditor had visited the site in Seattle and had raised no objections. A meeting of the board (including Governor Ferry) and the auditor on 9 October failed to resolve the impasse, so the board had no choice but to suspend all work on the campus. *Report of the University Land and Building Commissioners, 1892*, 22–26. A test case brought before the state Supreme Court resulted in a judgment that the auditor was correct: Without an appropriation the money could not be paid out of the state treasury. The legislature was not then in session, so interim measures could not be passed, and the project stopped. *P.I.*, 15 Nov. 1891, 3. "Report of the Board," Ferry Papers, 38–41 (published as: *Report of the University Land and Building Commissioners, 1892*, 26–28). *Washington Reports* 3 (Nov. 1891), 125–130 (case decided 14 Nov. 1891).

82. Boone apparently thought the project would eventually proceed, because he took the opportunity to visit campuses in the East and in California including Yale, Harvard, Brown, Cornell, Stanford, and California at Berkeley. He claimed that faculty members at these schools generally approved the plans and called the Administration Building design "splendid." Boone also later said that his firm had prepared plans for the dormitory building at their own expense. Boone and Willcox presented their invoice for $10,000 for architectural services (2.5% on the estimated $400,000 cost of the main building), but at least half of this went unpaid.

83. David McNichols, *Seattle Pacific University: A Growing Vision, 1891–1991* (Seattle: Seattle Pacific University, 1989), 9–22; also see: *P.I.*, 19 Sept. 1892, 5.

84. *Northwestern Architect* 9/11 (Nov. 1891).

85. *P.I.*, 1 Jan. 1893, 8.

86. Walt Crowley, *Seattle University: A Century of Jesuit Education* (Seattle: Seattle University, 1991): 19–29.

87. *P.I.*, 9 Jan. 1893, 8.

88. *P.I.*, 3 Apr. 1893, 7.

89. The extent to which the final detailing represents Parkinson's intentions is unknown. The project began without full funding in place. Although the cost was projected as less than $20,000, after the bank failures of May 1893, construction halted. It had proceeded only as far as the foundation and cornerstone (which was set on 16

April), although the needed materials had apparently been acquired. See: *P.I.*, 3 Apr. 1893, 7.

90. The upper floors of the building were gutted by fire in 1907; it was subsequently reconstructed for university use. The exterior was restored for the university's centennial in 1991, but the missing west-facing stair was not reconstructed.

91. A copy of House Bill No. 470, providing for revisions to the university site and the process by which construction on the new campus would be initiated, is found in the Meany Papers, Acc. No. 106–70–12. For a discussion of the process, see: Untitled, undated typescript, 1–9, Meany Papers, Acc. No. 106–70–12. Also see: *P.I.*, 19 Feb. 1893, 8; 20 Feb. 1893, 5; 12 Mar. 1893, 5. Meany, "History of the University," 81–89.

92. *P.I.*, 15 Aug. 1893, 5; 12 Oct. 1893, 8; 26 Oct. 1893, 8; 11 Nov. 1893, 3; 29 Nov. 1893, 3; 30 Nov. 1893, 4; 7 Dec. 1893, 8. The decision to use "slow burning" construction meant that the first building would have a heavy timber frame and that steel would not be required.

93. *P.I.*, 23 Dec. 1893, 5; 24 Dec. 1893, 5.

94. *P.I.*, 13 Feb. 1894, 5; 20 Feb. 1893, 2; 16 Mar. 1894, 8.

95. On Denny Hall construction history, see: *P.I.*, 11 Apr. 1894, 8; 17 Apr. 1894, 8; 11 May 1894, 8; 29 June 1894, 2; 8 Jan. 1895, 3; 24 Apr. 1895, 6; 29 Apr. 1895, 8; 2 Sept. 1895, 8. On the decision to name the building "Denny Hall," see: *P.I.*, 5 Sept. 1895, 5.

96. *P.I.*, 16 Mar. 1894, 8. Saunders would have known Sever Hall from his years in Cambridge, Massachusetts. Willis Ritchie's French Renaissance scheme for the Spokane County Courthouse was also selected in competition in 1894, suggesting a growing preference for eclectic designs drawing on Renaissance precedents (see chap. 7).

Because the bids for Denny Hall came in lower than expected (only $112,000), sufficient funds were available to build several other buildings, for which Saunders also provided designs, including the Observatory (1895), Gymnasium (1895, destroyed), and Power House (1895, destroyed). The Observatory was actually constructed using leftover stone not used for Denny Hall. See: Meany, "History of the University," 90–92.

97. "The exterior will be plain and substantial, it being the intention to convert the building into a business block when the site becomes too valuable for church purposes." *Times*, 10 Aug. 1889, 8.

98. Saunders and Houghton's "Project for a Church" appeared in *Northwestern Architect* 9/2 (Feb. 1891). From the date of the design as well as its size and general orientation, it might be conjectured that this was an early proposal for Plymouth Congregational Church.

99. For Plymouth Congregational Church design and construction, see: *P.I.*, 27 Mar. 1891, 5; 29 Mar. 1891, 3; 1 Aug. 1891, 8; 8 Sept. 1891, 8; 13 June 1892, 5.

100. *Times*, 26 June 1891, 6; *Northwest Magazine* 9/2 (Feb. 1891), 25; Corkey, *Seattle Churches*, 245. The only church that was actually constructed that might be characterized as Romanesque was Charles Alexander's unimpressive First Presbyterian Church (1893–94, destroyed), at Fourth and Spring (replacing the earlier building by Krumbein and Williams at Third and Madison, see: chap. 2), which featured a modified brick veneer facade, described as "Byzantine" in the press at the time. See: *P.I.*, 20 Mar. 1893, 8; 29 Jan. 1894, 5; also see: Corkey, *Seattle Churches*, 30–31.

101. For selection of the architects and their roles, see: Trinity Church Vestry minutes books: 1 July 1889: formation of building committee; 14 Feb. 1890: "Mr. Watson was instructed to write to an eastern architect and obtain plans from him for a stone church"; 31 Mar. 1890: "Mr. Watson is instructed to telegraph the Chicago architect Mr. Starbrook [*sic*], accepting his general plans of the church"; 13 Oct. 1889: Alexander is appointed as supervising architect; 8 Oct. 1891: "Chas. A. Alexander was appointed superintendent of construction during the erection of Trinity Parish Church."

Washington Churchman, Oct. 1891, n.p., contains a description of the building; *Washington Churchman,* Apr. 1892, n.p., mentions the roles of Starbuck and Alexander as well as Alexander's responsibility for the adjacent rectory. For interior description, see: *P.I.,* 6 June 1892, 5.

Henry F. Starbuck may have been known as a result of the publication of a drawing of his stone building for Trinity Episcopal Church, Michigan City, in *IA* 14 (Oct. 1889), 41. By 1895, Starbuck apparently moved to San Diego as he is listed in the San Diego Polk Directory in that year. He died in Alameda County, California, in 1935.

102. *P.I.,* 23 Aug. 1890, 3; for the dedication (no mention of the architect), see: *P.I.,* 20 July 1891, 5. Also see: Corkey, *Seattle Churches,* 165. This building burned about 1899. For Perrault and Mesnard, see: Isabel Gournay and France Vanlaethem: *Montreal Metropolis* (Toronto: Stoddart, 1998), 80. Mesnard and Perrault also furnished designs for St. Andrew's Roman Catholic Cathedral in Victoria, B.C. (1891–92). See: Martin Segger, *Victoria: A Primer for Regional History in Architecture* (Watkins Glen, N.Y.: American Life Foundation, 1979), 225. (Mesnard's name is misspelled as "Mesiard" in this text.) For Parkinson's school and rectory see: *P.I.,* 12 Feb. 1893, 8.

103. *P.I.,* 24 Oct. 1889, 3; 1 Jan. 1890, 13; Bagley, *History of Seattle* 1: 180–181; Frederic J. Grant, *History of Seattle, Washington* (New York: American, 1891), 335–336.

104. For Congregation Ohaveth Shalom: *P.I.,* 9 May 1892, 5; 18 Sept. 1892, 13. Corkey, *Seattle Churches,* 346 (misidentifies the location as Eighth and Spring).

105. A drawing of the wood row by J. A. DeProsse at Eighth and Columbia appeared in *Seattle Illustrated* (Chicago: Baldwin, Calcutt and Blakely, c. 1890), 21; newspaper citations for this project have not been found. For Towle and Wilcox wood rowhouses on Sixth Street between University and Union, see: *P.I.,* 1 Apr. 1890, 5; 1 Jan. 1891, 4; for their seven terrace houses at 1913–1925 Yesler Avenue, see: *P.I.,* 5 Oct. 1889, 5; 13 Nov. 1889, 4.

106. *P.I.,* 11 Mar. 1892, 8.

107. For Stone Row history, see: *P.I.,* 11 Mar. 1892, 8; 30 May 1892, 5; 7 July 1892, 5; 1 Aug. 1892, 5; 10 Oct. 1892, 8. For Parkinson's trade with Charles Hopkins to obtain the downtown site on which he built the Seattle Athletic Club building, see: *P.I.,* 27 Oct. 1892, 3; 3 Nov. 1892, 5.

108. *P.I.,* 27 Oct. 1892, 3. By 1904 these individual townhouses had been reconfigured as the Greystone Hotel.

109. After the turn of the century, some subdivisions would show streets following land contours or other topographically responsive organizations, but such practices rarely occurred before 1900.

110. Dennis A. Andersen and Katheryn H. Krafft, "Plan and Pattern Books: Shaping Early Seattle Architecture," *PNQ* 85/4 (Oct. 1994), 150–158.

111. *Times,* 19 Mar. 1890, 5; 26 June 1891, 6.

112. For the Scurry House, see: *P.I.,* 30 June 1889, 4. Later owners included Alden J. Blethen and Thomas S. Lippy. Also see: Margaret Strachan, "Early Day Mansions #20: John G. Scurry," *Times,* 14 Jan. 1945, magazine section, 3.

113. For Otto Ranke's obituary, see: *P.I.,* 16 Nov. 1892, 5. For Fisher's Ranke house, see: *P.I.,* 11 July 1890, 5; *NREBR* 1/2 (Mar.-Apr. 1891), 16. Later owners of the house included Moritz Thomsen and the Missionary Sisters of the Sacred Heart. Also see: Margaret Strachan, "Early Day Mansions #33: Otto Ranke," *Times,* 15 Apr. 1945, magazine section, 2.

114. *P.I.,* 11 Aug. 1889, 8; also see: Margaret P. Strachan, "Early Day Mansions #31: Rezin W. Pontius," *Times,* 1 Apr. 1945, magazine section, 2.

115. *Pacific Magazine* 4/6 (Dec. 1891), 176 (illus.), 177; *Seattle Illustrated,* 50–52; Judy Gellatly, *Mercer Island: The First 100 Years* (Mercer Island, Wash.: Mercer Island Bicentennial Committee, 1977), 20–24.

116. *Times,* 26 June 1891, 6; *AABN* 37 (17 Sept. 1892).

117. *P.I.*, 4 July 1892, 5; 15 Aug. 1892, 5.

118. The drawing of the Phinney House shows the extraordinary capabilities of the delineator A. B. Chamberlin. See: Ochsner, "A. B. Chamberlin," 140–141. This drawing is cited for its excellence by Eileen Michels; see: Michels, "Late-Nineteenth-Century Perspective Drawing," 307. Unfortunately, in this article, Chamberlin's name is incorrectly spelled "Chamberlain" and the location of the house is incorrectly given as "Woodland Park, Washington, DC."

119. *P.I.*, 30 May 1892, 5; *Architect, Builder & Decorator* 8/9 (Sept. 1894).

120. In 1902, architect August Tidemand designed a Romanesque Revival house for Thomas Russell at 923 14th Avenue North (now East). Russell managed the Tenino Sandstone Company.

121. On the impact of academic eclecticism and the comparative development of architecture in Seattle, Portland, and San Francisco, see: Jeffrey Karl Ochsner, "The Missing Paradigm," *Column 5* (student journal of the Department of Architecture, University of Washington), 1991, 4–11.

VII. Creating a Civic Presence:
Willis Ritchie and the Architecture of Public Buildings

1. Certain architects in the period achieved equal or greater local fame, such as Elmer Fisher in Seattle and Kirtland Cutter in Spokane, but only Ritchie had a significant statewide reputation prior to the late 1890s. Cutter eventually did achieve a statewide reputation, but not until the years after 1898 did he build substantial projects west of the Cascades. For these and other architects of the period, see Ochsner, ed., *Shaping Seattle Architecture*, 1–83.

2. Although family papers and records from Ritchie's office do not survive (with the exception of a single letterpress book, see: note 22), his prominence as an architect attracted sufficient attention such that published accounts make it possible to reconstruct a history of Ritchie's career. Brief biographical summaries of Ritchie's life and career appeared between 1890 and 1915, including those in *Pacific Magazine* 3 (Dec. 1890): 300–301; Harvey K. Hines, *An Illustrated History of the State of Washington* (Chicago: 1893), 362–64; Nelson W. Durham, *Spokane and the Inland Empire* (Spokane: 1912), 3: 122–23. All these sources include occasional inaccuracies and must be used with caution. A brief biography also appeared in a promotional publication, *A General Historical and Descriptive Review of the City of Seattle, Washington* (San Francisco: 1890), 27; however, this includes multiple misattributions and exaggerations and should, therefore, be regarded as unreliable.

3. For Saunders and Houghton's Hotel Eisenbeis in Port Townsend, see: Denison and Huntington, *Victorian Architecture of Port Townsend*, 19–20. For notices in Seattle of Saunders and Houghton projects, see: Hotel Eisenbeis: *P.I.*, 12 Apr. 1890, 6; hotel in Anacortes and buildings in Sedro Wooley: *P.I.*, 13 Aug. 1890, 3.

4. For Fisher's Lottie Roth Block (1890–91), Whatcom (now part of Bellingham), see: *P.I.*, 28 June 1890, 12 ("Roeder & Roth Block"). Unidentified projects by Fisher in Ellensburg and Yakima are noted in *P.I.*, 1 Jan. 1890, 22. After the Ellensburg fire in July 1889, the Ellensburg *Capital* listed the new buildings under construction and their costs, but did not include architects' names. Fisher made a visit to Yakima in 1890, but his work there was not identified in the Seattle paper; see: *P.I.*, 10 Apr. 1890, 8.

5. Fisher's responsibility for the design of the Mrs. Edmund R. Lowe house, Woodland, California (1890), is noted in the *Yolo Democrat*, 24 July 1890. The contractor was her son-in-law, Daniel McPhee, from Port Townsend. It may have been McPhee who recommended Fisher. (This information was brought to our attention by Daniel Wilkinson of the Woodland Historical Preservation Commission.) Fisher may also have been responsible for the design of a house in Alameda, California, but this has not been verified.

6. Undertaking the study of architecture through a correspondence school course

was not uncommon in this period. The most widely known correspondence program in architecture, however, that offered by the International Correspondence Schools, was first offered only in the 1890s, so the course taken by Ritchie remains unidentified. Later biographical summaries indicate that Ritchie wrote to James G. Hill, supervising architect of the U.S. Treasury, and Hill recommended a particular correspondence course; this cannot be verified.

Ritchie also later claimed to have designed his family's home, although he was only sixteen. The building still stands in Lima at 541 W. Wayne although it has been extensively expanded and altered; it is now the Chiles Funeral Home.

7. Experience in either Cincinnati or Toledo cannot be verified. Some later accounts indicated that Ritchie also worked in the Office of the Supervising Architect of the Treasury. However, Ritchie's name does not appear in the Federal Register for this period, nor is there any record of his employment in the National Archives. Further, when he later applied for the position of superintendent of the federal building in Wichita, he did not claim any prior experience in the Office of the Supervising Architect (see: note 18, below). It is, therefore, highly unlikely that Ritchie ever worked in the Office of the Supervising Architect. (Information provided by Bill Creech at the National Archives, and Antoinette Lee at the National Park Service.)

8. Ritchie's later biographical summaries mention designing "business houses and dwellings" in central Ohio towns including Bucyrus, Delphos, Ottawa, and Columbus Grove. Although the Ritchie family was prominent in northwest Ohio in the 1880s, correspondence with historical societies and libraries in these Ohio communities turned up no easily available verification of the projects Ritchie claimed as his designs. In the 1884 city directory for Lima, Ohio, Willis Ritchie's architectural office is located in the Faurot Opera House and his ad is in large bold type. At that time the Faurot block was the location of offices for many prominent businessmen in Lima, according to Jeanne Porreca of the Allen County Historical Society.

9. For general background on the development of the plains states including Kansas, see, for example, Robert G. Athearn, *High Country Empire: The High Plains and the Rockies* (Lincoln: University of Nebraska Press, 1960), especially sections 2 and 3. The growth of Winfield was regularly reported by the local newspaper. In 1884, Winfield's population was tabulated as 3,917 and in 1885 as 5,151. Winfield's boom was regularly reported in the paper, which by November 1885 had become a daily. In February 1886, the *Winfield Daily Courier* (*WDC*) carried an article heralding the city's "unrivaled prospects" and predicting that it would eventually surpass Wichita and grow to 100,000 in population. *WDC*, 11 Feb. 1886, 4. An entire issue of *WDC* devoted to a review of Winfield's progress was published on 24 Dec. 1886. The estimate of 9,000 population appeared in an article in *WDC*, 28 Sept. 1886, 2. The population given in the 1887 city directory was 8,500. This figure was also stated in a July 1887 issue of *The Illustrated Western World* (an illustrated weekly newspaper published in Kansas City, Missouri) that focused entirely on Winfield and Cowley County; see: *The Illustrated Western World* 15/2 (2 July 1887), n.p. (Research on Winfield and on Ritchie's Kansas career was greatly assisted by local historian Joan Cales.)

10. *Winfield Courier*, 16 July 1885, 1; 6 Aug. 1885, 1; 20 Aug. 1885, 3; 3 Sept. 1885, 1; 10 Sept. 1885, 4; 16 Oct. 1885, 4; *WDC*, 31 Oct. 1885, 4; 14 Nov. 1885, 4; 20 Nov. 1885, 4; 24 Nov. 1885, 4.

11. Longstreth, "Richardsonian Architecture in Kansas," 70–72.

12. On Winfield's stone, see *WDC*, 29 Nov. 1886, 2. Also see: *Illustrated Western World* 15/2 (2 July 1887) n.p.

13. *Winfield Courier*, 16 July 1885, 1; *WDC*, 31 Dec. 1885, 4; 23 Jan. 1886, 4; 9 Apr. 1886, 3; 19 Apr. 1886, 3; 1 Oct. 1886, 3; 11 Nov. 1886, 3; 12 Nov. 1886, 3; 22 Nov. 1886, 3.

14. For the Southwestern Kansas Methodist Episcopal college, see: *Winfield Courier*, 10 Sept. 1885, 3; 16 Oct. 1885, 4; *WDC*, 31 Oct. 1885, 4; 31 Dec. 1885, 4; 25 Mar.

1886, 3; 26 Apr. 1886, 2; 12 May 1886, 3; 11 Nov. 1886, 3; 10 Jan. 1887, 3; 28 Feb. 1887, 3. For the Winfield City Building, see: *WDC*, 20 Nov. 1885, 4; 24 Nov. 1885, 4; 9 Dec. 1885, 4; 22 Dec. 1885, 4; 23 Dec. 1885, 4; 21 Jan. 1886, 4; 27 Jan. 1886, 4; 9 Feb. 1886, 4; 13 May 1886, 3; 11 June 1886, 3.

15. A general description of Ritchie's firm and its success appeared in *WDC*, 24 Dec. 1886, 1.

16. Ritchie's work in Arkansas City is described in *WDC*, 23 Feb. 1886, 4; 8 Mar. 1886, 3; and in the *Arkansas City Traveller*, 11 Aug. 1886, 3; 8 Dec. 1886, 3; Unfortunately only a very incomplete run of the *Traveller* from this period survives. His buildings in Arkansas City have been destroyed.

Ritchie's Wellington project, the State National Bank Building (1886–87, destroyed), was noted in *WDC*, 27 Apr. 1886, 3; 19 May 1886, 3; the building is described in the *Wellington Monitor*, 10 June 1887, 2 (but Ritchie was not named).

Ritchie also designed the Barbour (now Barber) County Courthouse, Medicine Lodge (1886–87, destroyed); this is noted in *WDC*, 27 Apr. 1886, 3; 19 May 1886, 3; and in the *Medicine Lodge Cresset*, 29 Apr. 1886, 3. Thereafter, although the *Cresset* regularly reported construction of the courthouse until completion in March 1887, Ritchie was not mentioned again.

17. *WDC*, 16 Sept. 1886 2; 11 Nov. 1886, 3; 6 Dec. 1886, 2; 7 Jan. 1887, 4; 1 Feb. 1887, 3; 26 Feb. 1887, 3; 15 Mar. 1887, 3; 19 Mar. 1887, 3; 28 Jan. 1888, 3; 31 Jan. 1888, 1; 1 Feb. 1888, 3. See also: Rick McConn, "The Winfield Opera House" (1968), typescript in possession of Winfield Public Library. Ritchie may have intended a more ambitious design, as a drawing of the Board of Trade and Opera House building with a larger corner tower was shown on the cover of *Illustrated Western World* 15/2 (2 July 1887).

18. Ritchie's 14 Jan. 1886 letter of application and eleven letters of recommendation are found in the Federal Archives. (One letter recommending George Bird, of the Wichita firm Proudfoot and Bird, was also received.) National Archives RG 56, General Records of the Treasury Department, Entry 273: Applications and Recommendations for Appointments as Superintendents of Construction, 1853–1904. The 1887 Federal Register, under the Treasury Department, Office of the Supervising Architect, lists "Willis Alexander Ritchie" as "Superintendent of Construction" for Wichita, Kansas. (Information provided by Bill Creech at the National Archives.)

19. Ritchie's involvement with the Wichita federal building is noted in *WDC*, 12 Apr. 1886, 3; 13 July 1886, 3; 18 Nov. 1886, 2; 22 Nov. 1886, 3; 6 Jan. 1887, 3; 1 Feb. 1887, 3. The Wichita City directories for 1887 and 1888 included a listing for "Willis A. Ritchie, Supt. U. S. Bldg." Ritchie served only as superintendent of the courthouse and never attempted to establish an architectural office in Wichita.

20. On the Romanesque Revival in Wichita, see Richard Longstreth, "Richardsonian Architecture in Kansas" 75–78.

21. With Ritchie focusing on the Wichita Federal Building and on real estate interests (see: note 22, below), his practice was supervised by his chief assistant, Otto Weile; see: *WDC*, 26 Jan. 1886, 4; 28 Jan. 1887, 3. Largely under Weile's direction, the firm received commissions in Ashland, about 150 miles west of Winfield, and Meade, even farther west. On Ritchie's work in Ashland, see: *Clark County Clipper*, 19 May 1887, 8; 28 July 1887, 1; 25 Aug. 1887, 1; 3 Nov. 1887, 1; 5 Jan. 1888, 1; 12 Jan. 1888, 1. On the Meade City Hall and County Courthouse, see: *Meade Republican*, 24 Oct. 1888, [3]; 5 Dec. 1888, [2].

22. Ritchie became involved in real estate speculation in Winfield in early 1887, just as the Kansas boom was coming to an end. As a partner in a new real estate venture, Frank H. Greer & Company, he acquired land platted as "Ritchie's Addition," and began advertising lots for sale on 31 January. *WDC*, 28 Jan. 1887, 3; 31 Jan. 1887, 4.

That Ritchie incurred significant debts in Kansas is known from a February 1893 letter to his cousin, Thomas Eaton in Winfield, in which Ritchie indicated that a large portion of his personal income from his Washington State architectural practice was going toward paying off his Winfield debts and that he wished to be "through with my speculating experience." Ritchie also owed money to his father. See: Letter to Judge J. E. Ritchie, 29 Oct. 1892; letter to Thomas J. Eaton, 20 Feb. 1893, Willis Ritchie letterpress book; Manuscripts, Special Collections, University Archives Division, University of Washington Libraries.

23. On Ritchie's marriage to Etta Reid, see: *WDC*, 15 July 1887, 3. For the death of A. Lawson Reid, see: *WDC*, 28 Dec. 1888, 3; 29 Dec. 1888, 3; 4 Jan. 1889, 3.

24. *P.I.*, 4 July 1889, 4.

25. *P.I.*, 4 July 1889, 4; 1 Aug. 1889, 3; 7 Aug. 1889, 4; 3 Sept. 1889, 4; 3 Sept. 1889, 4; 14 Sept. 1889, 4.

26. *P.I.*, 7 Oct. 1889, 3; 10 Oct. 1889, 5; 11 Oct. 1889, 3; 3 Nov. 1889, 1; 5 Nov. 1889, 5.

27. *P.I.*, 3 Nov. 1889, 1.

28. For King County Courthouse construction, see: *P.I.*, 12 Nov. 1889, 8; 17 Nov. 1889, 5; 19 Nov. 1889, 8; 20 Nov. 1889, 5; 21 Nov. 1889, 8; 22 Nov. 1889, 8; 19 Jan. 1890, 8; 5 Feb. 1890, 5; 11 May 1890, 8; 22 Aug. 1890, 6; 4 Sept. 1890, 8; 16 Sept. 1890, 8; 25 Nov. 1890, 8; 14 Feb. 1891, 8; 18 Feb. 1891, 7; 6 June 1891, 12; 7 June 1891, 5. Also see: *West Shore* 15 (30 Nov. 1889), 364–65, cover (illus.).

29. On Ritchie's fire stations, see: chapter 6.

30. For Bowman house see: *P.I.*, 31 Aug. 1890, 3; *NREBR*, May 1891, 10; *Pacific Magazine* 4 (Aug. 1891): 72 (illus.).

31. *P.I.*, 6 Feb. 1890, 5; *Bellingham Bay Express* (hereafter *BBE*) 15 Apr. 1890, 3; 19 Apr. 1890, 4. Ritchie's winning the Whatcom Courthouse commission was also noted in the [Vancouver, Wash.] *Register*, 5 Mar. 1890, 3.

32. The construction of the Whatcom Courthouse was regularly reported: *BBE*, 29 Apr. 1890, 4; 6 May 1890, 1; 8 May 1890, 1; 20 May 1890, 1; 22 May 1890, 1; 24 May 1890, 1; 19 June 1890, 1; 1 July 1890, 1; 12 July 1890, 1; 17 July 1890, 1; 29 July 1890, 4; 13 Sept. 1890, 4; 30 Sept. 1890, 1; 21 Oct. 1890, 4; 6 Jan. 1891, 1; 7 Feb. 1891, 1. Also see: *West Shore* 16 (21 Mar. 1890), 357, back cover (illus.).

33. *Northwestern Architect* 9/5 (May 1891).

34. *BBE*, 6 May 1890, 1; 15 May 1890, 1; 19 June 1890, 1; 8 July 1890, 3; 12 July 1890, 1; 24 July 1890, 1; 2 Aug. 1890, 1; 14 Aug. 1890, 4; 19 Aug. 1890, 1; 21 Aug. 1890, 1; 28 Aug. 1890, 3; 16 Sept. 1890, 4; 2 Oct. 1890, 1; 4 Oct. 1890, 1; 9 Oct. 1890, 1; 16 Oct. 1890, 1.

35. *Ellensburg Capital*, 20 Mar. 1890, 3; 8 May 1890, 3.

36. The construction of the Ellensburg School was regularly reported: *Ellensburg Capital*, 29 May 1890, 2; 25 June 1890, 3; 10 July 1890, 3; 24 July 1890, 3; 31 July 1890, 3; 21 Aug. 1890, 3; 30 Oct. 1890, 3; 4 Dec. 1890, 3; 5 Mar. 1891, 3; 3 Sept. 1891, 2–3. Also see: *West Shore* 16 (5 July 1890): 838. Initially the State Normal School occupied the second floor, while the classrooms on the first floor served grade school students from Ellensburg.

37. *P.I.*, 14 May 1890, 3 (advertisement for submissions). Esther Knox, "A Diary of the Olympia School District, 1852–1976" (typescript in possession of Washington State Capitol Museum, Olympia), 14–17. Also see: *West Shore* 16 (5 July 1890): 840.

38. *Morning Leader* [Port Townsend, Wash.] (hereafter *ML*), 7 May 1890, 2; 8 May 1890, 4, 8; 27 June 1890, 8.

39. *ML*, 28 June 1890, 5; 2 July 1890, 1, 5. Ritchie's winning the Jefferson Courthouse was also noted in the [Vancouver, Wash.] *Register*, 21 May 1890, 3.

40. *ML*, 4 July 1890, 5.

41. *ML*, 8 July 1890, 8.

42. For the construction of the Jefferson County Courthouse: *ML*, 14 Aug. 1890, 5; 17 Sept. 1890, 5; 19 Sept. 1890, 4; 20 Sept. 1890, 4; 2 Oct. 1890, 8; 21 Nov. 1890, 8;

22 Nov. 1890, 8; 4 Mar. 1891, 4; 18 Mar. 1891, 4; 13 Apr. 1891, 4; 14 Apr. 1891, 4; 13 June 1891, 4; 16 June 1891, 4; 2 July 1891, 1; 3 July 1891, 4; 25 July 1891, 4; 1 Jan. 1892, 1; 20 Jan. 1892, 3; 28 Jan. 1892, 1; 2 Feb. 1892, 4; 9 Mar. 1892, 1; 31 Mar. 1892, 3; *Townsend Daily Leader,* 17 June 1892, 1; 24 June 1892, 1; 28 June 1892, 1; 16 July 1892, 2, 4; 23 July 1892, 1; 9 Aug. 1892, 2; 11 Aug. 1892, 1. The contract had called for the building to be completed by 1 April 1892, but it was not opened until July. Also see: *West Shore* 16 (9 Aug. 1890): 988, back cover (illus.).

43. Dennison and Huntington, *Victorian Architecture of Port Townsend,* 81.

44. *Morning Olympian,* 15 May 1891 (article typescript in possession of Washington State Capitol Museum, Olympia). John Rigby had won the construction contract initially, but by the time of the groundbreaking, the contractor was identified as Wright and Evans.

45. For Thurston County Courthouse construction: *Washington Standard* [Olympia], 28 Nov. 1890, 1; 19 Dec. 1890, 2; 23 Jan. 1891, 2; 6 Mar. 1891, 1; 3 Apr. 1891, 2; 15 May 1891, 2; 12 Oct. 1892, 2.

46. On the history of the Washington State capitol building, see Norman J. Johnston, *Washington's Audacious State Capitol and Its Builders* (Seattle and London: University of Washington Press, 1988).

47. *ML,* 12 Nov. 1890, 3, 5; on Soldiers Home construction history, see: *P.I.,* 22 Aug. 1890, 6; 29 Aug. 1890, 5; 31 Aug. 1890, 2; 27 Sept. 1890, 8; 21 Oct. 1890, 5; 6 Nov. 1890, 8; 9 Nov. 1890, 5. Also see: *West Shore* 17 (7 Mar. 1891): 154.

48. *P.I.,* 26 June 1891, 2.

49. *P.I.,* 1 Jan. 1891, 27. The value of Ritchie's projects seems even more impressive if inflation is accounted for. The consumer price index increased by a factor of about nine from 1890 to 1990. Using this figure suggests that Ritchie's projects would have a value of more than $7.7 million today. However some historians have suggested that building costs have inflated more rapidly, perhaps by as much as a factor of 40, so that Ritchie's buildings might be worth over $30 million today.

50. *ML,* 16 July 1890, 8; 22 July 1890, 8.

51. *P.I.,* 27 Apr. 1893, 2.

52. *Tacoma Morning Globe,* 12 June 1890, 3.

53. *Tacoma Morning Globe,* 15 June 1890, 4, 18 June 1890, 4.

54. *NREBR* 1/3 (May 1891): 10–11.

55. Parkinson, *Incidents,* 159–160. The building Parkinson won over Ritchie was the South Seattle School (see: chapter 6).

56. On Buchinger, see: *Seattle of To-Day* (Seattle, 1907?), 134, and Dennis A. Andersen, "Breitung & Buchinger," *Shaping Seattle Architecture,* 84–89. On Patterson, see: *P.I.,* 18 July 1894, 5, and Ochsner, *Shaping Seattle Architecture,* 350. Various Seattle city directories list Ritchie employees, including Patterson in 1890 and 1891, Buchinger from 1890 to 1892, Villeneuve in 1890, and Wert W. Reid (who was likely related to Ritchie's wife) in 1891. Villeneuve and Bungart are both mentioned in *ML,* 8 July 1890, 8.

57. *P.I.,* 16 May 1891, 5; [Vancouver] *Register,* 26 Feb. 1890, 3; 9 Apr. 1890, 2, 3; 30 Apr. 1890, 2; 14 May 1890, 2; 4 June 1890, 3; 11 June 1890, 3.

58. *Register,* Feb. 10, 1892, 3; for Clark County Courthouse construction history, see: *Register,* 2 July 1890, 3; 27 Aug. 1890, 2; 11 Mar. 1891, 3; 13 May 1891, 3; 20 May 1891, 3; 3 June 1891, 3; 5 Aug. 1891, 3. 9 Sept. 1891, 3; 7 Oct. 1891, 3; 18 Nov. 1891, 3; 2 Dec. 1891, 2; 10 Feb. 1892, 3; 9 Mar. 1892, 3.

59. *ML,* 17 July 1891, 1; *P.I.,* 20 July 1891, 8.

60. *P.I.,* 20 Nov. 1891.

61. *P.I.,* 13 Mar. 1892

62. Daniel Burnham to N. G. Blalock, 5 Jan. 1892; Burnham Papers, Art Institute of Chicago.

63. For a detailed discussion of Ritchie and the Washington State Building controversy, see: Ochsner, "In Search of Regional Expression."

64. Burnham's choice was clearly influenced by a theory of "regionalism" that had developed within the framework of "academic eclecticism," the newly emerging but soon to be dominant tendency in American architecture nationally. The academic eclectic movement was "eclectic" in that it focused on the *choice* of historical precedents as a basis for new work; it was "academic" in that it depended on knowledge gained primarily in the new architectural schools or in leading design offices as the basis for making such choices. Thus, Burnham's choice of Skillings's design over Ritchie's is evidence that Ritchie's Victorian background in architecture was becoming dated as the profession changed.

65. Ritchie's first listing as an architect was in Spokane: *Spokane Review* (hereafter *SR*), 23 Mar. 1892, 4.

66. On Parkinson and the Seattle Schools, see: chapter 6.

67. This was the Wallace School, Wallace, Idaho (1892–93, destroyed). See: School District Number 8, Shoshone County, Idaho, School Board minutes, 22 July 1891; 28 Feb. 1892; 11 Apr. 1892 (mentions Ritchie).

Ritchie is credited with the design of the Prescott School (1892–93, destroyed) and the Lincoln School (1892, 1894, destroyed) in Anaconda, Montana, in Hines, *An Illustrated History of the State of Washington*, 364. The buildings are discussed (but Ritchie is not mentioned) in *Anaconda Standard*, 12 Sept. 1892, 3; 26 Jan. 1893, 3; 20 Sept. 1897, 3. In late 1892, Ritchie was still trying to collect fees owed to him for his Anaconda school designs; see: Letter to Anaconda School Board, 2 Oct. 1892; Willis Ritchie letterpress book, University of Washington Libraries, Manuscripts, Special Collections, University Archives Division.

68. For a discussion of Ritchie's Spokane career, see: Jeffrey Karl Ochsner, "Willis A. Ritchie: Public Architecture in Washington, 1889–1905," *PNQ* 87/4 (Fall 1996): 204–211.

69. From 26 Jan. 1893 to 30 June 1893, Ritchie's name reappeared in the architects listing in the *P.I.*; he described his expertise as "public building and fireproof work" and gave office locations in both Seattle and Spokane.

70. *P.I.*, 22 Jan. 1893, 8.

71. *P.I.*, 24 Jan. 1893, 8.

72. On the King County Hospital construction history, see: *P.I.*, 22 Apr. 1893, 8; 11 June 1893, 7; 27 Sept. 1893, 4, 5; 1 Oct. 1893, 8; 4 Oct. 1893, 4; 5 Oct. 1893, 8; 9 Oct. 1893, 3; 11 Oct. 1893, 8; 17 Oct. 1893, 5; 9 Nov. 1893, 5; 11 Nov. 1893, 8; 12 Nov. 1893, 8; 15 Nov. 1893, 5; 16 Nov. 1893, 8; 17 Nov. 1893, 5; 21 Nov. 1893, 5; 25 Nov. 1893, 5; 15 Dec. 1893, 5; 17 Dec. 1893, 5; 25 Jan. 1894, 5; 30 Jan. 1894, 8; 4 Feb. 1894, 5.

73. See: Ochsner, "Willis A. Ritchie: Public Architecture," 206–211.

74. Henry-Russell Hitchcock and William Seale, "Notes on the Architecture," in *Court House: A Photographic Document*, edited by Richard Pare (New York: Horizon Press, 1978), 230, 231 (illus.).

VIII. Toward the Turn of the Century:
Seattle after 1895

1. *P.I.*, 17 July 1893, 6; 29 July 1893, 8.

2. Development in the American West was most dependent on financing from eastern banks. When money became tight, interest rates shot up, and new projects could not be financed. At the same time, the contracting economy and the lack of money made it harder to make necessary payments on existing mortgages and other loans. The effect of the depression was particularly severe in Seattle where the physical development of the city had been rapid, and the city was especially dependent on outside capital.

3. *P.I.*, 25 Dec. 1893, 3.

4. On the State Capitol competition, see: Norman J. Johnston, *Washington's Audacious State Capitol*, 15–19; see also Norman J. Johnston, "The 1893 Competition for Washington State's Capitol: New Evidence," *ARCADE: Northwest Journal for Architecture and Design* 9/5 (Dec. 1989/Jan. 1990): 10–11, 26. For all four finalists and Ware's report, see *IA* 23/5 (June 1894): 48, 54–55.

5. *P.I.*, 10 Jan. 1894, 5; 29 Jan. 1894, 2; 26 Mar. 1894, 5. This previously unknown project by Frank Lloyd Wright was initially announced as a hotel, but subsequently was revised to be an apartment building. Although in early January drawings were described as nearly complete, and bidding was reported as under way in late January, with a visit to Seattle by Frank L. Wright and C. P. Dose anticipated, the project died. No records or drawings for the project are found at the Frank Lloyd Wright Archives.

6. *Times*, 14 May 1911, 12. Permit values were listed for each year from 1889 to 1902 (when they again reached the 1889 level) as follows:
1889: $6,025,037; 1890: $4,451,354; 1891: $1,707,964; 1892: $1,372,973; 1893: $1,112,509; 1894: $467,171; 1895: $284,890; 1896: $201,081; 1897: $360,131; 1898: $906,445; 1899: $1,570,066; 1900: $3,263,022; 1901: $4,569,768; 1902: $6,325,108.

7. *P.I.*, 13 Mar. 1895, 3.

8. Washington State AIA Chapter Records; Manuscripts, Special Collections, University Archives Division, University of Washington Libraries. Parkinson was also listed as a member, but his residence was identified as Los Angeles.

9. *P.I.*, 16 Mar. 1894, 5.

10. For boycott of the Queen Anne School competition, see: chapter 6.

11. The number of architectural firms listed in Seattle city directories for this period charts the near collapse—and gold rush revival—of the architectural profession in Seattle: 1890, 30; 1891, 21; 1891–92, 30; 1892–93, 24; 1893–94, 27; 1894–95, 23; 1895–96, 14; 1897, 11; 1898, 10; 1899, 16; 1900, 24.

12. Polk's *Seattle City Directory* 4 (1892), 362; Fisher is listed as follows: "Fisher, Elmer H., res. The Abbott." The *Times* described Fisher as "a well-known architect and the popular proprietor of the Abbott Hotel" in the announcement of his wedding; see: *Times*, 18 Feb. 1893, 8.

13. *Times*, 7 Mar. 1892, 1; 9 Mar. 1892, 1.

14. For Fisher's marriage, see: *P.I.*, 15 Feb. 1893, 6; *Times*, 18 Feb. 1893, 8; for suit by Mary Smith, see: *P.I.*, 16 Mar. 1893, 2, 5; 18 Mar. 1893, 1; 9 Apr. 1893, 5; 12 Apr. 1893, 5; *Times*, 12 Apr. 1893, 8.

15. *P.I.*, 23 Apr. 1893, 5.

16. Fisher's new advertisement as an architect appeared in: *P.I.*, 6 May 1893, 6. The first report of bank failure appeared in *P.I.*, 10 May 1893, 2.

17. The text of Fisher's letter to Stimson reads: "For and in consideration of one dollar to me in hand paid I hereby sell to T.D. Stimson the following described goods now located in rooms 509 & 510 Stimson Bldg. Los Angeles: 1 desk, 1 counter with drawer and doors, 2 screens, 4 office chairs, 4 rugs, linoleum on floor, parquette flooring on floor, 2 stools & 4 cuspidors [signed:] E. H. Fisher, Los Angeles, California, June 3d 96." (This letter was discovered by Lawrence Kreisman in his research on the Stimson family. See: Lawrence Kreisman, *The Stimson Legacy* (Seattle: Willows Press, 1992), 41.)

18. John Parkinson wrote that Fisher "worked for me as an outside Supervisor and died there [in Los Angeles] in 1905." Parkinson, *Incidents*, 133. However, no death certificate has been discovered. Rumors have also surfaced of Fisher's interment in San Francisco, but these have not been substantiated. See: J. Kingston Pierce, "The Elusive Architect," *Seattle* 3/2 (Mar. 1994): 59.

19. *P.I.*, 9 Aug. 1893, 5.

20. *P.I.*, 20 Nov. 1891, 8.

21. For the career of John Parkinson, see: Tracy, "John Parkinson and the Beaux-

Arts City Beautiful Movement in Downtown Los Angeles," 210–442. The successor firm to Parkinson's practice continues in operation today as Parkinson Field Associates. The history of the firm in Los Angeles is presented in the publication *Parkinson Centennial, 1894–1994: 100 Years of the Parkinson Architectural Firm in Los Angeles* (Los Angeles: Parkinson Field Associates, 1994).

22. Augustus Heide (4 May 1862–?) was born in Alton, Illinois, and arrived in Washington in 1889. He practiced architecture in Tacoma and Everett in the early 1890s and in Los Angeles in the mid to late 1890s. DeNeuf and Heide formed their partnership in Seattle in 1901; it dissolved in 1906. DeNeuf moved to San Francisco in 1912 and died there in 1915. Heide remained in Seattle at least until 1914. His later life and career are unknown. For a list of some of the buildings of DeNeuf and Heide, see: Ochsner, ed., *Shaping Seattle Architecture*, 341.

23. Willcox's later career was traced through California State Library records including the *Index to the Architect and Engineer, 1905–1928*, and through city directory entries in the various cities in which he lived: Los Angeles, 1895–98; San Francisco, 1900–1912. Willcox's life and career after 1912 are unknown. However, his death on 1 February 1929 occurred at the veterans home in Yountville (near Napa), California, where he had been residing.

24. Although Skillings and Corner was listed in Seattle city directories through 1899, the firm was under James Corner's direction after 1897, when Skillings left Seattle for Dawson City, as part of the Klondike Gold Rush. Skillings's later career was traced through California State Library records including the *Index to the Architect and Engineer, 1905–1928*, and through city directory entries in the various cities in which he lived: Eureka, 1900–1910; San Jose, 1910–30. Skillings died in San Jose, 1 August 1939.

25. In its early years, the Minneapolis-based *Western Architect* (which began publication in 1902) frequently carried the work of Bertrand and Chamberlin. For example, after the drawing of the Doric column signed by Chamberlin appeared in September 1902, drawings of Bertrand and Chamberlin houses appeared in the January 1903, March 1903, and February 1904 issues. Other than the Doric column, these drawings must have been the work of drafters working in the firm; they mimic, but do not equal, Chamberlin's personal style.

Michels notes that once draftsmen moved into positions of ownership of architectural firms, they almost always stopped producing presentation renderings. Michels, "Late-Nineteenth-Century Perspective Drawing," 298.

26. Chamberlin died on 28 Sept. 1933. About Bertrand and Chamberlin, Torbert wrote: "The firm of Bertrand and Chamberlin was one of the most successful in Minneapolis in the early twentieth century. Their residences are characterized by a profuse use of classicized detail. Their warehouse buildings . . . are among the best and most understated in the city." Torbert, "Minneapolis Architecture and Architects, 1848–1908," 451.

27. In addition to the City Building and County Courthouse, Ritchie's later practice in Spokane included: Edison School, Spokane, 1893 (destroyed); Ridenbaugh Hall, University of Idaho, and Science Building (destroyed), University of Idaho, 1901–1902; and numerous residences. No works by Ritchie have been identified after 1912. He died in Spokane on 17 Jan. 1931. His obituary listed many of his buildings across the state, but none after 1902. For Ritchie's later life and career, see: Ochsner, "Willis A. Ritchie: Public Architecture in Washington, 1889–1905," 206–211.

28. For Boone's later career, see: Jeffrey Karl Ochsner, "William E. Boone," *Shaping Seattle Architecture*, 16–21.

29. For Saunders's later career, see: Jeffrey Karl Ochsner, "Charles W. Saunders," *Shaping Seattle Architecture*, 34–39.

30. For Houghton's later career see: Jeffrey Karl Ochsner and Dennis A. Andersen, "Edwin W. Houghton," *Shaping Seattle Architecture*, 46–51.

31. *P.I.*, 25 Sept. 1891, 8; 26 Sept. 1891, 8. Also see: chapter 6.

32. Charles Bebb to Thomas Burke, 23 Sept. 1892, Box 2–1, Burke Papers.

33. Bebb to Burke, 23 Dec. 1892, 25 May 1893, Box 2–1, Burke Papers.

34. Bebb to Burke, 14 June 1893, Box 2–1, Burke Papers.

35. Bebb to Burke, 22 June 1893, Box 2–1, Burke Papers.

36. Bebb to Burke, 19 July 1893, Box 2–1, Burke Papers.

37. The Denny Clay Company was founded in 1882 as the Puget Sound Fire Clay Company which principally produced sewer pipe. The company's major creditor, Arthur A. Denny, eventually took over the company and on 1 April 1892 the Denny Clay Company began operation. By 1900 it had become one of the leading suppliers of architectural terra-cotta on the Pacific Coast. In 1905, the company merged with the Renton Clay Company to become the Denny-Renton Clay & Coal Company. In 1925, this company was purchased by the Gladding, McBean Company of California, which had grown to become one of the largest terra-cotta producers in the world. Mark Smith, "The History of American Terra Cotta and Its Local Manufacture," in Lydia Aldredge, ed., *Impressions of Imagination: Terra-Cotta Seattle* (Seattle: Allied Arts of Seattle, 1986), 1–7.

Bebb appears to have been involved with the Denny Clay Company from its inception as Burke's letter to Bebb on 25 March 1892 included the following: "I am glad to hear that you have made such favorable arrangements with Mr. Denny in regard to the fire proofing works, and sincerely hope that you may make a success of it." The nature of Bebb's involvement prior to joining the company in fall 1893 is unknown. Burke to Charles Bebb, 25 Mar. 1892, Box 20, letterpress book 3, 509, Burke Papers.

38. *P.I.*, 10 Jan. 1894, 5. Bebb would, of course, have known Wright from the time when they worked together at Ader and Sullivan.

39. Charles H. Bebb opened his own practice in 1898, then formed the partnership of Bebb and Mendel with Louis Leonard Mendel (1867–1940) in 1901. This partnership was responsible for numerous Seattle structures including the Hoge Building, completed in 1911. Bebb was elected a Fellow of the American Institute of Architects in 1910. For Bebb and Mendel, see: David A. Rash and Dennis A. Andersen, "Bebb & Mendel," *Shaping Seattle Architecture*, 72–77.

40. In 1914, Bebb formed the partnership of Bebb and Gould with Carl Frelinghuysen Gould (1873–1939), an 1898 graduate of Harvard, who had attended the Ecole des Beaux-Arts from 1899 to 1903. Gould had come to Seattle in 1908 after working in the offices of D. H. Burnham, McKim, Mead & White and George B. Post. Bebb and Gould quickly became one of Seattle's leading firms. Bebb died 21 June 1942. For Bebb and Gould, see: T. William Booth and William H. Wilson, "Bebb & Gould," *Shaping Seattle Architecture*, 174–179.

41. For construction permits decline and recovery, see: note 6.

42. James Stephen (1858–1938) had actually arrived in Seattle in 1889 but received few commissions. The most significant portion of Stephen's career began after the turn of the century. See: Katheryn Hills Krafft, "James Stephen," *Shaping Seattle Architecture*, 58–63.

43. For Seattle's Carnegie Libraries, see: Thomas Veith, "Daniel R. Huntington," *Shaping Seattle Architecture*, 116, 118; David A. Rash, "Somervell & Cote," *Shaping Seattle Architecture*, 120, 123, 124; and Norman J. Johnston, "Harlan Thomas," *Shaping Seattle Architecture*, 127.

44. Surviving pre-1900 public school buildings include the B. F. Day School by John Parkinson, the Denny-Fuhrman School by Chamberlin and Siebrand (now part of the Seward School complex), and the Queen Anne School (now West Queen Anne School) by Skillings and Corner. All of these buildings have been enlarged; West Queen Anne School has been converted to residential condominiums.

45. On plan books and periodicals in Seattle after 1900, see: Dennis A. Andersen and Katheryn Hills Krafft, "Pattern Books, Plan Books, Periodicals," *Shaping Seattle*

Architecture, 64–71; and Andersen and Krafft, "Plan and Pattern Books," 150–158. Also see: Erin Doherty, "Jud Yoho and The Craftsman Bungalow Company: Assessing the Value of the Common House" (unpublished M. Arch. thesis, University of Washington, 1997).

46. The term "skid row" originated in Seattle. Mill Street (which later was named Yesler Avenue, and is now Yesler Way) was the original "skid road"; in pioneer Seattle, trees would be cut on the hills above the new town and "skidded" down Mill Street to Yesler's Mill. Eventually, as the center of downtown Seattle moved north, away from Pioneer Square, which became the site of economical lodging houses, the term was transmuted into "skid row" with its later reference to those who were "on the skids."

47. On the history of the preservation movement in Seattle, see: Kreisman, *Made to Last: Historic Preservation in Seattle and King County*. A brief summary of preservation in the city is included in: Jeffrey Karl Ochsner, "Introduction: A Historical Overview of Architecture in Seattle," *Shaping Seattle Architecture*, xxxvi–xl. For favorable comments on Seattle's preservation efforts, see: Delahanty and McKinney, *Preserving the West*, 156–163.

48. Woodbridge and Montgomery, *Architecture in Washington*, 110.

49. Of the major business blocks erected after the fire, Fisher's Pioneer Building, Saunders and Houghton's Bailey Building, and Parkinson's Seattle National Bank Building all survive in relatively intact condition. (The Pioneer Building is missing its seventh-floor tower, lost in the 1949 earthquake.) William Boone's New York Building was demolished in 1921 for a new Dexter Horton Building. Fisher's Burke Building survived until the 1960s when it was demolished for a federal office building; the arched entrance and fragments of the terra cotta ornament from the Burke Building were incorporated into the federal building plaza. Of Parkinson's Butler Block only the stone portions of the two street facades survive, incorporated into a parking garage on the site. Of William Boone's major Seattle projects only the Marshall-Walker Building still stands; Boone and Willcox's Frink Building also survives, although two additional floors were added in the twentieth century. Fisher and DeNeuf's Yesler (now Mutual Life) Building was further modified and enlarged after 1898; it, too, survives today. Many other post-fire buildings survive, as listed in the appendix.

50. D. H. Burnham's rejection of Willis Ritchie's Romanesque Revival design for the Washington State Building, which Burnham described as "commonplace," is discussed in chapter 7.

51. In addition one might add a "shingle-style Richardson"—the work in his time characterized as "modern colonial"—and the Glessner house interiors reflect an emerging "Arts and Crafts Richardson."

52. The persistence of Richardsonian Romanesque architecture in Texas and Kansas, for example, is remarked on by Henry and by Longstreth. See: Henry, "Richardsonian Romanesque in Texas," 58–59; Longstreth, "Richardsonian Architecture in Kansas," 84–85.

53. Montgomery Schuyler, *A Review of the Work of Charles C. Haight*, Great American Architects Series, No. 6 (New York: Architectural Record, July 1899; reprint edition, New York: DaCapo, 1977), 48.

Index

Buildings are indexed by their original or historical names. Present names, if different from these, are cross-referenced to historical names. When a building name is based on the name of a person, the name is indexed last name first (for example: Minor, T. T., School; Yesler, Henry, House). Buildings are indexed by name, by architect, and, for those outside Seattle, by location. Locations of buildings outside Seattle are listed with the building names. Seattle, as a location, is indicated only when necessary for clarity.